THE SINAI STRATEGY

Other books by Gary North

Marx's Religion of Revolution, 1968
An Introduction to Christian Economics, 1973
Foundations of Christian Scholarship (editor), 1976
Unconditional Surrender, 1981
Successful Investing in an Age of Envy, 1981
The Dominion Covenant: Genesis, 1982
Government By Emergency, 1983
The Last Train Out, 1983
Backward, Christian Soldiers?, 1984
75 Bible Questions Your Instructors Pray You Won't Ask, 1984
Coined Freedom: Gold in the Age of the Bureaucrats, 1984
Moses and Pharaoh: Dominion Religion Versus Power Religion, 1985
Negatrends, 1985
Conspiracy: A Biblical View, 1986
Unholy Spirits: Occultism and New Age Humanism, 1986

THE SINAI STRATEGY

Economics and the
Ten Commandments

Gary North

Institute for Christian Economics
Tyler, Texas

Copyright © 1986
Gary North

ISBN 0-930464-07-9

Cover design by George Grant
Cover illustration by Randy Rogers
Typesetting by Thoburn Press, Tyler, Texas

Published by
The Institute for Christian Economics
P. O. Box 8000
Tyler, Texas 75711

This book is dedicated to

Lewis Lehrman

philosopher, businessman, and
politician, who understands that
long-term, meaningful change must be
grounded in permanent moral principles.

TABLE OF CONTENTS

PREFACE

The day I finished the final reading (ha!) of the page proofs of *The Sinai Strategy*, I sat down and began editing a manuscript on the covenant by Ray Sutton. It is an insightful book, one which I suspect may provide Bible students with the fundamental framework for understanding the biblical concept of the covenant, which is the Bible's most important doctrine relating to the relationship between God and man.

As I was reading his chapter on the ten commandments, I was stunned. He had entirely missed the most important single piece of evidence for his thesis. So had I. So has every commentator I have ever read. What he had failed to see was that his five-point outline of the covenant, which he had developed independently of the ten commandments, fits them like a glove. More than this: it opens up the whole structure of the ten commandments.

My immediate thought was: "Here comes a major revision of *The Sinai Strategy*, and there goes $4000 in typesetting charges, plus two week's work on the index I just completed." The indexing upset me most. Above everything else associated with writing a book, I hate to index. Yet if I were to attempt to incorporate my discovery into the text, I would have to rewrite everything.

Or else I could change the Preface by adding a summary of Sutton's outline. So I went back to the page proofs to see how lengthy the Preface was. Guess what? No Preface. Nothing. It was listed right there in the Table of Contents, but there was nothing in the page proofs, nothing in my original manuscript, and nothing in my computer. I had forgotten to write a Preface. It would have been listed in the Table of Contents, but there would have been nothing in the book—a classic typographical error which would have rivaled the subtitle on the inside front page of the first printing of *Backward, Christian Soldiers?*, namely, *A Manual for Christian Reconstuction*. Not "reconstruction," but "reconstuction." (By the way, with over 14,000 copies sold, no one ever wrote in and commented on it. I didn't notice it either until I had the first copy in my hand; at that point, it took me under 60 seconds to spot it.)

So what I have decided to do is to take the easy way out. I am not going to rewrite this book. I am going to tell you here what the outline should have been, and you can insert it into the chapters mentally as you read. None of my conclusions should need revising, I hope. There is some space left at the end of most of the chapters, so I will add a few comments if necessary. The content of the book should not be affected, but the ability of the reader to "fit the pieces together" might have been easier if I had seen Sutton's manuscript earlier, assuming I would have spotted its applicability to the ten commandments.

The Covenant's Outline

What Sutton argues in the manuscript is that there is a five-part structure to both the Old Testament and New Testament covenants. He discovered this structure in the Book of Deuteronomy. I had never considered this structure before, nor had he considered it in detail, until just a few weeks ago, in October of 1985. But his discovery is going to reshape the way we understand the covenant. Here is the basic outline of the covenant throughout the Bible, from creation to Revelation:

1. Transcendence/immanence (redemption)
2. Hierarchy/authority (submission)
3. Ethics/dominion (stipulations)
4. Judicial/evaluational (sanctions)
5. Legitimacy/inheritance (continuity)

This may not seem to be a revolutionary insight, but it is. It is not possible for me to reproduce all of his arguments that support this interpretation, nor discuss all of its applications. Sutton's book is the bare-bones minimum, and the manuscript will be about 300 pages. He has had to cut it down in order to keep it this short.

He argues that this same structure is found in the suzerainty treaties of the ancient world. The king (suzerain) would initially announce his sovereignty over a nation, demand loyalty, impose sanctions for disobedience, offer protection for obedience, publish a law code, and establish the rules of succession. Sutton believes that these treaties were simply imitations of a fundamental structure of human government which is inherent in man's relationship with God.

1. *Transcendence/immanence (redemption)*

Some of the highlights include the following. In Genesis 1:1 we read, "In the beginning, God created the heaven and the earth." He is the Creator God. He is not part of the creation. Thus, the Bible announces the *Creator/creature distinction*. This distinction is fundamental to every aspect of life. God is not to be in any way confused with His creation. He is not part of a hypothetical "chain of being" with His creation. As the Psalmist put it: "For thou, LORD, art high above all the earth: thou art exalted far above all gods" (Ps. 97:9). "The LORD is great in Zion; and he is high above all the people" (Ps. 99:2). Perhaps the crucial verses in the Bible that deal with God's transcendence are Isaiah 55:8-9: "For my thoughts are not your thoughts, neither are your ways my ways, saith the LORD. For as the heavens are higher than the earth, so are my ways higher than your ways, and my thoughts than your thoughts."[1]

God is transcendent, but He is also immanent. He is not so far removed from His creation that He has no contact with it. Genesis 1:2 says that the Spirit of God hovered (moved) upon the face of the waters. This imagery of God as a bird hovering over its brood is found throughout the Old Testament. Deuteronomy 32:11 compares God's deliverance of Israel out of the wilderness to an eagle fluttering over her young. (This is amazingly similar to the suzerainty treaties that announced the power of the suzerain and his historical acts.) Psalm 91:4 reads: "He shall cover thee with his feathers, and under

---

1. Those who are familiar with the writings of Christian philosopher Cornelius Van Til will recognize that the Creator/creature distinction is Van Til's starting point: the *sovereignty of God* and therefore the *non-autonomy of man*. John Frame writes: "Van Til's apologetics is essentially simple, however complicated its elaborations. It makes two basic assertions: (1) that human beings are obligated to presuppose God in all of their thinking, and (2) that unbelievers resist this obligation in every aspect of thought and life. The first assumption leads Van Til to criticize the notion of intellectual autonomy; the second leads him to discuss the noetic [knowledge] effects of sin. . . . The initial description of presuppositionalism shows insight in the prominent place given to Van Til's critique of autonomy: that is, I think, the foundation of Van Til's system and its most persuasive principle. We must not do apologetics as if we were a law unto ourselves, as if we were the measure of all things. Christian thinking, like all of Christian life, is subject to God's lordship." Frame, "Van Til and the Ligonier Apologetic," *Westminster Theological Journal*, XLVII (1985), p. 282.

his wings shalt thou trust: his truth shall be thy shield and buckler."

Thus, the Bible denies both deism and pantheism. God is not like the god of deism who "winds up the universe" as a man winds up a clock, and then goes away, leaving it to its own preordained, impersonal devices. We do not live in a world of cosmic impersonalism. God is also not to be identified with His creation, as pantheism's god is. The creation *reflects* His glory; it does not participate in God. God is present with His creation; He is not part of it.

2. *Hierarchy/authority (submission)*

The second principle of the covenant is that of hierarchy/authority. The King of creation comes before men and demands that they submit to Him. God required Adam to obey Him. The relationship between God and man is therefore one of *command and obedience*. The covenant is therefore a *bond*. It is a *personal* relationship between responsible individuals. It is to be a *union*. But this union is not ontological. It is not a union of common "being." God is not some pantheistic being. Men are not evolving into God (Eastern religion). It is a personal relationship based on *authority and submission*.

3. *Ethics/dominion (stipulations)*

The third aspect of the covenant is its ethical quality. The terms of submission are ethical. The union between covenant-keepers and their God is an ethical union. The disunion between covenant-breakers and God is equally ethical: they are rebels against His law. Adam's fall into sin did not take place because he lacked some essence, some aspect of "being." He was created perfect. He fell willfully. He knew exactly what he was doing. "Adam was not deceived," Paul writes (I Tim. 2:14a).

This emphasis on ethics separates biblical religion from pagan religion. Man is supposed to exercise dominion, but not autonomous power. He is not to seek power through ritual, or through any attempted manipulation of God or the universe. Dominion is based on adherence to the law of God—by Christ, perfectly and definitively, and by men, subordinately and progressively. Thus, ethics is set in opposition to magic (what Van Til calls metaphysics).

We are not to misuse God's name in a quest for power over creation. To do so is to imitate God. God spoke the creation into existence by the power of His word. Man must not imitate God in this way.

4. *Judicial/evaluational (sanctions)*

The fourth aspect of the covenant is its judicial character. The essence of maturity is man's ability to render God-honoring judgment. God renders definitive judgment in His word, the Bible, and renders final judgment at the end of time. Man is to render analogous judgment progressively through time. During the creation week, God said "It is good" after each day. He *evaluated* His own work, and He *rendered judgment verbally.* God is the supreme King, but also the supreme Judge. When He *declares* a man innocent, because of His grace to the person through the gift of saving faith, God thereby imputes Christ's righteousness to him.[2] Without God's declaration of salvation, meaning without the imputation of Christ's righteousness to overcome the imputation of Adam's sin, there is no salvation.

When a covenant is "cut," men are reminded of both the blessings and the cursings attached to the covenant. There are oaths and vows. There are covenant rituals. There are visible signs and seals. We see this in the church (baptism, Lord's Supper), the family (marriage ceremony), and in civil government (pledge of allegiance, oath-taking of officers).

5. *Legitimacy/inheritance (continuity)*

Finally, there is the legitimacy/inheritance aspect of the covenant. There are covenantally specified standards of transferring the blessings of God to the next generation. In other words, the covenant extends over time and across generations. It is a bond which links past, present, and future. It has implications for men's time perspective. It makes covenantally faithful people mindful of the earthly future after they die. It also makes them respectful of the past. For example, they assume that the terms of the covenant do not change in principle. At the same time, they also know that they must be diligent in seeking to apply the fixed ethical terms of the covenant to new historical situations. They are respectful of great historic creeds, and they are also advocates of progress, creedal and otherwise. They believe in change *within the fixed ethical terms of the covenant.*

---

2. John Murray, *Redemption Accomplished and Applied* (London: Banner of Truth Trust; Grand Rapids, Michigan: Eerdmans, 1961).

xiv   THE SINAI STRATEGY

The Ten Commandments

What Sutton had not seen when he wrote his first draft was that the ten commandments adhere to this same structure, even its very numbering. More than this: once we recognize that this structure undergirds the ten commandments, we come to a remarkable insight: there really are two "tables" of the law. No, there was not a pair of stones, with five laws written on each. There were two tablets with all ten written on each. They served as copies, one for God and one for Israel, in much the same way as a modern sales receipt, which is implicitly modeled after God's covenant. But there were two separate sections of the ten commandments (literally: ten "words" [Deut. 4:13]). They were arranged along this same covenantal pattern in two separate sections, 1-5 and 6-10.

In the Bible, there is to be a *two-fold witness* to the truth. Conviction for a capital crime requires two witnesses (Deut. 17:7; Num. 35:30). Satan in the garden sought two human witnesses against God, to test God's word and therefore challenge it. There are two angelic witnesses for every demon, for Satan only took a third of the angelic host with him (Rev. 12:4). Revelation 8 provides a deeply symbolic description of God's earthly judgment. He sends angels to judge one-third of: trees, sea, creatures, ships, rivers, waters, sun, moon, stars. In short, two-thirds are spared. This is the testimony to God's victory, in time and on earth. The double witness pattern is basic to covenantal law and historic judgment.[3]

What we find is that the very structure of the ten commandments serves as a two-fold witness to the structure of the covenant. Sutton subsequently concluded that the first five-part pattern deals with the priestly functions, while the second five-part pattern deals with the kingly.

I. First Table (priestly)

The traditional distinction between the "two tables of the law" is based on 1) what man owes to God, namely, proper worship (first table) and 2) what man owes to his fellow man (second table). The problem has always come with the fifth commandment, which requires children to honor parents. This one seems to violate any

---

3. Gary North, "Witnesses and Judges," *Biblical Economics Today* (Aug./Sept. 1983).

five-five division between the God-oriented "first table" and the man-oriented or society-oriented pattern of the "second table." In fact, as we shall see, the fifth commandment is right where it belongs, on the "priestly side of the table."

1. *Transcendence/immanence (redemption)*

The first commandment begins with a description of who God is. He is the God who delivered Israel out of the land of Egypt, out of the house of bondage. Therefore, we must have no other gods before Him.

This God is the God of liberation — liberation in history. He is transcendent because he is the God of gods, the one true God who exercises absolute sovereignty. How do we know this? First, He says so in Genesis 1. Second, He offers evidence: His defeat of the gods of Egypt. In fact, because He is transcendent, He must be immanent. He is omnipresent. The Psalmist says: "Whither shall I go from thy Spirit? Or whither shall I flee from thy presence? If I ascend up into heaven, thou art there: if I make my bed in hell, behold, thou art there" (Ps. 139:7-8). Jeremiah writes: "Am I a God at hand, saith the LORD, and not a God afar off? Can any hide himself in secret places that I shall not see him? saith the LORD. Do not I fill heaven and earth? saith the LORD" (Jer. 23:23-24). Not only is He *generally present* throughout creation, He is *specially present* with His people. "For what nation is there so great, who hath God so nigh unto them, as the LORD our God is in all things that we call upon him for? (Deut. 4:7). He is a universal God, the God of creation, yet He is also the God of history. In short, this most high God is the God of *deliverance*. Therefore, men are to have no other gods before Him, meaning above Him.

2. *Hierarchy/authority (submission)*

He then forbids the use of graven images. Men bow down to their gods. This shows their subordination to them. God said that men are not to make graven images for themselves, nor are they to serve them. This would be an act of rebellion: removing themselves from the subordination to God, and substituting a rival god of their choice — their autonomous choice — to worship.

There is a warning attached: God is a jealous God who visits (sees, visits) the iniquity of men. There is also a promise: God also shows mercy to thousands (of generations) of those who love him and keep His commandments. *Keep His commandments*, therefore, and gain His mercy. He is in power over men, and He is in a position as a judge to dispense punishments and mercy. In short, *obey*.

3. *Ethics/dominion (stipulations)*

Do not take the name of God in vain. As I argue in the third chapter, by using the name of a society's god, rebellious men seek to *invoke power*. It is an attempt to manipulate that god in order to get him to do the will of man. God warns us against using His name in this way. To do so is to use His name in vain.

This does not mean that there is no power associated with God's name. On the contrary, there is immense power. This is why men are not to invoke this power autonomously. God promises to honor His name when it is used lawfully by church authorities, which is his ordained monopoly. The church alone can legitimately declare excommunication in the name of God. Thus, what we call "swearing" (profanity) is an unlawful attempt to manipulate God by rebellious men who assume the position of His ordained monopoly, the church. (See chapter three.)

The magician believes that "words of power" can be used to manipulate external events. Man seeks power by manipulating his environment. He attempts to become master of the creation by the use of secret phrases or techniques known only to initiates, whether witch doctors or scientists. Men seek *power through manipulation* rather than by ethics, obedience, and service to others.

The prohibition on the misuse of God's name cuts off magic at the roots. The commandment, being negative, is nonetheless positive: ethical. We are considering the priestly function here, however; the ethical and dominical aspects are more clearly seen in the eighth commandment, which parallels the third.

4. *Judicial/evaluational (sanctions)*

Sutton argues that the sabbath was the day of evaluation in the Old Testament. As I argue in chapter four, following James Jordan's exegesis, the sabbath was also the day of judgment by God. On that day, Satan tempted man. Thus, there had to be judgment. There was supposed to be judgment of Satan by Adam provisionally, and then by God upon His return that afternoon. Instead, Adam sided with Satan against God's word, and God returned to judge both man and Satan. But it was indeed judgment day. The sabbath was therefore a day of rendering judgment on the efforts of the previous six days. Men halted their normal labors and rested, as God had rested after His six-day efforts. In the New Testament, the church celebrates the Lord's Supper on the Lord's day, which is analogous to (but not the same as) the Old Testament sabbath. Each church member is to examine himself for the previous week's transgressions, making confession before God before taking communion (I Cor. 11:28-32). Paul's words are forthright: "For if we would judge ourselves, we should not be judged. But when we are judged, we are chastened of the Lord, that we should not be condemned with the world" (vv. 31-32). Those who judge themselves falsely can thereby come under God's earthly judgment, which is why Paul points to sickness and even death within the Corinthian church (v. 30). In short, the fourth commandment is judicial.

I also argue that the sabbath millennium is coming, and that this will be an era of rest and judgment, when God's people will take dominion by exercising godly judgment, thereby bringing Satan and his host under preliminary condemnation, in preparation for God's return at the end of the millennium to render final judgment.

5. *Legitimacy/inheritance (continuity)*

Honoring father and mother is required because of the testamental nature of the covenant. Men grow old and need care; they also transfer wealth and authority to successors. To this fifth commandment a promise is attached: long life in the land which God gives to us. This commandment seems to be man-oriented, and also a uniquely *positive* law, in contrast to the priestly negatives of the first four.[4] Nevertheless, if we see this law as essentially priestly in scope, then it places the family under the overall protection of the church, or in Old Testament times, under the protection of the priests. The priesthood, not the civil government, is the protector of the primary agency of welfare, the family, and therefore the church is the secondary agency of welfare, should the family prove incapable of providing for its own.

This is why Jesus cited the fifth commandment when He criticized the Pharisees for giving alms in public but not taking care of their parents (Mark 7:10-13). They were being unfaithful to their

---

4. The sabbath law was essentially negative: no work.

calling as sons. They were therefore illegitimate sons. Jesus was calling them *bastards*. He also told them that they were the sons of their father, the devil (John 8:44). Again, He was calling them illegitimate spiritual sons rather than sons of Abraham, which they proclaimed of themselves.

It should not be surprising that the church is required to care for "widows indeed," meaning 60-year-old women who have not remarried and whose younger relatives refused to support them (I Tim. 5:2-5). This is because the protection of the family is a priestly function. It should also not be surprising that the same passage says that the man who refuses to take care of his family is worse than an infidel (I Tim. 5:8). This is why the church can and should excommunicate such people. They come under the priestly ban.

It is clear that the civil government is not the economic protector of the family when it breaks down. The church is. The unwarranted growth of the welfare State in the twentieth century is therefore a manifestation of a satanic pseudo-family and a pseudo-priesthood of the modern messianic State. This development has paralleled the breakdown of the family, a breakdown which the State in fact subsidizes through tax-financed welfare programs; it has also paralleled the default of the church as the secondary agency of welfare.

II. Second Table (kingly)

There is no question that this second table of the ten is not ecclesiastical and priestly in focus but rather social (familial) and political. On the other hand, the second table is no less religious than the first table of the law. Both tables are inescapably religious. But the two are separated in terms of the *primary* locus of sovereignty: family and civil government, not church.

6. *Transcendence/immanence (redemption)*

It is illegal to kill men. Why? Because men are made in the image of God (Gen. 9:5-6). They reflect His transcendence in a way that animals and other aspects of the creation do not. *Man is uniquely symbolic of God.*

God is transcendent. He is untouchable, absolutely sovereign, and beyond challenge. Man, His image, is not equally sovereign or equally protected. To a limited extent, he is protected. Animals, for instance, are afraid of him (Gen. 9:2). Still, he is vulnerable to attack since Adam's fall. Thus, to attack man seems to be an indirect way to attack God. This is one reason why Satan tempted man in the first place. To a kill man unlawfully is an affront against the image of God.

I discuss "God's monopoly of execution," the civil government, in chapter six, but I failed to link this commandment with the first commandment. The transcendence of God is the basis of this commandment: the transcendent God must be worshipped, and His image must not be slain.

7. Hierarchy/authority (submission)

Adultery is prohibited. Adultery in the Bible is linked theologically to idolatry. Ancient pagan societies adopted ritual prostitution, sometimes in the temple or at the entrance to the temple. To break the marital covenant is the earthly equivalent of breaking the covenant with God. This was the message of the prophet Hosea. Adultery is the equivalent of worshipping a false god, an idol. This is why it is punished by execution (Lev. 20:10; Deut. 22:22). Like the sixth commandment, which is *analogous to* and *reflective of* the first commandment, so is the seventh analogous to and reflective of the second commandment: the worship of graven images. Ultimately, both violations are the worship of autonomous man, the worship of the products of man's rebellion.

The man is head of the household. He represents God before his wife and children. They are to obey him. His authority is analogous to and reflective of God's authority. The wife is functionally subordinate to the husband, just as the Son of God is functionally subordinate to the Father. The wife is not ethically inferior to the husband, just as the Son of God is not ethically inferior to the Father. There is hierarchy in the family, just as there is hierarchy in the Godhead itself. (This is what theologians call the "economical trinity," to distinguish it from the "ontological trinity," meaning the co-equal nature of the three Persons. Both doctrines are true, depending on what aspect of the trinity you are discussing.)

Adultery is a ritual denial of the faithfulness of Christ to His church, which Paul compares to a marriage (Eph. 5:22-33). It is a denial of the permanence of the hierarchical bond between Christ and the church.

Adultery is also a ritual denial of the trinity. It says that the covenantal bond between marriage partners is breakable. But this bond is analogous to the bond among the members of the trinity. Thus, it is a denial of the trinity, for if men can lawfully break the marriage covenant at will, then analogously, so can God break the covenant that binds the Persons of the godhead. This leads to polytheism, which is why polytheistic cultures of the ancient world so often had ritual prostitution. This ritual reflected the theological foundation of these cultures. Adultery is therefore a form of idolatry, and analogous to the idolatry which is prohibited by the second commandment. It is a denial of man's subordination to God.

8. *Ethics/dominion (stipulations)*

The eighth commandment protects private property. This is a fundamental aspect of dominion. While the third commandment prohibited using the Lord's name in vain — a denial of magic — this commandment prohibits any interference with another man's tools of dominion (his capital goods), and it also protects the fruits of his labor, consumer goods. Just as magic appropriates power to the magician, even though he has not served consumers in a market in order to gain his wealth, so does theft appropriate wealth that was not produced by the owner, or bought by the owner, or lawfully inherited by the owner.

The magician wants to manipulate the world in order to gain his ends apart from lawful service. This is why we find that in pagan cultures, envy, jealousy, and magic are closely linked.[5] The thief has a similar view of life: to enrich himself at the expense of others without voluntary exchange and service to the victim. Both the magician and the thief seek to escape the limits God has placed on them. Both seek power without covenantal faithfulness to the laws of God.

9. *Judicial/evaluational (sanctions)*

The ninth commandment prohibits false witness. This commandment implicitly refers to a law court. It is illegal to harm another person by testifying falsely to his character or his actions. Satan asked Adam and Eve to act against God's law — in short, to deny the integrity of God and the reliability of His word. God's judgment is imposed in terms of an accurate assessment of all the facts, and then these acts are evaluated by Him in terms of His law. He bears true witness to Himself and to the acts, thoughts, and motives of all men.

---

5. Helmut Schoeck, *Envy: A Theory of Social Behavior* (New York: Harcourt, Brace & World, [1966] 1970), chaps. 3, 4.

God does not bear false witness against others. In other words, He *evaluates* reliably. On the day of judgment, His judgment will be perfect. Meanwhile, in time and on earth, men are to "think God's thoughts after Him." They are to evaluate everything in terms of God's standards, and in terms of an accurate perception of external events. They are to regard history as God's product. To testify falsely against a truthful historical record is to violate the ninth commandment.

The link between the sabbath law and the false witness law is the day of judgment. Just as each person at the end of the week in Israel was supposed to evaluate his work, and whose rest was an acknowledgement of God's sovereignty over all of history, so is the commandment against false witness designed to force men to acknowledge God's sovereignty over history. Man does not create a new history by distorting the past. Man does not create a new future by distorting the past. Man only brings himself under condemnation by attempting such a crime against man and God.

10. *Legitimacy/inheritance (continuity)*

Coveting another person's goods is to covet the inheritance he will leave to his children. This also prohibits a premature coveting of parents' wealth by the children. Coveting is the first step to theft (eighth commandment). It is also a first step before adultery (seventh commandment, "thy neighbor's wife") and sometimes before murder (sixth commandment, e.g., David's murder of Uriah). Coveting is a denial of the ninth commandment, too: an implicit assertion of the illegitimacy of the present legal order which establishes the owner's rights to his property and his children's legal rights of inheritance. Evil men are tempted to misuse the courts to achieve their goals. Ahab's theft of Naboth's vineyard (I Kings 21) is representative: coveting led to the corrupting of justice through the hiring of false witnesses and then the murder of a righteous man.

The Jubilee law in Old Testament Israel was designed to reduce such coveting with respect to land. Land had to be returned to the lawful, legitimate heirs every 50 years (Lev. 25).

In effect, the covetous person regards himself as the true heir to his neighbor's patrimony. He wishes to dispossess the lawful heirs. He plots against history—the history which led to his neighbor's position and goods—in the name of his own autonomy.

Conclusion

The ten commandments are divided into two sections of five commandments each. The first section is priestly, while the second is kingly or dominical. Both sections reflect the same five-part aspect of the Deuteronomic covenant structure.

Is this structure permanent? Sutton traces it back to Adam, Noah, and Abraham. He traces it forward to David, Malachi, and Jesus' Great Commission. I find it also in the temptation of Christ by Satan, and in the trial of Jesus by the Jewish leaders.

Satan's Temptation of Jesus

The devil came to Jesus in the wilderness, and in three different challenges, he tempted Him (Matt. 4).

First Commandment: transcendence/immanence: Satan asked Jesus to worship him. This would have been a violation of the commandment to have no other gods before the God of the Bible. Jesus refused, citing Deuteronomy 6:13.

Second Commandment: hierarchy/authority: Satan asked Jesus to throw Himself off the top of the temple. Satan cited a promise of God as justification (Ps. 91:11). Jesus' reply: do not tempt God (Deut. 6:16). This is a matter of obedience. The next verse in Deuteronomy 6 is significant: "Ye shall diligently keep the commandments of the LORD your God, and his testimonies, and his statutes, which he hath commanded thee" (6:17). Again, He answered Satan's request with God's requirement to *obey* God by obeying God's law. He honored the covenantal principle of hierarchy/authority.

Third Commandment: ethics/dominion: Satan asked Him to command stones to turn into bread. This would have been a transgression of the third commandment: misusing the spoken word to gain power over creation, which is an imitation of God. He tempted Jesus to become a magician. Would He, as perfect humanity, feed Himself in His hunger by means of *a word of magic*? The answer was appropriately ethical: man lives by *the word of God*, a citation of Deuteronomy 8:3, the chapter which restated the terms of the covenant to Israel before they left the wilderness and entered the promised land.

Fourth Commandment: judicial/evaluational: Satan cited Psalm 91:11 in his temptation at the temple. He said, "for it is written." This was a variation of his temptation of Eve, where he also partially cited the word of God. Was he citing God's word correctly? He was promising

Jesus a covenantal blessing. Who was in a lawful position to offer covenantal blessings, Satan or God? Satan did not mention a curse, but it too was implicit in the covenant. Who would impose it, Satan or God? Jesus had to evaluate Satan's use of the Bible with respect to this decision in history. He then had to respond to Satan. Jesus pronounced judgment against Satan, as He did in each case, by citing the word of God accurately and appropriately.

It is possible to view the cross as Satan's self-deluded attempt to impose a curse on Jesus for not worshipping him. It was God's imposition of the curse against mankind in general on Jesus, who was innocent: the substitutionary atonement. This atonement gives rebellious men earthly life for a season and regenerate men both earthly life and eternal life. Yet it was Satan who initiated the historic process which led to the crucifixion when he entered into Judas and provoked him to evil (Luke 22:3). He must have believed that this would be to his own advantage. It is reasonable to interpret Satan's motivation in terms of the fourth commandment: the judicial imposition of the death penalty for Jesus' refusal to worship him.

Fifth Commandment: legitimacy/inheritance. Satan offered Jesus the kingdoms of this world. This implied that Jesus was not God's lawful heir. Had Jesus accepted this offer by paying Satan's price (worshipping Satan), He would thereby have imitated Adam, who lost his inheritance to Satan because of his transgression. Satan became a false heir (a squatter) because of Adam's transgression, and it was Jesus who was at last coming to reclaim His inheritance. He was calling Satan a false owner. He was calling Satan a bastard.

The Pharisees' False Covenant Lawsuit Against Jesus

At the trial of Jesus, the high priest asked Him if He was the Christ, the son of the Blessed. Jesus replied forcefully: "I am." (In the Greek, it reads *ego eimi*, a very strong emphasis.) He said they would see Him coming in the clouds of heaven (Mark 14:62). This meant God's clouds of judgment (fourth commandment). It meant the destruction of Jerusalem, just as it had meant the destruction of Egypt before: "Behold, the LORD is riding on a swift cloud, and is about to come to Egypt; the idols of Egypt will tremble at His presence" (Isa. 19:1). By implication, Jesus was calling them disobedient idolaters (second commandment). He was speaking as their heavenly Judge, meaning God, but they refused to honor Him and worship Him as

God (first commandment).

"Then the high priest rent his clothes, and saith, What need we any further witnesses? Ye have heard the blasphemy: what think ye? And they all condemned him to be guilty of death" (Mark 14:63-64). So they accused Jesus of blasphemy, which would have been a violation of the first commandment, had the accusation been true.

Let us consider the violations of the ten commandments in this trial. They refused to worship the transcendent Father of Jesus, for they refused to acknowledge that Jesus was God walking among them, a violation of the *first* commandment: transcendence/immanence (presence). They refused to obey Him, which was a violation of the *second* commandment: hierarchy/authority (obedience). The high priest was His accuser, and it was the high priest who spoke in the name of God. The court consented to this invocation of God's authority, a violation of the *third* commandment, ethics/anti-magic. The court brought a false charge against Him (blasphemy), a violation of the *ninth* commandment, because they did not evaluate His ministry properly, a violation of the *fourth* commandment, the sabbatical principle of judgment/evaluation. They unlawfully executed the son of God, deliberately (for He had told them that He was, in fact, the son of God), a violation of the *sixth* commandment. In doing so, they tried to appropriate His inheritance for themselves (Luke 20:13-15), which was a violation of the *fifth* commandment: legitimacy/inheritance. The root sin here was covetousness, a violation of the *tenth* commandment: legitimacy/inheritance. This attempted theft of His inheritance was also a violation of the *eighth* commandment, which prohibits theft. They broke the covenant, and in doing so, separated Israel from her husband, God, a violation of the command against adultery, the *seventh* commandment: hierarchy/authority (obedience).

God's law regarding perjury is clear: the false accuser is to receive the judgment which would otherwise have been visited on the condemned person (Deut. 19:16-19). Thus, God brought upon Israel in 70 A.D. the judgment which Israel had meted out to His son, the lawful heir.

Conclusion

The ten commandments are the archetypal summary of the two covenants of God, Old and New. They manifest the five component parts of the Deuteronomic covenant, and they manifest them twice, commandments 1-5 and 6-10. They provide a dual witness to the truth. By identifying all five elements of the covenant, we can better understand God's claim on all men in general and redeemed men in particular. These claims involve economic claims and requirements, as we shall see.

INTRODUCTION

A standard remark that we hear in Christian circles is this: "The Bible has answers for all of man's problems." The very first problem comes, however, when we begin to ask specific questions about the Bible's answers for specific problems in any one area of life. All of a sudden, people who only moments before had assured us that the Bible has the answers now begin to backtrack. "Well," they say, "the Bible has all the answers for man's *spiritual* problems."

This is a significant admission — *an admission of failure*. If the Bible has answers for only narrowly defined spiritual problems, and not for the concrete, day-to-day problems of economics, family relationships, politics, law, medicine, and all other areas of life, then we are faced with a terrible dilemma. Either these areas of life are not areas affected by the "spirit" — the so-called "spiritual" concerns — or else the Bible *doesn't* really have the specific answers that men desperately need in their daily decision-making. Either we live in a dualistic world — a world of totally separated parts: "spirit" and "matter" — or else we have been mistaken about the ability of the Bible to answer man's questions.

But what if we refuse to accept either of these possibilities? What if we still want to insist that the Bible does have answers for men's problems? There is a third possibility. The original statement is correct after all: the Bible *does* have answers to all of men's problems, but these answers are in the form of *first principles*. These biblical first principles apply to every area of life. Sometimes they apply specifically, such as the law, "Thou shalt not kill." In other situations, they apply in principle, such as the scientific principle that the universe is orderly. But they do apply, and without them, there can be no true knowledge of "the way the world works."

There is a fourth possibility. Sometimes the Bible presents very specific laws that modern men mistakenly believe no longer apply to

1

our era. Men misinterpret these Old Testament laws as temporary instructions given by God in ancient times — laws that no longer apply to the modern world. But what if God still intends for His people to honor these laws? What if these laws really *are* valid in modern times? What if the presumed dualism between spirit and matter is false in the case of specific biblical laws, as well as false in theory?

Spiritual Problems and Biblical Law

The original statement is true: the Bible provides the answer for every problem, not just "spiritual" problems. The Bible has answers for spiritual problems. What we need to understand is that *all of man's problems are spiritual problems.* The dualism of spirit and matter is an ancient heresy. It was called gnosticism in the ancient world, and it was a major rival philosophy to Christianity. Forms of it have revived throughout history. We need to reject it entirely. We need to recognize that man's so-called "earthly" problems are in reality spiritual problems, because when Adam rebelled, he *really* rebelled. It wasn't some Sunday morning rebellion; it was an "all week long" kind of rebellion. He rebelled in spirit, but this rebellion had an outward manifestation: eating the forbidden fruit. Was that forbidden fruit an earthly problem? Of course; Adam was an earthly creature. Was that forbidden fruit a spiritual problem? Of course, for Adam was a spiritual creature. Did God's judgment on Adam involve his flesh, not to mention his environment? Yes. Did God's judgment involve Adam's spirit? Yes. And what we say of Adam we also must say of ourselves, and of mankind in general. Every problem is a spiritual problem, for man's spirit is in ethical rebellion against God's Spirit.

Twentieth-century Christians have had a false view of spirituality because they have had an *incomplete view of sin.* They have failed to understand how comprehensive the effects of sin really are, and because of this, *they have not understood how comprehensive the redemption of Jesus Christ really is.*[1] They have failed to understand that the redemption of Jesus Christ involves both the spirit of man and the body of man. It also involves the redemption of the environment of man. In short, Jesus Christ *definitively* (once and for all) *removed the curse of God from redeemed men.* Since that curse was comprehensive, so is the removal of that curse. *Progressively,* redeemed men work out their salva-

---

1. Gary North, "Comprehensive Redemption: A Theology for Social Action," *The Journal of Christian Reconstruction*, VIII (Summer 1981).

tions with fear and trembling (Phil. 2:12). *Finally,* God will declare them righteous before all men and angels at the day of judgment, when the removal of the curse will be complete. In short, what was definitive at Calvary — Satan's defeat — is being progressively revealed in history, and will be finally revealed at the day of judgment and in eternity.

Because Christians in our day have failed to understand these fundamental biblical principles, they have misunderstood the meaning of "spiritual." David Chilton's comments are to the point: "When the Bible uses the term *Spiritual*, it is generally speaking of *the Holy Spirit*. . . . To be Spiritual is to be guided and motivated by the Holy Spirit. It means obeying His commands as recorded in the Scriptures. The Spiritual man is not someone who floats in midair and hears eerie voices. The Spiritual man is the man who does what the Bible says (Rom. 8:4-8). This means, therefore, that we *are* supposed to get involved in life. God wants us to apply Christian standards everywhere, in every area. Spirituality does not mean retreat and withdrawal from life; it means *dominion*. The basic Christian confession of faith is that *Jesus is Lord* (Rom. 10:9-10) — Lord of all things, in heaven and on earth. As Lord, He is to be glorified in every area (Rom. 11:36). In terms of Christian Spirituality, in terms of God's requirements for Christian action in every area of life, there is no reason to retreat."[2]

But how do we know that we are being Spiritual? By looking to the Bible in order to discover the principles of Spiritual living. What are these *permanent* principles called in the Bible? *The law.* Modern Christians may prefer to use some other word to describe these fixed, permanent principles — rules, guidelines, blueprints for living — but the Bible calls these principles the *law of God*. This is why faith in, respect for, and obedience to the law always accompany true Spirituality.

Let us return to the question at hand: Does the Bible speak to every kind of problem that man has? It does. While I believe in the third possibility, meaning that the Bible provides the only source of true principles of knowledge, with God the Creator as the only source of order, I believe also in the fourth possibility: the continuing validity of many Old Testament laws. We have ignored these laws in modern times, and we have paid a heavy price. We will pay an even

---

2. David Chilton, *Paradise Restored: A Biblical Theology of Dominion* (Tyler, Texas: Reconstruction Press, 1985), p. 4.

heavier price if we continue to discount the laws of God.

How do we know that a particular Old Testament law is no longer legally binding, let alone no longer morally binding, in New Testament times? There can be only one legitimate answer: *because the New Testament says so.* There should be a specific injunction that a particular law, or a particular class of laws, is no longer binding in New Testament times because Jesus' work of redemption has fulfilled it *and also annulled it.* If the New Testament does not reveal this, then the law still must be in force.³

Most Christians say that they believe in the ten commandments (the Decalogue). A few say that these laws no longer apply in New Testament times, but most Christians refuse to go this far. If we turn to the ten commandments, we should expect to find principles, as well as specifics, that give us guidance for evaluating the success or failure of our own time and civilization. If God threatens a civilization with judgment, just as He threatens individual sinners with judgment, then we ought to be able to discover laws that God expects us not to violate. If we turn to the ten commandments, we should be able to discover the foundational standards of biblical social order.⁴

At the very least, we should find in the ten commandments laws that apply to civil government and economics. After all, God delivered these laws to a nation that had experienced many decades of tyrannical slavery. God announced Himself as their deliverer in the very first commandment. Wouldn't we expect to find rules that govern economics and politics in these laws? The answer should be an unequivocal "yes."

Why is it, then, that so few commentators have ever addressed this problem? What *are* the political and economic laws of the ten commandments? Why don't commentators ask the two crucial questions:

1. How did these commandments apply in Old Testament times?

2. How should they apply today?

---

3. Greg L. Bahnsen, *Theonomy in Christian Ethics* (2nd ed.; Phillipsburg, New Jersey: Presbyterian & Reformed, 1984). For a shorter introduction, see Bahnsen, *By This Standard: The Authority of God's Law Today* (Tyler, Texas: Institute for Christian Economics, 1985).

4. R. J. Rushdoony, *The Foundations of Social Order: Studies in the Creeds and Councils of the Early Church* (Fairfax, Virginia: Thoburn Press, [1968] 1978).

The reason is fairly simple: they do not believe in the God of the Bible or God's revealed will for mankind, His law. This is especially true of seminary professors.

Useful Idiots

A good example of the professional drivel of modern antinomian "scholarship so-called" is a book by Walter Harrelson, *The Ten Commandments and Human Rights*. This book is as forthright and honest a defense of the ten commandments as the late Premier Konstantin Chernenko's book on human rights in the Soviet Union was for human rights in the Soviet Union.[5] What Harrelson and other academic "experts" on the ten commandments really want is to *escape* the ten commandments. Their faith is clear: better situation ethics than the restraining effects of God's law. As he says, "In contemporary, secularized Western society there is a wistful longing for such norms, upon which individual and family could depend in all circumstances. One reason for the rapid growth today of evangelical religion of a fundamentalist nature, or for the growth of charismatic religion, with its rigid personal and communal norms, is that such communities are thought to supply just norms. . . . We should know, however, that if we are to find a way to supply nourishment to meet this hunger, we have to do so with the utmost care. The gains of a contextualist and existentialist ethic are too numerous and too solid to be endangered by facile returns to absolutist norms. The enslavement of the human spirit in the name of religion is too well known in history. We dare not risk a recurrence of such enslavement out of fear that our society is about to collapse into normlessness. And the misuse of norms for the protection of the privileged is a perennial danger."[6]

Or, as another concerned student of biblical law and authoritarian regimes once asked: "Hath God said?"

But God *hath* said! God said that Egypt was the tyranny, not Israel. God showed the Israelites that Assyria and Babylon were the true threats to human rights, not His law. But in the name of Jesus, and in the name of human rights, today's academic specialists in the law of God come before us and warn us of the risks of asserting the

5. Konstantin U. Chernenko, *Human Rights in Soviet Society* (New York: International Publishers, 1981). This was published just before he became Soviet Premier.
6. Walter Harrelson, *The Ten Commandments and Human Rights* (Philadelphia: Fortress Press, 1980), p. 9.

eternal validity of an eternal law-order of an eternal God. They worry about offending the defenders of "a contextualist and existentialist ethic," meaning their old professors at Yale Divinity School (or wherever). They survey the strongholds of these situation ethicists, and rather than seeing the looming collapse of humanist civilization as the greatest opportunity in man's history for the triumph of God's law as the *only* possible substitute for this collapsing moral order, they urge faithful Christians to restrain themselves. Why, such efforts might embarrass these waffling theologians among their peers, and their peers are not the tithing people in the pews who pay their salaries, but the tenured atheists in the prestige divinity schools that awarded them their coveted (and low market value) doctorates. (I've got a Ph.D. myself; I know how little it is worth these days.)

In short, these fearful, obscure, and academically irrelevant drones, with their Ph.D.'s, their tenured seminary positions, and their minimal prospects for future employment if righteous Christian people ever purge the seminaries of heretics, now see what is coming: a revival of interest in God's law, and the rapid development of political skills on the part of those who take God's law seriously. They see their liberal, pleasant, tenured little world on the verge of disaster, for those naive people who have funded their rebellion — the little people in the pews — may soon catch on to their game. The court prophets are once again in trouble on Mt. Carmel. They saw what happened last time, and they are not happy about it.

Sadly, they have allies in the conservative camp: those who preach the irrelevance of the ten commandments in New Testament times. But pietism's influence is also waning in the latter decades of this century. The ecclesiastical irrelevance of the older pietistic fundamentalism is becoming pronounced. What has taken place in the United States since 1980 — really, since 1965 — has exposed the nakedness of the fundamentalist antinomians. They had no concrete, specifically biblical social answers for the radicals of the late 1960's, and they knew it. They went into retreat in the 1970's, and they are now being ignored into oblivion.

At last, conservative Christian laymen, and even a growing number of pastors, are beginning to see the light. They are beginning to understand the choices laid before them:

God's law or chaos
God's law or tyranny
God's law or God's wrath

Proof Texts, Blueprints, and Economic Antinomianism

What the ten commandments set forth is a *strategy*. This strategy is a *strategy for dominion*. The general principles of the ten commandments summarize the whole of biblical law. The case-law applications of Exodus 21-23 go on to illustrate ways in which the ten commandments are to be applied.[7] But the Decalogue itself is the master plan, the *blueprint* for biblical social order. These laws have very definite economic implications. This sort of thinking is foreign to virtually all modern Christian social and economic thinkers, whether conservative or liberal, Protestant or Catholic.

If I were to offer a single sentence of warning with respect to the misuse of the Bible by modern scholars, it would be this: *beware of doubletalk and outright gibberish*. I will put it even more bluntly: if you cannot understand what a theologian writes concerning a perfectly plain passage in the Bible, trust your instincts; you are probably being conned by a professional. These hypocrites for over two hundred years have made a lifetime occupation out of hiding their radical ideas behind a mask of orthodox language. They want to be low-risk revolutionaries, fully tenured, with their salaries provided by unsuspecting Christian sheep. Furthermore, they are, almost to a man (person?), desperate for public acceptance by secular scholars. They are humanists by conviction, even though they operate in the churches. If they forthrightly proclaimed the doctrines of the historic Christian faith without compromise, they would be ridiculed by humanist scholars. They fear this above all. So they write endless reams of convoluted language in order to hide the academic irrelevance of their concepts. (German theology is especially afflicted by this verbal constipation.) Their concepts are dangerous to orthodoxy and irrelevant to humanism, except as a tool of confusing the faithful. Liberal theologians are simply examples of what Lenin used to call "useful idiots."[8] They are middlemen for the humanists in a great deception of the faithful. They have been described best by David Chilton: "Modern theologians are like a pack of dogs who spend most of their time sniffing each other's behinds."

---

7. James B. Jordan, *The Law of the Covenant: An Exposition of Exodus 21-23* (Tyler, Texas: Institute for Christian Economics, 1984).

8. John P. Roche, *The History and Impact of Marxist-Leninist Organizational Theory: "Useful Idiots," "Innocents' Clubs," and "Transmission Belts"* (Cambridge, Massachusetts: Institute for Foreign Policy Analysis, 1984).

Roman Catholic Economic Antinomianism

The Lay Commission on Catholic Social Teaching is a conservative group which is made up of some of the most famous American Catholic social thinkers and political figures. Its study of Catholic economic thought announces on the opening page: ". . . Christian Scripture does not offer programmatic guidance for the concrete institutions of political economy."[9] It then cites "the great Catholic economist Heinrich Pesch, S.J." who proclaims that morally advanced societies will be better prepared to endure hard times, but "this does not mean that the economist should theologize or moralize in the treatment of his subject matter or, what is worse, try to derive an economic system from Holy Scripture."[10] This document was written specifically to counter the ultra-liberal proposed first draft of Catholic bishops regarding the U.S. economy. And what first principle regarding biblical authority governs the liberal bishops? The same as the one adopted by the Catholic lay conservatives: "Although the Bible does not and cannot give us simple and direct answers to today's complex economic questions, it can and must shape our vision of the meaning of economic life."[11] The conservatives cite the free market economists who they like, while the liberals cite the anti-free market non-economists who they like. No one appeals to biblical law.

Conservative Protestant Economic Antinomianism

Conservative Protestant philosopher Ronald Nash is opposed to liberation theology and Christian socialism. His book, *Social Justice and the Christian Church* (1983) is a ringing defense of capitalism. But not biblical capitalism. He appeals not to the Bible, but to universal standards of logic, universal truth that can be recognized by all right-thinking people. He begins with the implicit but unstated presupposition that the Bible is not sufficiently self-attesting and clear to provide generally agreed-upon conclusions; an appeal to universal logic is therefore necessary:

---

9. *Toward the Future: Catholic Social Thought and the U.S. Economy* (North Tarrytown, New York: Lay Commission, 1984), p. ix.

10. *Ibid.*, pp. ix-x.

11. "First Draft — Bishop's Pastoral: Catholic Social Teaching and the U.S. Economy," *Origins*, Vol. 14 (Nov. 15, 1984), p. 343. Published by the National Catholic News Service, Washington, D.C.

Chapter 6 considers what the Bible teaches about justice. This book intentionally rejects any proof-text approach to its subject. [But why should we expect to find autonomous proof in opposition to a biblical text? — G.N.] Many other treatments [but not all! — G.N.] of the topic purport to "discover" revealed truth about economic and social theory in the Bible and then deduce the appropriate applications of that truth to the contemporary scene. The great problem with the proof-text method is the extent to which the participants beg the question. [Beg what question? — G.N.] In most cases [but not all! — G.N.], what happens is that the writer finds some passage in the Old Testament that relates to an extinct cultural situation. [Is human reason eternally applicable, and biblical principles that undergirded the "extinct cultural situation" merely temporary? — G.N.] It is often the case [but not always! — G.N.] that such passages are ambiguous enough to give any interpreter problems. [Is human reason never ambiguous, and therefore more reliable than the "ambiguous" Bible? — G.N.] But before the reader knows it, the passage is used to prove the truth of socialism or capitalism. [Are serious Christians unable to determine good from bad exegesis in the case of biblical economic policy, so must we therefore appeal to "unambiguous" logic? And is the Bible equally ambiguous, and readers equally defenseless, with regard to everything else it speaks about? Must autonomous logic also be used to establish theological truths? — G.N.] This book takes a totally different approach. It assumes the unity of all truth. Truth in any area of human knowledge will be consistent with truth in every other area. [So why not begin, and end, with biblical revelation, since it is unquestionably true, while the speculations of men are unquestionably fallible in part? — G.N.][12]

Notice the qualifying phrases: "many other treatments," "in most cases," "it often is the case." Fine and dandy; then why not search for the *exceptions* to these generalities and adopt them when we find them? Why not search out those unique cases in which biblical texts *are* used properly by expositors, and then follow their lead? The answer is fairly simple: philosopher Nash does not believe that any Christian ever has successfully used the Bible to create a coherent, accurate, God-given and man-interpreted biblical economic framework. Furthermore, he obviously does not believe that such an effort *should* be attempted. *He* avoids the temptation, certainly. After all, why should we appeal to the Bible instead of appealing to universal human reason, which unlocks "the unity of all truth"? Implicitly, he is arguing that the Bible is not the bedrock universal; human reason

---

12. Ronald Nash, *Social Justice and the Christian Church* (Milford, Michigan: Mott Media, 1983), pp. 7-8.

is. Some people do not accept the Bible; presumably, all *rational* people will accept the findings of human reason. (Problem: given the low sales of his book, and the low sales of hundreds of other pro-free market economic books equally grounded in universal human reason, there are apparently a lot more irrational people around than people who refuse to accept the Bible. There are more people who just won't face "the universal truth" than those who reject biblical truth.)

As a devoted follower of the Protestant philosopher Gordon Clark, Dr. Nash rejects the idea of Van Til's presuppositional, Bible-based (i.e., "proof-text") approach to the intellectual defense of Christianity. He relies instead on the hypothetical natural, unbiased, and reliable reasoning abilities of natural (unregenerate) man. In short, he appeals to biblically unaided (autonomous) reason because of his personal preference and philosophical commitment. He then discovers what he regards as inescapably clear free market principles in the conclusions of autonomous human reason. Unfortunately, "radical Christians" somehow have escaped from this inescapably clear set of economic conclusions.

Liberal Evangelical Economic Antinomianism

Nevertheless, we find the same sort of "anti-proof text" reasoning in the camp of the "radical Christian" Protestants, the left-wing targets of Nash's book. In a symposium on Christian economics published by the neo-evangelical Protestant (and increasingly politically liberal) InterVarsity Press in 1984, three of the four contributors were defenders of more State planning and authority over the economy. I was the lone critic of the State. All three of the anti-market essayists explicitly denied that the Bible gives us any specifics concerning economics.

The fact that our Scriptures can be used to support or condemn any economic philosophy suggests that the Bible is not intended to lay out an economic plan which will apply for all times and places. If we are to examine economic structures in the light of Christian teachings, we will have to do it another way.[13]

The Old Testament gives detailed laws regulating economic relationships. Although *we need not feel bound by these laws*, the general concern of justice and

---

13. William Diehl, "The Guided-Market System," in Robert Clouse (ed.), *Wealth and Poverty: Four Christian Views of Economics* (Downers Grove, Illinois: InterVarsity Press, 1984), p. 87.

shalom found there is repeated in the New Testament and is meant for us.[14]

There is no blueprint of the ideal state or the ideal economy. We cannot turn to chapters of the Bible and find in them a model to copy or a plan for building the ideal biblical state and national economy.[15]

If this is true — if there are no biblical blueprints — then how can we, as Christians, come before a fallen, rebellious society which is threatened by the judgment of God, and announce confidently, "Thus saith the Lord"? How can we criticize specific economic sins with the confidence of the Old Testament prophets? How can we call men to repent, if we cannot say for certain what specific biblical laws they are violating? And more to the point, *how can we offer biblical alternatives?* How can we confidently affirm with Paul: ". . . God is faithful, who will not suffer you to be tempted above that ye are able [to bear]; but will, with the temptation also make a way to escape, that ye may be able to bear it" (I Cor. 10:13b)? Are we saying that God offers *no specific way* to escape? Are we saying that *any old way* will do, just so long as it feels right, just so long as it conforms to the recommended political and economic outlook of political liberals fifteen years ago (which they discarded five years later)?

David Chilton has called this attitude toward the Bible on the part of economic radicals, "The Case of the Missing Blueprints."[16] These "concerned Christians" reject modern free market capitalism in the name of "biblical justice," just as the "social gospel" promoters did two generations ago. Unlike the social gospellers, who really believed that the Bible teaches some form of socialism, they then turn around and tell us that the Bible does not provide a specific blueprint or outline of the godly economic system. The reason for their rejection of the Bible as a guide for economics is clear: they understand what the social gospel theologians should have understood but did not, namely, that *the Bible categorically affirms legal, moral, and economic principles that lay the foundations of a free market economic system.* They assert, with John Gladwin, "Scripture offers no blueprint for the form of modern government. This means that I will resist any idea that decentralized or privatized versions of management of the economy and the provision of services are necessarily more Christian

---

14. Art Gish, "Decentralist Economics," *ibid.*, p. 140. Emphasis added.
15. John Gladwin, "Centralist Economics," *ibid.*, p. 183.
16. David Chilton, "The Case of the Missing Blueprints," *The Journal of Christian Reconstruction*, VIII (Summer 1981).

than the centralized solution."[17] He sees that the Bible *does* teach such a decentralized and privatized view of society, so he rejects from the start any suggestion that this blueprint is still morally or legally binding on Christian societies.

InterVarsity Press in 1983 published one of its typically statist tracts in the name of Jesus. The author, a British Ph.D. from Cambridge who is now teaching theology in India, rejects the idea that Old Testament law is still literally binding in New Testament times. "In the economic sphere, the Old Testament paradigms provide us with *objectives* without requiring a *literal* transposition of ancient Israelite practice into twentieth-century society."[18] In other words, Old Testament law, which drastically limited the centralization of power by the civil government, is no longer supposed to bind the State.

Here is the two-part argument which virtually all of these wolves in sheep's clothing have adopted. First, the law's *objectives* are still binding, and the State must see to it that these objectives are achieved. Second, the *means* established by Old Testament law to achieve these objectives are rejected as being old fashioned or inappropriate for today's complex society, namely, men acting as individuals or as agents of the church, voluntary charitable societies, or families. In short, he proposes what virtually all academic Christian social commentators have proposed in this century: *the substitution of the State for society.* It is a common error in this century, and an exceedingly pernicious one.[19]

Wright states that "there are societies where the conditions of allegedly 'free' employees are pitiably more harsh and oppressive than those of slaves in Israel."[20] (He does not mention the giant slave societies created by the Communists.) "In such situations, the paradigmatic relevance of the Old Testament economic laws concerning work and employment can be taken almost as they stand. To introduce statutory rest days and holidays, statutory terms and conditions of employment, statutory protection from infringement of personal rights and physical dignity, statutory provision for fair

---

17. Gladwin, in Clouse, *op. cit.*, p. 181.
18. Christopher J. H. Wright, *An Eye for an Eye: The Place of Old Testament Ethics Today* (Downers Grove, Illinois: InterVarsity Press, 1983), p. 89.
19. Robert A. Nisbet, *The Quest for Community* (New York: Oxford University Press, 1952), p. 99.
20. Wright, pp. 79-80.

wages promptly paid, would revolutionize the face of economic life for multitudes of workers in some parts of the world. And all of these are drawn from the economic legislation of God's redeemed people, Israel."[21]

Such statutory actions would indeed revolutionize the face of economic life for multitudes of workers. It would guarantee their continuing unemployment in all legal markets. It would, if enforced universally, transfer a monopoly grant of power to industrial economies, and specifically to the monopolistic trade unions, whose members cannot stand the wage competition which is offered by Third World employees. "Statutory" is Dr. Wright's key word, and it is this word which was *not* used in the Old Testament. God, not the State, is sovereign. God issued His economic laws, and it is market competition and self-government under God's law, not statutes, that are supposed to govern men's economic actions in the vast majority of cases, as *The Dominion Covenant* volumes on the Pentateuch will demonstrate.

What is noticeable is Wright's hostility to the binding character of Old Testament law *literally* transferred to today's political institutions, for what that law would bind is the messianic State. Predictably, we find *antinomianism*—hostility to the continuing validity of God's revealed law—in close association with statism and a mania for legislation. What the Bible warns against above all—the divinization of man—and what its law-order undermines whenever it is taken seriously, the modern antinomians have implicitly accepted. The divinized State that the Bible's law-order militates against is the sacred cow of the intellectuals today. In short, there is a relationship between *false gods* and *high taxes*. These armchair socialists proclaim their allegiance to the "paradigmatic principles" of Old Testament law, but not its State-restricting specifics. They proclaim the "principle of the tithe," and then go on to promote massive compulsory taxation by the State. In short, they are devoted to Old Testament laws only on an ad hoc basis: whenever such verbal allegiance can be misdirected to glorify the authority of the State.

This same sort of social antinomianism also characterizes the so-called "cosmonomic" Christianity of the Dutch Calvinist philosopher, Herman Dooyeweerd and his followers. In their hands, the Bible becomes a manual of guild socialism or worse.[22] Liberation

---

21. *Ibid.*, p. 80.
22. See Appendix C: "Social Antinomianism."

theology appears in many circles under many names. In all instances, however, the underlying presupposition is the same: a denial of the New Testament validity of the law of God. This is why a
conservative such as Ronald Nash is incapable of responding forcefully enough to the liberals or the Dooyeweerdians.[23] By attacking
them at their weakest point, their antinomianism, he would thereby
disembowel himself.

Whose Word Is Sovereign?

What we discover is that contemporary Christian social commentators are agreed: the revealed law of God is not applicable in
New Testament times. This revealed law-order is somehow out of
date. It deals with "an extinct cultural situation." Antinomians view
the Old Testament as some sort of discarded first draft, "the word of
God (emeritus)." These commentators want to avoid the restrictions
that God has said must be placed on men, institutions, and governments, if freedom and justice are to prevail. How, then, will freedom
and justice be maintained? How will "the word of man (tenured)" establish and defend freedom and justice?

The biblical program is clear: *self-government under revealed biblical
law*, with various aspects of this law enforced by a *biblically revealed
system of decentralized courts*. There is no other valid program for the establishment and maintenance of biblically sanctioned government.
All other programs are aspects of false religions. Christians have
partially adopted false religions for two millennia. Christian social
thought has been syncretistic from the beginning. Christians have
failed in their attempt to establish freedom and justice for this very
reason.

With the rise of the Christian Reconstruction movement since
1973, this syncretism has at last been systematically challenged. Van
Til's presuppositional apologetic method, coupled with a renewed
interest in (and exposition of) biblical law, has opened the possibility
at last of the establishment of a self-conscious Christian civilization.
To accomplish this, Christians must go forward in terms of the law
delivered to man at Sinai.

---

23. Ronald H. Nash, *Dooyeweerd and the Amsterdam Philosophy* (Grand Rapids,
Michigan: Zondervan, 1962).

Conclusion

We see the "privatized" nature of the biblical social order in the eighth commandment: "Thou shalt not steal." But we also find the foundational principles of a free market economy in all the other nine commandments. The ten commandments are as fine a statement of the principles of liberty, including liberty of voluntary exchange, as we can find anywhere in the history of man. The Old Testament is an *anti-statist* document. It limits the civil government in the interests of personal *self-government*. Limited civil government is one of the two political preconditions of a free market economy. The other political precondition is *predictable law* which places limits on civil government, which the ten commandments and the case laws also provide.

The Bible does not teach a doctrine of salvation by law. In both the Old Testament and the New Testament, the doctrine is clear: "The just shall live by faith" (Hab. 2:4). The Bible teaches *dominion under God*, but it does not teach salvation by law. In contrast, all other religions teach either *salvation by law* or *salvation by mystical escape*, with the techniques of asceticism and mysticism serving as the "laws" that save man.[24] Humanism teaches salvation by law, and most forms of humanism in the twentieth century have been statist, for the State is clearly the highest and most concentrated form of power. Salvation by the State, or by an agency of the State,[25] is the common faith of twentieth-century humanists. This is why the Bible is repugnant to twentieth-century humanist man.

In the ten chapters that follow, you will learn more about the relationship between the ten commandments and economics. You will also learn more concerning the relation between the ten commandments and the dominion covenant.[26] The ten commandments certainly have implications outside of the realm of economics, but they surely have implications *at least* for economics. When men see how relevant the ten commandments are for economics, they should

24. Gary North, *Moses and Pharaoh: Dominion Religion vs. Power Religion* (Tyler, Texas: Institute for Christian Economics, 1985), Introduction.

25. R. J. Rushdoony, *The Messianic Character of American Education* (Phillipsburg, New Jersey: Presbyterian & Reformed, [1963]).

26. Gary North, *The Dominion Covenant: Genesis* (Tyler, Texas: Institute for Christian Economics, 1982).

gain new respect for the importance of the laws of God for all of life, but especially for the life of *dominion man*, the man redeemed by grace through faith in the one true Dominion Man, Jesus Christ.

1

LIBERATION ECONOMICS

God spake all these words, saying, I am the LORD thy God, which have brought thee out of the land of Egypt, out of the house of bondage. Thou shalt have no other Gods before me (Ex. 20:1-3).

God announced to the Hebrews that He had intervened decisively and miraculously in their lives. This intervention was intervention into history. It was also radically personal. The events of the Exodus cannot be cogently explained as a series of impersonal natural events.[1] There could be no doubt in the minds of the Hebrews of Moses' day that God had been the source of their liberation from Egypt. There was certainly no doubt in the minds of the people of the Canaanitic city of Jericho, as Rahab informed the spies a generation later (Josh. 2:10-11).

By identifying Himself as the source of their liberation, He announced His total sovereignty over them. A God who intervenes in history is not some distant God. He is a God of power. He possesses the power to reshape nations, seas, and history. No other god has this power; therefore, His people are required to worship only Him.

He was also their king. Middle eastern kings of the second millennium B.C. used a formula for announcing their sovereignty which was similar to God's announcement in Exodus 20:1, and also similar to God's announcement to Moses of His name (Ex. 6:2). Even when

---

1. One heroic but unsuccessful attempt to explain the exodus in terms of astronomical events is Immanuel Velikovsky, *Worlds in Collision* (New York: Doubleday, 1950), Pt. I. Velikovsky's *Ages in Chaos* (New York: Doubleday, 1952) deals with Egypt's chronology, and is a superior work. On the academic community's vicious attack on *Worlds in Collision*, see Alfred de Grazia (ed.), *The Velikovsky Affair* (New Hyde Park, New York: University Books, 1966). Cf. Gary North, "The Epistemological Crisis of American Universities," in North (ed.), *Foundations of Christian Scholarship: Essays in the Van Til Perspective* (Vallecito, California: Ross House Books, 1976), pp. 18-19.

their names were well known, they announced them in the introduction to their proclamations.[2] It also was customary for the king to record his mighty deeds.[3] To demonstrate the similarities between God's treaty with His people and the treaties of ancient monarchs, Cassuto summarizes the implicit assumptions of God's announcement: "*I*, the Speaker, am called *YHWH*, and I *am your God* specifically. Although I am the God of the whole earth (xix 5), yet I am also your God in the sense that, in consideration of this sanctification, I have chosen you to be the people of My special possession from among all the peoples of the earth (xix 6); and it is I *who brought you out of the land of Egypt*, not just bringing you forth from one place to another, but liberating you *from the house of bondage*. Hence it behooves you to serve Me not out of fear and dread, in the way that the other peoples are used to worship their gods, but from a sense of love and gratitude."[4] By asserting His sovereignty from the very beginning, as the thirteenth-century Jewish scholar Nachmanides said, God provided the reason for them to accept His commandments. Without acknowledging His sovereignty, they would not obey.[5]

Law and Liberation

He is a God of *power* and of *ethics*. Both of these aspects of God's being were revealed by His act of freeing the Hebrews from their Egyptian masters. Both love and awe-filled obedience are due to Him. The events of life are controlled by a God who can bring His words to pass. Cosmic personalism is inescapable in a created universe.[6] The Hebrews had this revelation of God's being as the historical foundation of their faith in God and His law-order. This law-order is summarized in the ten commandments that follow the introduction. The commandments are the foundation of righteous living. The whole of Old Testament law serves as a series of case-law applications of the ten.[7] Thus, they must be regarded as the basis of social

---

2. U. Cassuto, *A Commentary on the Book of Exodus* (Jerusalem: The Magnes Press, The Hebrew University, [1951] 1974), pp. 76-77.

3. *Ibid.*, p. 241.

4. *Idem.*

5. Ramban [Rabbi Moses ben Nachman], *Commentary on the Torah: Exodus* (New York: Shilo Publishing House, 1973), p. 286.

6. Gary North, *The Dominion Covenant: Genesis* (Tyler, Texas: Institute for Christian Economics, 1982), ch. 1: "Cosmic Personalism."

7. R. J. Rushdoony, *The Institutes of Biblical Law* (Nutley, New Jersey: Craig Press, 1973). James Jordan argues cogently that each of these case laws cannot easily

institutions and interpersonal relationships. Whatever the area of life under discussion — family, business, charitable association, military command, medicine, etc. — biblical law governs the actions of men.

Men can choose to ignore the requirements of the law. But God dealt definitively in Egypt and in the Red Sea with those who flagrantly and defiantly rejected the rule of His law. The Israelites had experienced firsthand the institutional effects of a social order governed by a law-order different from the Bible's. They had been enslaved. The God who had released them from bondage announced at Sinai His standards of righteousness — not just private righteousness but social and institutional righteousness. Thus, the *God of liberation* is simultaneously the *law-giver*. The close association of biblical law and human freedom is grounded in the very character of God.

The Hebrews could not have misunderstood this relationship between God's law and liberation. God identified Himself as the deliverer of Israel, and then He set forth the summary of the law structure which He requires as the standard for human action. *The God of history is the God of ethics.* There can be no biblical ethics apart from an ultimate standard, yet this standard is fully applicable in history, for it is the God of history who has announced the standard. Ethics must be simultaneously permanent and historically applicable. Permanence must not compromise the applicability of the law in history, and historical circumstances must not relativize the universality of the standard. The *dialectical tension between law and history,* which undermines every non-biblical social philosophy, is overcome by God, who is the guarantor of His law and also the guarantor of the social order which is governed by this law.[8] He is the *guarantor* of the law's permanent applicability because He is the *deliverer*, in time and on earth.

---

or automatically be subsumed under just one of the ten commandments. He writes that "any given case law may be related to more than one of the Ten Commandments, and so it would be an error to try to pigeon-hole the case laws under one Commandment each. In reality the case law as a whole comes under the Ten Commandments as a whole. Some case laws fit rather nicely under one or another of the Commandments, but most case laws seem to combine principles from several of the basic Ten." Jordan, *The Law of the Covenant: An Exposition of Exodus 21-23* (Tyler, Texas: Institute for Christian Economics, 1984), pp. 22-23.

8. R. J. Rushdoony, *The Foundations of Social Order: Studies in the Creeds and Councils of the Early Church* (Fairfax, Virginia: Thoburn Press, [1968] 1978).

The prophets of Israel repeatedly introduced their detailed critiques of Israel and Judah by first announcing that the God in whose name they were coming before the nation was the same God who had delivered them from Egypt.[9] Having made this identification, they would then go on to catalogue the sins of the nation—sins that were prohibited by biblical law. Ezekiel wrote: "Wherefore I caused them to go forth out of the land of Egypt, and brought them into the wilderness. And I gave them my statutes, and shewed them my judgments, which if a man do, he shall even live in them" (20:10-11). The New American Standard Version translates this final clause, "if a man observes them, he will live." In other words, the very foundation of life is the law of God, *if* a man truly lives in terms of this law. The prophets then listed the sins of the nation that were inevitably bringing death and destruction—the external judgment of God.

Biblical Law: God's Prescription for Healing

Does such a high view of biblical law in any way compromise the Christian doctrine of salvation by grace through faith? Not at all. Daniel Fuller has provided a helpful analogy of the relationship between biblical law and salvation by grace through faith. He describes God as a physician who prescribes a particular health regimen to patients. Jesus likened Himself to a physician with the task of healing mankind's sins (Matt. 1:21). "We avoid legalism to the extent that we acknowledge how truly sick we are and look away from ourselves and, with complete confidence in the Doctor's expertise and desire to heal us, follow his instructions (the obedience of faith!) *in order to* get well. We should understand that the entire business of our lives is the convalescence involved in becoming like Christ."[10] While a physician expects that patients will deviate occasionally from his prescribed program, he understands that a patient who consistently rejects his advice has lost faith in the physician and his program. "That is why the Bible emphasizes persevering faith."[11] This biblical faith looks toward the future, for saving faith is essentially "a confidence directed toward a future in which God will do and be all he has promised in the Bible."[12]

---

9. Isa. 43:3; Jer. 2:6; Hos. 13:4.
10. Daniel P. Fuller, *Gospel and Law: Contrast or Continuum?* (Grand Rapids, Michigan: Eerdmans, 1980), p. 118.
11. *Idem.*
12. *Ibid.*, p. 112.

"It should now be clear," Fuller continues, "why the necessity for obedience in no way clashes with *sola gratia* ('by grace alone'), for the Doctor is administering his cure just from the sheer joy he has in extending a blessing to others and in being appreciated for what he does. The Doctor does not bless people because they are the workmen who have rendered some necessary service to him which obligates him to reimburse them with medical care. It should also be clear why the obedience of faith is *sola fide* ('by faith alone'), for obedience is impelled wholly by faith and is not something added on to faith as though it were coordinate with it. . . . Finally, there should be no difficulty in understanding how the Doctor receives all the glory (*sola gloria*), the credit for the cures that are performed, and for the additional patients that flock to his clinic because of the glowing testimonies of those who have already experienced partial healing."[13]

Those who worship any god other than the God who reveals His standards in the Bible are worshippers of a false god. No other god, no other goal, no other standard is to replace men's faith in the living God who delivered Israel. God is primary; there is no secondary God. From this it follows that *those who proclaim a law-order alien to the one set forth in the Bible are thereby proclaiming the validity of the word of some other god.* They have become idolators — perhaps not conscious idolators, but idolators nonetheless. They are aiding and abetting the plans of men who worship another god. A god's personal (or impersonal) attributes are revealed by its law-order. *To proclaim a rival law-order is to proclaim a rival god.* Pluralism is political polytheism.

Biblical Economics and Liberation

Can men legitimately have confidence in the law of God in economic affairs? Yes. Why is this confidence justified? Because the same God who delivered Israel from the Egyptians also established the laws of economics. This means that the basis of these economic laws is not man, or random chance, or historical cycles, or the impersonal forces of history, but instead is the *sustaining providence of God.* The guarantor of the reliability of economic law is a personal Being who delivers His people from those who defy His law.

Biblical economics is liberation economics. Anti-biblical economics is therefore bondage economics. Those who present themselves as defenders of liberation economics, but who refuse to be governed in

---

13. *Ibid.*, pp. 119-20.

their economic recommendations by the concrete, explicit revelation of God concerning the laws of economics, are wolves in sheep's clothing. If they are proclaiming some variant of Marxism, socialism, interventionism, or other State-deifying economics, then they are the moral equivalent of the ancient Egyptians. They proclaim tyranny.

On the other hand, if they are proclaiming radical libertarianism as the only theoretical alternative to statism, then they are laying the foundations for an ethical and political backlash which will aid those who are seeking to expand the autononomous powers of the State. Men will not live under anarchy; libertinism (sexual and otherwise), which is necessarily a consequence of abolishing all civil laws (anarchism), creates the backlash. (Historically, the anarchists have allied themselves with statist revolutionaries at the beginning of a revolution, but have invariably been destroyed by their former allies after the latter have captured control of the coercive apparatus of the State. Communist Karl Marx and anarchist Michael Bakunin initially co-operated in the founding of the First International [International Workingmen's Association], the original international Communist revolutionary organization, but the two later split, and Marx and Engels in 1872 destroyed the organization which succeeded it, the Second International, by transferring its headquarters to New York City, rather than allow it to fall into the hands of Bakunin's followers.[14] In the case of the Russian Revolution, the anarchists were among the first dissidents to be arrested by the Cheka, Lenin's secret police.[15])

The Bible sets forth a true liberation theology, and it undergirds a true liberation economics. The specifics of this economic system are found in God's law. What is commonly called "liberation theol-

---

14. Franz Mehring, *Karl Marx: The Story of His Life* (Ann Arbor: University of Michigan Press, [1918] 1962), pp. 484-92. Bakunin hated communism because of its innate statism: "I am not a communist, because communism concentrates and swallows up in itself for the benefit of the State all the forces of society, because it inevitably leads to the concentration of property in the hands of the State, whereas I want the abolition of the State. . . ." Cited by E. H. Carr, *Michael Bakunin* (New York: Vintage, [1937] 1961), p. 356.

15. George Woodcock, *Anarchism: A History of Libertarian Ideas and Movements* (Cleveland, Ohio: Meridian, 1962), p. 219. See Part 8, "Anarchists in Prison," *The Anarchists in the Russian Revolution*, edited by Paul Avrich (Ithaca, New York: Cornell University Press, 1973). For an account of the anarchists in the Russian Revolution, see "Voline" (Vsevold Mikhailovich Eichenbaum), *The Unknown Revolution, 1917-1921* (New York: Free Life Editions, [1947] 1975). Voline was an anarchist who participated in the revolution.

ogy" in the latter decades of the twentieth century is very often warmed-over Marxism, or some sort of socialist economics.[16] Appeals are made by self-professed liberation theologians to the historic precedent of the Exodus, but few if any references are made to the many Old Testament case-law applications of the ten commandments. In fact, the continuing validity of Old Testament laws that deal with economic relationships is denied by liberation theologians; only those laws that *seem* to expand the economic power of the State — and there are very few of these in the Bible — are cited by liberation theologians. This "pick and choose" aspect of modern liberation theology — a choice governed by the standards of socialism and revolution rather than by the standards of orthodox theology — undermines the church's ability to reconstruct social institutions in terms of God's revealed word.[17]

Conclusion

Liberation and the law of God go together. God's announcement to His people that He is the God who delivered them from Egypt,

---

16. See David Chilton's review of José Míguez Bonino's book, *The Mutual Challenge to Revolution* (Grand Rapids, Michigan: Eerdmans, 1976), in *The Journal of Christian Reconstruction*, V (Summer 1978). The literature promoting liberation theology is large and growing rapidly. Orbis Books, the publishing arm of the radical Maryknoll organization (the Catholic Foreign Mission Society of America), produces an endless stream of paperback books on the topic. Recent publications are Leonardo & Clodovis Boff, *Salvation and Liberation: In Search of a Balance between Faith and Politics* (1984); Tissa Balasuriya, *Planetary Theology* (1984); Phillip Berryman, *The Religious Roots of Rebellion: Christians in Central American Revolutions* (1984); Elsa Tamez, *Bible of the Oppressed* (1982); Julio de Santa Ana (ed.), *Towards a Church of the Poor: The Work of an Ecumenical Group on the Church and the Poor* (1981), copyrighted by the World Council of Churches; Santa Ana, *Good News to the Poor: The Challenge of the Poor in the History of the Church* (1979). Neo-evangelical Protestant organizations that promote less openly revolutionary versions of liberation theology include *Sojourners* magazine and the Evangelicals for Social Action. Where two or three evangelical (including Baptist) seminary professors gather together, there you will probably find at least one person who promotes some version of this basic theology.

17. See Ronald J. Sider, *Rich Christians in an Age of Hunger* (2nd ed.; Downers Grove, Illinois: InterVarsity Press, 1984); Stephen Mott, *Biblical Ethics and Social Change* (New York: Oxford University Press, 1982). For a critique of Sider's book, see David Chilton, *Productive Christians in an Age of Guilt-Manipulators: A Biblical Response to Ronald J. Sider* (3rd ed.; Tyler, Texas: Institute for Christian Economics, 1985); Ronald H. Nash, *Social Justice and the Christian Church* (Milford, Michigan: Mott Media, 1983). The various branches of the Mott family, inheritors of a considerable fortune, have divided religiously and ideologically. Thus, we find George Mott publishing a book which is totally opposed to Prof. Stephen Mott's perspective. Stewart Mott, a political leftist, controls another Mott family trust and gives away money to various radical causes.

and then His presentation of the ten commandments, makes this connection between freedom and biblical law inescapably clear. The Christian economist who takes God's word seriously has a responsibility to begin to examine the case-law applications of God's law to see where economic issues are involved, and what requirements God sets forth for economic relationships. To abandon faith in the reliability of God's law in economics is to abandon faith in what the Bible proclaims as the only basis of liberation, namely, liberation under the sovereign power of God, who sustains the universe and calls all men to conform themselves to His ethical standards in every area of life, in time and on earth.

2

GRAVEN IMAGES AND COMPOUND JUDGMENT

Thou shalt not make unto thee any graven image, or any likeness of any thing that is in heaven above, or that is in the earth beneath, or that is in the water under the earth. Thou shalt not bow down thyself to them, nor serve them: for I the LORD thy God am a jealous God, visiting the iniquity of the fathers upon the children unto the third and fourth generation of them that hate me; and showing mercy unto thousands of them that love me, and keep my commandments (Ex. 20:4-6).

The second commandment is divided into two sections. The first section deals with the prohibition against graven images. The second section deals with the punishment and mercy of God. It is not initially clear just how these two sections are linked together. Possibly because of this confusion, the Lutheran Churches combine this commandment with the first commandment, so that the prohibition against worshipping other gods, the prohibition against graven images, and the promise of judgment and mercy are all considered as a single commandment. To get ten commandments, they divide the tenth, the prohibition against covetousness, into two: coveting the neighbor's house, and coveting the neighbor's wife, servants, and work animals.[1] This handling of the tenth looks strained, but the handling of the first two by other Protestant groups also initially looks strained. They do seem to be one unit, rather than a one-part commandment followed by a two-part commandment.

My treatment rests on my belief that the traditional Reformed and Anglican division is closer to the truth than the Lutheran. Deuteronomy 4:13 speaks of the necessity of obeying His covenant, which is ten commandments. The emphasis is on obedience to all

---

1. "The Ten Commandments," under "Lutheran Creeds," in John H. Leith (ed.), *Creeds of the Churches: A Reader in Christian Doctrine* (Chicago: Aldine, 1963), pp. 113-14.

ten, not the proper numbering of each one. What we need to do is to obey the whole of the passage, not quibble over how to divide up ten laws that we can supposedly now safely ignore, once we agree on the numbering. This is generally what twentieth-century Christianity has done: dismissed or at least ignored the whole of the passage in the name of a "higher morality," or a "flexible morality," or "the affirmation of grace," or in the name of dispensational theology. But God is more concerned about obedience to His laws than He is about our numbering of them.

The first commandment is clear: men are not to worship any other god. The first part of the second commandment is also clear: make no graven images. This is an application of the principle governing the first commandment, namely, that no rival gods are allowed. In other words, first there is faith in God and no other god; then there is an application of this faith into action (or better, inaction): no graven images. The second commandment is an application of the principle governing the first commandment.

One reason why we can legitimately conclude that these are two separate commandments (or at least that we are not doing violence to the text by treating this passage within the whole law as if it were two) is that both share a common feature: a *prohibition* and a *reason* for this prohibition. The first commandment gives a reason for obedience: God delivered Israel out of bondage in Egypt. The second commandment also gives a reason for obedience: God is the One who brings judgment against those who hate Him, and who also brings mercy and love to those who love Him.

It should be pointed out that the third, fourth, and fifth commandments also follow this pattern. The third says not to take the name of the Lord in vain, "for the LORD will not hold him guiltless that taketh his name in vain," (20:7b). The fourth prohibits work on the sabbath. In the Exodus version, the reason offered is that God created the world in six days and rested on the seventh. In the Deuteronomy version, the reason offered is that they had been bondservants in Egypt, and God had delivered them (Deut. 5:15). The fifth commandment, honoring parents, also has a reason for obedience: a promise of long life.

Thus, the first five commandments reveal a common pattern: commandment and explanation (or motivation). Because of this, it is reasonable to consider the prohibition against graven images as a separate commandment. The task of the expositor is to show why the reason God offers for man's obedience is consistent with the prohibition against graven images. I have divided my exposition into the following outline:

> I. No Graven Images
>> A. The Theology of Images
>> B. Rival World Orders
>
> II. The Compounding Process
>> A. The Iniquity of the Children
>> B. Mercy Unto Thousands

I. No Graven Images

The prohibition against worshipping graven images was unique in the ancient world. Whenever archaeologists dig up the remains of some ancient city, they find images of all kinds — in temples, in the palace of the king, and in the homes of the people. Ancient cultures were polytheistic, and the proliferation of civic and household images was a universal phenomenon. By prohibiting the use of graven images, God was separating the Israelites from the surrounding cultures. It was always the mark of rebellion when the Israelites began to worship graven images.

Images and Political Alliances

Because images were prohibited, it made political alliances with surrounding nations impossible during the periods in which Israel remained faithful and avoided images. In the ancient world, including the classical civilizations of Greece and Rome, political alliances involved a peace treaty between the gods of the city-states. Politics was fundamentally religious; citizenship was based on a man's right to participate in the religious rites of a particular city. He could participate only in the rites of his own city. Dual citizenship was impossible.

Where did the local gods come from? A Greek city-state could adopt local gods that were identified with certain families within the city. When a family consented to allow its deity to become the god of a city, it generally retained the hereditary right of priesthood for that deity.[2] Different cities would have local deities named Zeus or

---

2. Numa Denis Fustel de Coulanges, *The Ancient City: A Study on the Religion, Laws, and Institutions of Greece and Rome* (Garden City, New York: Doubleday Anchor, [1864] n.d.), pp. 124-25. Reprinted by Peter Smith, Glouster, Massachusetts, 1979.

Athena, but these were not the same gods.[3]

Warfare between cities was simultaneously warfare between the gods of each city. A conquered city had to be allowed to remain independent, or else it had to be destroyed. "There was no middle course," Fustel de Coulanges wrote. "Either the city ceased to exist, or it was a sovereign state. So long as it retained its worship, it retained its government; it lost the one only by losing the other; and then it existed no longer."[4] Understandably, this made warfare total. Soldiers burned crops because the crops were dedicated to other gods. Cattle were slaughtered. The sacred fires of the defeated city and its households were extinguished. There was no sense of duty towards the enemy.[5]

What about peace treaties between cities? They were religious acts. The ceremony of the treaty was conducted by the priests of each city. "These religious ceremonies alone gave a sacred and inviolable character to international conventions. . . . With such ideas it was important, in a treaty of peace, that each city called its own gods to bear witness to its oaths. . . . Both parties tried, indeed, if it was possible, to invoke divinities that were common to both cities. They swore by those gods that were visible everywhere — the sun, which shines upon all, and the nourishing earth. But the gods of each city, and its protecting heroes, touched men much more, and it was necessary to call them to witness, if men wished to have oaths really confirmed by religion. As the gods mingled in the battles during the war, they had to be included in the treaty. It was stipulated, therefore, that there should be an alliance between the gods as between the two cities. To indicate this alliance of the gods, it sometimes happened that the two peoples agreed mutually to take part in each other's sacred festivals. Sometimes they opened their temples to each other, and made an exchange of religious rites."[6]

Fustel de Coulanges wrote about Greece and Rome, but similar theologies reigned in the Near East. Thus, it was impossible for Israel to make covenants of peace with the foreign nations and still remain faithful to God. "Thou shalt make no covenant with them, nor with their gods" (Ex. 23:32). The nations of Canaan had to be

3. *Ibid.*, p. 150. Cf. Jane Harrison, *Prolegomena to the Study of Greek Religion* (New York: Meridian, [1903] 1960), ch. 1.

4. *Ibid.*, p. 205.

5. *Ibid.*, pp. 205-6.

6. *Ibid.*, pp. 208-9.

utterly destroyed (Ex. 23:27), for their altars had to be destroyed (Ex. 34:13). "Speak unto the children of Israel, and say unto them, When ye are passed over Jordan into the land of Canaan, then ye shall drive out all the inhabitants of the land from before you, and destroy all their pictures, and destroy all their molten images, and quite pluck down their high places; and ye shall dispossess the inhabitants of the land, and dwell therein; for I have given you the land to possess it" (Num. 33:51-53). It was also forbidden for the Israelites to intermarry with foreigners who were not under the covenantal authority of God (Deut. 7:3-4).

How could God deny His own sovereignty? He was the God who had delivered His people from Egypt, demonstrating that He was no local god, but a God over all kingdoms. Pharaoh had not conquered God by subjugating His people. Pharaoh had wanted to negotiate with God through Moses, but God had issued a non-negotiable demand to let His people go for one week to worship Him.[7] When Pharaoh refused to capitulate, God destroyed him. No self-proclaimed human divinity could come before God as an equal. No common rites were possible between God's people and the foreign gods of pagan cities.

It was this issue which got the early church into a life-and-death confrontation with Rome. Members were willing to be honest citizens, but they could not be citizens in Rome's view. They refused to participate in the rites of the Empire. The Roman pantheon was filled with the gods of the various conquered nations, which was the basis of the peace treaty between Rome and its subject peoples, but neither Israel nor the church could conform to the ritual terms of this treaty. Israel was scattered in the diaspora in the second century A.D., and the church was intermittently persecuted until Constantine's era. This is why Fustel could write, "The victory of Christianity marks the end of ancient society."[8]

When God told the Israelites they could not make graven images or worship them, He was announcing the terms of the dominion covenant. There had to be religious separation in Israel. They were to be isolated culturally from pagan nations. But the prohibition was more than a means to separate the Israelites culturally from their

---

7. Gary North, *Moses and Pharaoh: Dominion Religion vs. Power Religion* (Tyler, Texas: Institute for Christian Economics, 1985), ch. 10: "Total Sacrifice, Total Sovereignty."

8. *The Ancient City*, p. 389.

neighbors. It was a call to *conquest*. There could be no peace treaties with the people dwelling in the land which God had given to them; God imposes unconditional surrender or ultimate extinction.[9]

A. The Theology of Images

Man is made in God's image. He has power over the creation as a lawful subordinate to God. But rebellious man is not content to remain a steward to God, a subordinate creature. He wants autonomy. At least, he wants to operate under some creature other than God. So man makes an image, thereby imitating God, who made man, His image. This image is a *point of contact* between man and the supernatural being associated with the image. The image represents the supernatural being. Man has an integral part in the formation of this being's point of contact. Man believes that he participates in the work of the divinity by giving shape to its image.

Ironically, man worships something less than man when he worships an idol. He worships power — power which is limited to the period of history prior to Christ's final judgment. But man himself is God's image. Redeemed men (the church) will eventually judge the angels (I Cor. 6:3). Therefore, in an attempt to imitate God's original creativity by making an image — just as God made man in His image — men identify themselves with the eschatological fate of some fallen angel, for the graven image serves as a point of contact with some fallen angel. *Men thereby identify themselves with ultimate impotence and death:* "Their idols are silver and gold, the work of men's hands. They have mouths, but speak not. Eyes have they, but they see not. They have ears, but they hear not. Noses have they, but they smell not. They have hands, but they handle not. Feet have they, but they walk not. Neither speak they through their throat. They that make them are like unto them; so is every one that trusteth in them" (Ps. 115:4-8; cf. 135:15-18).

Fallen man wants a mediator between himself and God. He wants that mediator to be the work of his own hands. This is an attempt to make himself a co-equal with God, or at the very least, a co-participant with God in their "mutual struggle" against the unpredictable forces of nature and history. The idea that there is a God-ordained mediator who was not the product of men's hands — a

---

9. Gary North, *Unconditional Surrender: God's Program for Victory* (rev. ed.; Tyler, Texas: Geneva Divinity School Press, 1983).

"stone cut out without hands" (Dan. 2:34)—is repulsive to fallen man. Such a concept of God denies man's own sovereignty and places him at the mercy of God exclusively. He would rather worship some other kind of god. As Rushdoony writes, "the only God they can tolerate is on[e] who is immersed in history, one who is Himself a product of natural process and is working together with man to conquer time and history. God and man are thus partners and co-workers in the war against brute factuality."[10]

Representing God

God was not to be represented visually by the people of the Old Testament because He had not yet appeared as the Incarnation, the perfectly human mediator between God and men who perfectly represented God (John 14:9).[11] Any pre-Christian attempt on the part of man to picture God would have been an assertion of divinity on the part of man, for only Jesus Christ has seen God, because He is of God (John 6:46). It would have meant that fallen man had seen the face of God. But to view God meant death, as the Hebrews had been told (Ex. 19:21). Not even Moses was allowed to see God's face (Ex. 33:23). Men could have painted a burning bush, which was a manifestation of God, or produced a sculpture of Jacob wrestling with the theophany (Gen. 32:24-32), but there was no way they would have been able to represent God in His Person as a divine being. Men violated this prohibition by representing God in the form of animals, worshipping creatures as if they were the creator (Rom. 1:23).

---

10. R. J. Rushdoony, *The Biblical Philosophy of History* (Nutley, New Jersey: Craig Press, 1969), pp. 3-4.

11. Can we legitimately represent Jesus? Men did see Him. If a camera had been available to one of His followers, He could have been photographed. He was not an apparition. Someone could have made a sculpture of him, or a painting. But no one did. Should we guess concerning His appearance? We make guesses at what other biblical figures looked like. Moses, since the days of Michelangelo, has come to be thought of in a particular way. But Moses was a man, not divine. So we face a dilemma: Jesus Christ was both human and divine. We can legitimately represent Him in His *work* on earth. He was an historical figure. On the other hand, representations of Christ with a pagan halo around His head are not historical representations of His humanity, and are therefore illegitimate. (On the pagan origins of halos in medieval art, and their relationship to the occult phenomenon of the "human aura," see "aura," in Nandor Fodor, *Encyclopedia of Psychic Sciences* [New Hyde Park, New York: University Books, (1934) 1966], pp. 17-18; Lewis Spence, *Encyclopaedia of Occultism* [New Hyde Park, New York: University Books, (1920) 1960], pp. 50-51.) Also, any use of icons or paintings that "aid" us in the worship of God—aids that supposedly provide a *point of contact* between the worshipper and God—are illegitimate.

An idol is a means of negating the Creator-creature distinction. Men believe that they can approach God, placate God, and even control God through bowing to an idol. Yet idols are radically distinct from God, as this passage tells us: men are not to worship any aspect of the creation, whether in heaven, on earth, or under the earth.[12]

Idols are weak. The Hebrews had seen that idols had not protected the Egyptians, and their children would see that the idols of the Canaanites would be equally impotent. At best, idols put men into contact with demonic beings that can manifest power, but nothing comparable to the awesome power of God. These rites place men into bondage to underworld spirits that can control them, even as men hope to control the spirits and the external environment by means of idol worship.

God forbade the use of tools in the construction of His altar. "Ye shall not make with me gods of silver, neither shall ye make unto you gods of gold. An altar of earth thou shalt make unto me, and shalt sacrifice thereon thy burnt offerings, and thy peace offerings, thy sheep, and thine oxen: in all places where I record my name I will come unto thee, and I will bless thee. And if thou wilt make me an altar of stone, thou shalt not build it of hewn stone: for if thou lift up thy tool upon it, thou hast polluted it. Neither shalt thou go up by steps unto mine altar, that thy nakedness be not discovered thereon," (Ex. 20:23-26).[13] The Hebrews were not allowed to design and build at their own discretion the shape of the place of atonement before God. God provided the raw materials, and they were not to reshape them.

When the early church spread the gospel, the image-makers suffered financial losses. Acts 19 records the confrontation between the evangelists and the silversmiths who made the images of the temple of Diana. The leader of the craft guild, Demetrius, warned his colleagues: "Moreover ye see and hear, that not alone at Ephesus, but almost throughout all Asia, this Paul hath persuaded and turned away much people, saying that they be no gods, which are made with hands" (v. 26). The gospel had negative economic consequences for the pagan craftsmen of idols.

The prohibition of graven images was not a universal condemna-

---

12. I am indebted to Prof. John Frame's class syllabus, *Doctrine of the Christian Life*, for these insights.
13. Deut. 27:5; Josh. 8:30-31.

tion of all religious images. The tabernacle had images of the cherubim (Ex. 25:18-22) and bowls shaped like almonds (Ex. 25:33-34).
The cherubim were not "cherubs" in the modern sense — not ruddy-
faced children. They had four faces: a man's, an ox's, an eagle's, and
a lion's (Ezk. 1:10). The temple actually had a large basin supported
by twelve oxen (I Ki. 7:25), yet bulls were a familiar part of pagan
worship. But the permitted likenesses were spelled out by God and
limited to the Old Testament house of God. Men were not acting autonomously when they put these likenesses in the tabernacle. In
short, these specified likenesses were *symbols*, not icons. As symbolic
of God and His relationship with man, they rested on the doctrine
of creation, the absolute distinction between Creator and creation. The
icon, in contrast, points to a supposed scale of being, an ontological
link between God and the image. This is the theology of magic.

Icons and Magic

Let us consider an Old Testament example of a legitimate use of
an image for religious purposes. It is one of the strangest events in
the Bible. The setting, however, was only too typical an event in the
life of that first generation in the wilderness. They had made a vow
with God to deliver a Canaanitic nation into their hands, if they in
turn utterly destroyed the city. He did, and they did. The victory
was complete (Num. 21:1-4). Then they journeyed around Edom,
and once again they grew discouraged. They made their standard
complaint: "And the people spake against God, and against Moses,
Wherefore have ye brought us up out of Egypt to die in the wilderness? For there is no bread, neither is there any water: and our soul
loatheth this light bread" (Num. 21:5).

This time, God responded in anger. He sent fiery serpents
among them to bite them. Many of them died (21:6). They repented.
Moses then prayed for them (v. 7). God instructed him to make an
image of a fiery serpent and place it on a pole. Every one who looks
at it after he is bitten will live, God told Moses (v. 8). He made the
image, and God's word came true: merely looking at it saved their
lives (v. 9).

Was this magic? No, for God had instructed them *on a one-time
basis* to follow this *one-time ritual*. The use of the serpent on a pole was
not to become part of Israel's worship. Moses had been instructed by
God to make such an image. Of all images, this one is the one which
we would assume could never be made legitimately. The serpent be-

came a universal symbol in pagan civilizations. The Sumerian god Ningishzida was the son of the healing god Ninazu, and he was represented by a pair of snakes entwined around a rod. This god was worshipped in Babylon in the late Bronze Age era in which the Exodus took place.[14] In Greece, the symbol of a snake was also associated with divine healing: Asklepios, a snake-god, was their god of healing. He was symbolized as a snake wrapped around a staff.[15] We still see the Sumerian snakes' use as a symbol of healing: the medical profession's symbol is a pair of intertwined snakes on a pole. Yet God instructed Moses to construct a snake image.

Why was this image not an icon? Because it was used in an actual historical event. This is the key which unlocks the New Testament era's standard of the proper use of images. Now that God has come in the flesh and has manifested Himself among men, it is legitimate to represent God by making representations of Jesus Christ. How can such statues or paintings be kept from becoming magical talismans, amulets, or icons? *By placing the representations in a Bible-revealed historical setting.*

We do not know what Jesus looked like. We know that He was sufficiently nondescript that the Jews paid Judas to identify Him. So we cannot legitimately represent Jesus apart from recognizable historical settings from the Bible. The historical setting is the identifying mark of who the image represents. It points also to a *one-time only* event in man's history. In this way, the image does not readily become a *continuing incarnation.* It does not readily become a link in the present between the worshipper and the object of his worship. Thus, the presence of statues or paintings or stained glass windows in a church need not be violations of the second commandment. But when these images are used as links between the present worship of God in prayer, except as a way to *recall* the memory of some mighty act of God, they become idols.

The use of icons as *mediating instruments* between worshippers and God does involve elements of the forbidden practice, but this is not always a *self-conscious* defiance of the second commandment.[16]

---

14. E. A. Wallis Budge, *Amulets and Talismans* (New Hyde Park: New York: University Books, [1930?] 1961), pp. 488-89. "The snake sloughs its skin annually, and so suggested the ideas of renewed life and immortality to the ancients" (p. 489).

15. Harrison, *Prolegomena,* p. 341.

16. The iconoclastic controversy in Byzantium in the eighth century A.D. was a war by the emperors against the use of icons in the church. As Ladner noted in 1940, this was a political struggle. The emperors wanted a monopoly over the use of icons. The icons of the emperors in public places were to be the manifestation on earth of material aspects of God's kingdom. In short, "they did not wish to permit on this

Eastern orthodoxy and Roman Catholicism are marked by practices that are rebellious in this regard, but this may not always be self-conscious rebellion. The leadership of both churches has unquestionably failed in the past to limit the use of images within the worship ceremonies to strictly historical settings. By failing to limit the use of visual representations of Jesus or the "saints" — historical figures from the Bible — to their historical settings, churches have thereby implicitly or explicitly encouraged the misuse of images. They have not warned the worshippers that the use of images is to be historical, not ontological. They are to remind men of the deliverances in history by God of His people. They may be used to remind men of the power of God in history, and to reinforce their faith in God's power in the affairs of this world. They may not be used to link a specific worshipper with a specific mediator who is represented by the image so closely that the very presence of the image is the source of the mediation. In other words, worshippers can easily be lured into substituting magic for Christian faith.

We can understand how easy it is for a believer to make this illegitimate substitution when we examine the case of Moses' tapping of the rock in order to bring forth water for the Israelites. Moses tapped the rock in order to get water out of it. Why? He had once been told by God to smite a rock in order to bring water out of it (Ex. 17:6), and he made a false conclusion: that God rewards the man who properly manipulates the talismans or implements of ritualistic power. He concluded that a one-time *historical* link between tapping a rock and getting water out of it was in fact an ontological link between ritual precision and desired effect. He was lured into heresy. The influence of the power religion of Egypt was still strong in his thinking. He began to think in terms of ritual rather than ethics, of the precise repetition of a familiar formula rather than obedience to God's revealed word. In short, Moses adopted magic in place of biblical religion.

God knew that this shift in Moses' thinking had taken place. This is why He tested Moses. He told Moses in the desert of Zin to take the rod and gather the assembly, and then *speak* to the rock before

---

earth any other but their own image or more exactly the imagery of their own imperial natural world." Gerhard B. Ladner, "Origin and Significance of the Byzantine Iconoclastic Controversy," *Medieval Studies*, II (New York: Sheed & Ward, 1940), p. 135. Cited in R. J. Rushdoony, *The One and the Many: Studies in the Philosophy of Order and Ultimacy* (Fairfax, Virginia: Thoburn Press, [1971] 1978), p. 179.

their eyes, "and thou shalt bring forth to them water out of the rock" (Num. 20:8). Moses did not believe God. He relied instead on ritual. He concluded that adherence to a form (formula) which had produced results in the past is the key to tapping God's power. So he tapped the rock in order to "tap" God's power. He even added a touch of his own—literally: a second tap of the rod. "And Moses lifted up his hand, and with his rod he smote the rock twice: and the water came out abundantly, and the congregation drank, and their beasts also. And the LORD spake unto Moses and Aaron, Because ye believed me not, to sanctify me in the eyes of the children of Israel, therefore ye shall not bring this congregation into the land which I have given them" (vv. 11-12).

A legitimate symbol reminds us of what God is *like* by revealing what kinds of physical blessings God has given to His people. Its prohibited pagan equivalent is the amulet or talisman, which commands a god's obedience because of the presence of the object, or because of ritual precisely performed by man. It assumes that both the god and man are under the bondage of ritual, but that man can impose his will on the god through manipulating a talisman or other implement of power. Budge writes: "The use of amulets dates from the time when animism or magic satisfied the spiritual needs of man. Primitive man seems to have adopted them as a result of an internal urge or the natural instinct which made him protect himself and to try to divine the future. He required amulets to enable him to beget children, to give him strength to overcome enemies, visible and invisible, and above all the EVIL EYE, and to protect his women and children, and house and cattle; and his descendants throughout the world have always done the same. When the notion of a god developed in his mind, he ascribed to that god the authorship of the magical powers which he believed to be inherent in the amulets, and he believed that his god needed them as much as he himself did. He did not think it possible for his god to exist without the help of magical powers. . . . The gods became magicians, and employed magic when necessary, and dispensed it through their priests to mankind."[17]

A legitimate image of a Bible event reminds men of what God has *done*. An icon is the hypothetical representation of a person out of the Bible—a representation which offers the worshipper power

---

17. Budge, *Amulets and Talismans*, pp. xv, xvi.

over today's events because it manifests the *displayed power* which the person represented by the image once possessed. It is an illegitimate device because it is used in worship which assumes that the worshipper can directly appropriate the power which was *once revealed historically* in the life of the person represented by the image. It is not biblically significant that the person represented by the image once possessed such power; what *is* significant is that he was *placed under grace* and received power sufficient to perform his God-assigned task or sufficient to demonstrate God's power in history. The basis of this gift of power was not the precision of his ritual performance, or his special place on the hypothetical (and nonexistent) chain of being between God and man, but rather *his position in history*, meaning his place in the providentially controlled history of God's people. Worshippers should never forget that the biblical personality represented by the image never used an image to appropriate the power he received. There are no indications that worshippers in the Old Testament or New Testament church used images of historic persons to aid them in their prayers and devotions.

Similarly, our possession of power is not based on our ability to repeat precise rituals, or on our position in the "chain of being." Our power is dependent on the providence of God. Thus, it is *obedience*, not ritual, which is essential. It is *ethics*, not power, which is our goal. It is the kingdom of God, not the kingdom of man, which is our primary goal (Matt. 6:33). Thus, the use of images to enhance our power by bringing us closer to God *metaphysically* or *ontologically* is illegitimate. Images are to bring us closer to Jesus Christ *ethically*. To reduce the likelihood of our misusing images, they must be kept *historical* in their frame of reference. They must remind us of what God once did for people who verbally and ethically proclaimed biblical religion, not what He did for people who ritually proclaimed the power religion. What God did *to* the latter is what faithful worshippers wish to avoid.

As I have said, the improper use of icons, candles, or other objects used in worship is not always self-consciously magical. In the world of occultism, on the other hand, we still find a self-conscious acceptance of the old religion of images. The revival of an occultist political order under Nazism indicates that the lingering traces of occultism can be revived at any time.[18] If occultism continues to ex-

18. In early 1984, I was told by a Christian living in Austria that in the train stations where teenagers are forced to congregate (because of the State requirement

pand its influence, we can expect to see more examples of the ancient practice of image-worship.

B. Rival World Orders

There are invariably close links among the image, the god represented by the image, and the social order of the society which worships this god. Bowing down to an idol means the acceptance of that god's law-order. "Thou shalt not bow down to their gods, nor serve them, nor do after their works; but thou shalt utterly overthrow them, and quite break down their images" (Ex. 23:24). To *bow down to any deity* means to *walk in his ordinances*. "After the doings of the land of Egypt, wherein ye dwelt, shall ye not do: and after the doings of the land of Canaan, whither I bring you, shall ye not do: neither shall ye walk in their ordinances" (Lev. 18:3). The history of Israel testifies to the inescapable link between gods and their social orders: "They did not destroy the nations, concerning whom the LORD commanded them, but were mingled among the heathen, and learned their works. And they served their idols: which were a snare unto them. Yea, they sacrificed their sons and daughters unto devils" (Ps. 106:34-37).

Making a graven image means to participate in the creation of *a new world order*. This new world order is in opposition to God's world order. A different god is elevated to a position of sovereignty. In the Old Testament era, this meant that some demonic being became the source of health and prosperity. In modern civilization, which is the historical product of Christianity, most men no longer worship demons explicitly. They attribute sovereignty to impersonal forces of history (Marxism), or forces of the unconscious (Freudianism), or the spirit of the *Volk* (Nazism), or the impersonal forces of nature (Darwinism's explanation of pre-human evolution). Modern man has attempted to become what C. S. Lewis prophesied: *the materialist magician.*[19] Ultimately, *man is the sovereign agent*, by means of: the Party (Marxism), economic planning (Fabianism), genetic manipulation (eugenics), conditioned response training (behaviorism), psychoanalysis (Freudianism), the Führer (Nazism), higher consciousness techniques (New Age transcendentalism), compulsory public

---

that they travel to distant centralized high schools) there are three types of literature available for purchase: cheap pulp edition "western" novels, hero stories from Norse mythology, and pornography.

19. C. S. Lewis, *The Screwtape Letters* (New York: Macmillan, [1961] 1969), p. 33. These "letters from a senior devil" were first published during World War II.

education (progressive education), scientific planning (Darwinism), or scientific management (Taylorism).[20]

Satan did not tempt Adam and Eve to worship him openly; he only asked them to violate the law of God. The violation of God's law was the equivalent of worshipping Satan. Only when he approached Christ did he ask to be worshipped (Luke 4:7). *The worship of man and his works is essentially the worship of Satan.* In short, man the idol-maker and idol-worshipper is man the Satan-worshipper. Humanism is inescapably satanism, which is why satanism revives during periods of humanistic dominance.[21]

The construction of a world order which is opposed to the one set forth by God is therefore theologically comparable to constructing a graven image. There may be no official graven image at first. Men may not be asked to bow down to it at first. But the substitution of the ordinances of man for the ordinances of God is the heart of idol-worship. It is an assertion of *man's autonomy,* which ultimately results in *the subordination of man to the ordinances of Satan.* The society of Satan does not need graven images to make it operational.[22]

It is a testimony to the impact of Christianity on Western culture that graven images have all but disappeared. Humanists have adopted faith in the original promise of Satan to Eve, namely, the impossible offer of autonomy to man, but they do not bow down to graven images. To make a profession of faith in man's autonomy is to become *ethically subordinate to Satan* (but inescapably under the overall sovereignty of God).[23] Men who believe that they worship no god have nevertheless conformed themselves sufficiently to Satan's standards to warrant eternal punishment, and to that extent, Satan is pleased. In worshipping the works of their own hands, they refuse to worship God. Their idols are not explicitly religious or explicitly

---

20. Gary North, "From Cosmic Purposelessness to Humanistic Sovereignty," Appendix A in *The Dominion Covenant: Genesis* (Tyler, Texas: Institute for Christian Economics, 1982).

21. On the occultism of the Renaissance, see Frances Yates, *Giordano Bruno and the Hermetic Tradition* (New York: Vintage, [1964] 1969). On the occult background of nineteenth-century revolutionism, see James Billington, *Fire in the Minds of Men: Origins of the Revolutionary Faith* (New York: Basic Books, 1980). On the link between humanism and occultism in the United States, especially after 1964, see Gary North, *None Dare Call It Witchcraft* (New Rochelle, New York: Arlington House, 1976).

22. R. J. Rushdoony, "The Society of Satan," (1964); reprinted in *Biblical Economics Today*, II (Oct./Nov. 1979).

23. Gary North, *Dominion Covenant: Genesis*, p. 92.

rebellious ritually. They do not celebrate their faith by adopting the ancient rituals of satanism, namely, by making graven images.[24] Worshipping graven images would make manifest their ultimate theology, so in this respect Christianity has influenced humanism and has restrained it.

II. The Compounding Process

We come now to the reason given for the prohibition against constructing graven images. The reason is that God is a jealous God. What kind of God is that? It is a God who visits the iniquity of the fathers on subsequent generations of ethical rebels. It is also a God who shows mercy to generations of covenantally faithful people. The presence or absence of graven images testifies to the spiritual condition of the two ethically distinct and *ritually distinct* types of people.

The heart of the description of the jealous God is the *covenantal process of compound growth:* growth unto judgment and growth unto dominion. History is linear. It develops over time. What goes before affects what comes after. Nevertheless, it does not *determine* what comes after. God determines both the "before" and the "after." God is sovereign, not the forces of history. But the criteria of performance are ethical. We know which covenant we are in by evaluating the external events of our lives in terms of God's list of blessings and curses (Deut. 28).

A. The Iniquity of the Children

"[F]or I the LORD thy God am a jealous God, visiting the iniquity of the fathers upon the children unto the third and fourth generations . . ." (Ex. 20:5b). This verse is frequently misunderstood. It does not say that God punishes sons for the sins of their fathers. The Bible's testimony concerning the responsibilities of children for the sins of their fathers is clear: "The fathers shall not be put to death for the children, neither shall the children be put to death for the fathers: every man shall be put to death for his own sin" (Deut. 24:16). This principle was reaffirmed by Ezekiel: "The soul that sin-

---

24. C. S. Lewis' magnificent novel, *That Hideous Strength* (1945), presents a literary prophecy of a coming fusion of power-seeking modern science and power-seeking ancient demonism. This experiment ends in the novel with the destruction of the scientists: one by a suicidal but consistent application of modern dualistic psychology (Frost), another as a blood sacrifice to a demonic god-head whose scientific "creator" never suspected (until the moment of his death) that it was anything but a strictly scientific phenomenon (Filostrata).

neth, it shall die. The son shall not bear the iniquity of the father, neither shall the father bear the iniquity of the son: the righteousness of the righteous shall be upon him, and the wickedness of the wicked shall be upon him" (Ezk. 18:20). We therefore must interpret the unique phrase, "visiting the iniquity of the fathers upon the children," in terms of this clearly stated principle of judgment.

What we have in view here is a covenantal framework of reference. The Hebrews had just come out of Egypt. They and their ancestors had labored under slavery. The year of release had not been honored by their captors. Year after year, the Egyptians had built up their cities by the use of Hebrew labor. This capital base kept expanding. The wages that would have been paid to free laborers, as well as the capital that was to be given to slaves in the year of release (Deut. 15:13-14), was retained by succeeding generations of Egyptians. Thus, the later generations became the beneficiaries of the compounding process.[25] They were richer, they supposed, than their ancestors because they possessed the visible manifestations of labor extracted illegally over decades.

Then came God's judgment. With the compound growth of the visible benefits came the compound judgment of God. Both had built up over time. The final generation suffered incomparable judgment because they had not repented, made restitution voluntarily, and freed the Hebrews. For God not to have judged that final generation in terms of the benefits they had received illegally — benefits conveyed to them as a continuing legacy from their ancestors — would have been an injustice on the part of God.

Repeated Iniquities

The iniquities of the fathers were repeated by the sons. The fathers escaped the full temporal retribution of God. In this sense, God showed them mercy, in time and on earth. But the sons also did not repent. They continued in the sins of their fathers. If anything, they enjoyed the luxury of sinning even more flagrantly, because they were the beneficiaries of a larger capital base — a capital base of evil.

How long will God allow the sins of the heirs to go on? Unto the third and fourth generation. How long had the Hebrews been under

---

25. Gary North, *Moses and Pharaoh*, ch. 6: "Cumulative Transgression and Restitution."

the dominance of Egypt? Three generations.[26] The historical precedent should have been obvious to any Hebrew in Moses' day. God
visits the iniquity for several generations. He *punishes* iniquity, according to one possible translation. He *numbers* iniquities, according to
another.[27] It can also mean *remember* (I Sam. 15:2).

The sons of the final generation in Egypt indulged in the sins of
their fathers. The same sins were popular. God numbered or
remembered these sins. This is the meaning of "visiting the iniquity."
He visits and sees the sins, generation after generation. A satanically
covenantal society becomes skilled in certain sins. There is a systematic specialization in particular evils. Men are creatures. They are
limited. *Men have to specialize in order to achieve their goals.* This is as true
of sinfulness (and righteousness) as it is of economic production. As
time goes on, the sinners get very good at what they are doing. Their
unique cultural sins compound over time. As God put it with
reference to the iniquity of the Amorites, their cup had to be filled up
before the heirs of Abraham could inherit the promised land (Gen.
15:16b). The cup of iniquity of the Egyptians filled up one generation
(40 years) before the cup of the Amorites filled up. Thus, in the
fourth generation (Kohath's generation to Joshua's), Israel returned
to Canaan, just as God had promised (Gen. 15:16a).

The compounding process which builds up the *capital base of iniquity* explains Isaiah 65:7: "I will repay your iniquities, yours and
your fathers, all at once, says the LORD, because they burnt incense
on the mountains and defied me on the hills; I will first measure out
their reward and then pay them in full" (NEB). It is not that the sons
have broken with the sins of the fathers, but nonetheless are going to
be judged in terms of their fathers' rebellion. On the contrary, it is
that the sons have become *even more efficient* in sinning. Mercy had
been shown to the fathers in not destroying them. The fathers had
been able to pass down a *legacy of evil* to the sons. Thus, the sons
suffer for their own sins, but their sins are more deserving of judgment, for this final generation has not repented in thankfulness for the
mercy shown to their fathers by God. The final generation exists only

---

26. Kohath, Moses' grandfather, was alive before the descent into Egypt (Gen.
46:11). His son was Amram (Ex. 6:18), Moses' father (Num. 26:59). For a discussion
of the problem of the period of Israel's sojourn in Egypt, see Donovan Courville, *The
Exodus Problem and its Ramifications*, 2 vols. (Loma Linda, California: Challenge
Books, 1971), I, pp. 137-41.

27. Num. 1:44; 4:37, 41, 45, 46, 49.

because God had not destroyed their fathers, yet they refuse to repent. God's massive judgment is just, for their sin is greater. Why? Because, first, they did not repent in the face of God's mercy to their fathers, and second, because they have inherited a legacy of evil which has built up over time — a covenantal inheritance of death.

B. Mercy Unto Thousands

In contrast to the compounding process of evil, which is cut short after a few generations, stands God's promise to show mercy to thousands of those who keep His commandments. Cassuto interprets this to mean *thousands of generations*. Nachmanides translates it: "He showeth mercy unto the thousandth generation."[28] The contrast is between few generations and many — so many that it really means eternity. He cites Deuteronomy 7:9: "Know therefore that the LORD thy God, he is God, the faithful God, which keepeth covenant and mercy with them that love him and keep his commandments to a thousand generations."[29] The next verse is also significant, although Cassuto neglects it: "And repayeth them that hate him to their face, to destroy them: he will not be slack to him that hateth him, he will repay him to his face" (Deut. 7:10).

This is one of the most optimistic concepts in the Bible. What God is saying is that *the works of evil will be cut short,* sometimes after three or four generations, and sometimes immediately. The process of compound growth for the sinners will not go on forever, in contrast to the compounding process for the righteous. The evils of the sinners overtake them; their cup becomes full and they are destroyed. But for the righteous man and the righteous society, the cup runneth over (Ps. 23:5b). Even the now-empty cup of the vanquished wicked — the economic base in which sin was finally filled to the brim — is inherited by the righteous. "A good man leaveth an inheritance to his children's children: and the wealth of the sinner is laid up for the just" (Prov. 13:22b).

Could the Hebrews really have understood all this? In general, yes. Abraham had been told that the fourth generation would inherit the land of Canaan. This was the generation that succeeded Moses' generation. The children of the Exodus were told this explicitly by

---

28. Ramban, *Commentary on the Torah: Exodus* (New York: Shilo Publishing House, 1973), p. 300.

29. U. Cassuto, *A Commentary on the Book of Exodus* (Jerusalem: The Magnes Press, The Hebrew University, [1951] 1974), p. 243.

God, with respect to the external blessings that He was about to give them, and were reminded of their covenantal responsibility to obey His law and teach it to their children (Deut. 6:5-9).

> And it shall be, when the LORD thy God shall have brought thee into the land which he sware unto thy fathers, to Abraham, Isaac, and to Jacob, to give thee great and goodly cities, which thou buildest not, and houses full of good things, which thou filledst not, and wells digged, which thou plantedst not; when thou shalt have eaten and be full; Then beware lest thou forget the LORD, which brought thee forth out of the land of Egypt, from the house of bondage (Deut. 6:10-12).

The compound growth rate of evil is temporary. Such growth is always brought into judgment by God. The "positive feedback" of growth is always overturned by the "negative feedback" of judgment — sometimes overnight, as in the case of Babylon when it fell to the Medo-Persian Empire (Dan. 5). The compound growth rate of righteousness is long term. More than this: it is *perpetual.* God shows mercy to thousands of generations, meaning throughout history and (symbolically) beyond history. But this growth process does include history; generations are historical phenomena. There can be intermittent departures from faith which interrupt the growth process. But the contrast is between a *brief period* of three or four unrighteous generations and a *stupendously long period* of mercy to those who love God and keep His commandments. The magnitude of the growth period of mercy and mercy's works is enormous, compared with the growth period of evil.

Exponential Righteousness

The implication should be obvious: *the capital base of righteousness will grow to fill the earth over time.* Even a little growth, if compounded over a long enough period of time, produces astronomically large results — so large, in fact, that exponential growth points to an eventual final judgment and an end to time, with its cursed, scarce creation.[30] The righteous widow's two mites (Luke 21:2-4), if invested at 1% per annum over a thousand generations, would be worth more than all the wealth on earth. In other words, the concept of "a thousand generations" is symbolic; it means everything there is, a total victory for righteousness. Furthermore, this victory is no overnight

---

30. See Gary North, *Moses and Pharaoh,* ch. 17: "The Metaphor of Growth: Ethics"; cf. North, *Dominion Covenant: Genesis,* pp. 174-76.

affair; it comes as all growth processes come for a society: step by step, line upon line, here a little, there a little.

The sheer magnitude of righteousness' compounding capital base will inescapably overcome the feeble capital structure of iniquity, as surely as God's army will overcome Satan's. Men who work diligently and faithfully in terms of God's law can legitimately have confidence in the snowball effect of their efforts. There can be a comparable snowball effect for rebellious societies, but rebellion's snowball eventually is melted by the heat of God's fury. Four generations of compounding — even "leveraged" compounding — cannot match a thousand generations of compounding.

Kingdoms: Simultaneously Internal and External

It is difficult to interpret Exodus 20:4-6 in terms of the idea that Satan's kingdom grows externally, but God's kingdom grows only internally. If Satan's kingdom is essentially external and cultural, rather than both internal ("spiritual") and external, then why did Satan demand that Jesus worship him? On the other hand, if God's kingdom is essentially internal ("spiritual") and not also external and cultural, then why does He demand visible conformity to His commandments? Even more important, why does God promise external blessings to those who conform themselves to his law (Deut. 8:1-13), and warn against the lure of the religion of autonomous man when those blessings tempt men to forget God (Deut. 8:14-20)? Why should God tell His people not to worship graven images, and then immediately thereafter list all the external blessings — agricultural and military blessings, plus peace — that they can confidently expect if they obey this commandment (Lev. 26:1-12)? The answer should be obvious. *Both kingdoms are simultaneously internal ("spiritual") and external*; the spirit and the flesh are interconnected. Both kingdoms operate in the supernatural realm and in the temporal realm. Both seek dominion over the creation. Both have periods of growth, internally and externally. But Satan's kingdom is cut down early, "in the midst of its prime," so to speak, just as Jesus was cut off in the midst of His prime, and the animals sacrificed in the Old Testament were cut off in the midst of their prime,[31] so that God's kingdom might

---

31. Young turtledoves or young pigeons (Lev. 5:7), young bullocks (Ex. 29:1; Num. 28:11, 19), a three-year-old heifer, goat, and ram (Gen. 15:9), a virgin heifer which has never been yoked (Deut. 21:3), and the archetype of all sacrifices, the lamb (Gen. 22:7; Ex. 12:3-5; etc.).

have long life and not suffer the judgment of Satan's kingdom.

The comparative growth rates are, of course, symbolic. Egypt's case was literal, and the Hebrews should have recognized the power of God to bring His word to pass. Nevertheless, some pagan societies have gone on in their rebellion far longer than four generations. The Roman Empire is one historical example, although the Pax Romana lasted less than two centuries before the Empire began to be subjected to major crises. The point is, *compared to the long-term growth of God's kingdom, in time and on earth as well as beyond the grave, Satan's earthly kingdoms are short-lived*. The mercy which God shows to pagan kingdoms by not bringing judgment on them the moment they transgress His law is ultimately a form of judgment. They receive common grace, meaning an unmerited and temporary gift of an extension of time without judgment, but this only increases the magnitude of the eventual wrath of God.

We should not expect to see Satan's kingdom cut down overnight in the future, after having attained a position of universal dominion. The process of growth for Satan's kingdom is not continuous. The "negative feedback" phenomenon of external judgment repeatedly cuts back the growth of Satan's external dominion long before it achieves worldwide dominion. These verses point to a far different future: the steady growth of Christ's kingdom as the *leaven of righteousness* overwhelms and replaces the God-hindered leaven of Satan's kingdom.[32]

The Gambler

Satan's kingdom does manifest itself intermittently during temporary periods of exceedingly rapid growth, but this growth cannot be sustained for "a thousand generations." The growth rate of Satan's kingdom is the growth rate of the gambler who has a string of successful bets, or the highly leveraged (indebted) investor who predicts the market accurately for a time and multiplies his wealth with borrowed money. Such growth is rapid, but it cannot be sustained. It is the growth rate of a person who has limited time, and who must make his fortune in one lifetime. He requires rapid growth, for he has no faith in long-term growth over many generations. The compound growth rate must be high, and it must be rapid, for it will not last for long.

---

32. Gary North, *Unconditional Surrender*, pp. 183-92.

Paganism and gambling are closely linked philosophically, especially in periods of declining social order. Rushdoony writes: "Gambling comes to have a religious prominence and passion in the minds of men, so that it is more than a mere pastime: it is a hope for life. . . . The gambler denies implicitly that the universe is under law; he insists that 'all life is a gamble,' and a falling brick can kill you, and totally meaningless events always surround you, because chance, not God, is ultimate. Since chance, not God, rules the universe, causality does not prevail. It is therefore possible to get something for nothing, and the gambler, knowing what the odds are, nevertheless expects chance to overrule law and enrich him."[33] The gambler believes in law-overcoming chance, or luck. Such an outlook was dominant during the Roman Empire, and it destroyed the foundations of classical civilization.[34]

Such an outlook is also the ideology of the revolutionary. Faith in the great revolutionary discontinuous event, the run of successful bets, or the overnight "killing" in the market marks the *short-run view of fallen man*.[35] Continuity holds no promise of victory for him, for he knows that *time and continuity are his great enemies*. The run of luck for a gambler cannot hold; the law of averages (statistical continuity) eventually reasserts itself. Similarly, the traditions and habits of men (social and ethical continuity) thwart the revolutionary; if the revolutionaries cannot capture the seats of central power overnight, in a top-down transfer of power to the newly captured central gov-

---

33. R. J. Rushdoony, *Politics of Guilt and Pity* (Fairfax, Virginia: Thoburn Press, [1970] 1978), p. 217.

34. Charles Norris Cochrane, *Christianity and Classical Culture: A Study of Thought and Action from Augustus to Augustine* (New York: Oxford University Press, [1944] 1957), p. 159.

35. Karl Marx, who spent most of his life in self-imposed poverty, inherited a fortune in 1864. As the money was being sent in chunks, Marx invested in the stock market. He wrote to Engels on July 15: "If I had the money during the last ten days, I would have been able to make a good deal on the stock exchange. The time has come now when with wit and very little money one can make a killing in London." As his biographer reports, a year later he was again begging for money from Engels. Robert Payne, *Marx* (New York: Simon & Schuster, 1968), p. 353. Marx was supported entirely by Engels from the early 1870's until his death in 1883.

In contrast to Marx's profligate, gambling ways was his uncle, Lion Philips, who despised his nephew. Philips founded the Philips Company, which is still one of the largest manufacturing companies in Europe. In the United States, it is known as the North American Philips Company, or Norelco. In the early 1960's, this innovative firm invented the audiocassette tape and tape recorder, which launched a technological revolution. Compound growth was still operating at Philips.

ernment, they fear that all will be lost.[36]

Even a successful revolution is threatened by institutional continuity: lethargy, corruption, bureaucracy. This has been the fate of
the Soviet Union.[37] To overcome these results, communists have argued for the necessity of continual revolutions. Trotsky[38] and Mao[39]
both called for a continuing series of revolutions, echoing the instruction given to Communist proletarians by Karl Marx in 1850:
"Their battle cry must be: The Revolution in Permanence."[40] Billington has traced the idea back to the Bavarian Illuminati.[41]
(Jefferson used similar language: "What signify a few lives lost in a
century or two? The tree of liberty must be refreshed from time to
time with the blood of patriots & tyrants. It is its natural manure."[42]
He was writing of Shays' rebellion, the reaction against which
became one of the main motivations of the Constitutional convention. Yet here was Jefferson, writing: "God forbid we should ever be
20 years without such a rebellion.")

God's people, on the contrary, should have faith in both time and
continuity.[43] God governs both. The steady efforts of the godly man
accomplish much. God's word does not return to Him void (Isa.
55:11). Through the covenantal community, over time, each man's

---

36. Lenin wrote a secret message from his hiding place to the Bolshevik Central
Committee on Oct. 8, 1917, a few days before the Communists captured Russia. It
outlined the tactics for the capture of power. He ended his letter with these words:
"The success of both the Russian and the world revolution depends on two or three
days' fighting." "Advice of an Onlooker," in Robert C. Tucker (ed.), *The Lenin Anthology* (New York: Norton, 1975), p. 414.

37. Konstantin Simis, *USSR: The Corrupt Society: The Secret World of Soviet Capitalism* (New York: Simon & Schuster, 1982); Michael Voslensky, *Nomenklatura: The
Soviet Ruling Class* (Garden City, New York: Doubleday, 1984).

38. *The Age of Permanent Revolution: A Trotsky Anthology*, edited by Isaac Deutscher
(New York: Dell, 1964).

39. "Revolution was the proper occupation of the masses, Mao believed, for only
through perpetual revolution could he realize his vision of an egalitarian collective
society." Dennis Bloodworth, *The Messiah and the Mandarins: Mao Tsetung and the Iron-
ies of Power* (New York: Atheneum, 1982), p. 187.

40. Marx, "Address of the Central Committee to the Communist League" (1850),
in Karl Marx and Frederick Engels, *Selected Works*, 3 vols. (Moscow: Progress Publishers, [1969] 1977), I, p. 185. A similar call was made by Tolstoy: ". . . the only
revolution is the one that never stops." Cited by James Billington, *Fire in the Minds of
Men: Origins of the Revolutionary Faith* (New York: Basic Books, 1980), p. 417.

41. Billington, *op. cit.*, p. 597, note 309.

42. Jefferson to William S. Smith, Nov. 13, 1787, from Paris; in *Thomas Jefferson:
Writings* (New York: Library Classics of America, 1984), p. 911.

43. See North, *Moses and Pharaoh*, ch. 12: "Continuity and Revolution."

efforts are multiplied, for "thousands of generations." The regenerate person should expect a long-term return from his efforts: the establishment and steady expansion of the kingdom of God, in time and on earth, and then beyond the grave.

Conclusion

The prohibition against graven images is fundamentally a prohibition against man's worshipping the works of man. When man worships an image created by man, he cannot worship the Creator, whose image man is. He is worshipping something less than man. All men should see this, but only regenerate men do. The *prohibition of graven images* should therefore be understood as the *repudiation of humanism* (Ex. 20:4). All forms of *idolatry* are ultimately variations of *self-worship,* for it is man, as a self-proclaimed sovereign being, who asserts the right to choose whom he will worship in place of God. Man, the sovereign, decides.

Men are called to exercise dominion over all creatures, but ethically rebellious men worship images of creatures (Rom. 1:22). Sometimes these images are graven images; sometimes they are mirror images. In either case, men bow down to the creation. What appears to be an *act of human autonomy* — worshipping the creation of one's own hands — is ultimately an *act of subordination to the dark one* who is supposed to be judged by men, not worshipped by men, and who will be judged by God's people (I Cor. 6:3).

The fulfillment of the dominion covenant is based on simultaneous *subordination and rulership*.[44] Men are to be under God and over the creation. There is no escape from the governing principle of subordination and fulfillment. It is an inescapable concept. The questions are: To whom will men be ethically subordinate, and over what will they exercise dominion? Whose ethical yoke will men wear: Christ's or Satan's? Men cannot operate without an ethical yoke. Whose law-order will they uphold and conform themselves to?

When men worship the creature, including man, they are worshipping Satan, who is temporally and temporarily the most powerful of creatures. *They have adopted a religion of exclusively temporal power.* Supernatural forces may or may not be invoked, but the goal is the same: the acquisition of temporal power. Anton Szandor LaVey, the founder of the Church of Satan in the mid-1960's, has put it well:

---

44. Gary North, *Dominion Covenant: Genesis,* ch. 7.

"Anyone who pretends to be interested in magic or the occult for reasons other than gaining personal power is the worst kind of hypocrite."[45] This is the heart and soul of all Baal worship. But Satan's rule is doomed. It can grow in influence culturally for short periods, but ultimately temporal judgment comes, as it came to the Egyptians. The capital investment of the idol-worshippers is eventually squandered, destroyed, or inherited by the faithful.

On the other hand, when men worship God, they place themselves within a covenantal framework which is guaranteed for "thousands of generations." They can take dominion over the external realm because they operate in terms of God's tool of dominion, His law. Time and continuity are not the enemies of God's people, for long-term growth eventually brings prosperity to the spiritual, covenantal heirs of the faithful. The *continuity of faith* over time brings the *continuity of expansion* over time, spiritually and culturally.

Men are to seek covenantal dominion, not autonomous power. Dominion comes through obedience to God. God possesses ultimate authority. Man cannot escape being subordinate to something ultimate, and this ultimate something is God. By refusing to make graven images, the ancient Hebrews ritually affirmed that their covenantal yoke was imposed by God, not by themselves.

To whom will a man or society be subordinate: God or Satan? Will a man become part of God's hierarchy or, as C. S. Lewis puts it in his *Screwtape Letters*, part of Satan's "lowerarchy"? Whose covenantal yoke will men wear, Christ's or Satan's? There is no escape from yokes; the question is: Whose? The issue of hierarchy and obedience is crucial in this commandment. God commands men to worship Him, and not to attempt to escape subordination to Him by seeking autonomy. Worshipping anything other than God is an affirmation of autonomy, for man autonomously determines for himself that he will worship something other than God. The second commandment prohibits man from setting up any visible manifestations of a representative of any supernatural authority other than God.

---

45. Anton Szandor LaVey, *The Satanic Bible* (New York: Avon, 1972), p. 51.

3

OATHS, COVENANTS, AND CONTRACTS

Thou shalt not take the name of the Lord thy God in vain; for the Lord will not hold him guiltless that taketh his name in vain (Ex. 20:7).

The third commandment generally receives very little space in commentaries. R. J. Rushdoony's *Institutes of Biblical Law* (1973) devotes only 27 pages to this commandment out of the 636 pages that are devoted exclusively to explaining the ten commandments. While Rushdoony's comments are frequently to the point, since he has recognized several of the underlying relationships between profane speech and profane religion, the very sparseness of his comments testifies to the historic absence of attention to the third commandment on the part of commentators. There is no large body of previously developed material for the contemporary commentator to respond to.

The standard interpretation of this verse in the twentieth century is that the essence of this commandment is to prevent swearing, with swearing narrowly defined as foul language, or cursing: using God's name to emphasize a point. Swearing is thus understood as a loose and socially offensive form of language. The definition of swearing or cursing in this century centers on the misuse of language, not in the sense of calling on the power of God—legitimately or illegitimately—to achieve one's goals, but rather in the sense of inappropriately using God's name as a kind of verbal amplifier. In short, the interpretation of this verse focuses on oaths as *obscenities* rather than on oaths as *profanities*, although the English word "profanity" is now used almost exclusively as synonymous with obscenity. This limits the usefulness of the modern concept of profanity.

Profanity as Invocation

Biblically, *profanity* is an aspect of *profane worship*. As Rushdoony points out, the word is derived from two Latin words, *pro* (before, or

51

in front of) and *fanum* (temple), meaning "before or outside the temple."[1] Profane worship takes two forms: *first*, the attempt to escape from God's final judgment by means of the attainment of power apart from God's law, and *second*, the attempt to escape from God's final judgment by means of an escape from power and a release from the dominion covenant, an attempt which is equally opposed to God's law. In short, profane religion is either *power religion* or *escapist religion*.[2] However, profane speech of the kind prohibited by the third commandment is almost always formally the invocation of power, and therefore formally an assertion of power.

Profanity is unquestionably a misuse of language, for it involves the *verbal invocation* of a false god, and therefore it involves the worship of a false god. This is why the prohibition against the vain use of God's name is included in the ten commandments immediately after the first two commandments, which prohibit the worship of false gods. Profane speech calls upon the name of the God of the Bible in a profane way. It implies that God can be called upon by rebellious man—either individually or collectively—in order to add His power to the programs of rebellious man.[3]

Swearing in the Bible involves far more than obscenity. Indeed, it is difficult to find a single example in the Bible of a violation of this commandment where someone used obscene language, meaning language that is inappropriate because it is perceived in polite society as being crude. This does not mean that using God's name in vain is not crude. But when men think "bad manners" or "obscene language" when they hear someone using the name of God unthinkingly as an expletive, they thereby reveal their own failure to understand the primary reason for the third commandment. They have focused on the secondary or tertiary reasons. The issue is not primarily a question of propriety or etiquette; it is a question of the improper invocation of power.

Solemn Curses and Solemn Oaths

Solemn oaths are taken in the name of God. There are definite restrictions on the taking of such oaths. They are confined to state-

---

1. R. J. Rushdoony, *The Institutes of Biblical Law* (Nutley, New Jersey: Craig Press, 1973), p. 107.
2. Gary North, *Moses and Pharaoh: Dominion Religion vs. Power Religion* (Tyler, Texas: Institute for Christian Economics, 1985), Introduction.
3. C. S. Lewis' profound novel, *That Hideous Strength* (New York: Macmillan, 1945), is an account of just this sort of profane quest for power: a fusion of self-proclaimed autonomous man's scientific power with the occult power of false gods.

ments before judicial bodies exclusively appointed by God to execute His judgment, the institutional church, the civil government, and (under certain circumstances) the family. Each agency can legitimately enforce sanctions against oath-breakers, and they do so in the name of God. The civil government can lawfully impose physical sanctions, and the institutional church can lawfully impose spiritual sanctions. The family can impose both physical sanctions (the rod) and spiritual sanctions (the father's blessing). There are three forms of curses: civil, ecclesiastical, and familial.

This is not to argue that sanctions are not simultaneously spiritual and physical. The civil government enforces its law by fines, physical punishment, or execution. Yet these physical punishments point to a future and permanent spiritual punishment by God, for the oath-breaker is involved in a violation of God's law. Civil authority is ultimately derived from God, so a violation of Bible-based civil law necessarily involves a transgression of the covenant. Similarly, the church enforces its spiritual sanctions by separating people physically from the sacraments. This punishment points to an eternal future punishment which involves physical separation from God and His resurrected church — punishment which is unquestionably physical in nature (Rev. 20:14), and not simply spiritual.

The essence of the third commandment is the defense of God's three institutional monopolies that can legitimately pronounce curses in God's name: the church, the civil government, and the family. The civil government pronounces the curse of *earthly* punishment in the name of God, and so does the family (Gen. 49:3-7). The church pronounces the curse of *eternal* punishment in the name of God. Individuals and associations other than these three monopolies are prohibited by God from exercising autonomous power by invoking God's name in a curse.

Curses as Imperatives

Consider a familiar violation of this commandment in English, the expletive, "God damn you." It is used thoughtlessly, usually in anger. Biblically speaking, the phrase is an imperative: the invocation of the ultimate biblical curse, a calling upon God to execute His judgment to destroy eternally a personal opponent. It should not be understood as simply a breach of good manners, a violation of biblical etiquette. It is a verbal expression of personal outrage or disgust which is prohibited precisely because it invokes the ultimate power of God for distinctly personal ends. In other words, *it is an attempted misuse of power.* Even Michael the archangel avoided such language when he confronted Satan himself, for he dared not "bring against him a railing accusation, but said, The Lord rebuke thee" (Jude 9b).

This is not to say that all cursing is prohibited. The commandment reads, "thou shalt not take the name of the Lord thy God *in vain.*" God's name may be invoked for God-ordained ends. Cursing within a God-ordained context is therefore legitimate. Indeed, it is *mandatory.* Excommunication is such a curse. Jesus established certain procedural rules of church discipline in Matthew 18. "Verily I say unto you, Whatsoever ye shall bind on earth shall be bound in heaven: and whatsoever ye shall loose on earth shall be loosed in heaven," (v. 18). This element of *verbal "binding"* is the very essence of cursing, for it is more than verbal. It is real — eternally real. Thus, the loose language which we call cursing is prohibited, precisely because biblical cursing is the language of *binding.* The power to curse is the exclusive possession of the church, for the church is God's monopolistic human agency of eternal judgment, both for men and angels (I Cor. 6:3).

Adam did not pronounce the preliminary judgmental curse against Satan in the garden, but he was required by God to have done so. Mankind does not escape the task of executing judgment because of the Fall. Redeemed mankind—the church—becomes both the earthly and heavenly agent of pronouncing judgment against Satan, his angelic followers, and his human followers. God executes final judgment, but redeemed mankind pronounces preliminary judgment. God's "earnest" or down payment to His church of this coming authority—an original authority which was given to Adam in the garden—is the church's present ability to bind and loose on earth as it is in heaven and will be at the final judgment.

The church in effect issues a warning: "God damn you, *unless* you repent." It is an *imperative*—a calling upon God—since the phrase is not in the active voice, "God damns you." It is to serve as a warning to the offender, not a final judgment. It calls upon the heavenly Judge to honor the church's word, which He promises to do. The church in its earthly capacity cannot execute judgment against a man's soul, for the possibility of repentance always exists, as far as the church can see. Instead, the church casts out the man's body from the presence of the church, and therefore from the sacramental presence of God. This is what is meant by Paul's phrase, "to deliver him to Satan." Paul wrote concerning the necessity of the church's judging the incestuous Corinthian church member: "To deliver such an one unto Satan for the destruction of the flesh, that the spirit may be saved in the day of the Lord Jesus" (I Cor. 5:5). Excommunication is therefore what we call a *solemn curse*. It is issued in solemnity by a *judicial agency*. Solemn curses are biblically legitimate, but only under very limited circumstances.

Solemn Oaths

Individuals can legitimately take solemn oaths in lawful judicial proceedings, either in front of a church court or a civil court. Oaths that invoke *God's name*, and therefore implicitly acknowledge God's *power to curse*, are frequently required from individuals prior to their giving of testimony in judicial proceedings held by the civil government. We sometimes refer to these oaths as *self-maledictory*. They call forth God's judgment on the verbal promoter of falsehood, and this judgment is eternal and institutional (church and civil government).

Civil oaths are judicially binding. To lie under oath — deliberately to offer testimony known to be false — is perjury, and the biblical punishment for perjury is the imposition by the State of the same penalty that would have been brought upon the proposed victim of the perjury (Deut. 19:16-21). It is not judicial oaths as such that are prohibited by God; it is *false* oaths. A false oath in God's name is true *profanity*. "And ye shall not swear by my name falsely, neither shall thou profane the name of thy God: I am the LORD" (Lev. 19:12). It involves profanely calling upon God to *certify the false words* of rebellious man, thereby *empowering his programs*.

Rushdoony quite properly points to the relationship between swearing and revolution.[4] Men are forbidden to curse their parents; it is a capital offense (Ex. 21:17). Blasphemy, another capital crime (Lev. 24:16), is wicked language directed against God.[5] In his section, "The Oath and Society," he concentrates on the much narrower question: the oath and civil government.[6] He argues that a false oath is an assault on society and social order, an assault on the life of the society.[7] The existence of a mandatory oath has important implica-

---

4. Rushdoony, *Institutes*, pp. 106-11.
5. *Ibid.*, p. 108.
6. *Ibid.*, pp. 111-15.
7. *Ibid.*, p. 114.

tions for civil government: "The oath in God's name is the 'legal recognition of God' [writes T. Robert Ingram] as the source of all things
and the only ground of all being. It establishes the state under God
and under His law. The removal of God from oaths, and the light
and dishonest use of oaths, is a declaration of independence from
Him, and is warfare against God in the name of the new gods, apos-
tate man and his totalitarian state."[8]

Covenant and Curse

What is missing from Rushdoony's analysis is any discussion of
the relation of the oath and the institutional church. An oath is
always a self-maledictory act. The archetype is the oath of covenantal membership in the body of Christ. Men bind themselves
covenantally to the church by means of an oath. This oath can legitimately be made by parents in the name of children,[9] but the oath is
always present in the covenant. When this oath is broken, either verbally (profession of another faith) or by external acts in defiance of
biblical law (the terms of the covenant), the church must excommunicate the oath-breaker. In short, *where there is an oath, there is also
implicitly a curse.* Without the presence of a curse, there can be no
oath. Even after the final judgment, there is always a curse: on
redeemed mankind *historically* in the person of Jesus Christ, the
perfect man, and on covenant-breaking mankind *eternally* in the lake
of fire (Rev. 20:14). The doctrine of eternal punishment is therefore
inherent in the doctrine of the covenant. It was Adam's implicit
denial of this inescapable relationship which brought on the curse.

*The exercise of the curse of excommunication by the church is the only legiti-
mate manifestation in society of the imperative use of God's name in judgment.*
The church, as God's monopolistic agency of corporate worship, the
sole possessor of the sacraments, is the only institution which can
lawfully call down the warning of the ultimate curse of God, eternal
punishment, and therefore it alone can lawfully enforce institutionally God's criteria of ethical reconciliation to Him. *Therefore, the
use of God's name in an imperative eternal curse in private speech is an infringement on the monopoly power of the church.* It is a public act of rebellion.
Even the civil magistrate cannot lawfully pronounce the judgmental
imperative, "God damn you."

---

8. *Ibid.*, p. 115.

9. Meredith G. Kline, *By Oath Consigned: A Reinterpretation of the Covenant Signs of
Circumcision and Baptism* (Grand Rapids, Michigan: Eerdmans, 1968), ch. 6.

Oaths, Vows, and Subordination

Implicit in any vain use of God's name is the invocation of the self-maledictory oath. The oath brings the judgment of God over the oath-taker. A self-maledictory oath is appropriate only when taken before biblically sanctioned courts that are carrying out their God-ordained tasks. It does not result in God's judgment if the testimony of the oath-taker is true, to the best of his knowledge.

There are also other oaths that are taken directly before God, called vows. Such oaths made unto the Lord can legitimately invoke His name, for they, too, are self-maledictory. Vow-taking was a common practice in the Old Testament and is still legitimate in New Testament times. A vow cannot legitimately be taken autonomously by unmarried or married women. They must report the terms of their vows to their fathers (unmarried women) or husbands (married women). The man who has been placed over them can override the vow within twenty-four hours (Num. 30:3-8). A widow, however, is the head of her household. Her vow carries the same force as a man's: God can require it of her (Num. 30:9). There are biblical laws associated with the various oaths made unto God.[10] They have to be kept as vowed.

What about promises? Are they in the same category as vows and oaths? A promise is an assurance of truthfulness to third parties. Unlike an oath sworn before a civil or ecclesiastical court, and also unlike a vow made directly to God, promises are not to mention God or any "near-God" place or thing. A self-maledictory oath may invoke God's name under biblically specified conditions, but *promises are not self-maledictory oaths under God*, and therefore must not mention God's name. To use God's name in this way is to misuse the name of God — to take God's name in vain — for God's name is used to impress third parties with the reliability of a man's word. To invoke God's name means that you have placed yourself directly under one of God's three legitimate monopolies of enforcement. The sovereign agency can therefore enforce the terms of the covenant. In short, if there is no *direct, immediate subordination* in a law-court situation, a self-maledictory oath is invalid and therefore prohibited.

Marriage requires a covenantal oath, for the family is a monopolistic agency sanctioned by God. It is therefore marked by

---

10. Lev. 7:16; 22:21-23; 27:1-13; Num. 6 (Nazarite vows); 15:3-8; Deut. 12:17-19; 23:18, 21-22.

legally enforceable vows, either implicitly under God or explicitly under God (Mal. 2:14). The New Testament compares the marriage bond with the bond between Christ and His church (Eph. 5:22-33; I Pet. 3:1-7). Where God's name is invoked, both marriage partners come under the self-maledictory conditions of God's covenant oath structure. Where God's name is explicitly invoked, both church and State can impose their respective sanctions against covenant-breakers within the marriage. Where God's name is not invoked, then the civil government becomes the sole enforcer. But it must be understood that marriage is a monopolistic institution established by God, and God requires the civil government to impose the harshest of sanctions against adulterers: death (Lev. 20:10; Deut. 22:22).

Oaths vs. Anarchy

What is forbidden, then, is the use of God's name to create an *illusion of reliability.* The reliability of performance which is associated with the self-maledictory oath may not legitimately be transferred autonomously by men to their daily affairs and activities. Thus, Jesus warned His listeners in His "sermon on the mount":

> Again, ye have heard that it hath been said by them of old time, Thou shalt not forswear thyself, but shalt perform unto the Lord thine oaths: But I say unto you, Swear not at all; neither by heaven; for it is God's throne: Nor by the earth; for it is his footstool: neither by Jerusalem; for it is the city of the great King. Neither shalt thou swear by thy head, because thou canst not make one hair white or black. But let your communication be, Yea, yea; Nay, nay: for whatsoever is more than these cometh of evil (Matt. 5:33-37).

There has long been confusion concerning the frame of reference of Christ's words. Did he condemn all oaths that invoke God's name? Obviously not; this would have been a denial of the legitimacy of God's three monopoly governments that are founded on His covenant with man. Any interpretation which argues that Jesus was abolishing all oaths that invoke God's name is implicitly anarchical, for the civil government and the institutional church (and sometimes the family) can lawfully require those subject to them to invoke God's name *and therefore God's curse* when they are about to offer testimony to the respective court. This increases the likelihood of honest testimony from those who fear the God who knows men's hearts. Only those governments specifically authorized by God to require

the self-maledictory oath have the lawful authority under God to extract a God-naming oath.[11] Nevertheless, these three monopoly governments do possess this authority. To deny this authority to them is
implicitly to assert the *autonomy of man*. This is why the Westminster
Confession of Faith (1646) states: "Yet it is a sin to refuse an oath
touching any thing that is good and just, being imposed by lawful
authority" (XXII:III).

Such a denial has been made at various times by various
Anabaptist groups from their beginnings in the early sixteenth century. In the name of a "higher obedience to the words of Jesus," they
refuse to invoke God's name and therefore simultaneously refuse to
place themselves under God's potential curses, as administered on
earth by the civil government. They thereby implicitly assert the autonomy of the individual conscience from any God-ordained civil
government. Sometimes radical Anabaptists have explicitly made
this assertion of their own autonomy, but it is always implicit in their
theology.

Penalties

The question eventually must be raised: Is it a criminal offense to
take the name of the Lord in vain? When people curse their parents,
it unquestionably is a capital crime (Ex. 21:17). The son or daughter
is under the lawful jurisdiction of the family. The integrity of the
family must be maintained by the threat of death. Clearly, cursing
God (blasphemy) is a comparable crime, and is therefore a capital
crime (Lev. 24:16).

What about the integrity of the church? What if someone who is
not a member of the church publicly curses the church? Is the State
required to apply the same sanction? The person may not be
covenantally subordinate to the particular church, or any church,
unlike the subordinate child who curses a parent. There is no specific
reference to any civil penalty for cursing anyone but a parent or
God, nor is there any civil penalty assigned for using God's name in
vain. Then is there a general prohibition against cursing? On what
grounds could a church prosecute a cursing rebel?

One possible answer is the law against assault. Battery involves

---

11. In the Old Testament, it appears, the father of the bride was the sovereign
agent of a marriage. Thus, marriage vows were taken before him by the couple. See
James B. Jordan, *The Law of the Covenant: An Exposition of Exodus 21-23* (Tyler, Texas:
Institute for Christian Economics, 1984), p. 150.

physical violence against a person, but assault can be verbal.[12] A threat is made. A curse is a threat: calling the wrath of God down upon someone. Another approach is the law against public indecency. A third: cursing as a violation of the victim's peace and quiet. Restitution could be imposed by the civil magistrate to defend a church or an individual who is victimized by cursing.

What about cursing a civil magistrate? It is clear that this is an act of rebellion analogous to someone in the military who is insubordinate to his superior officer. A citizen or resident alien is under the lawful authority of the civil government. By publicly challenging this authority, the person becomes a criminal rebel. There is no explicit penalty assigned to this crime. We know, however, that public flogging is lawful, up to forty lashes (Deut. 25:3), yet no crime in the Bible ever explicitly requires public physical punishment, except on an eye-for-eye basis, or the unique case of the woman who has her palm split[13] in response to her specific prohibited physical violence against her husband's opponent in a fight (Deut. 25:11-12). The punishment for cursing a civil magistrate is therefore left to the discretion of the magistrates or a jury. It might be public flogging; it might be a fine imposed in lieu of public flogging.

Obscenity and Impotence

What about taking God's name in vain, but not in the form of a curse? What about obscenity in general? Obscenity also constitutes a form of public violence against third parties. It is obscene behavior. It is an infraction of moral sensibilities, comparable to disrobing publicly. It is an aggressive act against biblical social order. It must be viewed as an immoral act, however common this act has become in the twentieth century. It therefore should be subject to prosecution in the civil courts.

Should every instance of obscene language be prosecuted? No. Language is subtle. Certain occasional uses of a word that in some (or many) contexts would be regarded as obscene or profane are sometimes not so regarded by the general public. There are also shades of meaning and emphasis in language. Consider a traditional sentence in American political history: "Men will be governed by God, or, by God, they will be *governed*." The second "by God" could

---

12. *Oxford English Dictionary,* "assault," definition #2.
13. Her palm was to be split, not cut off, as the King James mistakenly implies. James B. Jordan, *Law of the Covenant,* p. 118.

be seen to be a misuse of God's name. Yet it may not be. The underlying message is theologically profound: without subordination under God men will find themselves subordinate to the tyranny of other men. The acceptance of this principle by the Christian West has always been the foundation of Western liberty.[14] The phrase, "by God, they will be governed," is a warning—the forceful communication of a political condition to be avoided at all costs.

Thus, to require civil punishment for every possible infraction of the third commandment would be to require perfection on the part of the listeners and the judges. It would also waste precious public resources in endless litigation. But there is no doubt that continued obscenity, as well as illegitimate cursing, must be regarded as an attack on Christian social order. A jury of twelve people (the Anglo-Saxon traditional number) has the right to evaluate the circumstances and contexts, and then make a civil judgment.

Language and Dominion

James Jordan argues that language is the first stage of dominion. "If we do not have a word for a certain thing, we cannot readily come to grips with it."[15] Language is also the first stage of creativity. "God created via the Word. All cultures and societies are shaped by verbal concepts. This is why proclamation of the Gospel is the foundation stone of Christian society."[16]

When rebellious men seek to infuse their language with power, they often turn to the use of obscenities. Rushdoony links this with the pagan quest for *power from below*. "Godly oaths seek their confirmation and strength from above; ungodly swearing looks below for its power. Its concept of the 'below' is Manichaean to the core: it is material. Hence, ungodly swearing finds its power, its 'below,' in sex and in excrement. The association is significant. Even while protesting the 'Puritanism' of Biblical morality, the ungodly reveal that to them sex and excrement are linked together as powers of the 'underworld' of the unconscious, the primitive, and the vital."[17]

---

14. R. J. Rushdoony, *The Foundations of Social Order: Studies in the Creeds and Councils of the Early Church* (Fairfax, Virginia: Thoburn Press, [1968] 1978), ch. 7: "The Council of Chalcedon: Foundation of Western Liberty."
15. Jordan, *Law of the Covenant*, p. 132.
16. *Ibid.*, p. 133.
17. Rushdoony, *Institutes*, p. 109.

What actually takes place is that this particular quest for power from below brings verbal impotence. The shocking words cease to shock. They become boring. Yet the speaker finds that he can no longer express himself without them. He has grown accustomed to calling attention to his ideas and opinions by means of obscenities, but his language becomes steadily debased. His words no longer attract. They even repel.

Henry Miller wrote books that shocked the public, and brought in the censors, in the middle third of the twentieth century. His *Tropic of Cancer* and other books were suppressed for a time as pornographic. He defended his books against this accusation. What he was, he claimed, was a writer of obscenity, not pornography. He stated boldly that *Tropic of Cancer* "is not a book. This is libel, slander, defamation of character. This is not a book, in the ordinary sense of the word. No, this is a prolonged insult, a gob of spit in the face of Art, a kick in the pants of God, Man, Destiny, Time, Love, Beauty . . . what you will."[18]

There can be no doubt about Miller's impulse. It was religious to the core. He had in mind the salvation of man. In a well-titled 1946 essay, "The Time of the Assassins," he stated his soteriology quite well: "The road to heaven leads through hell, does it not? To earn salvation one has to become innoculated with sin. One has to savour them all, the capital as well as the trivial sins. One has to earn death with all one's appetites, refuse no poison, reject no experience however degrading or sordid."[19] This theology is familiar. It is a resurrection of the chaos cults of the ancient world.

His vision of the artist was messianic, but always within the framework of the religion of revolution: "Ultimately, then, he [the artist or poet] stands among his own obscene objurations like the conqueror midst the ruins of a devastated city. He realizes that the real nature of the obscene resides in the lust to convert. . . . Once this vantage point is reached, how trifling and remote seems the accusations of the moralists! How senseless the debate as to whether the work in question was of high literary merit or not! How absurd the wrangling over the moral or immoral nature of his creation!"[20] In short, "I am my own savior."[21]

18. Henry Miller, *Tropic of Cancer* (New York: Grove Press, [1934] 1961), p. 2.
19. Miller, "The Time of the Assassins" (1946), in *Selected Prose* (London: Macgibbon & Kee, 1965), II, p. 122.
20. Miller, "Obscenity and the Law of Reflection," (1947), in *ibid.*, I, p. 366.
21. Miller, *The World of Sex* (New York: Grove Press, 1959), p. 20.

Control over language is a training ground for dominion. The person who cannot control his tongue, the Bible says, is in danger (James 3:2-10). The context of James' remarks is the anomaly of blessing and cursing out of the same mouth. Failure to control the tongue reflects a failure to exercise self-government under law. The lack of self-government can lead to other kinds of deviant behavior, and ultimately can lead to the imposition of civil penalties against violent behavior. The inability to express oneself also produces frustration, and this frustration can lead to violence. Escalating emotions in an obscenity-filled shouting match become the stepping stone to violence. The continual use of obscene language is therefore a manifestation of *lower-class culture*. Lower-class culture decapitalizes civilization.[22] So do pornography and its moral first-cousin, obscenity.[23]

Thus, we find that the quest for power as such leads to impotence. Long-term power is derived solely from God, as a gift from God for obedience. Biblical dominion religion seeks the kingdom of God and attains external success (Matt. 6:33). Power religion uses language from below to increase its power temporarily, and it thereby loses power. This is the paradigm of power religion which I use throughout my studies of Exodus. It applies to the field of language, just as it does to all other areas of life.

Deceptive Contracts

We now come to the more explicitly economic portion of the chapter. When Jesus warned people not to invoke God's name, or the name of some "near-divine" object, he was warning them against creating a *false sense of trust* on the part of other people. For instance, consider a person who agrees to perform a specified service for a specified price. "You can count on me. My word is my bond. I agree to perform the service." This is a case of "Yea, yea." But what if he escalates his rhetoric? What if he says, "I am absolutely trustworthy. I swear on the Bible that I will fulfill the terms of our agreement. But I want payment in advance."

He has sworn on the Bible. So what? If he is a God-fearing man, he will avoid such language, unless he is ignorant about God's word.

---

22. Edward Banfield, *The Unheavenly City* (Boston: Little, Brown, 1970), pp. 53-54, 62-64.
23. R. J. Rushdoony, *The Politics of Pornography* (New Rochelle, New York: Arlington House, 1974), ch. 13: "Decapitalization."

If he is a deceiver, he might very well use such a phrase. The Bible becomes a tool in his tool kit of deceptive techniques. He enlists God's name, by implication, in this deception. He extracts money in advance because the buyer believes that the seller will be too afraid not to perform the promised service. Or perhaps the use of religious-sounding language calmed the buyer into believing that this is a man familiar with God's blessings. In any case, vaguely religious and ignorant people can become victims of those who take the name of God in vain.

Such language involves *fraud*. A person poses as God-fearing, yet his very language belies his claim. But the ignorant person is deceived. This is a recapitulation of Satan's temptation of Eve in the garden. He used God's name and religious-sounding language in order to calm Eve's sense of insecurity. Because of the misleading use of language, Eve believed that her risks were lower than they really were. In business contracts, the misuse of religious language accomplishes the same thing: *a reduction in the buyer's perceived risk*. The deal seems less risky than it really is because of the seller's use of religious language, at least less risky in the mind of the superstitious or ignorant person who is unfamiliar with the third commandment or Jesus' sermon on the mount.

A Performance Bond

The word of God is sure. Similarly, the word of the Christian should be his bond. A bond is a legal guarantee of performance. A bonded employee is someone who has been certified by a third party as being able and willing to perform his job honestly. If he fails, the bonding agent is subject to penalties. He must make restitution to the victimized employer. The employee's bonding was one reason why the employer hired him. The employer trusted the employee because the bonding agent said the person was trustworthy. The bonding agent is therefore financially responsible for the honest performance of the employee.

What is the economic function of the bonding agent? He reduces risks, for a fee. He expends time and money in a specialized search for clues regarding a person's performance. The employer buys the results of this specialized knowledge. The bonding agent receives a return on his investment of his specialized knowledge and his time. But if his techniques of investigation are faulty, or if his judgment of the data is faulty, then he stands to lose. He will have to pay a higher-than-average number of insurance payments to victimized employers.

A Christian should be a lower-risk employee. He believes in God. He believes that God's word is reliable and sure. He imitates Christ. He performs his agreed-upon tasks on time and at the level of quality as is customary in his profession, and perhaps above that level. He is not supposed to be an inefficient or unreliable employee. He is supposed to be doing all things for the glory of God, performing his tasks of the dominion covenant.

A Christian's word should be worth more in the marketplace than other men's words. If this is not a characteristic feature of Christian service, then there is a glaring deficiency in the church's level of instruction and discipline. When a Christian says "yea," then the other person can rely on that "yea." He can make a budget for the future which includes predictable performance on the part of his Christian suppliers of goods and services. He can more accurately plan for the future. This makes his plans less expensive. There is therefore less waste in the economy. God's resources are allocated more efficiently. In short, *there should be less risk when we rely upon the promises of Christians.*

The Name of Christ

Christians since New Testament times have borne the name of Christ (Acts 11:26). They say, "I am of Christ." This is not a violation of the third commandment. But if they attempt to create a market in terms of the name of Christ, they must be ready to sacrifice in order to honor that name. To use God's name explicitly in commercial ventures requires above-average performance, what some have called "going the extra mile." To swear to a contract, verbal or written, explicitly by using God's name, is a violation of the third commandment. It is a misleading use of a covenantal oath which is biblically limited to self-maledictory affirmations in front of God's monopolistic agencies of government, civil and ecclesiastical.

Covenants and Contracts

Here we discover a fundamental distinction between contracts and covenants. A contract is made between individuals or organizations on the basis of mutual self-interest. The terms of a contract are governed by the written and customary laws of the civil government. The contract may or may not be enforceable in civil courts. But a private contract does not legitimately involve the use of a self-maledictory oath, implicitly or explicitly, since no God-ordained sovereign institution has initially bound the parties by means of such an oath. Oaths may be required in the future by a sovereign government if a dispute concerning the terms of the covenant or the performance of the contracting parties drives the antagonists into civil court. Originally, however, the two contracting parties are not in possession of God's grant of monopoly authority. A business is not institutionally sovereign in the way that the church or civil government is.

The Family Covenant

If this analysis of a contract is correct, then we have additional evidence that marriage is a covenant rather than a contract, for marriage implicitly involves a self-maledictory oath. The traditional English marriage vow has both parties affirm that they will remain married, "till death do us part." Death can come as a result of adultery when the civil government enforces God's law on the offenders (Lev. 20:10; Deut. 22:22). Because the civil government is required by the Bible to become the enforcing agent of capital punishment at the request of the injured party, it can legitimately establish legal criteria of evidence that demonstrate that a marriage has taken place. In the West, the civil government establishes agents—justices of the peace, judges, and even pastors in their capacity as people who can marry couples—to take the oaths from the contracting marriage partners. In the era when families were the contracting agents, they also had a grant of monopolistic power with respect to the management of their own affairs. Churches also assert sovereign authority when performing marriages.

The biblical penalty for adultery is death (Lev. 20:10; Deut. 22:22). The terms of the self-maledictory oath are invoked by the injured marriage partner against the offending partner. Capital punishment is not mandatory, however: Joseph, a just man, decided to put Mary away privately, without bringing her before the authorities publicly (Matt. 1:19). Joseph, as the injured party, had the option of deciding the proper response: mercy or judgment. But the injured spouse clearly possesses this decision-making ability. He can decide whether to bring the suspected covenant-breaker before the public authorities. The family is to this extent the bearer of a monopoly grant of legitimate power.[24]

There are limits on this grant of familistic power. Roman law authorized the father to sell children into slavery or even execute them.[25] This law was not changed until the era of Justinian, a Christian Emperor of the sixth century.[26] No such authority existed in Israel. In the case of the incorrigible delinquent (a rebellious glutton-drunkard), the family was required to bring him before the men of the city, who would then execute him (Deut. 21:18-21). There is no mention of a family member's casting the first stone, which was required of all other witnesses to a capital crime. (Deut. 13:6-9). There was one exception: a family member was required to cast the first stone in the case of the execution of a member who had attempted to lead him or her into idolatry (Deut. 13:6-9).

The Business Contract

Men can make better use of their scarce economic resources by co-operating in the activities of production. The idea behind a business contract is that such co-operation involves costs, especially unknown future costs. A contract reduces the area of uncertainty by formalizing the various responsibilities of the co-operating entrepreneurs. *A contract therefore is a cost-reduction device.* Men can learn to trust one another to fulfill the terms of the contract. Self-government becomes easier, since everyone has a clearer idea of what is expected from him. This greater certainty of performance frees up resources that would otherwise have to be expended in policing the venture.

The contract may have penalties for non-performance written into it. These are analogous to, but not identical to, the self-maledictory aspect of a covenant. The contract cannot legitimately call upon God to uphold the terms of the contract. Depending on the circumstances, the ultimate earthly enforcing agency might be the civil government, or an agreed-upon arbitration organization, or even the church (I Cor. 6), but a truly sovereign agency cannot delegate its sovereignty in advance without thereby transferring its

24. The question may arise: Does the civil magistrate or other third party possess this right? The scribes and Pharisees brought a women "taken in adultery, in the very act" (John 8:4). Was this legal? Jesus never challenged them concerning this decision on their part. It is suspicious, however, that they did not bring the man.

25. Edward Gibbon, *The History of the Decline and Fall of the Roman Empire*, Milman edition, 5 vols. (Philadelphia: Porter & Coates, [1776-88]), III, p. 683.

26. *Idem.*, note 106.

character as a sovereign agency to the recipient. For example, the transfer of the seal of government involves also the transfer of governmental sovereignty to the recipient. But this transforms the contract-making ability of the recipient organization into a covenant-making ability.

In short, a *covenant* testifies to the existence of a *higher sovereignty.* Biblically sanctioned self-maledictory oaths are administered by such a sovereignty; it possesses more than a contractual sovereignty. It possesses *covenantal sovereignty.* This is why the explanations of the origins of civil government by all so-called social contract theorists are categorically incorrect. The three governments ordained by God — ecclesiastical, civil, and family — were not the product of a hypothetical historical social contract among sovereign individuals. They are the covenantal creations of the Creator God. They are not organizations that were created by the equivalent of business contracts.

From "Brotherhood" to "Otherhood"

This is a phrase adopted by the sociologist-historian Benjamin Nelson.[27] He uses the so-called "Weber thesis" to provide an interpretation of the transition from feudalism to capitalism. The historical documentation and debates surrounding this thesis are not the main issue at this point.[28] What is important is the concept of the *non-covenantal voluntary association.*

As the West became increasingly Christian during the Middle Ages, men could deal with each other because they belonged to a universal church. Christian associations steadily replaced pagan brotherhoods and tribes. The medieval world was a world of mutual loyalties, very often written down. Feudal contracts were military and civil covenants, however. What steadily replaced these covenants was the contract, especially the business contract.

The Protestant Reformation destroyed the ecclesiastical unity of the medieval world, but it did not destroy trade. On the contrary, trade increased.[29] Men who did not share membership in a common

---

27. Benjamin Nelson, *The Idea of Usury: From Tribal Brotherhood to Universal Otherhood* (2nd ed.; University of Chicago Press, 1969).

28. Gary North, "The 'Protestant Ethic' Hypothesis," *The Journal of Christian Reconstruction*, III (Summer 1976).

29. On the growth of trade and commerce in this period, see the magisterial study by French historian Fernand Braudel, *Civilization and Capitalism, 15th-18th Cen-*

church or a common city could still truck and barter with each other, even in the absence of a universal currency (though gold coins circulated increasingly, especially after 1500). It was men's adoption of contracts which partially substituted societally for the destruction of a common church covenant.

Consider the benefits provided by the contract. Men whose ends are radically different, or even opposed, can trade in the marketplace in order to capture the benefits of the division of labor. Because the contract spells out mutual obligations, men can make better plans concerning the future. But a contract, because it is not a covenantal document, can bring together people of varying religious beliefs and practices. The division of labor expands, and so does specialization. Per capita output increases. Had men been limited to exchanges within the covenanted "brotherhood," their markets would have remained small. The division of labor is limited by the extent of the market.[30] Therefore, their per capita wealth would have remained small. But contracts allow men to exchange with members of an "otherhood."

When Protestantism shattered the universal Roman Church covenant, it simultaneously destroyed the institutional presupposition of a universally Christian West. But the West's economic institutions not only remained, they developed and expanded. Had the covenant concept remained dominant, the economic development of the modern world would have been drastically retarded. While there were unquestionably various law systems operating in the Christian West, including the law merchant, as Harold Berman's *Law and Revolution* makes clear,[31] the use of the business contract as an implement of social co-operation would probably have been retarded. The voluntary contract held the West together economically, even though religious opinions began to vary widely. Had men relied exclusively on covenantal relationships to achieve their goals, we would almost certainly still be a rural society made up of uncooperative, religiously hostile villages.

---

tury, 3 vols. (New York: Harper & Row, 1979), and his earlier work, *The Mediterranean and the Mediterranean World in the Age of Philip II*, 2 vols. (2nd ed.; New York: Harper & Row, [1966] 1973).

30. Adam Smith, *The Wealth of Nations* (1776), ch. 3.

31. Harold Berman, *Law and Revolution: The Formation of the Western Legal Tradition* (Cambridge, Massachusetts: Harvard University Press, 1983).

Pseudo-Covenants

There is always a tendency for Satan to imitate God. Satan establishes pseudo-covenants, just as he establishes pseudo-churches. Pseudo-covenants are not limited to forthrightly pagan associations, such as the Mafia or secret societies. Parachurch groups, especially those that are "communalist" in structure, frequently adopt discipline procedures that are appropriate only for covenanted churches that possess the ultimate spiritual sanction, the power of excommunication. Pseudo-covenant parachurch organizations can fall into a very dangerous trap, the adoption of a pseudo-excommunication ritual which seemingly has the same authority as the church's excommunication. This can escalate into "brainwashing" or other kinds of emotional manipulation, since the non-church organization is itself autonomous and not clearly under the threat of corporate excommunication. An implicit oath of allegiance operates within these autonomous groups, and sometimes even explicit self-maledictory oaths.

Because they rely on a pseudo-covenant, they usually fail to adopt the legitimate and efficient practice of writing contracts, since they assume that there will be no necessity of contracts in a "fellowship." The problem is, the "fellowship" is not in fact a covenantal institution, so without voluntary contracts, the details of "right relationships" get very clouded in a crisis, especially where two or more strong-willed people are at loggerheads. Under such conditions, a "charismatic" leader can begin to exercise illegitimate power precisely because there are neither contractual nor true covenantal restraints on him. Such pseudo-covenant parachurch organizations have a marked tendency to disintegrate, and this disintegration leads in one of two ways: to the disappearance of the organization, or to the centralization of a "remnant" of the older organization. Neither result is planned, but both are common.

Conclusion

The prohibition against taking the name of God in vain has implications for several areas: civil, familial, and ecclesiastical covenants; private contracts, both business and associational (voluntary societies); public language and therefore public law; and literature. The essence of the prohibition was the question of ultimate sovereignty. Who is sovereign: God, man, or rival gods?

By invoking the name of his god, a man seeks to harness that god's power. God warns men to invoke only His name, and only under restricted situations. By using God's name thoughtlessly, His followers debase that name. To misuse God's name is to substitute power religion for dominion religion, and this inevitably leads to impotent religion and the destruction of civilization.

By invoking God's name, men implicitly are attempting to arrogate God's power to themselves — power which resides solely in His ordained institutions of monopolistic authority. These institutions are exclusively marked by self-maledictory oaths, which in turn announce the sovereignty of God. Of these three institutions — church, family, and civil government — only the church can invoke God's name in a curse, and this curse is imperative, not final: a warning of what is to come, unless a person repents. The church enforces its discipline by invoking this curse, implicitly or explicitly, when it separates former members from the communion table.

A covenant is not a contract. It rests on higher authority, and it invokes a higher penalty for non-fulfilment of terms. Therefore to swear by God or any aspect of the creation in a *contractual* situation is to use God's name in vain. To do this is to create the illusion of more reliable performance because of the presence, implicit or explicit, of a pseudo-self-maledictory oath. This involves deception, and should be penalized by civil statutes governing fraud.

These biblical distinctions between covenants and contracts necessarily involve a rejection of any social contract theory of civil (or any other) government. Government is of God, not of men. Only God, as Creator, has absolutely sovereign authority and power. Both authority (legitimacy) and power are delegated to man by God. By upholding the sanctity of His name, all governments thereby testify to this subordination. One aspect of this upholding is the enforcement of the law against the misuse of God's name. To misuse God's name is clearly an act of ethical rebellion, but it is also an act of revolution. Adam, the first human revolutionary, is the model. He failed to pronounce judgment in the name of God against the tempter. He thereby necessarily pronounced judgment in his own name — and by implication, in Satan's name — against God. The third commandment is a warning to mankind to exercise judgment judiciously in every area of life, including language. The third commandment is not simply a restriction against obscene language in particular; it is a prohibition against revolutionary language in general.

4

SABBATH AND DOMINION

Remember the sabbath day, to keep it holy. Six days shalt thou labour, and do all thy work: But the seventh day is the sabbath of the LORD thy God: in it thou shalt not do any work, thou, nor thy son, nor thy daughter, thy manservant, nor thy maidservant, nor thy cattle, nor thy stranger that is within thy gates: For in six days the LORD made heaven and earth, the sea, and all that in them is, and rested the seventh day: wherefore the LORD blessed the sabbath day, and hallowed it (Ex. 20:8-11).

We come now to one of the most difficult of all exegetical and application problems in the Bible, the question of the meaning and enforcement of the sabbath. Only the proper interpretation and application of the tithe principle is equally as difficult and controversial an economic question. Both issues involve the question of what man is required to forfeit in order to honor God.

Several questions must be considered. First, what is the meaning of "rest"? Second, what is the meaning of "sabbath"? Third, is the Lord's Day the same as the sabbath? Fourth, what was the focus of the sabbath in Old Testament times: rest or worship, or both? Fifth, how extensive were the restrictions against working in Old Testament times? Sixth, are these same restrictions still required by God in New Testament times? Seventh, who or what agency is to enforce sabbath requirements in New Testament times? In short, where is the *locus of sovereignty* for sabbath enforcement? Eighth, if the Old Testament's prohibitions had been enforced throughout the history of the West, could the modern, industrialized West ever have come into existence?

In order to keep this introductory chapter sufficiently short and uncluttered with technical problems, I have decided to add an appendix on the economics of sabbath-keeping. I cover questions four

72

through eight in the appendix. In this chapter, I devote more space to the meaning of rest and its relationship with dominion, and secondarily, the problem of the sabbath in New Testament times. I argue here that the sabbath principle is related closely to communion with God, and that both are closely related to dominion.

Autonomy and Creation

God alone is absolutely sovereign. He is also the Creator. This link between absolute sovereignty and original creation is reflected in man's nature as the image of God. Man is subordinately sovereign and subordinately creative, or we might say, *re*-creative. He exercises dominion over the creation because he is subordinate to God. He can never be at the top of the pyramid of power. Only God can occupy that position. To attempt to occupy it means the attempt to become divine.

When Adam rebelled, he believed that he had the opportunity of becoming as God, knowing (determining) good and evil (Gen. 3:5). His ethical rebellion was an assertion of human autonomy, a conscious decision to substitute his own authority and judgment for God's. Was Adam's word sovereign, or was God's?

That single forbidden tree, with its forbidden fruit, was a symbol of Adam's subordination, meaning his lack of original sovereignty. He did not have control over that one sphere of the creation. Only God possessed absolute control over everything, including control over both Adam and that tree. By asserting his right to eat from that tree, Adam was announcing unilaterally the legitimacy of his quest for total power — the power to control anything and possibly even everything, as if he were God. If he could achieve such control, through autonomous knowledge and autonomous power, then God could not fully control man. Man is therefore truly autonomous and potentially divine, Adam declared by his act of defiance. The sign of his autonomy was his *power*: the power to eat rebelliously without suffering the predicted consequences. Adam adopted a *power religion* in place of God's required *dominion religion* — a dominion process based on ethics.

Adam probably ate of the forbidden tree on that first sabbath. The serpent beguiled Eve (II Cor. 11:3), and Adam listened to his beguiled wife. She was deceived; he was not (I Tim. 2:14). Rather than initially rebuking the serpent, thereby passing preliminary judgment against Satan, and awaiting God's return to the garden to pass final judgment against him, Adam attempted to render autonomous judgment. By asserting such autonomy, he thereby rendered judgment against God's word and in favor of the serpent's announced estimation of the low or zero likelihood of God's punishment for Adam's disobedience.

Adam and Eve could have refused to accept Satan's evaluation of the effects of eating from the tree. They could have waited for God to return and pass judgment against the intruder, and then sit down with them to eat of the tree of life. This communion meal with God was postponed by their rebellion and their subsequent ejection from the garden. The celebration of Passover and the Lord's Supper points to a future meal with God after He pronounces final judgment against sin and Satan's forces, but it also points back to the "meal that might have been."

Rest: God's and Man's

Adam's rebellion was linked to the question of the sabbath. God had created the world, including Adam, in six days, and He rested the seventh day. The sabbath day was man's first full day of life. This day began with rest, since God's original creation activity had ended the day before. Man was the capstone of God's creation, the final species to be created, but he was nevertheless under God's sovereignty as a creature. The whole creation, except for one tree, had been delivered into Adam's hand. The day after the sabbath, the "eighth day," meaning the eighth day after God first announced, "Let there be light," Adam was to have gone forth to subdue the earth as God's subordinate.

Rest means something different for God than it means for man. God rested on the seventh day, after His work was over, and after He had pronounced judgment on it, announcing its inherent goodness. For God, rest is a testimony of His absolute independence. He created the world out of nothing. It is dependent on Him; He is in no way dependent on it. For creatures, on the other hand, rest means subordination. Rest means that God is absolutely sovereign, and that man is absolutely dependent on God. Man begins with rest, for he is subordinate. God ended with rest, for He is absolutely sovereign.

Adam did not rest in his position of dependence under God. To have accepted the first day of the week as God's gift of rest, to have admitted that the creation was finished, would have meant the acceptance of man's perpetual position as a *re-creative* sovereign, not an originally creative sovereign. It would have meant that Adam accepted his position as a creature. The restriction placed upon Adam by God meant that divinity is forever closed to man. Adam refused to accept this. *He could not abide in his God-given rest, precisely because it was God-given.* He wanted rest on his own terms. *He wanted rest as an originally creative sovereign.* He wanted his rest at the end of man's week, for God had inaugurated a day of rest at the end of His week.[1]

Resting the Land

On the seventh day, God rested. Adam should also have rested (his first full day). Thus, for one day in seven, the land is to rest. There was to have been no direct personal attention of man or God to the care of the land. The general personal sovereignty of God undergirds all reality, but there was to have been no visible management of the land on that day. It, too, was to have rested. It, too, was to have been free to develop apart from constant direct attention by another. In this sense, nature was analogous to Adam, for God had departed and left him physically alone.

This should have pointed to man that he was not ultimately sovereign over nature. The land continued to operate without man's active supervision. If man rebelled against God, the land would come under a curse, but if Adam remained ethically faithful and enjoyed his rest, the land would suffer no damage from its day of solitude. The forces of nature were never intended to be autonomous from man, but they were nevertheless not entirely dependent on man. This pointed to another source of nature's daily operations: a law-order created by God which did not require man or God to be physically present for its continued operation.

After the fall of man, nature was cursed (Gen. 3:17-18). The Mosaic law imposed an additional form of sabbath on Israel: every

---

1. Gary North, *The Dominion Covenant: Genesis* (Tyler, Texas: Institute for Christian Economics, 1982), ch. 5. I have subsequently come to the conclusion that Adam sinned on the sabbath, rather than on the day following the sabbath, in contrast to the arguments I presented in the first edition of *Genesis*. The "eighth-day covering" — the eighth-day circumcision of all Hebrew males (Lev. 12:3) and the eighth-day separation from the animal mother of the firstborn male (Ex. 22:30) — makes sense if we regard the evening of the day as the beginning of the next day. "And the evening and the morning were the first day" (Gen. 1:5b). When God came at the end of the seventh day, He judged them and then covered them, in preparation for their departure from the garden. They would spend the evening and night of the eighth day outside the protection of the garden. Thus, their second day (God's eighth day) was their first day of labor outside the garden, the curse placed on their assertion of autonomy.

seventh year, the land was not to be worked, for man was not to do agricultural work (Lev. 25:2-7). It was called a sabbath of the land. Like that first day in the garden, the land was to be free from man's care. This pointed to the sovereignty of God over creation.

In that same year, the law was to be read to the assembled nation (Deut. 31:10-13). All debts of Hebrews were cancelled (Deut. 15:1-11). All Hebrew slaves (except criminal slaves who were repaying debts, and permanent slaves who had voluntarily covenanted with a family) were to be released (Deut. 15:12-18). Biblical law and freedom go together. They are tied ritually to a sabbath.

Defining "Sabbath"

What is the meaning of "sabbath"? Scholars debate this point. The Hebrew term means, at the very least, a cessation from activity. It is an *intermission*. God ceased from the activity of creation on the seventh day, a sign to man that the environment had been delivered to man in a completed form, though not historically developed. Man would henceforth work with this environment to subdue it, but this environment is a gift of God. The first week's seven-day pattern is to be an eternal pattern—a covenantal symbol of man's subordination to God. Man is to labor six days and rest one day.

Man's week began with rest. Adam, however, was not content with this pattern, since it began with God's rest from His labors, which implied that man's labors must begin with an acknowledgment of the sovereignty of God. He wanted to become as God, which meant that he chose to imitate God's week: six days of labor followed by a day of rest. Man would be a creator for six days, and then he would enjoy his rest at the end of the week, after his efforts had been brought to completion by his own hand.[2] The seventh day

---

2. Writes Meredith Kline: "For on the seventh day God rested from his work of creation, and this Sabbath of God is a royal resting and enthronement on the judgment seat. One indication that God's Sabbath-rest consequent to the finishing of his cosmic house was an enthronement is that the Scriptures present the converse of this idea; they portray God's enthronement in his micro-cosmic (temple-) house as a Sabbath-rest. Thus, when Isaiah makes his challenging comparison between the earthly temple built by Israel and the creation temple of heaven and earth built by God at the beginning, he introduces the Sabbath-rest imagery of the creation history as a parallel to God's throne house: 'The heaven is my throne, and the earth is my footstool: Where is the house that ye build unto me? And where is the place of my rest (*menuhah*)?' (Isa. 66:1; cf. II Chron. 6:18; Acts 7:49)." Kline, *Images of the Spirit* (Grand Rapids, Michigan: Baker Book House, 1980), p. 111. Man, in his assertion of divine sovereignty, acted as though he himself had created the universe, using it

of rest would be a man-made sabbath. Man would rest from his autonomous labors.

What Adam did not count on was God's response to this rebellion: the curse of the ground. He also did not count on the advent of his own mortality, even though God had warned him that he would surely die if he disobeyed. His time on earth was shortened, while his work was increased. His work was made burdensome, mixed with his own sweat. The ground would supply him with life, but at the same time, his life would be, in effect, poured into the ground. To dust man now returns. Man's rest was taken away; his labor is now cursed. By this curse of the ground and this shortening of man's days, man is made to see that he will never be able to complete his work by himself; it requires God's grace. Without a God-imposed day of rest—without God's *re-creating grace*, in other words—dominion-driven man would work himself to death: spiritually, culturally, and historically. Without God's grace, Adam was a dead man. He would never achieve rest, not even in the grave, for there is no spiritual rest for the wicked beyond the grave. The sign of God's grace is the sabbath day, a promise both of re-creation and the eternal rest to come.

Choices and Costs

What are some of the economic implications of a day of rest? Man's world is a world of costs and benefits, of *choices* made in terms of these costs and benefits. It costs men the forfeited income that a day of rest involves, but it also brings them benefits. *Leisure is a consumer good*, and it has a market value, namely, forfeited income. A day of rest may increase human efficiency which results in increased total weekly production (and therefore increased income). Furthermore, God's covenantal promises are available to those who are faithful to the terms of the covenant, so these *promised blessings for obedience* must also be added to the visible, immediate blessings of man's external rest. These promised blessings are not always acknowledged by those who are not aware of, or not confident concerning,

---

as a throne of his own. He would bring judgment, deciding between God's word and Satan's word. He, like God, would rest at the end of his creative week. But while man was created to enjoy a seventh-day royal resting—God's seventh day—and to sit at God's table for a royal meal, man was not to do so apart from beginning with the enjoyment of a first-day, creature's, vice-gerent resting. He is to begin his week with rest.

God's covenant with His people. They tend to underestimate the benefits of honoring one day of rest in seven. In the Old Testament economy under the Mosaic law, the people of Israel were placed under severe restrictions against sabbath violations. The benefits of rest were in force, but God saw fit to raise the costs of disobedience, thereby encouraging men to remain faithful to the sabbath principle. All those who lived under the civic administration of God's covenant had to obey. The penalty was stiff: "Six days shall work be done, but on the seventh day there shall be to you an holy day, a sabbath of rest to the LORD; whosoever doeth work therein shall be put to death. Ye shall kindle no fire throughout your habitations upon the sabbath day" (Ex. 35:2-3). This same penalty was later reinforced during the wilderness period, when a man who was caught gathering sticks on the sabbath was executed by stoning at the express command of God (Num. 15:32-41). No one could miss the message: God wants men to honor the sabbath principle.

The death penalty, when enforced, imposed a tremendous cost on sabbath violators. While all men in Israel were expected to understand the nature of the covenant, with external blessings assured for external conformity to the terms of the covenant, nevertheless, God relied on the "stick" as well as the "carrot." The promised benefits were less visible, and therefore more to be taken on faith, than the promised punishment. The punishment was visible and the sanctions were permanent. A man with weak faith still had an incentive to obey.

New Testament Alterations

What about New Testament times? Is the Old Testament sabbath still in force? The church has never given a straightforward answer to this question. The church has generally celebrated the first day of the week as the Lord's day (the Day of the Lord), and Christians have often linked certain Old Testament provisions concerning the sabbath with the New Testament's day of rest. From the church's beginning, God's "eighth day" (Adam's first working day of the week) was honored as the day of worship[3] (Acts 20:7; I Cor. 16:2a), although it took perhaps a century for the first day of the week to be

---

3. Wilfrid Stott, in Roger T. Beckwith and Wilfrid Stott, *The Christian Sunday: A Biblical and Historical Study* (Grand Rapids, Michigan: Baker Book House, [1978] 1980), ch. 12: "The Theology of the Christian Sunday: The Eighth Day"; cf. pp. 64-69.

regarded by most Christians as the sole and exclusive day of worship.[4] This day has also been honored as a day of rest.

Capital Punishment

But what about the penalty? Has the church maintained that the death penalty should still be enforced on all members of society? The answer is unquestionably *no*; the church has never required the civil government to execute sabbath violators, although occasionally some commentator does.[5] The church has enforced its own laws, even excommunication, on sabbath violators. It has also recommended that the civil government fine violators, or punish them in other ways. But throughout the history of the church, the vast majority of expositors and church officials have hesitated to call for the death penalty. They have, by word and deed, admitted that *there has been a fundamental transformation of the civil aspects of sabbath law.*

Typical of this approach to sabbath law in the New Testament

---

4. Seventh Day Adventist scholar Samuele Bacchiocchi has argued that it was only in the late second century that the Christians, especially in Rome, began to celebrate the first day of the week (Lord's day) exclusively as the day of rest and worship, in order to distinguish themselves from the Jews: *From Sabbath to Sunday: A Historical Investigation of the Rise of Sunday Observance in Early Christianity* (Rome: Pontifical Gregorian University Press, 1977), p. 2. This study is an impressive work of historical scholarship, though far less distinguished as a work of reliable biblical exposition. I would guess that the reason why the Pontifical Gregorian University awarded Dr. Bacchiocchi his doctorate and published his dissertation is that he presents the Roman Church as the source of the change "from sabbath to Sunday," thereby attesting to the historical authority of the Roman Church. Church officials were understandably unconcerned about his arguments against all interpretations of New Testament passages that attest to the first day of the week ("Sunday") as the day of rest and worship. The authority of the Roman Church, rather than the evidence of Scripture, was the crucial criterion in the minds of the churchmen. This, in fact, had been the familiar argument used by Rome against the Reformers: If *sola scriptura* really is your guide, they asked, why don't you keep the Saturday sabbath? Luther's opponent, John Eck, used this argument with great skill. It was repeated in the Zurich Disputation, the Baden Disputation, and at both the pre-Reformation debates in Geneva in 1534 and 1535: Daniel A. Augsburger, "Pierre Viret on the Sabbath Commandment," *Andrews University Seminary Studies*, 20 (Summer 1982), p. 92. Andrews University is a Seventh Day Adventist school. For a brief but penetrating critique of Bacchiocchi's thesis, see R. J. Bauckham, "Sabbath and Sunday in the Post-Apostolic Church," in D. A. Carson (ed.), *From Sabbath to Lord's Day: A Biblical, Historical, and Theological Investigation* (Grand Rapids, Michigan: Zondervan-Acadamie, 1982), pp. 270-73.

5. Examples are the continental Protestant Reformer Heinrich Bullinger in the late sixteenth century and the American Puritan Thomas Shepherd in the mid-seventeenth: R. J. Bauckham, "Sabbath and Sunday in the Protestant Tradition," in Carson (ed.), *From Sabbath to Lord's Day*, pp. 319, 326 (note 98).

era is John Murray's statement. Mr. Murray was a leading twentieth-century Calvinist scholar, and a Scot — a Scot whose views on the sabbath were too lax to gain favor in the Scottish Free Kirk, so he came to the United States to teach. He acknowledged the "element of truth" in the statement "by good men, that we do not now under this economy observe the Sabbath as strictly as was required of the people of Israel under the Old Testament." For one thing, they were not allowed to kindle a fire. For another, the death penalty was imposed. "Now there is no warrant for supposing that such regulatory provisions both prohibitive and punitive bind us under the New Testament. This is particularly apparent in the case of the capital punishment executed for Sabbath desecration in the matter of labour. If this is what is meant when it is said that observance is not as strict in its application to us as it was under the Mosaic law, then the contention should have to be granted."[6] Murray, however, offered no exegesis to explain how the requirement of sabbath observance has survived, but without the civil sanctions attached to Mosaic sabbath law.

F. N. Lee, a South African Calvinist sabbatarian who, like Mr. Murray, left his native land to teach in other English-speaking nations, writes in his doctoral dissertation on the sabbath (1966) that the capital punishment provisions of the sabbath law have been abrogated. "It is important to realize that these aspects of the weekly sabbath, even though they were ordained by God, were only of temporary ceremonial and/or political significance, and were not intrinsically normative for the permanent weekly sabbath as such, although they were certainly temporarily normative for the Sinaitic weekly sabbath of Israel from Sinai up to the death and resurrection of Christ in which events all these aspects were fulfilled."[7] (Lee has begun to alter his position since the time of publication of his dissertation in the early 1970's. He tells me that he believes that Old Testament law is still in force in this age, but he is not yet ready to recommend, categorically, that the death penalty should be imposed in all cases of sabbath violations, although continued willful desecration might be sufficient reason to execute the rebel, he says.[8])

---

6. John Murray, "The Sabbath Institution" (1953), in *Collected Writings of John Murray*, 4 vols. (Carlisle, Pennsylvania: Banner of Truth, 1976), Vol. I, p. 211.

7. F. N. Lee, *The Covenantal Sabbath* (London: Lord's Day Observance Society, 1972), p. 30.

8. Cf. F. N. Lee, *Christocracy and the Divine Savior's Law for All Mankind* (Tallahassee, Florida: Jesus Lives Society, [1979]), p. 7.

Timing the Sabbath

Lee's book is a comprehensive treatment of the sabbath question. It raises many interesting points. One of them relates to the timing of the sabbath. Three distinct positions have been maintained by Christians historically: the sundown-to-sundown sabbath, the midnight-to-midnight sabbath (which Lee holds), and the sunrise-to-sunrise sabbath (which I hold).[9] The inability of commentators to agree on this point obviously poses difficulties for those who might recommend nationwide or civil sanctions against sabbath violators.

The Hebrews celebrated the sabbath of the day of atonement from evening to evening (Lev. 23:32), and we presume that the other sabbaths were similarly celebrated. The sabbath in Jesus' day was begun at sundown (Mark 15:42). The Jews wanted the bodies of the dead to be removed before the evening (John 19:31). Nevertheless, we need not assume that Old Testament practices regarding the sabbath are still binding on the New Testament church, since the change of the day represents a fundamental break with the past. Christian scholars have not generally believed that the New Testament day of rest begins at sundown on Saturday evening, although some, including certain Puritan groups, have argued that it does.

The case for the sundown-to-sundown sabbath is based primarily on Old Testament law.[10] The case for the midnight-to-midnight sabbath is more problematical, resting on the idea of midnight being the midpoint between evening and morning. Jesus rose before the sun did, since the women came at the dawn to Jesus' tomb (Matt. 28:1; Luke 24:2), and the tomb was already empty. Finally, the firstborn of Egypt were slain at midnight (Ex. 12:29). Deliverance, in other words, was based on an event which took place at midnight.[11]

Promise and Deliverance

My commitment to a sunrise-to-sunrise New Testament Lord's day is based on the theme of promise and deliverance. The Hebrews were to begin their celebration of the Passover at sundown. The Passover lamb was slain in the evening (Ex. 12:6), and nothing was to remain by the next morning (12:10). The Passover feast looked in faith to the coming deliverance. The promise of God was sure. The

---

9. Lee, *Covenantal Sabbath*, p. x.
10. *Ibid.*, p. 39.
11. *Ibid.*, p. 74.

Israelites began the feast in the evening; they had been told that by the next morning, they would be delivered. The basis of deliverance, the death of Egypt's firstborn, came at midnight, but the actual deliverance came later, for Pharaoh then called Moses and Aaron by night and ordered the Israelites out of the land. They had to return to the people and convey Pharaoh's message. Then, hastily, the people gathered together their belongings, taking their unleavened (ready for cooking) bread. They had no time for preparing food (12:39). This points to an early morning deliverance.

Long before the exodus, Jacob had wrestled with the theophany of God through the night, fighting for His blessing. They wrestled "until the breaking of the day" (Gen. 32:24). Jacob received the blessing, the thigh wound, and his new name, Israel, at daybreak (32:25-28). Thus, Israel's deliverance (the Day of the Lord) came as the sun rose. But the struggle had begun at night (32:22-24).

God's righteousness is equated with the sun in several instances. Perhaps the most forthright is Malachi 4:2: "But unto you that fear my name shall the Sun of righteousness arise with healing in his wings; and ye shall go forth, and grow up as calves of the stall." Again, "He shall be as the light of the morning, when the sun riseth, even a morning without clouds; as the tender grass springeth out of the earth by clear shining after the rain" (II Sam. 23:4). "Arise, shine; for thy light is come, and the glory of the LORD is risen upon thee. For, behold, the darkness shall cover the earth, and gross darkness the people: but the LORD shall arise upon thee, and his glory shall be seen upon thee. And the Gentiles shall come to thy light, and the kings to the brightness of thy rising" (Isa. 60:1-3). "Then shall we know, if we follow on to know the LORD: his going forth is prepared as the morning . . ." (Hos. 6:3a). The righteousness of the faithful is also compared to morning: "The course of the righteous is like the morning light, growing brighter till it is broad day" (Prov. 4:18; NEB; cf. Jud. 5:31). Israel is to be delivered at the rising of the sun, the coming of light when there previously had been gross darkness.

The theme that Israel is delivered with the rising of the sun on the seventh day corresponds with the idea that Adam rebelled on the morning of the seventh day, and that man needs grace early in the morning. The New Testament reveals a similar message. The women came to the tomb at dawn, not at sundown the evening before, when the third day began officially, according to later Hebrew law. Furthermore, the day of Pentecost came seven weeks later, according to Mosaic law (Lev. 23:16). The disciples were meeting together, and the Holy Spirit came upon them (Acts 2:1-5). Speaking in many foreign languages, they communicated the gospel to a multitude (2:6), each in his own language (2:8). Critics charged that they were drunk with "new wine" (2:13). Peter's response is significant: "For these are not drunken, as ye suppose, seeing it is but the third hour of the day" (2:15). In other words, it was about three hours after the dawn. Peter was saying that these men had not had time to get drunk. People were not gathering to hear the gospel three hours after sundown, for then Peter's words would have been meaningless. Obviously, an evening of drinking might have preceded a nighttime outpouring of the Spirit. If we assume that dawn was around six o'clock in the morning, then "the third hour of the day" would have been about 9 A.M. This corresponds to the Roman sundial, which marked noon as the sixth hour.[12]

The Communion Meal

There are other pieces of data that point to a sunrise-to-sunrise Lord's day. Jesus met with His disciples on the evening of His resurrection (John 20:19), eating with them (Luke 24:41-43). This communion meal took place after the sun had gone down. He had already eaten with two disciples at Emmaus, approximately seven miles from Jerusalem (Luke 24:13: Berkeley Version), and this meal took place as the sun was setting (Luke 24:29-30). These two disciples then walked from Emmaus to Jerusalem in order to meet with the other disciples. Then Jesus appeared to the whole group (Luke 24:33-34). Yet this meeting is described as having taken place "the same day at evening, being the first day of the week" (John 20:19a). John was not using the Hebrew day, sundown to sundown, as his measure of the first day.

Paul's lecture to the church at Troas took place on the Lord's day. "And upon the first day of the week, when the disciples came together to break bread, Paul preached unto them, ready to depart on the morrow; and continued his speech until midnight" (Acts 20:7). He departed at the "break of day" (20:11b).

The evening meeting was a communion feast, as was the first

---

12. Leon Morris, *The Gospel According to John* (Grand Rapids, Michigan: Eerdmans, 1971), p. 158n.

evening of Christ's resurrection. After the day was spent, men gathered together to partake of the Lord's supper. We know also that Paul criticized the Corinthian church for its drunkenness at the Lord's table. "For in eating every one taketh before other his own supper: and one is hungry, and another is drunken" (I Cor. 11:21). They had not been drinking early in the morning, any more than the disciples on the day of Pentecost had been drinking in the morning. The Corinthian church members had been drinking too much in the evening, prior to the communion meal.

We celebrate communion on the Lord's day. We know that the early church celebrated communion in the evening. There is no evidence that the early church met for communion the night before the Lord's day, i.e., on Saturday evening. The first communion feasts took place on the evening of the Lord's resurrection, at Emmaus and Jerusalem, and in the latter case, the sun must have gone down before the meal. They did not take communion with Christ the day after His resurrection. Communion is taken on the Lord's day. Hence, we should count the New Testament day of rest from sunrise to sunrise ("Sunday" morning to "Monday" morning).

It is obvious, however, that most modern churches have not been rigid in this regard. Few of them ever discuss the matter. Among more sabbatarian denominations, the timing of the beginning of the sabbath is left to the discretion of individual members. Except on Easter, churches do not ask their members to be in their seats at daybreak. Nine o'clock, the hour that the Holy Spirit fell upon the church at Pentecost, is about as early as most churches require attendance.

The Passover celebrated by Jesus and His disciples looked forward to deliverance, just as the Passover meal in Egypt looked forward to deliverance. The communion feast of the church looks back, knowing that deliverance has come, and it dates the Lord's day with the risen sun. The communion feast is the capstone of a day of rest. As such, it then looks forward ritually to a week of work beginning the following day, the continuation of men's efforts to fulfill the terms of God's dominion covenant. *Passover points to dominion.* As Christ announced at the Passover, "I appoint unto you a kingdom, as my Father hath appointed unto me; That ye may eat and drink at my table in my kingdom, and sit on thrones judging the twelve tribes of Israel" (Luke 22:29-30).

We no longer look forward to deliverance from bondage; we look forward to *dominion*. Dominion begins with our labor on the day following the Lord's day of rest, just as it was supposed to begin for Adam. The communion meal, like the Passover meal, is to be *celebrated in the evening*. Also like the Passover meal, *it looks forward to the next morning*. But the victory is behind us. Deliverance came definitively at Calvary. We are strengthened in our faith the night before we are to go forth to exercise dominion, just as the Hebrews were strengthened in body by their Passover meal the night before God delivered them from bondage.

The Sabbatical Year

The church has never honored a sabbatical year, nor has any civil government. The land is not rested, debts are not cancelled, and the whole law is not read publicly before the gathered nation. Why not?

The New Testament has internalized the locus of sovereignty for the enforcement of the sabbath. Men are to rest the land, but not as a nation, and not simultaneously. The civil government honors Paul's dictum that some regard one day (or year) as equal to any other, and some regard one as special, to be set apart for rest.

A farmer might decide to rest his whole farm one year in seven. An alternative arrangement would be to rest one-seventh of his land each year. A Dutch-American immigrant informed me that at the beginning of the twentieth century, it was common in Holland for land owners to lease their agricultural land with a provision that each year, one-seventh of the land would not be planted.

With respect to debt, the civil government does not select one year in seven for the cancellation of all debts. What it probably should do is to declare that it will not enforce any debt obligation beyond the seventh year, on the assumption that long-term debt is prohibited by the Bible. This would also apply to the government's own debt structure. This would prohibit the building up of huge debt obligations that are never intended to be repaid. It would also reduce a major political impetus for inflation: debtors trying to defraud creditors. It would remind men that we are limited creatures and should not presume to look beyond seven years of productivity. Men might still continue to write debt contracts beyond seven years, but these contracts would not be enforceable in a civil court, and creditors would face higher risks of default. Creditors would become wary. This limitation on contracts is the biblical society's equivalent of the libertarian restriction against life-long contracts, which most libertarians equate with slavery and therefore reject as immoral and illegal.[13]

The Sabbath Millennium

As we approach the close of the twentieth century, and the coming of a new millennium, we can expect to see a growing apocalypticism, both Christian and humanistic. The year 2000 has been a focus of concern by humanists since at least the era of the French Revolution.[14] The year 2001 inaugurates the third millennium after Christ, and almost simultaneously, we expect to see the seventh millennium (if the world is just about 6,000 years old). This new millennium can easily be correlated with the "third day-seventh day" symbolism of rest and resurrection. We are in a very real sense approaching a *new Sinai*, a new sixth-day covenant which will inaugurate the seventh-day millennium. A new Sinai should be marked by a rediscovery of Old Testament law, which is precisely what has happened since 1973, when Rushdoony's *Institutes of Biblical Law* was published. For the first time in New Testament church history, there is a systematic attempt to defend and apply the principles of Old Testament law to New Testament society, but without the mixture of Greek categories of natural law. If this truly is the "evening before the Sabbath," then we can expect the millennial sabbath to follow. James Jordan's analysis of the symbolism of "third day-seventh day" is significant in this regard:

The process of covenant renewal with man dead in sins and trespasses must involve resurrection. . . . To be cleansed, therefore, is to undergo resurrection. This is the meaning of the cleansing rituals of Leviticus 11-15, and other places. The covenant can only be reestablished with resurrected men, so the people were to cleanse themselves before the third (sixth) day, when the covenant was to be made (Ex. 19:10-14). . . .

And so, God drew near on the third day (after God's announcement to Moses on the fourth day), which was the sixth day of the week, to renew covenant with men. It was not the New Covenant that God was renewing at Sinai, but the Old Adamic Covenant. It was the Old Covenant temporarily and provisionally reestablished in the sphere of temporary, provisional, ceremonial (New Covenant) resurrection. It was temporary; but just as the original Adamic Covenant had pointed forward to sabbath rest,

_____

13. See Chapter 7, subsection: "Libertarian Contracts."
14. Robert Nisbet, "The Year 2000 and All That," *Commentary* (June 1968).

so the renewed Adamic Covenant at Sinai pointed forward to the work of Christ and the Future New Sabbath Covenant to come.

It was the third day, and the third month (19:1, 16). For the significance of this we need to look at Numbers 19:11-12. The man who is unclean from contact with a corpse is to be cleansed on the third day and again on the seventh day. This *double resurrection pattern* is found all through the Scriptures. For instance, in John 5:21-29, Jesus distinguishes a first resurrection, when those dead in sin will hear the voice of Christ and live (v. 25); and a second resurrection, when those in the grave will come forth to a physical resurrection (v. 29). The *first resurrection* comes in the *middle of history* to enable men to fulfill the duties of the old creation. The *second resurrection* comes at the *end of history* to usher men into the new creation.

Jesus was raised on the third day, thereby inaugurating the New Covenant in the midst of the week of history. Christians live between the third and seventh days of history, Spiritually resurrected and in the New Covenant, but physically mortal and assigned to complete the tasks of the Old Adamic Covenant. The fact that the law was given at Sinai on the third day, and in the third month, was a provisional anticipation of the third-day resurrection yet to come in Christ.

The third-day resurrection was only provisional under the Old Covenant, so it had to be repeated year after year. Thus, every year, the third day after Passover, there was a waving of the first fruits before the throne of God (Lev. 23:5, 7, 10, 11). This was a prophecy of the resurrection of our Lord Jesus Christ, which came three days after Passover. Jesus' third-day resurrection, however, was not provisional but definitive, and never to be repeated. [15]

The Prophesied Thousand Years

Consider the millennial implications of Jordan's analysis. Sometime around the year 2000, there will be a one-time-only fusion of symbolic "days." The sixth "day" (millennium) comes to a close. This symbolically closes the six days of fallen mankind's labor. The sixth was also the day on which God created man and delivered the dominion mandate to him. As Jordan points out, the sixth day was also the day of re-covenanting between God and man at Sinai. On that day, God's law was delivered to Israel.

Simultaneously with this closing of the sixth "day" will be the closing of the second "day" (millennium) since the death of Jesus Christ. On the third day, He was resurrected. On this third day, true

---

15. James B. Jordan, *The Law of the Covenant: An Exposition of Exodus 21-23* (Tyler, Texas: Institute for Christian Economics, 1984), pp. 56-58.

life — life beyond the grave — was manifested. On the evening of the day of resurrection He took communion with His disciples. He spent two days in the grave, and then He visibly triumphed over death.

A "day" of rest, and a "day" of resurrection life: this is what the seventh millennium appears to offer. Furthermore, beyond it lies the eighth "day," which points to the culmination of creation: the new heavens and new earth. The new creation was definitively established by Christ's "eighth-day" resurrection. The church's switch in the day of rest-worship from Seventhday to Firstday meant that Eighthday is the day of the new creation. In short, the symbolism fits together. This will become increasingly apparent to a growing number of Christians as the year 2000 draws near.

The idea that the six days of the week and six millennia are linked symbolically was common opinion in the very early church. Barnabas wrote concerning the sixth day of God's creation: "Attend, my children, to the meaning of this expression, 'He finished in six days.' This implieth that the Lord will finish all things in six thousand years, for a day is with Him a thousand years. And He Himself testifieth, saying, 'Behold, to-day will be as a thousand years.' Therefore, my children, in six days, that is, in six thousand years, all things will be finished."[16] It is not clear to me whether he believed that the final judgment would come 6,000 years after Christ's era, or that the whole period of fallen man's life on earth lasts a total of 6,000 years. What is clear is that he believed that the 6,000-year period is significant. Then comes the eighth day: ". . . when, giving rest to all things, I shall make a beginning of the eighth day, that is, a beginning of another world. Wherefore, also, we keep the eighth day with joyfulness, the day on which Jesus rose from the dead."[17]

We should expect to find that people will begin to listen to biblical teaching concerning such themes as death and resurrection, work and rest, six days and one day, decline and dominion, defeat and victory, Old Covenant and New Covenant, as we approach what I call *the sabbath millennium and millennial sabbath.* Christians need to be in a position to explain the nature of the transition to a new stage in the manifestation of *Christ's new world order,* which was established during His lifetime, and was made visible by the fall of

---

16. *The Epistle of Barnabas,* ch. XV, in *The Ante-Nicene Fathers,* edited by Alexander Roberts and James Donaldson, 14 vols. (Grand Rapids, Michigan: Eerdmans, 1973, reprint), I, p. 146.

17. *Ibid.,* p. 147.

Jerusalem in 70 A.D.[18] The old humanism has bet a great deal on the inauguration of a humanist millennium, the dream of a humanist New World Order. So has New Age humanism.[19] When these dreams do not come true, and the premillennial expectations of fundamentalists concerning the imminent Rapture also do not come true, men will again begin to ask: "What must we do now?" Francis Schaeffer's title, *How Shall We Then Live?*, will be *the* religious question of the next two decades.

The millennium as such is not limited to a thousand years. The millennium as millennium began with the fall of Jerusalem — the end of the old order. The interim transitional period was called "the last days."[20] It could extend well into the "eighth day," or eighth millennium, which will begin sometime around the year 3001. But there could very easily be a *specific manifestation* of the millennium as well as the general manifestation. The specific manifestation would be exactly what Revelation 20 refers to, a thousand years in which Satan will be uniquely chained up and rendered civilizationally impotent. It would be most fitting if this full-blown restraining period would begin in precisely the period that the humanists and occultists have looked to for centuries as the beginning of their millennial reign.

There are several theological problems with predicting the inauguration of the long-awaited sabbath millennium sometime around the year 2000. One is that the world may be older than 6,000 years. Another is that there could be a period of "Babylonian captivity" in between the year 2000 and the full manifestation of victory — a 70-year period comparable to the era between the birth of Christ and the fall of Jerusalem. A third problem is that the symbolism of the week, however convenient, really has no clear temporal manifestation in terms of millennia.[21] Symbolic convenience, after all, is not necessarily the focal point of God's work in time. But the most important problem will appear if, in fact, a great period of worldwide conversions does begin close to the year 2000 (or 2070). This is the subsequent risk of prophesying the advent of the "eighth day" — the second coming — close to the year 3000 (or 3070). But the attempt to

18. David Chilton, *Paradise Restored: A Biblical Theology of Dominion* (Tyler, Texas: Reconstruction Press, 1985).

19. Alberto Villoldo and Kenneth Dychtwald, *Millennium: Glimpses into the 21st Century* (Los Angeles: Tarcher, 1981).

20. Chilton, *Paradise Restored*, ch. 13.

21. This, by the way, is James Jordan's opinion: *Geneva Review*, No. 18 (March 1985), p. 1.

date His return is improper, for only the Father in heaven knows the date; not even Jesus, as perfect humanity, knew it (Matt. 24:36). So the question must be asked: What could follow the seventh millennium, other than the final judgment, if the seventh millennium is in fact the millennial sabbath?

The Conversion of the Jews

One possibility of what might follow the sabbath millennium is the conversion of the Jews and an indeterminate period of blessings that will result. Paul wrote: "Now if the fall of them be the riches of the world, and the diminishing of them the riches of the Gentiles; how much more their fulness? . . . For if the casting away of them be the reconciling of the world, what shall the receiving of them be, but life from the dead?" (Rom. 11:12, 15).

Romans 11:11 says: "I say then, Did they stumble that they might fall? God forbid: but by their fall [trespass] salvation is come unto the Gentiles, to provoke them to jealousy." The salvation of the gentiles, however important, is subordinate to the more important phenomenon: *to provoke the Jews to jealousy.* John Murray comments: "Paradoxically, the unbelief of Israel is directed to the restoration of Israel's faith and the fall of Israel to their reclamation. . . . The idea is that the Jews observing the favour and blessing of God bestowed upon the Gentiles and the privileges of the kingdom accruing therefrom will be moved to emulation and thereby induced to turn to the Lord."[22]

There is a close relationship between faith and external blessings, both individually and corporately. Therefore, Paul predicts that the conversion of the gentiles will bring blessings to them. The eventual *fulness* of the gentiles will produce a triple response in the Jews: first jealousy, then a desire to participate in the blessings, and finally their conversion to Christ. Their conversion, in turn, will bring an unprecedented era of blessing to the whole earth. "For if 'fulness' conveys any idea it is that of completeness. Hence nothing less than a restoration of Israel as a people to faith, privilege, and blessing can satisfy the terms of this passage. The *argument* of the apostle is not, however, the restoration of Israel; it is the blessing accruing to the Gentiles from Israel's 'fulness.' The 'fulness' of Israel,

---

22. John Murray, *The Epistle to the Romans,* 2 vols. (Grand Rapids, Michigan: Eerdmans, 1965), II, p. 77.

with the implications stated above, is presupposed and from it is drawn the conclusion that the fulness of Israel will involve for the Gentiles a much greater enjoyment of gospel blessing than that occasioned by Israel's unbelief. There thus awaits the Gentiles, in their distinctive identity as such, gospel blessing far surpassing anything experienced during the period of Israel's apostasy, and this unprecedented enrichment will be occasioned by the conversion of Israel on a scale commensurate with that of their earlier disobedience. We are not informed at this point what this unprecedented blessing will be. But in view of the thought governing the context, namely, the conversion of the Gentiles and then of Israel, we should expect that the enlarged blessing would be the expansion of the success attending the gospel and of the kingdom of God."[23]

Some commentators have believed that the conversion of the Jews will inaugurate the millennium. For instance, the State of Israel might fall to some military invader, and the Zionist dream would at last collapse, leading to mass conversions of Jews. (Simultaneously, the theology of dispensationalism would collapse; dispensationalists have "bet the farm" on the State of Israel's place in the fulfillment of Bible prophecy.) Such a course of events is certainly conceivable. A period of blessing would follow. This could inaugurate a visible millennium. But if this does happen, then there will be a temptation for people to believe that a thousand years later, Christ will return. We are back to the major exegetical-symbolic problem.

It is possible, however, that this conversion of the Jews will take place after the millennial sabbath, after the fulness of the Gentiles has produced so stupendous a civilization that the Jews will have something visible to be jealous about. They have little culturally to be jealous about with respect to the visible performance and productivity of Christian gentiles in the latter decades of the twentieth century. Therefore, gentiles can look forward to the conversion of the Jews at the end of the millennial sabbath, with exponential blessings taking place as a result.

What will these blessings be? Paul is silent. This might lead some forecasters to predict that the ultimate blessing is final judgment unto sin-free existence — in short, the return of Christ in judgment, and the creation of the post-resurrection world. This would return us to

---

23. *Ibid.*, II, p. 79.

the temptation of dating Christ's return, something which has always led the church into the pitfall of short-term thinking and planning. At this point, we are not sure what these blessings will be. What we are sure of is that the Jews as a covenantal, identifiable (but not necessarily national) people will be converted to Christianity before the end of time, and that historically unprecedented blessings will be the direct result.

The best answer is: we cannot be sure in advance. If blessings abound, if revival comes, and if we can reasonably date the changes around 2000 (or 2070), then we can imagine the end of time around 3000, but we cannot be sure. Symbolism is not "chronology in advance." Expectations are one thing; precise timetables are another.

Conclusion

The sabbath points to the fulfillment of the dominion covenant, as well as the judgment by redeemed mankind of the enemies of God. The rest which was long ago promised by God is symbolized in the sabbath. A weekly sabbath is God's "earnest" — His down payment — on the cosmic sabbath to come. Ours is a Firstday sabbath, or Sunday sabbath, in New Testament times. We begin the week with rest, as Adam was supposed to but did not. Adam wanted to create by his own efforts the conditions of man's rest, and he never rested again.

The economic implications of the sabbath are extensive. This is why of necessity I have added an appendix on the topic. The key question, however, is this: *In New Testament times, where is the locus of sovereignty for the enforcement of sabbath law?* If I am correct in my conclusion that Paul has lodged this sovereignty with the *individual conscience* rather than with church government or civil government, then there is no legitimate role in New Testament times for "blue laws," or other sabbatarian legislation. This conclusion represents a major break with historic Protestantism and should be understood as such. It is a major theological step which needs to be discussed in detail by Christian commentators.

If commentators decide that mine is not a legitimate conclusion from Paul's writings, then the locus of sovereignty issue must be dealt with in detail. Who is to impose sanctions? What sanctions? Under what conditions? How will those who must impose sanctions deal with the multiple economic problems raised by compulsory legislation? These problems are discussed in greater detail in Appendix

A. This issue has been skirted for centuries. There has been no consistent answer—sabbatarian, "continental sabbath," or otherwise—concerning the final locus of sovereignty for sabbath enforcement. Until it is faced and dealt with in a manner sufficiently clear for the writing and enforcement of sabbatarian statutes, in church or State, the issue will remain muddled and an exegetical embarrassment for Christians. It will not be resolved successfully by the election of Christian politicians. They need guidelines for sabbath legislation, and these guidelines have yet to come forth from the 2,000-year-old church.

5

FAMILISTIC CAPITAL

Honor thy father and thy mother: that thy days may be long upon the land which the LORD thy God giveth thee (Ex. 20:12).

Paul tells us that this is the first commandment to which a promise is attached (Eph. 6:3). What does it mean, "that thy days may be long upon the land which the LORD thy God giveth thee"? It is a promise given to the *nation*. It is a collective promise, not an individual promise as such. God does not promise that every single child who shows honor for his parents will enjoy long life, nor does He assure us that every single dishonoring child will die young. Esau went against his parents' wishes when he married Canaanite women (Gen. 26:34-35), yet he lived to be at least 120, for he and Jacob buried Isaac, who had died at age 180 (Gen. 35:29), and they had been born when Isaac was 60 years old (Gen. 25:26). Joseph was alive at this time, and the Bible speaks of Joseph as the son of Jacob's old age (Gen. 37:3). In the case of Esau, a dishonoring child lived into old age. Abel, who honored God, and who presumably honored his parents as God's representatives, was slain by his violent brother, who in turn survived to establish a pagan civilization (Gen. 4).

What God does promise is that a *society* in which the *majority* of men do honor their parents will be marked by the long life expectancy of its members. This longer life span will be statistically significant. The society will enjoy, for example, lower life insurance premiums in every age bracket compared with the premiums in cultures that are marked by rebellion against parents. In other words, the risk of death in any given year will be lower, statistically, for the average member of that age bracket. Some will die, of course, but not so many as those who die at the same age in a parent-dishonoring culture.

The promise is significant. It offers long life. The very first promise that is connected to a commandment is long life. This is in-

94

dicative of men's desire to survive into old age. *Men want to live.* It is a universal desire, though it is marred or distorted by the effects of sin. All those who hate God love death (Prov. 8:36). Nevertheless, a standard expression of honor in the ancient Near East, especially in pagan civilizations, was reserved for the king: "O king, live forever" (Dan. 2:4; 5:10; 6:21). When God attached this particular blessing to this commandment, He could be assured of its initial attractiveness in the eyes of men. Life is a blessing for the faithful, and it is desired even by the unfaithful. It is not a burden to be borne patiently by steadfast "pilgrims" who are stoically "passing through life." Life is not just something to pass the time away. It is a *positive blessing.*

We know that the promise to Abraham was that he would have many children, meaning heirs throughout time (Gen. 17:4-6). We know that a large family is a blessing (Ps. 127:3-5). We know that one of the promised blessings for the godly is that miscarriages will be reduced in a nation which is seeking to conform itself to God's law (Ex. 23:26). The demographic implication of the biblical perspective should be obvious: a *large and growing population.* When godliness simultaneously increases both the birth rate and the survival rate, the godly society will experience a population explosion. What God sets forth in His word is simple enough, though both Christians and pagans in the late twentieth century have refused to believe it: *one sign of His pleasure with His people is a population explosion.*[1] It is not a guarantee of His pleasure. Ungodly societies can temporarily sustain a population explosion, especially when they have become the recipients of the blessings of God's law (for example, Western medical technology or the availability of inexpensive wire mesh window screens[2]) apart from the ethical foundations that sustain these blessings. Nevertheless, sustained population growth over many generations is one of God's external blessings, and these blessings cannot be sustained long term apart from conformity to at least the external, civil, and institutional requirements of God's law.

Long life is a biological foretaste of eternal life. It is an earthly down payment by God. It points to eternal life. It is also a capital asset which enables men to labor longer in their assigned task of subduing

---

1. Gary North, *Moses and Pharaoh: Dominion Religion vs. Power Religion* (Tyler, Texas: Institute for Christian Economics, 1985), ch. 1: "Population Growth: Tool of Dominion."

2. Peter F. Drucker, *Management: Tasks, Responsibilities, Practices* (New York: Harper & Row, 1972), p. 330.

their portion of the earth to God's glory. *Long life is an integral part of the dominion covenant.*

Since the fulfillment of the dominion covenant involves filling the earth, it is understandable why long life should be so important. It is one critical factor in the population expansion which is necessary to fulfill the terms of that covenant, the other being high birth rates. God has pointed clearly to the importance of the family — indeed, *the central importance of the family* — in fulfilling the terms of the dominion covenant. The parents receive the blessing of children (high birth rate), and the children secure long life by honoring their parents. Or, to put it even more plainly, a man gains the blessing of long life, including the ability to produce a large family, by honoring his parents. The way in which the people of a civilization define and practice their family obligations will determine their ability to approach the earthly fulfillment of the dominion covenant. Without a close adherence to this, the fifth commandment, no society can hope to receive and *keep* the capital necessary to fulfill the terms of the dominion covenant, especially the human capital involved in a population explosion.

Parental Sovereignty

Parents possess limited, derivative, but completely legitimate sovereignty over their children during the formative years of the children's lives. When children reach the age of civil responsibility, one sign of their maturity is their willingness to establish families of their own (Gen. 2:24). Responsibility therefore steadily shifts as time goes on. Eventually, the aged parents transfer economic and other responsibilities to their children, who care for them when they are no longer able to care for themselves. The man in his peak production years may have two-way financial responsibilities: to his parents and to his children. Maximum responsibility hits at an age when, because of economic and biological patterns, a man attains his maximum strength. This shift of responsibility is mandatory, given the mortality of mankind. The Bible provides guidelines for the proper transfer of family responsibility over time.

The requirement that men honor their parents preserves the *continuity of the covenantal family*, and therefore it preserves the *continuity of responsibility*. The totally atomistic family unit is probably impossible; where it exists, the culture which has created it will collapse.[3] *Mutual*

---

3. For an historical example of just such a social collapse, see Colin Turnbull, *The Mountain People* (New York: Simon & Schuster, 1973).

obligations bind the family units together. Parents have an obligation to lay up wealth for their children: ". . . for the children ought not to lay up for the parents, but the parents for the children" (II Cor. 12:14b). Parents are not to squander their children's inheritance.

It should also be recognized that each of the children has a legitimate claim to part of the patrimony, unless disinherited because of his rebellion against parents or his personal immorality. The eldest son is entitled to a double portion of the estate (Deut. 21:15-17). Why does the eldest son inherit this double portion? A reasonable explanation is that he is the person with the primary responsibility for the care of his parents.[4] The English system of primogeniture — in which the eldest son inherited all of the landed estate — was clearly unbiblical, and the breakdown of that system in the nineteenth century was a step forward for England. Such a system places too much responsibility on the eldest son, leaving the other children bereft of capital, but also psychologically free of economic obligations toward the parents. It cuts off most of the children from the mutual obligations of the covenantal family.

Economic obligations should flow in both directions: toward the children in their early years, toward the parents in their later years, and back toward the children at the death of the parents, when the family's capital is inherited by the survivors. In short, children inherit, but parents must first be provided for.

The Continuity of Capital

The biblical law-order is a unity. Blessings and responsibilities are linked. Without the coherence of comprehensive biblical law, blessings can become *curses*. We can apply this insight to the fifth commandment. Assume that a son honors his parents during their lifetime. He receives the blessing of long life. Nevertheless, he neglects to teach his own children the requirements of this commandment. He also wastes his own estate in a present-oriented orgy of consumption. He miscalculates his own life expectancy. He runs out of money before he runs out of time. He has nothing to live on in his old age. His fortune is gone, and his own children know it. The break in the family between generations is now a serious threat to him. His children know that he has abandoned them by squandering

---

4. R. J. Rushdoony, *The Institutes of Biblical Law* (Nutley, New Jersey: Craig Press, 1973), p. 180.

the family estate, so they in turn abandon him to poverty in his old age, when he most needs assistance. The blessing of long life then becomes a curse to him. He slowly rots away in abject poverty.

Capital, if familistic in nature, is less likely to be squandered. In a truly godly social order, the familiar rags-to-riches-to-rags progression of three generations, from grandfather to grandchildren, is not supposed to become typical, despite the fact that the *legal possibility* of "rags-to-riches-to-rags" is basic to the preservation of a free society. The example of a man who pulls himself up out of poverty, only to see his children squander his fortune, leaving his grandchildren destitute, is neither normative nor normal in a Christian social order. The godly do not lay up treasure for the ungodly; the reverse is true (Prov. 13:22). *Wealth in the long run flows toward provident and productive citizens who exercise dominion in terms of biblical law.* Therefore, these dual obligations, from fathers to sons and from sons to fathers, are an important aspect of the biblical tendency toward economic growth over many generations.

Fathers have economic incentives to expand the family's capital base, and they also have an incentive to train up children who will not dissipate the family's capital. The *continuity of capital*, under God's law, is promoted by the laws of inheritance-honor. This preservation of capital is crucial for long-term economic development.

In order to preserve family capital over time, godly parents must train their children to follow the ethical standards of the Bible. The biblical basis for long-term expansion of family capital is ethical: *character* and *competence*. But this ethical foundation for long-term family capital growth is not acceptable to anti-biblical cultures. They want the fruits of Christian culture without the roots. Thus, we find that civil governments often take steps to preserve *already existing* family fortunes at the expense of those productive families that are ready and willing to make their economic contribution to the production process. A phenomenon which is supposed to be the product of ethics and education — the expansion of family capital over many generations — is *temporarily* produced by the use of State power. This substitution of power for ethics is characteristic of Satan's religions — not power as the product of biblical ethics ("right eventually produces might"), but power as an alternative to biblical ethics ("might makes right").

The pagan imitation of a godly social order frequently involves the use of *legislated barriers to entry*. Those who have achieved economic success seek political power in order to restrict their competitors from displacing them.[5] This phenomenon has been described as "pulling up the ladder after you've reached the top." Primogeniture was one such restriction, which held together the great landed estates of England for many centuries. Other sorts of restrictions prevail in the modern "mixed" economy, all of them hostile to the great engine of progress under capitalism, *price competition*.[6] These restrictions include: tariffs or import quotas,[7] prohibitions against price competition (price floors) in the name of protecting market stability,[8] or protecting the consumer from trusts,[9] minimum wage laws (another price floor),[10] restrictions against advertising (still another kind of price floor),[11] compulsory trade unionism,[12] restrictions on

5. Gabriel Kolko, *The Triumph of Conservatism: A Reinterpretation of American History, 1900-1916* (New York: Free Press of Glencoe, 1963). Kolko is a "New Left" historian. He argues that the American Progressive movement, which promoted government regulation of the trusts in the name of protecting the consumers, was supported by large businesses that were seeking legislated protection from new competitors. For further evidence on this point, see James Weinstein, *The Corporate Ideal in the Liberal State, 1900-1918* (Boston: Beacon Press, 1968); Clarence Cramer, *American Enterprise: Free and Not So Free* (Boston: Little, Brown, 1972), chaps. 10-14.

6. Gary North, "Price Competition and Expanding Alternatives," *The Freeman* (August 1974).

7. Gary North, "Buy American!" *The Freeman* (January 1981). The relationship between monopolies and tariffs was explained as long ago as 1907: Franklin Pierce, *The Tariff and the Trusts* (New York: Macmillan, 1907).

8. Mary Peterson, *The Regulated Consumer* (Ottawa, Illinois: Green Hill, 1971); Dan Smoot, *The Business End of Government* (Boston: Western Islands, 1973).

9. D. T. Armentano, *Antitrust and Monopoly: Anatomy of a Policy Failure* (New York: John Wiley & Sons, 1982); Harold Fleming, *Ten Thousand Commandments: A Story of the Antitrust Laws* (New York: Prentice-Hall, 1951). See also Pierce, *The Tariffs and the Trusts, op. cit.*

10. Walter Williams, *The State Against Blacks* (New York: McGraw-Hill New Press, 1982), ch. 3. This book also covers occupational licensing, regulation by the states, taxicab licensing, and trucking regulation.

11. Yale Brozen, *Advertising and Society* (New York: New York University Press, 1974); George Stigler, "The Economics of Information," *Journal of Political Economy*, LXIX (June 1961); Yale Brozen, "Entry Barriers: Advertising and Product Differentiation," in Harvey J. Goldschmidt, *et al.* (eds.), *Industrial Concentration: The New Learning* (Boston: Little, Brown, 1974); David G. Tuerck (ed.), *The Political Economy of Advertising* (Washington, D.C.: American Enterprise Institute, 1978); Tuerck (ed.), *Issues in Advertising: The Economics of Pursuasion* (Washington, D.C.: American Enterprise Institute, 1978).

12. Gary North, "A Christian View of Labor Unions," *Biblical Economics Today*, I (April/May 1978); Philip D. Bradley (ed.), *The Public Stake in Union Power* (Charlottesville: University of Virginia Press, 1959); Sylvester Petro, *Power Unlimited: The Corruption of Union Leadership* (New York: Ronald Press, 1959).

agricultural production,[13] state licensing of the professions,[14] zoning laws,[15] and the most blatant and universally accepted restriction, immigration quotas.[16] All of these statist economic restrictions reduce people's freedom of movement — geographically, economically, and socially. They all involve the misuse of the otherwise legitimate monopoly of State power in order to restrict individual and social progress and personal responsibility.[17] The result of such legislation, if continued and enforced, is the universal destruction of freedom, as the State regulators steadily squeeze away the monopoly profits received by the early members of the protected group. This is especially true of State-licensed professionals, such as physicians.[18]

---

13. William Peterson, *The Great Farm Problem* (Chicago: Regnery, 1959); Clarence B. Carson, *The War on the Poor* (New Rochelle, New York: Arlington House, 1969), ch. 4: "Farmers at Bay."

14. Reuben A. Kessel, "Price Discrimination in Medicine," *Journal of Law and Economics*, I (October 1958); Milton Friedman, *Capitalism and Freedom* (Chicago: University of Chicago Press, 1962), ch. 9: "Occupational Licensure."

15. Bernard H. Siegan, *Land Use Without Zoning* (Lexington, Massachusetts: Lexington, 1972).

16. Gary North, "Public Goods and Fear of Foreigners," *The Freeman* (March 1974). An example of special pleading favoring immigration restrictions is Roy L. Garis, *Immigration Restriction: A Study of the Opposition to and Regulation of Immigration Into the United States* (New York: Macmillan, 1928). Such restrictions, had they been passed into law and enforced prior to 1924, would have greatly reduced American economic growth. On the multiple cultural and economic contributions of several immigrant groups — Germans, Irish, Italians, Jews, Blacks, Puerto Ricans, Mexicans, and orientals — see Thomas Sowell, *Ethnic America: A History* (New York: Basic Books, 1981). He covers similar material in a condensed way in *The Economics and Politics of Race: An International Perspective* (New York: William Morrow, 1983), but adds new material on the performance of immigrant groups in other societies. On the spectacular economic miracle of the city of Miami, Florida, as a result of heavy immigration from Cuba after 1960, see George Gilder, *The Spirit of Enterprise* (New York: Simon & Schuster, 1984), ch. 5.

The political-economic problem today is twofold: 1) new immigrants in a democracy are soon allowed to vote, and 2) they become eligible for tax-financed "welfare" programs. In the Old Testament, it took several generations for members of pagan cultures to achieve citizenship (Deut. 23:3-8), and there were very few publicly financed charities, the most notable being the third-year tithe (Deut. 14:28-29). Thus, mass democracy has violated a fundamental biblical principle — that time is needed for *ethical* acculturation of pagan immigrants — and the result of this transgression has been *xenophobia*: the fear of foreigners, especially immigrant newcomers. Cf. Gary North, "Two-Tier Church Membership," *Christianity and Civilization*, 4 (1985).

17. Walter Adams and Horace M. Gray, *Monopoly in America: The Government as Promoter* (New York: Macmillan, 1955); George Reisman, *The Government Against the Economy* (Ottawa, Illinois: Caroline House, 1979).

18. Gary North, "Walking Into a Trap," *The Freeman* (May 1978).

Another result is the reduction of per capita productivity, and therefore per capita wealth, even for those who appeared initially to be favored by the legislation.

Compound Interest

The importance of the continuity of capital can be seen in any example involving compound interest. Let me say from the beginning: we cannot expect to see this compound interest phenomenon continue uninterrupted in any family forever. We also cannot expect to see annual rates of growth over 1% for centuries at a time. As I like to point out, the 4 billion people on earth in 1980 would multiply to over 83 trillion in a thousand years, if the rate of population growth were 1% per annum. But the fact remains, the longer the compound growth phenomenon continues, the smaller the annual percentage increase needs to be in order to produce spectacular results.

Let us assume that we are dealing with a given monetary unit. We can call it a *talent*. A young married man begins with 100 talents. Say that he multiplies this capital base by 2% per annum. At the end of 50 years, the couple has 269 talents. Let us assume that the heirs of the family multiply at 1% per annum, on the average, throughout each subsequent family's lifetime. After 250 years, if the growth rates both of people and capital persist, the total family capital base is up to 14,126 talents. Divided by 24 family units, each family now has 589 talents. This is almost a 6-fold increase per family unit, which is considerable. We now have 24 family units, with each family possessing almost six times the wealth that the original family started out with, even assuming that each heir has married someone who has brought no capital into the marriage.

What if the capital base should increase by 3%? At the end of 50 years, the original couple would have 438 talents, over a 4-fold increase. This is quite impressive. But at the end of 250 years, the family would possess 161,922 talents, over 1,600 times as large. Even divided by 24 family units, the per family capital base would be 6,747 talents, or over 67 times larger than the original capital base of 100 talents.

Consider the implications of these figures. A future-oriented man — a man like Abraham — could look forward to his heirs' possessing vastly greater wealth than he ever could hope to attain personally. This is the kind of vision God offers His people, just as he offered to Abraham: heirs two or three generations later who will be numerous and rich. God offers a man the hope of substantially increased wealth during his own lifetime, in response to his covenantal faithfulness, hard work, and thrift. But God also offers the covenantal family truly vast increases in per family wealth, if the disciplined economic growth per family is maintained. The covenant community increases its control of capital, generation by generation, piling up ever-greater quantities of capital, until the growth becomes exponential, meaning astronomical, meaning impossible. Compound growth therefore points to the fulfillment of the dominion covenant, the subduing of the earth. It points to the end of cursed time.

(It might be appropriate at this point to clarify what I mean when I speak about a covenant society amassing huge numbers of monetary units called talents. If we are speaking of a whole society, and not just a single family, then for all of them to amass 6,747 talents per family in 250 years, there would have to be mass inflation — the printing of billions of "talent notes." I am speaking not of physical slips of paper called talents; I am speaking of goods and services of *value*. The 100 talents per family, multiplied by all the families in the society, would not be able to increase; instead, *prices would fall* in response to increased production of 3% per annum. Eventually, if the whole society experiences 3% per annum economic growth, given a fixed money supply, prices would begin to approach zero. But prices in a cursed world will never reach zero; there will always be economic scarcity [Gen. 3:17-19]. In fact, scarcity is defined as a universe in which total demand is greater than supply at zero price. So the assumption of permanent compound economic growth is incorrect. Either the growth process stops in the aggregate, or else time ends. That, of course, is precisely the point. Time *will* end.)

A man whose vision is geared to dominion, in time and on earth, has to look to the years beyond his lifetime. He cannot hope to build up his family's capital base in his own lifetime sufficient to achieve conquest. If he looks two or more centuries into the future, it becomes a conceivable task. Only a handful of men can expect to amass a fortune in a single lifetime. If a man's time perspective is limited to his own lifetime, then he must either give up the idea of family dominion, or else he must adopt the mentality of the gambler. He has to "go for the big pay-off." He must sacrifice everything for capital expansion, risking everything he has, plus vast quantities of borrowed money, on untried, high-risk, high-return ventures. He must abandon everything conventional, for an investor earns only conventional returns (prevailing interest rate) from conventional ventures. The man's world becomes an endless series of all-or-nothing decisions.[19] He "puts it all on the line" time after time.

Carnegie and the Patron State

During the final decades of the nineteenth century in the United States, a group of entrepreneurs collectively known in the history textbooks as "the robber barons" created the modern industrial economy.[20] Never before had a nation experienced economic growth on a scale as great as the United States experienced from 1870 to 1900. Enormous fortunes were made and lost and made again. Output quadrupled between 1867 and 1897, while the population doubled, from 37 million to 72 million. The wholesale price index fell by a hundred points, or 60%, from 168 to 68 — and this was accomplished in spite of the tripling of the money stock, from $1.3 billion to $4.5 billion.[21] The vast increase in per capita output meant an increase in per capita wealth — doubling in one generation, something that few people living in previous periods of man's history could have believed possible.

The secret of success for the entrepreneurs of the late nineteenth century was *efficiency*. They cut costs. They cut prices. They broadened their markets by making goods available to millions of buyers who could not have bought at the older prices. By increasing the size of their firms, by adapting new techniques of cost accounting, and by discovering new sources of power, raw materials, and communications, these men created a whole new world. The social costs were high for some groups (e.g., Chinese immigrant males in California

---

19. This is the world of modern entrepreneurship. Only a few people can make huge fortunes. Still, the rest of us benefit from their initiative and uncertainty-bearing: Gilder, *The Spirit of Enterprise.*

20. Matthew Josephson, *The Robber Barons: The Great American Capitalists, 1861-1901* (New York: Harcourt, Brace, [1934] 1962). For a more balanced view of this era, see Edward C. Kirkland, "The Robber Barons Revisited," *American Historical Review*, LXVI (October 1960). For a specific case study, see Allan Nevins' multi-volume study of John D. Rockefeller.

21. There was, however, a drop in the so-called velocity of money — turnover, or money transactions per unit of time — of 50%. This helped offset the price inflation effects of the monetary expansion. The money and income data are from Milton Friedman and Anna J. Schwartz, *A Monetary History of the United States, 1867-1960* (National Bureau of Economic Research, published by Princeton University Press, 1963), charts 3 and 8, pp. 30, 94-95. The population figures are found in *Historical Statistics of the United States, Colonial Times to 1957* (Washington, D.C.: Bureau of the Census, 1960), p. 7, Series A 1-3.

in the second half of the nineteenth century, for whom there were no marriageable women[22]), but the huge immigration from Europe indicated that millions of newcomers believed the costs were worth it. The dream of rags to riches was still basic to the American vision. Men like John D. Rockefeller, J. P. Morgan, and Andrew Carnegie became living legends, both to admire and to despise. The archetype cost-cutter was probably Carnegie. He arrived in this country in 1848 at the age of 12 or 13. He, his brother, and his parents had come from Scotland. His parents had been poverty-stricken radicals. Their son picked up many of their opinions. "As a child," he later said, "I could have slain king, duke, or lord, and considered their death a service to the state."[23] When he was 14, he worked 12 hours a day in a textile mill. At 16, he was a skilled telegraph operator. At 17, he was the assistant to a high official of the Pennsylvania Railroad, one of the largest firms in the world (it became the largest in 1865, when Carnegie left it at age 30). At age 20, he was appointed the general superintendent of the railroad's western division. He went on to create the largest manufacturing organization in the world, Carnegie Steel, and in January, 1901, he sold the company to J. P. Morgan for $480,000,000; $220,000,000 of this was his.[24] (The price of gold was then fixed at $20 per ounce; the average household in the United States at that time earned a little under $1,000 per year.)[25] This was not a cash sale, but involved long-term bonds. Nevertheless, Morgan contacted him a few days after the deal was transacted. "Mr. Carnegie, I want to congratulate you on being the richest man in the world."[26]

How had he accomplished this? By systematically cutting costs, year after year. He never ceased looking for new manufacturing processes to cut costs. His other tactic was brilliant and daring. He expanded production and improved production facilities during economic depressions of the period.[27] By 1900, he had become the

---

22. Thomas Sowell, *Ethnic America: A History*, pp. 140-41.
23. Cited in Clarence Cramer, *American Enterprise: Free and Not So Free*, p. 425.
24. Louis M. Hacker, *The World of Andrew Carnegie, 1865-1901* (Philadelphia: Lippincott, 1968), p. 424.
25. There were approximately 16 million households in the United States in 1900: *Historical Statistics of the United States, Colonial Times to 1957*, p. 15, Series A 242-244. National income was in the range of $15 billion: *ibid.*, p. 139: Series F 10-21.
26. Harold C. Livesay, *Andrew Carnegie and the Rise of Big Business* (Boston: Little, Brown & Co., 1975), p. 188. I have relied heavily on this book for Carnegie's biography.
27. Clarence Cramer, *American Enterprise*, pp. 426-27.

largest steel producer in the world, and was in a position to bankrupt most of his competitors. He was producing steel for $12 a ton, and hiding behind the tariff which allowed him to sell at $23.75 a ton.[28] Carnegie, the "rugged individualist," was a high tariff man (as every steel producer in recorded U.S. history has been), and agitated strongly for the McKinley tariff in the early 1890's.[29] Of course, his U.S. competitors also hid behind that import wall, but it did them no good with Carnegie's ability to underprice them. J. P. Morgan took the firm, merged it with others, and the result was the U.S. Steel Company. Morgan stopped Carnegie's competition by buying him out. Immediately, the new trust announced a price increase to $28 a ton.[30]

What did Carnegie do with the money? Over the next 19 years, he gave it all away.[31] This is what sets him apart from all the other "robber barons" of his day. He had achieved his goal. He had become fabulously wealthy in an era of falling prices and no income taxes, when the average family earned less than $1,000 a year. But he did not pass this wealth along to his heirs, for he left little money behind. He married late, at age 53, and had one daughter. His vision was limited to what he could accomplish with his capital within his own lifetime. He knew that only an *elite* could do much in one brief lifetime.

Carnegie's "Essay on Wealth"

Carnegie set forth his opinions concerning wealth and the responsibilities of those who possess it in a memorable essay, published in 1889. Predictably, he did not see wealth as the product of adherence to a biblical law structure, given his rejection of all supernatural religion. He was a religious evolutionist. He once described his conversion to Darwinism: "Light came in as a flood and all was clear. Not only had I got rid of the theology and the supernatural,

---

28. *Ibid.*, p. 427.

29. Mark D. Hirsch, *William C. Whitney: Modern Warwick* (New York: Archon, [1948] 1969), p. 410.

30. Cramer, p. 428.

31. He gave millions away to create libraries throughout the United States. I did some of my research on this chapter in a Carnegie library. Interestingly enough, the copy of Carnegie's autobiography, listed in the card catalogue, was missing from the shelves, probably permanently. He also set up several tax-exempt foundations. The total gifts may have reached $300,000,000, given the interest returns on the original principal, which he also gave away.

but I had found the truth of evolution. 'All is well since all grows better' became my motto, my true source of comfort. Man was not created with an instinct for his own degradation, but from the lower he
had risen to the higher forms. Nor is there any conceivable end to his
perfection. His face is turned to the light, he stands in the sun and
looks upward."[32] Not the family, not God's covenantal law-order, but
the impersonal processes of evolution will bring progress. Wealth is
the product of competition, and the fittest survive. Carnegie was a
devoted follower of Herbert Spencer's brand of evolutionism, with
this exception: unlike Spencer, he did not fear the effects of charity.
He saw charitable activities as obligations of the rich, who would
give direction to the masses. What he called "the law of competition"
raises society and is the source of progress. "But whether the law be
benign or not, we must say of it, as we say of the change in the conditions of men to which we have referred: It is here; we cannot evade
it; no substitutes for it have been found; and while the law may
sometimes be hard for the individual, it is best for the race, because
it insures the survival of the fittest in every department."[33] *Cosmic impersonalism* rules the world of man.

Carnegie pulled no punches in his defense of elitism. "We accept
and welcome, therefore, as conditions to which we must accom-
modate ourselves, great inequality of environment, the concentra-
tions of business, industrial and commercial, in the hands of a few,
and the law of competition between these, as being not only beneficial, but essential for the future progress of the race. Having accepted these, it follows that there must be great scope for the exercise
of special ability in the merchant and in the manufacturer who has to
conduct affairs upon a great scale."[34] The market process is to be left
alone; *individualism* must be the ruling principle of production and
distribution. Communism cannot work. We must defend the ideas of
"Individualism, Private Property, the Law of Accumulation of
Wealth, and the Law of Competition; for these are the highest
results of human experience, the soil in which society so far has produced the best fruit."[35]

So far, Carnegie sounds very much like the typical proponent of

---

32. Livesay, pp. 74-75.
33. Carnegie, "Wealth," (1889); in Gail Kennedy (ed.), *Democracy and the Gospel of Wealth* (Boston: D. C. Heath, 1965), p. 2.
34. *Idem.*
35. *Ibid.*, p. 3.

rugged individualism, or social Darwinism. But his frame of reference was both very short and very long: the individual's lifetime and the eternal evolutionary process. In between, the laws of Individualism, Private Property, and Accumulation of Wealth do not apply. Once a man dies, the State must move in and confiscate the bulk of the dead man's estate — in the name of the people. With this doctrine, Carnegie broke with nineteenth-century social Darwinism.

"There are but three modes in which surplus wealth can be disposed of. It can be left to the families of the descendants; or it can be bequeathed for public purposes; or, finally, it can be administered during their lives by its possessors." Carnegie overwhelmingly favored the third approach. He absolutely rejected the idea that rich men should bequeath their capital to their children. Children should be provided for *"in moderation."*[36] Leaving one's wealth in a will to the public often does not work, since the executors may not use the funds as the testator had hoped.[37] What is needed, therefore, is a *massive tax on inherited wealth.* "The growing disposition to tax more and more heavily large estates left at death is a cheering indication of the growth of a salutary change in public opinion. . . . Of all forms of taxation, this seems the wisest. Men who continue hoarding great sums all their lives, the proper use of which for public ends would work good to the community, should be made to feel that the community, in the form of the state, cannot thus be deprived of its proper share. By taxing estates heavily at death the state marks its condemnation of the selfish millionaire's unworthy life."[38] A man's children *must* be expropriated.

Here is the theology of the *pseudo-family.* The public, or community, is narrowly (and improperly) defined as the civil government, meaning organized political power. The State is entitled to "its proper share," and that share is large. The hoarder is living "an unworthy life." He set forth no limits on such taxation: "It is desirable that nations should go much farther in this direction. Indeed, it is difficult to set bounds to the share of a rich man's estate which should go at his death to the public through the agency of the state, and by all means such taxes should be graduated, beginning at nothing upon moderate sums to dependents, and increasing rapidly as amounts swell. . . ."[39] This vision has been universally accepted by

---

36. *Ibid.*, p. 3.
37. *Ibid.*, p. 4.
38. *Idem.*
39. *Idem.*

voters and civil governments in the twentieth century. The State has replaced the family as the lawful heir of the rich.

Carnegie the Benefactor

What Carnegie never understood was that the wealth he possessed was the result of his enormous contribution to human welfare. Before Carnegie, steel had not been used in construction projects, except for bridges and railroads. Because of his relentless cost-cutting techniques, the "age of steel" became a reality throughout the industrial world. Millions of people became the beneficiaries. In contrast, his philanthropies, such as free public libraries, his peace foundation, and similar projects, became places of employment for the middle-class bureaucrats who used his wealth to promote the religion of secular humanism.[40] It was Carnegie the "hoarder," the "wage suppressor" — in short, *Carnegie the reinvestor of profits* — who benefited the world. When he began to give away his wealth, he found (or at least we have found) that his skills were limited. His elitism trapped him. Carnegie the producer, not Carnegie the donator, was the great benefactor.

His scheme, he argued, was the "true antidote for the temporary unequal distribution of wealth, the reconciliation of the rich and the poor. . . ." It would produce "a reign of harmony." He even adopted a Marxist-like concept of surplus wealth. Under the sway of his system, "we shall have an ideal state, in which the surplus wealth of the few will become, in the best sense, the property of the many, because administered for the common good, and this wealth, passing through the hands of the few, can be made a much more potent force for the elevation of our race than if it had been distributed in small sums to the people themselves." The *radical elitism* of his perspective should be obvious. The man of wealth must live unostentatiously (although Carnegie himself had several mansions), "shunning display or extravagance; to provide moderately for the legitimate wants of those dependent on him; and after doing so to consider all surplus revenues which come to him simply as trust funds, which he is called upon to administer, and strictly bound as a matter of duty to administer in the manner which, in his judgment, is best calculated to produce the most beneficial results for the community — the man

---

40. On the revolutionary and elitist ideas promoted by the Carnegie Foundation, see William P. Hoar, *Architects of Conspiracy: An Intriguing History* (Boston: Western Islands, 1984), ch. 7.

of wealth thus becoming the mere agent and trustee for his poorer brethren, bringing to their service his superior wisdom, experience, and ability to administer, doing for them better than they would or could do for themselves."[41]

He warned against "indiscriminate charity." Echoing Benjamin Franklin, he said, "In bestowing charity, the main consideration should be to help those who will help themselves. . . ." In short, "Individualism will continue, but the millionaire will be but a trustee for the poor; entrusted for a season with a great part of the increased wealth of the community, but administering it for the community far better than it could or would have done for itself."[42]

The irony of this is that Carnegie, in order to finally cash in his investment and begin giving away $300,000,000 (Cramer estimates that he eventually gave away $350 million, including $62 million in the British Empire),[43] sold out to J. P. Morgan, knowing that Morgan was about to establish a giant conglomerate steel trust that was composed of companies whose profits were being wiped out by Carnegie's cost-cutting tactics.[44] Carnegie had served as a trustee of the masses by his activities as an entrepreneur; he abdicated that position of trusteeship in the name of philanthropy, where he had few skills. As a producer, he had increased the wealth of millions of steel users, allowing them to benefit from his efforts as *they* chose. He never understood this, or if he did, his elitism overwhelmed his understanding.

Darwinian Elitism

The sort of blatant elitism which Carnegie espoused did not survive the onslaught of socialistic and interventionist thought which has been the predominant position of twentieth-century intellectuals. Elitism survived, but not blatant, visible elitism. His sort of modified social Darwinism still contained too strong an element of individualism. Once Carnegie acknowledged the validity of confiscatory estate taxation by the civil government — obtaining "its proper share" — his case for private property was lost. The pseudo-family could not wait until the death of the testator. It could not rely on his

---

41. "Wealth," p. 7.
42. *Ibid.*, p. 8.
43. Cramer, p. 429.
44. Robert Hessen, *Steel Titan: The Life of Charles M. Schwab* (New York: Oxford University Press, 1975), pp. 111-18.

good judgment in distributing his wealth before his death. What was needed was a graduated income tax, Social Security taxes, and numerous other sorts of taxes. No one could be legally entitled to escape — not the rich, not the middle class, and not the poor. After all, if the State is a family, it is *everyone's* family. If it is a trustee, as every family should be, it is a trustee for everyone.[45]

It is significant that before he died, Carnegie abandoned his professed faith in the free market, and became a promoter of the statist Darwinism of the Progressive movement. Intellectually, this shift was first promoted, and promoted eloquently, by Lester Frank Ward, an early sociologist, whose book, *Dynamic Sociology* (1883), was an attack on individualistic Darwinism in the name of the Darwinism of central planning.[46] Progressivism's influence increased steadily after 1900. The leaders of the Progressive movement almost without exception adopted some version of Ward's Darwinism, including the business leaders who were supposedly the targets of the crusading zeal of the reformers. It was marked by a shift from individualism to collectivism and State economic planning and regulation.

Carnegie became a proponent of corporate licensing by the Federal government. By 1908, price competition was still plaguing the older steel firms, and Carnegie (the best of the old competitors) remarked: ". . . it always comes back to me that Government control, and that alone, will solve the problem . . ."[47] He had learned how valuable the Federal government could be in protecting the capital of established, large corporations. He understood the nature of the corporate State. He recognized the means by which his heralded elite could direct the affairs of "little people." Perhaps he at last perceived why the market could no longer be trusted: it gives too much power to the masses, who by their day-by-day decisions to buy or not to buy determine who among the producers is the "fittest" to survive.

---

45. R. J. Rushdoony, "The Family as Trustee," *The Journal of Christian Reconstruction*, IV (Winter 1977-78).

46. For an analysis of Ward's book, see Gary North, *The Dominion Covenant: Genesis* (Tyler, Texas: Institute for Christian Economics, 1982), pp. 297-318. Cf. Henry Steele Commager, *The American Mind* (New Haven: Yale University Press, 1950), ch. X; Sidney Fine, *Laissez Faire and the General Welfare State: A Study of Conflict in American Thought, 1865-1901* (Ann Arbor: University of Michigan Press, [1956] 1964), pp. 253-64.

47. Cited by Kolko, *Triumph of Conservatism*, p. 173.

Trusteeship: Which Family?

The continuity of capital is obviously threatened by the rise of the familistic State. It establishes itself as the trustee for all men, from womb to tomb. It therefore demands support from those who receive its protection. Like a father, or better yet, like a distant uncle who guides the fortunes of an orphaned nephew, the State must administer the funds, always taking a large portion of those funds as a necessary fee for services performed.

As men steadily begin to perceive the implications of the familistic State, they seek to hide their assets from its tax collectors. Men try to find ways to pass along wealth to their legitimate heirs, and the State, as the enraged illegitimate heir, relentlessly searches for ways of closing off escape hatches. The new "parent" must not be deprived of its support from every member of the family. And once the capital is collected, it is dissipated in a wave of corruption, mismanagement, bureaucratic salaries, and politically motivated compulsory charity programs. Men see the erosion of their capital, and they seek to hide it away. They recognize what the pseudo-family of the State will do to the inheritance of their children. Still, because of their own entrenched envy, they are unable to turn back. They and their parents and grandparents accepted the philosophical justifications of "soaking the rich" by means of the ballot box, but now that price inflation has pushed everyone into higher tax brackets, they are horrified by what they find. They have now been snared themselves, but they seem unable to turn back, for to turn back would involve an admission of the immorality and inefficiency of the "soak the rich" programs of twentieth-century democratic politics.

Permanent Children

The modern messianic State would like to make permanent wards of its citizens. This is a primary justification for the State's existence today. It must administer the inheritance for the benefit of children. But the children are *perpetual servants*, and a growing army, increasingly dependent upon the coercive wealth redistribution of politics. What we have here is a reversal of the New Testament teaching concerning sons and servants. "Now I say, That the heir, as long as he is a child, differeth nothing from a servant, though he be lord of all. But is under tutors and governors until the time appointed of the father" (Gal. 4:1-2). The State's bureaucrats do not recognize what every human parent must eventually recognize, namely, that he is going to become weak, and that he must encourage *independence on the part of his heirs* if he is to secure safety for himself in his old age. The State, by making men permanent children, guarantees its own demise, for the children cannot forever support the "trustee State," if the State has, in effect, institutionalized the voters.

The family *is* a trustee. By acknowledging the legitimacy of the laws of the family, men honor God, although the unregenerate do so unwittingly and in spite of their professed theology of autonomy before God. External blessings flow to those who honor God's laws. By establishing a tradition of honoring parents, sons increase the likelihood that in their old age their own children will protect them from the burdens of old age. The risks that life poses to the old are therefore minimized. The familistic welfare structure is *reciprocal* and *personal*. It is undergirded by revealed law and by family tradition. It need not rely heavily on the far weaker support of *sentiment* — an important aspect of the religion of humanism. [48] The growth of capital within the family increases each succeeding generation's ability to conquer nature to the glory of God, including the infirmities and vulnerabilities of old age.

The statist pseudo-family cannot permit this sort of challenge to its self-proclaimed sovereignty. The modern State has therefore laid claim to ownership of the children through the tax-supported public school system. [49] Children are obviously a form of family capital. They are to be trained, which involves costs to the parents. But the parents have a legitimate claim on a portion of the future assets of the children. The relationship involves costs and benefits for both generations. Neither side needs to buy the love of the other, any more than men need to buy the love of God. Each generation gives,

---

48. Herbert Schlossberg, *Idols for Destruction: Christian Faith and Its Confrontation With American Society* (Nashville, Tennessee: Thomas Nelson Publishers, 1983), pp. 43-47.

49. Pastor Everett Sileven of the Faith Baptist Church of Louisville, Nebraska, became a national celebrity in 1982 because of a much-publicized battle with the Nebraska Board of Education. Sileven spent four months in jail for his refusal to shut down his unaccredited church educational ministry ("church school"). During the battle in 1982, one state legislator told him privately that since members of his church had asked for and had been granted marriage licenses by the state of Nebraska, that these families were therefore the creation of the state, and that any children produced by such licensed families were the property of the state. The state therefore had the authority to determine the character of the education these children received.

and each receives. The relationship is both personal and economic. But today the modern State intervenes. It provides the children's education. It lays claim to future payments (taxes) by the children when they have reached maturity. Of necessity, it must try to buy the love (votes) of those children when they reach maturity. The children often remain subservient to the State-parent, unwilling to launch independent lives of their own, given the costs of breaking the financial and emotional tie with the welfare office. Children, the covenant family's primary resource, are stolen by the modern State. The State promises old age support. The State promises health care for the aged. The State provides State-financed and State-licensed education for the young. The State attempts to replace the benefits of the family, and simultaneously must require the same sort of financial support from the adults during their productive years. The relationship is impersonal and economic. The relationship is, by law, coercive and bureaucratic.

Impersonalism and Capital Consumption

This disastrous attempt of the civil government to replace the functions of the covenant family eventually destroys the productive mutual relationships between generations. It destroys the personal bond, making the *young in general* legally responsible for the *old in general*. The family name — so central to the life of a godly social order — is erased, and computerized numbers are substituted. The incentives for families to preserve their capital, whether for old age or for generations into the future, are reduced, for each generation's economic future is no longer legally bound to the success and prosperity of the children. "Eat, drink, and be merry, for tomorrow there will be government checks." But the dissipation of family capital, when it becomes a culture-wide phenomenon, destroys economic productivity, which in turn destroys the tax base of the State. The State cannot write the promised checks, or if it does, the monetary unit steadily grows worthless, as fiat money inflates the price level.

By abandoning the principle of family responsibility, the modern messianic State wastes a culture's capital, destroys inheritance, and makes more acceptable both euthanasia (which reduces the expense of caring for the unproductive elderly) and abortion (which reduces the expense of training and caring for the unproductive young). Lawless men, in their productive years, increasingly refuse to share their wealth with dying parents and squabbling children. They look only at present costs, neglecting future benefits, such as the care which the unborn might provide them in their old age. *They have faith in the compassionate and productive State* — the great social myth of the twentieth century. They want its benefits, but they never ask themselves the key question: *Who will pay* for their retirement years? Not the shrinking number of children, who are even more present-oriented, even more conditioned by the statist educational system, even more unwilling to share their wealth with the now-unproductive aged of the land. With the dissipation of capital, the productive voters will resist the demands of the elderly. *The generations go to war against one another — the war of politics.*

The pseudo-family State is an agent of social, political, and economic bankruptcy. It still has its intellectual defenders, even within the Christian community, although its defenders tend to be products of the State-supported, State-certified, and State-aggrandizing universities. *This pseudo-family is suicidal.* It destroys the foundations of productivity, and productivity is the source of all voluntary charity. It is a suicidal family which will pay off its debts with inflated fiat currency. Its compassion will be limited to paper and ink.

The impersonalism of the modern pseudo-family, along with its present-orientation — a vision no longer than the next election — will produce massive, universal failure of the welfare system. It has already done so. The rapid escalation of Federal anti-poverty programs has created more poverty, except for the middle-class bureaucrats who operate the programs.[50] The great economic experiment of the twentieth century is almost over, and all the college-level textbooks in economics, political science, and sociology will not be able to justify the system, once it erodes the productivity which every parasitic structure requires for its own survival. Like the Canaanitic cultures of Joshua's day, the end is in sight for the modern, messianic, welfare State economies. They have decapitalized their envy-driven, guilt-ridden citizens. Only to the extent that citizens hide their economic assets or vote to reverse the politics of envy will they escape the clutching hand of today's spendthrift, senile pseudo-parent.

Conclusion

It is imperative for Christians to abandon the religion of humanism. It is imperative that they fulfill their responsibilities as members

---

50. Charles Murray, *Losing Ground: American Social Policy, 1950-1980* (New York: Basic Books, 1984).

of a covenantal community. It is imperative that they see to it that their old people, as well as their young people, are not in any way dependent upon the services of a declining welfare State. To become dependent on such an institution is to become a slave. Worse than that: it is to become dependent on a master whose resources are almost spent. When men and women honor their fathers and mothers — financially, spiritually, and institutionally — they will have begun the painful but mandatory journey out of slavery. They will have begun to amass family capital for yet unborn generations.

The question is inescapable in any society: *Who shall inherit?* The key issue in the fifth commandment is therefore the question of *legitimacy*. Every institution faces the question of continuity over time. The biblical pattern for the family is to become representative for all other institutions: the legitimate heir is the one who does the explicit will of the righteous parent. (We even call the major testamentary instrument a "will.") God the Father establishes these eternal standards of performance, including the laws of inheritance. We must begin by honoring the laws of family inheritance.

We must decapitalize the State. The alternative is for the State to decapitalize us. If we are dependent on the State for its support, we are necessarily fostering the decapitalization of the family. *The first and crucial step in decapitalizing the State is to cease calling for favors from the State.* It is to create alternative, voluntary, biblical institutions that will replace the pseudo-compassion of the messianic State. If the covenant communities refuse to accept this challenge, then they will see their capital dissipated by the spendthrift managers of the humanistic State. The archetypal bastard will then inherit the inheritance of the righteous.

This will not come to pass. "A good man leaveth an inheritance to his children's children: and the wealth of the sinner is laid up for the just" (Prov. 13:22). God has made it clear: the bastard should not and will not inherit. We shall overcome.

6

GOD'S MONOPOLY OF EXECUTION

Thou shalt not kill (Ex. 20:13).

The usage, though not the grammar, of the Hebrew translated here as "kill" (*ratsach*) indicates murder or manslaughter. It means "to dash to pieces," but it is used in Numbers 35 and Deuteronomy 4:42 to indicate accidental manslaughter. The biblical definition of murder is the willfull execution of one man by another, unless the execution is sanctioned by the civil government; it is referred to as the shedding of man's blood (Gen. 4:10). It is an act of man in rebellion against God.

The prohibition against the shedding of man's blood applies even to murderous animals (Gen. 9:5). Guilty animals are to be stoned to death, the Mosaic law's most common means of public execution (Ex. 21:28). Because owners are covenantally responsible for the administration of their property, if the owner of the beast had been warned beforehand that the animal was dangerous, he also must be executed. He is permitted to buy his life by the payment of restitution, however: the only capital crime in biblical law for which economic restitution is legitimate (Ex. 21:29-30). Because all ownership is covenantal, *economic responsibility* is necessarily *personal*.

There are no exceptions based on idiocy, temporary insanity, temporary anger, or anything else. Unless it can be proved that the death came as a result of an accident—no premeditation—the criminal is to be executed. The willful shedding of man's blood must be punished by the civil government by execution.

The Image of God

Man's life is protected because he is made in the image of God. Genesis 9:6, the passage which teaches this doctrine, has either a double meaning (my conclusion), or else we must choose between

116

two different interpretations. "Whoso sheddeth man's blood, by man shall his blood be shed: for in the image of God made he man." The explanatory clause — "for in the image of God made he man" — can be understood in two different ways. *First*, it explains the nature of the violation: man's life is uniquely important to God, since man is made in God's image. An assault on man is an assault on the image of God. *Second*, the clause explains why men, by means of the civil government, are required to execute bloody judgment on murderers. Man is made in the image of God; therefore, as God's image, mankind can bring judgment in the name of God, the supreme Judge who executes final judgment. Man is God's agent who exercises God's delegated authority. He is an agent of the King. He is to exercise dominion over the earth.[1]

Man is made in the image of God. He is therefore a royal agent, and as such, he deserves protection. Christ's parable of the rebellious husbandmen who slew the owner's emissaries, including his son, rests on the principle of God's ultimate sovereignty and the authority which He delegates to all men (Matt. 21:33-40). Murder is rebellion, but a special kind of rebellion: lashing out at God's very image, the capstone of His creation. This is the most probable interpretation of the clause in terms of why murder is a capital crime. It explains why man-killing animals are to be executed (Gen. 9:5).[2]

Vengeance belongs to God (Deut. 32:35; Rom. 12:19; Heb. 10:30). It is His monopoly. He avenges the blood of his servants (Deut. 32:35-43). Individual men do not have the right to act as executioners except by law: "Thou shalt not avenge, nor bear any grudge against the children of thy people, but thou shalt love thy neighbor as thyself" (Lev. 19:18). The context of this oft-quoted final clause is clearly the administration of judgment. When God establishes His monopoly, transgression brings judgment. This boundary must be respected. We see an example of this — indeed, *the* example

---

1. Greg L. Bahnsen, *Theonomy in Christian Ethics* (2nd ed.; Phillipsburg, New Jersey: Presbyterian & Reformed, 1984), p. 444.

2. Because of the unnecessary exclusiveness of Bahnsen's interpretation of Genesis 9:6, which I discuss below, I need to stress the point that the right of the civil government to execute an animal should not be surprising, and the biblical defense of this right does not require any detailed exegesis, given the dominion covenant. It is not that the image of God in man uniquely empowers the civil government to execute animals; it is simply that the image of God in man is the reason why it is so heinous an act to kill a human being — so heinous that not even a "morally neutral" animal can escape the penalty. What the passage stresses is the *responsibility* of the civil government to execute an offending beast, not its authority to do so.

— in the garden of Eden. By challenging God's single, exclusive, and temporary monopoly in the garden, namely, the tree of the knowledge of good and evil, Adam and Eve rebelled, for they were attempting to play God, to usurp His position over creation. It was an attempt to worship an image: the image of God in man.

The *prohibition of graven images* in the second commandment should therefore be understood as the *repudiation of humanism* (Ex. 20:4). All forms of *idolatry* are ultimately variations of *self-worship*, for it is man, as a self-proclaimed sovereign being, who asserts the right to choose whom he will worship in place of God. Man, the sovereign, decides.

Critics of capital punishment could argue that men are not to avenge, and that we view capital punishment as a transgression of God's sole and exclusive monopoly of execution. This argument is wrong. The institution of civil government *is* entrusted with this responsibility. The individual may not execute another man, as if he were an autonomous agent of judgment, but the covenanted political community may. In fact, this power reduces the likelihood of blood vengeance by close relatives of the slain. Why does the State have the right to slay transgressors? Bahnsen explains: "The reason offered is that man is the *image of God*: man can accordingly carry out God's judgments on a creaturely level. Thinking God's thoughts after Him, man judges and penalizes after the commandment of God; man is properly *like God* his Father and Judge when he too judges crimes as God does. . . . Man should do this as well on his level as a creature, not in personal vindictiveness (i.e., such judgment does not apply to interpersonal affairs: 1 Thess. 5:15; 1 Pet. 3:9; Matt. 5:39; Rom. 12:17ff.), but as a matter of *social justice* (i.e., it is the *magistrate's* duty to punish criminals for the good of society: Rom. 13:1-4). The man created in God's image who has the responsibility of rule in human government (not citizens, not the church) is required to punish violators of God's law for the welfare of his country; he has the right to do this because he is the image of God and has God's law to direct him."[3]

I disagree with him in his assertion of an overly narrow focus of Genesis 9:6. He argues that it is not the death penalty as such which is the focus of Genesis 9:6, but the right of the civil government to *inflict* this penalty. "Instead of smoothly saying 'his blood is to be shed

---

3. *Ibid.*, p. 443.

by man' the verse reads '*by man* his blood is to be shed.' We stumble
over the 'by man' due to its obtrusion and conspicuousness. Man's
being made as God's image explains the infliction of the death penalty
by man." In other words, "the proper question at Genesis 9:5f. is:
what *right* has *man* to retaliate against the murderer? Genesis 9:6
gives the rationale: man is God's image."[4]

Bahnsen's interpretation is an attempt to force us to choose between two views: 1) the image of God in man as the *cause* of the death
penalty — the reason why such a harsh penalty must be imposed —
and 2) the image as the justification of the civil government's God-
given authority to *inflict* the penalty. I do not choose between the two
interpretations; I choose them both. The image of God in man
makes sacred the life of man, assuming he has not transgressed the
law in a capital crime, but it also legitimizes the execution of the
transgressor in the case of murder. Both the *reason for* the death penalty against murderers and the *requirement of* capital punishment by
the civil government are explained by the presence of the image of
God. But there is a stronger emphasis on the image of God in man as
the reason why murder must be punished by the death penalty, as I
have already argued (footnote 2): the execution of man-killing animals required by Genesis 9:5 points more clearly to the magnitude
of the crime than it points to the right of the civil government to
inflict the supreme earthly penalty. But ultimately it points to both.

Delegated Monopoly

God has shared His monopoly of execution with men. The final
power of death is held by Jesus Christ. "I am he that liveth, and was
dead; and, behold, I am alive for evermore, Amen; and have the
keys of hell and of death" (Rev. 1:18). It is He who triumphed over
death (I Cor. 15). Christ is the *go' el*, the kinsman-redeemer who is
also the family avenger of blood (Num. 35:19). Satan himself could
not take Job's life without God's permission (Job 3:6). Only the creator of life has the original right to destroy life; only He can establish
the standards by which man's life may be legitimately removed, including the standards of execution by the civil government.

The biblical view of the State unquestionably and irrefutably
affirms the right and obligation of the State to execute men, for the
Bible sets forth God's law. God has delegated this power to the State.

---

4. *Ibid.*, p. 444.

It cannot lawfully be neglected—certainly not in the name of a "higher, more compassionate" interpretation of God's holy law. *To deny the legitimate, derived, or ministerial sovereignty of the State in this regard is to deny the original sovereignty of God.* It is to call into question God's law, the image of God, the protection this image is entitled to, and the responsibility of State officials under God. The denial of capital punishment is, in a very real sense, an attempt to deny God's right of final execution, the imposition of the penalty of the second death, eternal punishment in fire (Rev. 20:14). Such a position denies the right of God to offer murderers an earthly, institutional "down payment" or "earnest" which points to and affirms the reality of their future eternal punishment to come. Furthermore, by denying this right of execution to the State, the opponents of capital punishment are implicitly turning over the power of execution (as distinguished from the right of execution) to murderers and rebels. It reduces their risk of permanent bodily judgment.

Anarchists, rebels, warlords, and criminals all resent the superior authority of civil government. Such authority points to a higher authority and the final judgment. Man's very image is repulsive to murderers, for it also points to the subordination of man's very being to a sovereign God. Man's image of God points to *man's subordinate responsibility*, but a lawful authority as a ruler over creation. It points to *dominion*. Satan and his followers loathe this image. They loathe it and love death (Prov. 8:36). But the image of God in man, when regenerate, is a death-defying image.

The Question of Deterrence

Do the opponents of capital punishment really play into the hands of the criminal classes? Does a society without capital punishment really transfer power into the hands of the lawless? Consider these facts. A murderer in the state of California is eligible for parole in seven years.[5] In Massachusetts in the early 1970's, where no one had been executed since 1947,[6] the median time served in prison for homicide was under 30 months.[7] As Prof. James Q. Wilson notes: "And even in states that practice the death penalty, the chances of a murderer's being executed have been so small that a rational mur-

---

5. Frank G. Carrington, *The Victims* (New Rochelle, New York: Arlington House, 1975), p. 6.
6. James Q. Wilson, *Thinking About Crime* (New York: Basic Books, 1975), p. 192.
7. *Ibid.*, p. 166.

derer might well decide to take the risk. There were eight thousand murders in 1960, but only fifty-six executions; thus, a murderer's chances of being executed were only about one in one hundred forty. After 1960 the number of executions dropped sharply, thus improving his chances."[8]

Scholars debate endlessly about whether or not the death penalty deters crime. Mafia members apparently have weighed the evidence and have discovered that *swift, predictable execution* does indeed influence people's behavior. Those who act as informers to the civil authorities wind up dead. This has made it difficult for civil authorities to find witnesses who will testify in court against criminal syndicates. The use of the threat of execution by secret societies of many varieties indicates just how effective the death penalty is in modifying people's behavior. Criminal societies, unlike modern scholars, may not have access to statistical data and complex explanations, but their members think they have adopted an effective approach to the "deviant behavior" problem. They may not have many footnotes, but they are still nearly immune to successful prosecution by the civil government. Capital punishment works well for them.

Humanism has steadily eroded the rule of God's law. The humanists have, again and again, substituted alternative punishments for those specifically required by the Bible. They have substituted long-term imprisonment for economic restitution to the victim by the criminal. They have substituted life imprisonment for the death penalty. They have substituted parole in three years for life imprisonment. The results have been disastrous.[9]

Society wants social order. Without this order, too many scarce economic resources must be assigned to crime prevention and safety programs. What voters want is a system of prevention which maintains personal freedom for the innocent and which does not bankrupt civil government.

There is little doubt that the vast majority of crimes go unpunished. Very few criminals are apprehended; few of these are brought to trial; few of these are convicted; few of these serve complete sentences. But eventually, most criminals are caught. When they are "off the market," they are not victimizing the innocent. How can society reduce the number of very serious crimes, given the reality of

---

8. *Ibid.*, p. 192.

9. Jessica Mitford, *Kind and Unusual Punishment: The Prison Business* (New York: Knopf, 1973).

minimal convictions? One answer is the death penalty.

Murder is a major crime. Victims are permanently disenfranchised. Thus, societies throughout history have imposed the death penalty. Even when a criminal knows that he may not be caught and convicted, the presence of the death penalty serves as a deterrent. If he is caught—if "his number comes up"—then the punishment is permanent. Those who believe in a chance universe are willing to take chances. All criminals do take chances if they believe that the odds are in their favor. But losing a bet against capital punishment is something else. Losers don't get to "play the game" again.

When societies raise the stakes to criminals by imposing capital punishment for capital crimes, they thereby reduce the likelihood of criminals' committing these crimes. Furthermore, those who do murder and who are convicted are not set free to kill again. While any single instance of criminal behavior may not be punished, eventually the professional criminal gets caught and convicted. If he is executed, all future crimes by this specialist in brutality are eliminated.

Society itself must not become brutal. By adhering to biblical law, a society can specify which crimes are capital and which involve paying restitution. But for those crimes that are specified as capital, the biblical commonwealth can reduce their likelihood even in an imperfect penal system which does not operate in terms of perfect knowledge. It raises the stakes so high that risk-taking criminals prefer to commit other sorts of crimes. The imperfection of the legal system is offset by the risk of *permanent* loss to the murderer.

In Defense of Stoning

Consider the mode of execution. The Old Testament specifies stoning as the proper mode in most cases (Lev. 20:2; Deut. 17:5). In the case of the sabbath-breaking gatherer of sticks, the whole congregation stoned him to death (Num. 15:36). Presumably, the phrase "whole congregation" refers to representatives of the twelve tribes, and not millions of people. Even the killer ox is to be stoned to death (Ex. 21:29). Witnesses of the capital crime are to cast the first stones (Deut. 17:7; Acts 7:58). But the whole community is to be involved. Adult males of the city are all to participate (Deut. 21:21). If the city is too populous, then it would appear to be legitimate to select representatives, but only because of the logistical problem.

Why stoning? There are many reasons. *First*, the implements of execution are available to everyone at virtually no cost. *Second*, no one blow can be traced to any person.[10] In other words, no one citizen can regard himself as "the executioner," the sole cause of another man's death. Psychologically, this is important; it relieves potential guilt problems in the mind of a sensitive person. The fact that public executioners in Western history wore masks indicates another problem: the threat of social ostracism (and socially imposed guilt) against a lone individual who does the community's "dirty business." Those who abstain from the "dirty business" of enforcing God's law have a tendency to elevate their behavior as being more moral than the executioner's, where in point of fact such abstention is itself immoral.

Third, public stoning makes it clear to everyone that the whole community is responsible for the prevention of criminal behavior. God holds the city responsible, which is why representatives of the city in Old Testament times had to offer a slain heifer as a covering if the criminal could not be found. "And all the elders of that city, that are next unto the slain man, shall wash their hands over the heifer that is beheaded in the valley: And they shall answer and say, Our hands have not shed this blood, neither have our eyes seen it. Be merciful, O Lord, unto thy people Israel, whom thou hast redeemed, and lay not innocent blood unto thy people of Israel's charge. And the blood shall be forgiven them" (Deut. 21:6-8). There is a collective responsibility in biblical law in several instances. Execution of criminals is therefore to be collective.

Fourth, executions are to be personal, not impersonal. The condemned man has the right to confront his executioners face to face. He does not die in seclusion, a faceless entity who dies at the hand of a faceless entity. He receives justice in a public, personal fashion.

The *fifth* and by far the most important reason is that stoning is literally a means of crushing the murderer's head by means of a rock, which is symbolic of God.[11] This is analogous to the crushing of the head of the serpent in Genesis 3:15. This symbolism testifies to the final victory of God over all the hosts of Satan.

Stoning is therefore integral to the commandment against murder. It allows men to execute God's justice, but not in a way that might lead an individual to believe that he, and he alone, has the right to take justice into his own hands. Executions are community

---

10. I have heard it argued that the person was killed by one huge stone that was dropped·on him or rolled on him. I doubt this. The Pharisees took up stones to throw at Jesus to stone him (John 8:59).
11. Deut. 32:3-4, 15, 18, 30-31, 37; I Sam. 2:1-2; II Sam. 22:2-4, 32, 47; 23:1-4.

projects—not with spectators who watch a professional executioner do "his" duty, but rather with actual participants. Execution is not to become a profession. It is not to be performed by a callous professional in a mask, who sees his job as just an occupation. The hangman, the masked expert at beheading men, or the official who throws the switch on the electric chair, or the man who releases the cyanide capsules: all are to be avoided by a consistently biblical social order. No man is to view himself as the community's hired "angel of death." Every citizen, beginning with the witnesses, is to see himself as a lawful agent of execution, if and when a criminal is convicted of a capital crime.

Western civilization has been marked by an *increasing depersonalization* in the area of capital punishment. Criminals were executed for centuries in public squares by masked axemen. They were hanged, sometimes after anti-biblical torture, in public squares. These events were almost sporting events, and pickpockets always did a lively business, even at the hangings of other pickpockets. Toward the end of the nineteenth century, the executions began to go indoors. By the early twentieth century, modern technology combined with modern jurisprudence to produce the indoor execution, where only a handful of observers attended. Often, they would become sick at the sight. By the latter decades, this impersonalism finally collapsed. The death penalty was seen as "inhumane," and the advent of "lifetime" sentences with paroles displaced the death penalty in most instances of capital crimes. A steady progression toward greater impersonalism finally led to repulsion on the part of political leaders and moral spokesman for humanism, leaving defenders of capital punishment to defend a long-corrupted imitation of biblical execution.

The grim reality is that personalism has been retained in such lawless acts as gangland murders and hangings by vigilante groups. In these cases, private citizens "take the law into their own hands," which is to say that they deny the legitimacy of the existing civil government. They execute vengeance apart from the sanction of the civil government. They arrogate to themselves God's monopoly of execution—a monopoly that he has placed into the hands of civil magistrates.

That modern Christians never consider the possibility of the reintroduction of stoning for capital crimes indicates how thoroughly humanistic concepts of punishment have influenced the thinking of Christians. If humanistic concepts of *punishment* have persuaded

Christians that there was something sinister about the Old Testament's specified mode of execution, then we should not be surprised to discover that humanistic concepts of *justice*, including economic justice, have also become influential in the thinking of Christians. Christians have voluntarily transferred their allegiance from the infallible Old Testament to contemporary God-hating and God-denying criminologists and economists. They have traded their birthright for a mess of pottage — or, given the nature of modern criminology's propaganda, for a pot of message.

Conclusion

That God has delegated this right to execute to the civil government indicates that this institution has legitimate power. It can protect men from kidnapping, a capital crime (Ex. 21:16). It can also protect men from the spread of disease, especially killer diseases, by means of imposing a quarantine (Num. 5:1-4; Lev. 13-15). The *police power of the State* is to serve as one of the foundations of *social stability*. It thereby permits men to apply time and capital to their callings. It offers *legal predictability*, which is vital to the flourishing of personal freedom and economic development. Most important, the right of the civil government to take a man's life under specified conditions is apt to remind men of the ultimate Judge who gives the gift of life, but who also retains the right to remove life from those who rebel against Him. The civil government's monopoly of execution testifies to God's absolute hostility against sin, especially the sin of striking out against God's own image.

This is an extremely important point. Man's life is to be protected, not because each man possesses a hypothetical absolute and original right of ownership over his own person (the fundamental assertion of most libertarian and anarcho-capitalist theoreticians), but because God is absolutely sovereign and the absolute owner of all things, including men. He will not permit His image, man, to be mortally wounded without imposing a form of judgment which, in time and on earth, is analogous to that final judgment beyond the grave. Peter speaks of "the grace of life" (I Pet. 3:7); to destroy human life is to reject grace. Murderers have no place in God's inheritance (Gal. 5:21; Rev. 21:8).

7

THE YOKE OF CO-OPERATIVE SERVICE

Thou shalt not commit adultery (Ex. 20:14).

As in all covenantal institutions, marriage necessarily involves the restraining factor of *discipline*. It is therefore a form of *bondage*. The Bible teaches that all creatures are bound by God through intermediaries established under His authority. *All life is bondage.* In Egypt, the people of God were in bondage. God delivered them: "I have broken the bands of your yoke" (Lev. 26:13b). Rebellion against God leads to the reimposition of earthly bondage under God's enemies—an external manifestation of a spiritual condition (Deut. 28:48). The book of Judges is an account of this process. When the Israelites fell away from God and began to worship the deities of the surrounding Canaanite nations, they were brought under the domination of these foreign nations. They "had their noses rubbed" in the cultures of God's enemies, until they cried out for deliverance.[1] Therefore, men must bear a yoke of some kind: God's or Satan's. They are commanded to take up Christ's yoke, for it is a light and easy one (Matt. 11:29-30). Men are always in *ethical bondage*, for they always serve either God or Mammon, the god of this world (Matt. 6:24). Men must do the work of some master. There is no such thing as a free (autonomous) man. Man is always *subordinate*.[2]

The Yoke of Marriage

The yoke of marriage, like all yokes, is a *yoke of labor*. This is one reason why Christians are cautioned to shun marriages with someone of another religious faith: labor performed by the partners must

---

1. James B. Jordan, *Judges: God's War Against Humanism* (Tyler, Texas: Geneva Ministries, 1985).
2. Cf. Gary North, *Unconditional Surrender: God's Program for Victory* (2nd ed.; Tyler, Texas: Geneva Divinity School Press, 1983).

126

ultimately be at cross purposes (II Cor. 6:14).[3] There is a *fundamental ethical separation* between believers and unbelievers, so the work of the believing partner is necessarily compromised. The Old Testament prohibition against ethical dualism within covenantal institutions can be seen in the case-law application regarding oxen (clean beasts) and donkeys (unclean): they were not to be yoked together (Deut. 22:10). If this rule is binding with respect to plowing, how much more binding in marriage!

A yoke provides *balance and direction* for both laborers. In the case of beasts of burden, the yoke multiplies the output of the two animals, and it also provides the master with a means of guiding their efforts. Neither animal can stray from its master or its partner. Each beast's labor should therefore complement the productivity of the other. The analogy of the yoke holds true for marriage. The seeds of the kingdom are sown in an orderly, productive, efficient manner. Marriage is a yoke of service.

The establishment of the marriage bond is an affirmation of interpersonal *communion*. Genesis 2:24 presents the concept of two persons' becoming one flesh, which is a distinctly theological description of the marriage bond. The act of physical union is a symbolic affirmation of this personal communion. Fornication (premarital sexual union) and adultery (post-betrothal sexual union with a partner other than one's mate) are both prohibited by God's law. The Bible sets forth explicit theological reasons for this prohibition, namely, God's ownership of mankind, and His specific design of the body for morality rather than immorality (I Cor. 6:13-20). Other implications are easy to discern. Fornication and adultery are symbolic affirmations of the legitimacy of communion outside of the marital covenant. Paul cites Genesis 2:24 in his presentation of the analogy between marriage and salvation: Christ's love for His church is like a man's love for his wife (Eph. 5:22-31).

Adultery is the symbolic rejection of Christ's covenant with his church, an assertion of the impermanence of Christ's love and commitment to His people. But even more fundamental is the foundation of all interpersonal relationships, the Trinity. The very Godhead is personal: total personalism in mutually self-exhaustive communion. The bond among the Persons of the Trinity is eternal.

---

3. A slogan might be: "Marriage should be for the purposes of the cross, not at cross purposes."

Adultery is therefore a symbolic denial of the permanence of the Trinity, as well as being a symbolic denial of the permanence of Christ's love for His church. Thus, when Adam and Eve sinned against God, they felt shame with particular intensity regarding their private parts, and they immediately hid them from each other, thereby introducing a symbolic barrier between themselves which reflected the new *ethical barrier* between themselves and God. It is not surprising that the Bible specifies the death penalty for adultery (Lev. 20:10; Deut. 22:22). It is also not surprising that pagan nations in antiquity, being *polytheistic*, were marked by *ritual prostitution* near or inside the temples: many gods, many covenants, many communions.

Marriage is a *covenantal* institution. It is established by the exchange of vows, both implicit and explicit. These vows are three-way vows initially: man and wife under God. Relationships with children and parents are also involved. Because of the covenantal nature of these vows, their terms are subject to enforcement by external human institutions: family, church, and civil government. No one who violates these vows can legitimately escape the judgment of these earthly institutions, nor can he escape ultimate retribution (Gal. 5:19-21).

Adultery

Adultery is a straightforward denial of the legitimacy of God's covenantal yoke. It is a denial of permanent communion, a denial of binding contracts, and a denial of the permanence of God's grace in election. It is ultimately *a denial of the Trinity* — an assertion of the interpersonal unfaithfulness of the Persons of the Godhead. Adultery affirms the autonomy of man and the impermanence of man's institutions. It affirms that God's special love for His redeemed people is at bottom unpredictable and impermanent. In short, adultery affirms that Christ's love for His church is grounded in chance and lawlessness. *Adultery is a symbolic assertion of a radically false theology.* The ministry of the prophet Hosea was God's explicit and symbolic refutation of the theology of adultery.

Adultery disrupts the covenantal bonds of the family unit. It thwarts the proper administration of God's system of familistic capital. Based on mistrust, unfaithfulness, and a rejection of the restraints of verbal promises, adultery shatters the yoke of service. The result is predictable: the dissipation of familistic capital.

Vows are permanent. They cannot be revoked if they are made

to God. "If a man vow a vow unto the LORD, or swear an oath to bind his soul with a bond; he shall not break his word, he shall do according to all that proceedeth out of his mouth" (Num. 30:2). A woman's vow is binding 24 hours after her father (if she is single) or her husband has heard of it and has not revoked it (Num. 30:3-8). The vow of a widow or a divorced woman stands (Num. 30:9). Because of the covenantal nature of the vow to God, God holds the vow-taker responsible for the fulfillment of the vow. God is sovereign, and He holds men responsible.

Permanent or household slavery in the Old Testament was a vow taken voluntarily. The slave who wished to remain in his master's house beyond the sixth year, or beyond the jubilee year, could do so. The master drove an awl through the slave's ear and into the door (Deut. 15:17). It was a bloody symbol of a permanent relationship, even as the blood on the doorpost at the Passover was a sign of a family's permanent relationship with God (Ex. 12:7). The slave was no longer a chattel slave but an adopted son of the house.

Marriage involves the same bloody sign; the "tokens of virginity" of the Old Testament were almost certainly the bloody cloth of the wedding night, which was presented to the wife's father in order to protect her from the charge of premarital sexual activity made by a lying husband (Deut. 22:13-17). The cloth of verse 17 bore the mark of her virginity; it must have been blood. The blood of the circumcised male was also a covenantal sign of permanence.[4]

Time and Crime

Yoked beasts clearly *belong* to someone. The same is true of yoked marriage partners. They serve some master. The marriage is a covenant bond, metaphysically under God, but *ethically* under either Satan or God. The partners build for the future: a future under God or a future dominated by Satan. The yokeless beast is a wild beast; the family yoke domesticates each partner, rather like the yoke on beasts of burden.

The efforts of the marriage partners can be directed toward the *future*, for the family extends into the future through the children and the expansion of family capital. This future-oriented nature of the family adds incentives for thrift, careful planning, hard work, and

---

4. See Gary North, "The Marriage Supper of the Lamb," *Christianity and Civilization*, 4 (1985).

economic growth. Each partner can rely on the assistance of the other, as well as the compassion of the other in times of crisis. This frees up the minds of both partners, for each knows that the other is there to help. What would otherwise be "uneven plowing" by one is smoothed out by the effect of the "yoke": the family goes forward, day by day, despite the occasional failings of either of the partners. While yoked together, neither partner can stray far without the other; neither can go his or her own way without regard for the other.

One of the most eloquent affirmations of the social value of marriage comes from George Gilder. "The short-sighted outlook of poverty stems largely from the breakdown of family responsibilities among fathers. The lives of the poor, all too often, are governed by the rhythms of tension and release that characterize the sexual experience of young single men. . . . Civilized society is dependent upon the submission of the short-term sexuality of young men to the extended maternal horizons of women. This is what happens in monogamous marriage; the man disciplines his sexuality and extends it into the future through a woman's womb. The woman gives him access to his children, otherwise forever denied to him; and he gives her the product of his labor, otherwise dissipated on temporary pleasures. The woman gives him a unique link to the future and a vision of it; he gives her faithfulness and a commitment to a lifetime of hard work. If work effort is the first principle of overcoming poverty, marriage is the prime source of upwardly mobile work."[5]

Gilder also reports that when marriages fail, the now-unencumbered husband may revert to the lifestyle of singleness. "On the average, his income drops by one-third and he shows a far higher propensity for drink, drugs, and crime." Thus, he concludes, "The key to the intractable poverty of the hardcore American poor is the dominance of single and separated men in poor communities."[6] Crime and social pathology in general increase when family cohesion decreases. This has been documented in literally thousands of sociological studies.[7] The problem for the conventional social scientist is that there are no generally acceptable measures that the civil government can take that will increase the stability of the family. As

---

5. George Gilder, *Wealth and Poverty* (New York: Basic Books, 1981), p. 70.
6. *Ibid.*, p. 71.
7. Urie Bronfenbrenner, "Origins of Alienation," *Scientific American*, Vol. 231 (Aug. 1974).

political scientist James Wilson says, "I cannot imagine any collective action we could take consistent with our civil liberties that would restore a moral consensus . . ."[8]

There is one step, however, which could be taken without violating civil liberties. In fact, it would increase civil liberties by reducing the size of the State. It is the step which the politicians believe that they dare not consider, yet which must eventually be considered: the abolition of all forms of State welfare payments, especially aid to dependent children. This is the recommendation of Charles Murray, whose 1984 book, *Losing Ground*, reveals the extent of the moral and social bankruptcy of the Federal welfare programs. Murray makes clear what is taking place. The State is subsidizing immorality, and immorality is disrupting the society. In 1960, approximately 224,000 children in the United States were born to single mothers; in 1980, over 665,000 of these children were born.[9] This increase has been especially marked within the black community. From 1950 through 1963, just before the "Great Society's War on Poverty" began, black illegitimate births rose slowly from 17% of all black births to 23%. In 1980, a staggering 48% of all live births among blacks were to single women.[10] Furthermore, a growing proportion of all illegitimate children are being born to teenagers.[11] This, it should be pointed out, has taken place during the period in which compulsory "sex education" courses were being established in the government school systems.

In 1950, about 88% of white families consisted of husband-wife households, and about 78% of black families did. In a single year, 1968, the percentage for black families slipped from 72% to 69%, and in the next five years, it dropped another six percentage points. By the end of 1980, the proportion was down to 59%.[12] As Murray says, "a change of this magnitude is a demographic wonder, without precedent in the American experience."[13] "As of 1980, 65 percent of all poor blacks who were living in families were living in families headed by a single female. The parallel statistic for whites was 34 percent."[14]

---

8. James Q. Wilson, *Thinking About Crime* (New York: Basic Books, 1975), p. 206.

9. Charles Murray, *Losing Ground: American Social Policy, 1950-1980* (New York: Basic Books, 1984), pp. 125-26.

10. *Ibid.*, p. 126.

11. *Ibid.*, p. 127.

12. *Ibid.*, pp. 129-30.

13. *Ibid.*, p. 130.

14. *Ibid.*, p. 132.

What about low-income blacks—not just the hard-core poor? These are people with incomes equal to or up to 25% above the defined poverty level. "In 1959, low-income blacks lived in families very much like those of low-income whites and, for that matter, like those of middle- and upper-income persons of all races. Barely one in ten of the low-income blacks in families was living in a single-female family. By 1980, the 10 percent figure had become 44 percent." This was higher than the percentage common among poor whites. [15]

Murray's conclusion is eloquent, and it gets right to the point: the presence of long-term poverty is not primarily a function of family income. It is a function of morality, time perspective, and faith regarding economic causes and effects. "Let us suppose that you, a parent, could know that tomorrow your own child would be made an orphan. You have a choice. You may put your child with an extremely poor family, so poor that your child will be badly clothed and will indeed sometimes be hungry. But you also know that the parents have worked hard all their lives, will make sure your child goes to school and studies, and will teach your child that independence is a primary value. Or you may put your child with a family with parents who have never worked, will be incapable of overseeing your child's education—but who have plenty of food and good clothes, provided by others. If the choice about where one would put one's own child is as clear to you as it is to me, on what grounds does one justify support of a system that, indirectly but without doubt, makes the other choice for other children? The answer that 'What we really want is a world where that choice is not forced upon us' is no answer. We have tried to have it that way. We failed. Everything we know about why we failed tells us that more of the same will not make the dilemma go away." [16]

The defenders of modern socialism, or the welfare State, have closed their eyes for three generations or more to the testimony of the Bible, and also to the testimony of the statisticians. They cling to a demonic view of stewardship, with the pseudo-family of the State at the head of the financial household. The result has been the destruction of families and the productivity and social peace produced by the family.

---

15. *Idem.*
16. *Ibid.*, p. 233.

Binding Contracts and Economic Growth

Covenants are binding. If men refuse to accept this truth, the possibilities for economic development in a society are thereby reduced. The historic link between the biblical idea of binding covenants and the West's idea of binding contracts is obvious enough. The covenant of marriage supports the institution which was the first to implement the division of labor. Without the predictability associated with contracts, the division of labor is hampered. Contracts involve the sharing of the fruits of combined labor. Nowhere is this more apparent than in the family unit. The basis of the idea of a contract, like the idea of a covenant, is *personal faithfulness*. It begins with the Trinity, extends to the relationship between Christ and His church, undergirds the family, and makes long-term economic co-operation possible. The covenant is binding analogous to the way that a vow is binding. A contract, which does not have the same authority as a covenant or a vow to God, nevertheless is analogous. If the model of permanence for contracts, namely, the vow or the covenant, is denied true permanence, then how much less permanent are contracts!

When J. D. Unwin examined the relationship between monogamy and cultural development, he found that in every society that he studied, the absence of monogamy guaranteed the eventual stagnation or retrogression of that society. [17] The Bible provides us with the information concerning man that allows us to understand why such a relationship between monogamy and culture should exist. The promise of external blessings is held out to those societies that covenant themselves with God, and which enforce the terms of that covenant, biblical law. The archetypal symbol of the rejection of God's covenant is adultery. The old business rule is close to the truth: "A man who cheats on his wife will probably cheat on anybody." It may not hold true in every single instance of adultery by a businessman, but when a society accepts adultery as "business as usual," business will not long retain its character as an enterprise marked by binding contracts. Honest business will become increasingly unusual, and litigation costs will rise, as men seek to enforce contracts. This represents needless waste — needless from the point of view of the dominion covenant. Lawyers prosper and multiply — a sign of a collapsing culture.

---

17. J. D. Unwin, *Sex and Culture* (New York: Oxford University Press, 1934). Cf. Unwin, "Monogamy as a Condition of Social Energy," *The Hibbert Journal*, XXV (July 1927); reprinted in *The Journal of Christian Reconstruction*, IV (Winter 1977-78).

Sowell on Contracts

Thomas Sowell has pointed to the importance of rigid, formal, and enforceable rules regarding marriage. His insights are brilliant. "Society itself may need to guarantee that certain relationships will remain rigid and inviolate in all but the most extraordinary circumstances. Much socially beneficial prospective action will not take place, or will not take place to the same extent, without rigid guarantees. The heavy investment of emotion, time, and resources necessary to raise a child would be less likely in a society where the child might at any moment, for any capricious reason, be taken away and never seen again. Such behavior is rejected not only for its retrospective injustice but also for its *prospective* effect on parental behavior. Not only will the state forebear from such behavior; it will use severe sanctions against private individuals who do such things (kidnappers). This rigid legal framework of parent-child relationships provides the protective setting within which the most flexible kinds of parent-child social relationships may develop."[18]

Sowell immediately proceeds to the questions of property and ownership. "Similar considerations apply across a spectrum of other social arrangements, particularly those involving long and large individual investments of efforts for prospective personal and social benefits. Property rights introduce rigidities into the use of vast amounts of many resources—by excluding all but the legal owner(s) from a serious voice in most of the decisions made about the disposition of the resources—on the assumption that such losses as are occasioned by this rigidity are more than offset by the gains in prospective behavior by people acting under these guarantees."[19] There is a socially indivisible link between rules protecting the integrity of the family and rules protecting private property. The civil government must enforce these rules.

Christians who are familiar with the commandment against coveting should understand this important link between family and property. "Thou shalt not covet thy neighbour's house, thou shalt not covet thy neighbour's wife, nor his manservant, nor his maidservant, nor his ox, nor his ass, nor any thing that is thy neighbour's" (Ex. 20:17). Socialism is as much a threat against the family's integrity as

18. Thomas Sowell, *Knowledge and Decisions* (New York: Basic Books, 1980), p. 31.
19. *Idem.*

adultery is a threat to the integrity of the free market's contractual order.

Sowell's analysis is superb. If the following paragraph were understood and implemented by societies that regard themselves as Christian—and even by societies that do not regard themselves as Christian—the world would prosper economically. Writes Sowell: "Someone who is going to work for many years to have his own home wants some fairly rigid assurance that the house will in fact belong to him—that he cannot be dispossessed by someone who is physically stronger, better armed, or more ruthless, or who is deemed more 'worthy' by political authorities. Rigid assurances are needed that changing fashions, mores, and power relationships will not suddenly deprive him of his property, his children, or his life. Informal relationships which flourish in a society do so within the protection of formal laws on property, ownership, kidnapping, murder, and other basic matters on which people want rigidity rather than continuously negotiable or modifiable relationships."[20]

Libertarian Contracts

A major theoretical dilemma for the modern libertarian or anarcho-capitalist is the problem of the lifetime contract. Each man is seen as the absolute owner of his own body. He therefore can legitimately make contracts with other men that involve his own labor services. *He is absolutely sovereign over his own person.* This is the theoretical foundation of almost all libertarian thought. "The central core of the libertarian creed, then, is to establish the absolute right to private property of every man: first, in his own body, and second, in the previous unused natural resources which he first transforms by his labor. These two axioms, the right of self-ownership and the right to 'homestead,' establish the complete set of principles of the libertarian system."[21]

But then there arises the problem of slavery: *the lifetime contract.* Man, the absolute sovereign agent, seems to be able to *sign away his autonomy* in such a contract. To say that man cannot legitimately sign such a contract—that such a contract is not morally or legally binding—is to say that there are limits placed on this autonomous sovereignty of man. This is the libertarian's version of the old ques-

---

20. *Ibid.*, p. 32.
21. Murray N. Rothbard, *For a New Liberty: The Libertarian Manifesto* (rev. ed.; New York: Collier, 1978), p. 39.

tion: "Is God powerful enough to make a rock so heavy that He cannot lift it?" The libertarians ask: "Is man sovereign enough to make a contract so binding that he cannot break it?" The theist is not particularly bothered by the real-life applications of the God-rock paradox, but the libertarian faces several paradoxical problems that are only too real. First, how long is a contract really binding, if lifetime contracts are illegitimate? Forty years? Four years? Four weeks? When does the absolute sovereignty of a man to make a binding contract come into conflict with the absolute sovereignty of a man not to be bound by any permanent transfer of his own will? Lifetime slavery is immoral and illegal in a libertarian framework. A libertarian must argue that such a contract should always be legally unenforceable. But what about a ten-year baseball contract? Second, and more to the point, what about marriage?

Murray Rothbard, the most consistent and innovative of the libertarian economists, has stated his position with his usual clarity: ". . . a man cannot permanently transfer his will, even though he may transfer much of his services and his property. As mentioned above, a man may not agree to permanent bondage by contracting to work for another man for the rest of his life. He might change his mind at a later date, and then he cannot, in a free market, be compelled to continue working thereafter. Because a man's self-ownership over his will is inalienable, he cannot, on the unhampered market, be compelled to continue an arrangement whereby he submits his will to the orders of another, even though he might have agreed to this arrangement previously."[22] In the footnote to this final sentence, he adds: "In other words, he cannot make enforceable contracts binding his future personal actions. . . . This applies also to *marriage contracts*. Since human self-ownership cannot be alienated, a man or a woman, on a free market, could not be compelled to continue in marriage if he or she no longer desired to do so. This is regardless of any previous agreement. Thus, a marriage contract, like an individual labor contract, is, on an unhampered market, terminable at the will of *either one* of the parties."[23]

The libertarian concept of absolute self-ownership as the foundation of all economic exchanges sinks into oblivion when it hits the

---

22. Murray N. Rothbard, *Man, Economy, and State* (New York: New York University Press, [1962] 1975), I, p. 142. (I am using the original Van Nostrand edition, which was printed in two volumes.)

23. *Ibid.*, I, pp. 441-42; footnote 35. Emphasis in original.

libertarian concept of the illegitimacy of lifetime contracts. The libertarian's universe could not bind a man to perform any sort of future labor service. It certainly could not require him to love, cherish, and support a recently abandoned wife. She may have given him her youth in the days of her beauty—her "high-yield capital" stage, or her "high exchange value capital" stage—but once this capital is gone, she is without legal protection. Thus, the *radical impermanence of libertarian contracts* would threaten the social fabric of any society so shortsighted as to adopt this utopian philosophy as its foundation. The *future-orientation* provided by the safety of permanent vows in a godly society could not exist in a consistently libertarian society. There would be no institutional means of enforcing the terms of covenants, and this would eventually reduce men's confidence in the enforceability of shorter-run contracts. A society which rejects the binding nature of *covenants* will not long retain the economic blessings of binding *contracts*.

Conclusion

The *protection* of man's life, wife, and property is what a biblical social order offers. The woman is protected, too. The time perspective of such a society will be longer term than a social order (disorder) characterized by adultery, divorce, illegitimate births, and single-parent households. Whenever a social order is marked by successful attacks against private property and also by the removal of stringent sanctions against adultery, the social order in question has departed from the standards set forth in the Bible. It has adopted an anti-biblical religion, whatever the official pronouncements of its leaders, including its church leaders.

A survey of 950 religious teachers and counsellors which was conducted by the University of Houston in 1984 revealed that of the 500 who responded to the questionnaire, 40% did not believe that premarital heterosexual sex is immoral, and that 87% believed that adultery should not be a crime.[24] When the religious and political leaders of a society begin to wink at adultery, they will soon enough wink at coercive wealth redistribution, confiscatory taxation, and

---

24. Associated Press story, *Tyler Morning Telegraph* (Dec. 28, 1984). Sixteen percent said that adultery is not morally wrong, 9% were uncertain, and 75% said it is morally wrong. But almost none of them thinks the civil government has any role in punishing adulterers. Only 53% said that the legal system ought to limit marriage to people of opposite sexes.

the compulsory retraining of children by statist planners. In fact, we can expect to see these leaders not only wink at such invasions of both the family and property, but also actively pursue these policies. There are too many adulterers in the highest seats of civil government and in the pulpit.

In the sixth commandment, we are told that man's life is sacrosanct, for man is made in God's image. In the seventh, we are told that the marriage covenant is also sacrosanct, for it reflects the covenantal bond of Christ with His church, and even the covenantal bond within the trinity.

The yoke of co-operative service necessarily involves a hierarchy: husbands possess lawful (though biblically specified) authority over their wives. But this possession is mutual, Paul tells us: the man's body belongs to the wife, and her body belongs to him (I Cor. 7:4). The husband's authority is therefore limited. Each of the partners belongs to God, whose ownership is absolute. But God's ultimate authority is reflected in the husband's authority. This hierarchy reflects the hierarchy of God the Father over God the Son. Thus, the seventh commandment parallels the second: there must be authority, hierarchy, and obedience.

8

THE RIGHTS OF PRIVATE PROPERTY

Thou shalt not steal (Ex. 20:15).

It has long been recognized by Christian commentators that the biblical case for private property rests more heavily on this passage than on any other passage in the Bible. Individuals are prohibited by biblical law from forcibly appropriating the fruits of another man's labor (which includes his ideas), or his inheritance. The civil government is required by the Bible to defend a social order based on the rights of private ownership. The various laws requiring restitution that are found in Exodus 22 explicitly limit the State in its imposition of sanctions against thieves, but there can be no doubt that it is the civil government which is required to impose them.

Rights of ownership mean that God transfers to specific men and organizations the sole and exclusive ability to use specific property for certain kinds of ends, and the State is to *exclude* others from the unauthorized use of such property. Property *rights* therefore refer to *legal immunities* from interference by others in the administration of property. The duties associated with dominion are more readily and effectively achieved by individuals and societies through adherence to the private property system, which is one reason why the Bible protects private ownership. *Private property is basic to effective dominion.*

The only conceivable biblical argument against this interpretation of the commandment against theft would be an assertion that the only valid form of ownership is ownership by the State, meaning control by bureaucracies established by civil law. But to argue along these lines demands evidence that the Bible, both Old Testament and New Testament, authorized the public (State) ownership of all goods. There is not a shred of evidence for such a view, and massive evidence against it. The tenth commandment prohibits coveting the property of a *neighbor,* which is plain enough. The biblical social

order is a social order which acknowledges and defends the rights —
legal immunities — of private property. This prohibition binds individuals and institutions, including the State.

God's Ownership, Man's Personal Stewardship

The foundation of property rights is the ultimate ownership of all
things by God, the Creator. God owns the whole world. "For every
beast of the forest is mine, and the cattle upon a thousand hills. I
know all the fowls of the mountains: and the wild beasts of the field
are mine. If I were hungry, I would not tell thee: for the world is
mine, and the fulness thereof" (Ps. 50:10-12). God's sovereignty is
absolute. The biblical concept of property rests on this definition of
God's authority over the creation. The Bible provides us with data
concerning God's delegation of responsibility to men — as individuals
and as members of collective associations — but all human sovereignty, including property rights, must be understood as *limited,
delegated, and covenantal* in nature.

Christ's parable of the talents presents the sovereignty of God in
terms of the analogy of a *loan* from a lord to his servants. The servants
have an obligation to increase the value of the capital entrusted to
them. They are directly responsible to their lord, who is the real
owner of the capital. *Ownership* is therefore *stewardship*. Men's rights of
ownership are delegated, covenantal rights. God's "loan" must be repaid with capital gains, or at the very least, with interest (Matt.
25:27). Each man is fully responsible before God for the lawful and
profitable administration of God's capital, which includes both spiritual capital and economic capital (Luke 12:48). This is one of Christ's
"pocketbook parables," and while it was designed to illustrate God's absolute sovereignty over the affairs of men, it nevertheless conveys a secondary meaning, namely, the legitimate rights of private ownership.

God distributed to Adam and Eve the resources of the world.
They were made covenantally responsible for the care and expansion of this capital base when God established His dominion covenant with them. This same covenant was reestablished with Noah
and his family (Gen. 9:1-7). In the originally sinless condition of
Adam and Eve, this initial distribution of the earth's resources could
be made by God in terms of an *original harmony of man's interests*.[1] This

---

1. Gary North, *The Dominion Covenant: Genesis* (Tyler, Texas: Institute for Christian Economics, 1982), ch. 8: "The God-Designed Harmony of Interests."

harmony included *hierarchy*, for Eve was functionally subordinate to Adam (though not ethically inferior).[2] The God-designed harmony of interests was never an equalitarian relationship. It is not equalitarian in the post-Fall world. The church, as the body of Christ, is similarly described in terms of an organic unity which is supposed to be harmonious, with each "organ" essential to the proper functioning of the whole, yet with each performing separate tasks (I Cor. 12). All are under Christ, the head of the church (Eph. 5:23).

God's universe is orderly. *There is a God-ordained regularity in economic affairs.* There is a predictable, lawful relationship between personal industriousness and wealth, between laziness and poverty. "How long wilt thou sleep, O sluggard? When wilt thou arise out of thy sleep? Yet a little sleep, a little slumber, a little folding of the hands to sleep: So shall thy poverty come as one that travelleth, and thy want as an armed man" (Prov. 6:9-11). "Wealth gotten by vanity shall be diminished: but he that gathereth by labour shall increase" (Prov. 13:11). This applies to individuals, families, corporations, and nations. Not every godly man or organization will inevitably prosper economically, in time and on earth, and not every evil man will lose his wealth during his lifetime (Luke 16:19-31), but in the aggregate, there will be a significant correlation between *covenantal faithfulness* and *external prosperity.* In the long run, the wealth of the wicked is laid up for the just (Prov. 13:22). This same principle applies to national, cultural, and racial groups (Deut. 8). Covenantal law governs the sphere of economics. Wealth flows to those who work hard, deal honestly with their customers, and who honor God. To argue, as the Marxists and socialists do, that wealth flows in a free market social order towards those who are ruthless, dishonest, and blinded by greed, is to deny the Bible's explicit teachings concerning the nature of economic life. It is a denial of the covenantal lawfulness of the creation.

The Theology of the Welfare State

Critics of the capitalist system have inflicted great damage on those societies that have accepted such criticisms as valid. Men have concluded that the private property system is rigged against the poor and weak, forcing them into positions of permanent servitude. Historically, on the contrary, *no social order has provided more opportunities for upward social mobility than capitalism.* The remarkable advance of

2. *Ibid.*, pp. 91-92.

numerous immigrant groups, but especially of Eastern European Jews, in the United States from 1880 to 1950, is historically unprecedented.[3] Today, the policies of the welfare State are making lifetime dependents out of a substantial minority of citizens.[4] The modern welfare system is deeply flawed, not simply because it uses coercion to take income from the employed, but because it destroys the will of the recipients to escape from the welfare system.[5] The politics of welfare is also leading to class conflict. George Gilder's words are eloquent in this regard: "A program to lift by transfers and preferences the incomes of less diligent groups is politically divisive — and very unlikely — because it incurs the bitter resistance of the real working class. In addition, such an effort breaks the psychological link between effort and reward, which is crucial to long-run upward mobility. Because effective work consists not in merely fulfilling the requirements of labor contracts, but in 'putting out' with alertness and emotional commitment, workers have to understand and feel deeply that what they are given depends on what they give — that they must supply work in order to demand goods. Parents and schools must inculcate this idea in their children both by instruction and example. Nothing is more deadly to achievement than the belief that effort will not be rewarded, that the world is a bleak and discriminatory place in which only the predatory and the specially preferred can get ahead. Such a view in the home discourages the work effort in school that shapes earnings capacity afterward. As with so many aspects of human performance, work effort begins in family experiences, and its sources can be best explored through an examination of family structure. Indeed, after work the second principle of upward mobility is the maintenance of monogamous marriage and family."[6]

Biblical Cause and Effect

The biblical perspective on marriage, like the biblical perspective

---

3. Cf. Thomas Sowell, *Race and Economics* (New York: David McKay Co., 1975), Pt. II.

4. George Gilder, *Wealth and Poverty* (New York: Basic Books, 1981), chaps. 6-13.

5. Charles Murray, *Losing Ground: American Social Policy, 1950-1980* (New York: Simon & Schuster, 1984).

6. Gilder, *Wealth and Poverty*, pp. 68-69. Gilder's book is second only to Murray's *Losing Ground* as a study of the welfare State and its destruction of the avenues of private economic advancement. It is not equally good on questions of fiscal and monetary policy. For a critique of Gilder's recommended monetary policies, see Gary North, *The Last Train Out* (Ft. Worth, Texas: American Bureau of Economic Research, 1983), pp. 9-13.

on the foundations of economic growth, points to both ideas: the relationship between *work and reward*, and the central importance of the *family bond*. Men are told to have faith in the work-reward relationship, which encourages them to take risks and invest time and effort to improving their own personal work habits. The Bible tells us that such efforts will not go unrewarded, whether on earth or in heaven (I Cor. 3). The habits of discipline, thrift, long hours of effort, investment in work skills, and the instruction of children in this philosophy of life will not be wasted, will not be "capital down the drain." On the contrary, the Bible teaches that *such an approach to life is the very essence of the dominion covenant.*

When philosophies contrary to the philosophy of capital accumulation and private economic dominion are encountered, Christians should recognize them for what they are. When men are taught that the capitalist system is rigged against them, that they have a legal and moral right to welfare payments, and that those who live well as a result of their own labor, effort, and forecasting skills are immoral and owe the bulk of their wealth to the poor, we must recognize the source of these teachings: the pits of hell. This is Satan's counter-philosophy, which is expressly intended to thwart godly men in their efforts to subdue the earth to the glory of God. This radically anti-biblical philosophy is not simply a matter of intellectual error; it is a *conscious philosophy of destruction*, a systematically anti-biblical framework which is calculated to undercut successful Christians by means of false guilt and paralysis. That such teachings are popular among Christian intellectuals in the latter years of the twentieth century only testifies to further their abysmal ignorance — indeed, their judicial blindness (Matt. 13:14-15) — concerning biblical ethics and economic theory. Christians have adopted the politics of envy from the secular humanists, especially in college and seminary classrooms. We live in an age of guilt-manipulators, and some of them use Scripture to their evil ends.[7]

Theft and Market Value

Christian commentators have, from earliest times, understood that the prohibition of theft, like the prohibition against covetousness, serves as a defense of private property. Theft is an autono-

---

7. David Chilton, *Productive Christians in an Age of Guilt-Manipulators: A Biblical Response to Ronald Sider* (3rd ed.; Tyler, Texas: Institute for Christian Economics, 1985).

mous, willful act of economic redistribution, and therefore it is a denial of the legitimacy and reliability of God's moral and economic law-order.

The immediate economic effect of widespread theft in society is the creation of insecurity. This lowers the market value of goods, since people are less willing to bid high prices for items that are likely to be stolen. Uncertainty is increased, which requires that people invest a greater proportion of their assets in buying protection services or devices. Scarce economic resources are shifted from production and consumption to crime fighting. This clearly lowers per capita productivity and therefore per capita wealth, at least among law-abiding people. Theft leads to wasted resources.

The internal restraints on theft that are provided by godly preaching and upbringing help to reduce crime, thereby increasing per capita wealth within the society. *Godly preaching and active church courts against theft* are therefore forms of *capital investment* for the society as a whole (what the economists call "social overhead capital"), for they release scarce economic resources that would otherwise have been spent on the protection of private and public property. Such preaching and church court actions also reduce the necessary size of the civil government, which is important in reducing the growth of unwarranted State power.

What is true about the reduction of theft is equally true concerning the strengthening of men's commitment to private property in general. When property rights are carefully *defined* and *enforced*, the value of property increases. Allen and Alchian, in their widely used economics textbook, have commented on this aspect of property rights. "For market prices to guide allocation of goods, there must be an incentive for people to express and to respond to offers. If it is costly to reveal bids and offers and to negotiate and make exchanges, the gains from exchange might be offset. If each person speaks a different language [as at the tower of Babel—G.N.], if thievery is rampant, or if contracts are likely to be dishonored, then negotiation, transaction, and policing costs will be so high that fewer market exchanges will occur. If *property rights* in goods are weaker, ill defined, or vague, their reallocation is likely to be guided by lower offers and bids. Who would offer as much for a coat likely to be stolen?"[8] The

8. Armen A. Alchian and William R. Allen, *University Economics: Elements of Inquiry* (3rd ed.; Belmont, California: Wadsworth, 1972), p. 141.

authors believe that the *higher market value* of goods that are protected by strong ownership rights spurs individuals to seek laws that will strengthen private-property rights. Furthermore, to the extent that private-property rights exist, the *power of the civil government* to control the uses of goods is thereby *decreased*. This, unfortunately, has led politicians and jurists to resist the spread of secured private-property rights.[9]

There is no question that a society which honors the terms of the commandment against theft will eventually enjoy greater per capita wealth. Such a society rewards honest people with greater possessions. This is as it should be. A widespread hostility to theft, especially from the point of view of self-government (self-restraint), allows men to make more accurate decisions concerning what they want to buy, and therefore what they ought to produce in order to offer something in exchange for the items they want. Again, quoting Allen and Alchian: "The more expensive is protection against theft, the more common is thievery. Suppose that thievery of coats were relatively easy. People would be willing to pay only a lower price for coats. The lower market price of coats will understate the value of coats, for it will not include the value to the thief. If the thief were induced to rent or purchase a used coat, the price of coats would more correctly represent their value to society. It follows that the cheaper the policing costs, the greater the efficiency with which values of various uses or resources are revealed. The more likely something is to be stolen, the less of it that will be produced."[10] When communities set up "neighborhood watches" to keep an eye on each other's homes, and to call the police when something suspicious is going on, the value of property in the community is increased, or at least the value of the property on the streets where the neighbors are helping each other. By lowering the benefits to criminals, property owners increase the value of their goods.

A Critic Responds

When I referred to the passage by Alchian and Allen in my essay in *Wealth and Poverty*, a collection of four Christian views (the book's cover says) on economics, the lone essay which defended the unhampered free market, one of the anti-market respondents was

---

9. *Idem.*
10. *Ibid.*, p. 239.

horrified. In the name of Jesus, he attacked the idea of the biblical sanction of private property, and my defense of the economics of crime prevention, with the following line of argumentation: "The less thievery there is, the more the value of private property increases and the less able the poor are to buy it. In capitalism, the more 'moral' a people are, the more the poor are oppressed."[11] He is not joking. He expects us to take him seriously. The culprit is capitalism, in Gish's view. It is capitalism which hurts the poor, even when crime goes down, since capitalism lowers the value of goods when crime goes up. Less thievery means that the poor are exploited in capitalism. If this is the best that Christian communalists and egalitarians can come up with in their ideological struggle against private ownership, then the intellectual battle is just about over.

I cannot resist citing Oscar Wilde's definition of a cynic: "a man who knows the price of everything and the value of nothing." This is Mr. Gish's problem. What Mr. Gish does not understand is that thieves reduce the value of *everyone's* property, both rich and poor, but especially the poor who live in ghettos where crime is rampant. Gish's comment reveals that he has failed to understand the economic reasoning behind Allen and Alchian's conclusion. It is not that *prices* necessarily go up when crime is reduced (although they may), thereby excluding the poor; it is that the *value* of goods goes up, including the value of property owned by the poor. The poor get richer, not poorer. Gish confuses increases in the value of property with increases in the cost of living. Mr. Gish is so red-faced in his hatred of capitalism that he cannot understand a simple economic argument. If the poor now enjoy property that is worth more, why are they oppressed under capitalism? They aren't, *unless they are eaten up by envy*, and hate to see the rich also get richer—hate it with such intensity that they would give up their own increases in order to tear down the rich.

The decrease in the value of property as a result of theft would also occur in a socialist economy. Official prices might not change— who knows what a socialist planning board might do to prices in response to crime?—but the value of goods would drop. This has nothing to do with the structure of a particular economy; it has everything to do with the effects of crime on people's assessment of

---

11. Art Gish, "A Decentralist Response," in Robert Clouse (ed.), *Wealth and Poverty: Four Christian Views on Economics* (Downers Grove, Illinois: InterVarsity Press, 1984), p. 75.

the costs of holding goods. If criminals are raising the costs of holding goods, then the value of the goods falls. In other words, *costs of ownership* rise, so the *value of the items owned* drops. If I own an item that was worth five ounces of gold before the crime wave hit, but it now costs me three ounces of gold a year to store it or otherwise protect it, the net value of that item to me will drop in my calculations. I may be willing to sell it today for two ounces of gold, or even less. Its *price* has dropped only because its *value* to me and to potential buyers has *dropped first*. This is so incredibly simple that only a professional capitalism-hater could miss it. Mr. Gish missed it.

Similarly, if the crime wave stops, and it costs me only an ounce of silver to store it or otherwise defend it—the same storage fee that I paid before the crime wave hit—its value to me will rise. Now I may not be willing to sell it for under five ounces of gold. Others may offer me five ounces because they, too, see its increased net value to them. The crime wave is over. The price rises because the costs of ownership have fallen. Prices "return to normal," meaning closer to those that prevailed before the crime wave, because *value* has "returned to normal."

The wealth of the poor increases. The market value of the items they own also goes up. It may even go up more, since the poor may have been the targets of the criminals even more than the rich. In any case, the cost of defending their goods, proportional to the market value of those goods, was probably far higher during the crime wave than the protection costs for the rich were, proportional to the value of their goods. The poor probably will experience a more rapid percentage increase in net worth if theft goes down. The poor suffered more when the crime wave hit, so they gain more when it finally is reduced. This is so incredibly simple that only a professional capitalism-hater could miss it. Mr. Gish missed it.

The increased value of private property in a society which prosecutes theft would also take place in response to preaching against theft, if hearers take seriously the sermons. Gish continually moralizes against theft (theft by ruling elites) in the passage immediately preceeding his outraged protest against capitalism. He blames capitalism for raising the cost of living to poor people whenever theft is reduced. Implicitly, he must be arguing that under socialism (or local communal ownership) reducing theft will not lead to higher prices.

Value and Price

Let us consider the effects of a wave of theft on market prices. If we understand what is going on in this scenario, we probably have a firm grasp of economic theory. It can serve as a good example. Mr. Gish may even understand it. Under capitalism, any *additional* self-government and self-restraint against theft will tend *initially* to raise the market price of goods above which prevailed prior to the wave of thefts. So will any cost-effective increases in the civil government's war against thieves. Let us look at the sequence of events.

First, the wave of thefts begins. Assume that it is national in scope and horrendous. People are afraid to leave their homes. They reduce the number of shopping trips. They put more money in the bank, since banks are perceived to be safer against bank robbers than homes are against burglars. In other words, they decide to buy fewer stealable goods. Demand for consumer goods therefore drops.

On the other hand, the supply of available goods *initially* rises. Stolen goods that would not have been offered for sale by their owners at the older, higher prices, begin to enter the resale markets. These goods carry price discounts. Honest producers of goods must compete by lowering their prices. Production of new goods drops. New goods producers begin to go into bankruptcy and start selling goods at huge discounts. Then, after they sell off inventories, some of them stop producing.

In short, prices drop because the value of goods has dropped. Why has the value of goods dropped? Because the *costs of ownership have risen.* If you raise costs, you should expect reduced demand. This is what we do see: the demand for consumer goods drops. This is especially true for poor people, who are more vulnerable to theft and violence in their communities. The value of their presently owned goods is drastically reduced because the costs of ownership for them have been drastically increased.

As I have already pointed out, Mr. Gish is not used to this sort of economic reasoning, so he resorted to his knee-jerk policy of criticizing capitalism for the evils of both increased crime and decreased crime. In good times and bad times, capitalism is evil. He is not alone in his hostility to capitalism. It is the characteristic feature of literati everywhere.[12]

---

12. Ludwig von Mises, *The Anti-Capitalist Mentality* (Princeton, New Jersey: Van Nostrand, 1956).

Falling prices are not the end of the story. *Second*, prices subsequently start to rise, because buyers can no longer locate sellers of new goods. Too many sellers have gone out of business. The burglars hit them, too. The costs of production rose for them, since producers are owners, too. Furthermore, thieves find that owners have bought burglar alarms, locks, and guard dogs. The costs of being a burglar also rise, so there is less burglary. The availability of stolen goods drops. The initial discounts disappear. Stolen goods start to command higher prices. Fewer goods are bought and sold, but for those necessities that do remain on the shelves, their prices will be much higher. *Consumer dollars will be chasing a smaller number of goods*, so prices of these goods tend to rise. If the crime wave persists, prices of goods actually brought to market rise higher than they had been before, since fewer goods are available. Most people continue to be worse off as a result of the crime wave.

We need to ask ourselves: How are poor people benefited if prices are pushed *initially* lower by criminal behavior (reduced demand coupled with lower prices for stolen goods)? How are they benefited when the uncertainties associated with theft must be dealt with? What benefit is the high rate of theft in, say, New York City's black ghetto, Harlem? I have visited apartments in Harlem, with their expensive doors and intricate locks. It is profitable for sellers of anti-burglary devices, but not for any other law-abiding citizen. Prices of other consumer goods are initially lowered because of money that must be spent on locks, burglar alarms, and insurance. But they do not remain low. Buyers need to lure sellers into high-risk markets where theft is common. People in Harlem wind up having to pay far higher prices than in other areas of New York City because costs of doing business are high (you might get killed), and it is expensive to lure sellers into the area. Consumer choices are drastically limited; there are no supermarkets in Harlem; only small "mom and pop" stores that issue credit and know their customers. Harlem's problem is not capitalism; Harlem's problem is that too many criminals and people with short-run perspectives live (and prey) there.[13]

What if the crime wave ends? We now come to phase *three*. There will still be an increase in prices, as buyers seek to lure back potential

---

13. On short-run perspectives in black ghettos and the grim effects, see Edward Banfield, *The Unheavenly City: The Nature and Future of Our Urban Crisis* (Boston: Little, Brown, 1970), pp. 53-54, 124-28.

sellers. *Initially,* prices will rise, but they will not rise as high as they would have risen *had the crime wave not come to an end.* It is this phase of the economic process that Gish singles out and criticizes: the recovery phase. He blames capitalism for high prices. But he ignores phase four.

Fourth, if the criminals are kept out of the crime business, the high prices being offered by buyers will lure manufacturers back into the markets. Manufacturers are given accurate signals about true consumer demand. As they target specific markets and their output increases, prices will again fall back closer to where they had been prior to the crime wave. Never forget: *producers need accurate signals concerning true consumer demand.* This is what the free market gives them. Prices enable producers to assess more accurately the value in the marketplace of all scarce resources. They can then make better decisions about production.

This is what the critics of capitalism simply will not admit: that producers respond to higher consumer prices by producing more goods and services to meet the new demand, unless the costs of production rise as fast or faster. If it becomes safer to own goods, and people want to buy additional goods, then prices may rise initially. But this is not the end of the story, except in books written by socialists and free market critics. The question is: What happens next? What happens next in a free market society is greater output of the newly demanded goods. This new production tends to *lower* consumer prices.

Socialism's War Against Price Signals

We might ask Mr. Gish: What would be the result of similar self-restraint or civil government restraint against theft in a socialist society which had previously been hit with a crime wave? If government bureaucrats set most prices (price ceilings), and they keep prices fixed in both the crime wave and the recovery phase (which is likely, since they are probably as ignorant of market pricing as Mr. Gish is), then the ethics-induced increased *value* of consumer goods will not send a *price* signal to producers to produce more goods. They will not respond rapidly to the new conditions of higher value for goods because the bureaucrats hold down official (legal) prices.

True, citizens who no longer are victimized by thieves are benefited. Thus, there is a net social benefit in socialist societies (as in all societies) from a reduction in theft. But far from this crime reduction's leading to an indirect benefit for the poor, it leads nowhere in particular in the official, State-controlled markets. The market value of goods rises in the black market, where prices more closely match true value to buyers and sellers, but not in the State-controlled markets. Only to the extent that poor people have greater skills in entering the black market will poor people be favored by the indirect economic effects of a reduction in theft.

In all likelihood, the poorest members of society will not be well-informed black marketeers. Thus, the reduction of theft by private individuals in a socialist economy tends to augment the flow of consumer goods flowing into an illegal market which is dominated by people with specialized skills in illegal bargaining. The primary beneficiaries are those people who trade in the illegal markets. This is the curse of all socialist economies: those people who become dependent on the State to deliver the goods become the victims of bureaucratic incompetence, and those who ignore the official markets and who enter black markets become the winners. It is a good lesson in economics. (I am sure my critic's answer would be that socialist governments ought to pass more laws against black markets.)[14]

Conclusion

We want sellers to respond to our offers for goods or services. At the same time, we as producers want to know what buyers are willing and able to pay for our goods and services. The better everyone's knowledge of the markets he deals in, the fewer the resources necessary for advertising, negotiating, and guessing about the future. These "released" resources can then be devoted to producing goods and services to satisfy wants that would otherwise have gone unsatisfied. The lower our transaction costs, in other words, the more wealth we can devote to the purchase and sale of the items involved in the transactions.

One transaction cost is the defense of property against theft or fraud. God therefore steps in and offers us a "free good": an inescapable system of punishment. To the extent that criminals and potential criminals believe that God really does punish criminal behavior, both on earth and in heaven, their costs of operation go up.

---

14. The economic ignorance that underlies the arguments of my critic is monumental. Yet such ignorance is representative of the published books and essays of "socially concerned," Christian college-educated, seminary-trained social thinkers in the American and British evangelical community in the 1980's.

When the price of something rises, other things being equal, less of it will be demanded. What if we can raise the "price" of crime? Less criminal behavior will be the result of a widespread belief in God's judgments, both temporal and final. *God raises the risks to thieves.* When the commandment against theft is preached, and when both the preachers and the hearers believe in the God who has announced His warning against theft, then we can expect less crime and greater per capita wealth in that society. God's criminal justice system is flawless, and it is also inescapable, so it truly is a free good—a gift from God which is a sign of His grace. *This is one aspect of the grace of law.*[15] It leads to increased wealth for those who respect His laws.

Theft at the Ballot Box

We have dealt so far primarily with the question of criminal behavior by private individuals or organized criminal societies. But the economic analysis that applies to theft by private individuals also applies to theft by the civil government. The commandment against theft does not read: "Thou shalt not steal, except by majority vote." We need to have private-property rights respected not just by criminals, but also by individual citizens who find that they can extract wealth from others by means of State power. Furthermore, private property rights must be respected by profit-seeking businesses that would otherwise petition the State for economic assistance: tariffs, import quotas, below-market interest rate government loans, and so forth. To violate this principle is to call for the so-called "corporate State," another form of the welfare State—fascism, monopoly capitalism, or whatever.[16] Whenever such a system has been constructed,

15. Ernest F. Kevan, *The Grace of Law: A Study in Puritan Theology* (Grand Rapids, Michigan: Baker Book House, [1976] 1983). (I am going by the book's title page; the cover says *A Study of Puritan Theology.*)
16. An example of just such a proposal for the corporate State is a highly touted and well-reviewed book by Robert B. Reich, *The Next American Frontier* (New York: Times Books, 1983). The author recognizes the evils of the hidden subsidies (Chapter 9), but his solution is for more direct collusion between industry and State. A similar book is Felix G. Rohatyn, *The Twenty-Year Century: Essays on Economics and Public Finance* (New York: Random House, 1983).
   For examples of the close alliance between monopoly capitalists and the Communists, see Antony Sutton, *Wall Street and the Bolshevik Revolution* (New Rochelle, New York: Arlington House, 1974); Joseph Finder, *Red Carpet* (New York: Holt, Rinehart, Winston, 1983); Charles Levinson, *Vodka Cola* (London: Gordon & Cremenosi, 1978).
   On the relationship between monopoly capitalists and the Nazi movement, see Antony Sutton, *Wall Street and the Rise of Hitler* (Seal Beach, California: 76 Press,

it has led to reduced productivity and an increase in bureaucracy. The politicians are simply not competent enough to plan for an entire economy.[17] To promote such a system of State planning and protection of industry is an illegitimate use of the ballot box, meaning democratic pressure politics.

Property and Voting

Let us consider an example which has been debated from the Puritan revolution of the 1640's until today: *the property qualification for voting*. At the Putney Debates of Cromwell's New Model Army in 1647, Ireton, Cromwell's son-in-law, debated Rainsborough, the representative of the democratic faction, the Levellers. (The Levellers were not communists, but they were committed to a far wider franchise. The communists in the English Revolution were the Diggers, who called themselves the "True Levellers."[18]) Rainsborough argued that since all men are under the laws of a nation, they deserve a voice in the affairs of civil government. Ireton countered with a ringing defense of property rights. A man must have some stake in society, meaning property to defend, if he is to be entrusted with the right to vote. Men without permanent interests in the society — property, in other words — are too dangerous when handed the power of civil government. The property qualification is crucial to preserve society in a democratic order. "And if we shall go to take away this, we shall plainly go to take away all property and interest that any man hath either in land by inheritance, or in estate by possession, or in anything else. . . ."[19]

Two centuries later, Karl Marx concluded much the same, except that he favored the abolition of the property qualification for voting, precisely *because* it would destroy private property: ". . . the state as a state abolishes *private property* (i.e., man decrees by *political*

1976); Charles Higham, *Trading With the Enemy: An Exposé of the Nazi-American Money Plot, 1933-1949* (New York: Delacorte Press, 1983). There is little evidence that German big business financed Hitler: Henry Ashby Turner, Jr., *German Big Business and the Rise of Hitler* (New York: Oxford University Press, 1985).

17. *The Politics of Planning: A Review and Critique of Centralized Planning* (San Francisco: Institute for Contemporary Studies, 1976). See also Don Lavoie, *National Economic Planning: What Is Left?* (Cambridge, Massachusetts: Ballinger, 1985), a detailed criticism of the idea of central planning.

18. Christopher Hill, *The World Turned Upside Down: Radical Ideas During the English Revolution* (New York: Viking, 1972), ch. 7.

19. A. S. P. Woodhouse (ed.), *Puritanism and Liberty, Being the Army Debates* (1647-9) (London: Dent, 1938), p. 53.

means the *abolition* of private property) when it abolishes the *property* qualification for electors and representatives. . . . Is not private property ideally abolished when the non-owner comes to legislate for the owner of property? The *property qualification* is the last political form in which property is recognized."[20]

Lord Macaulay, the English historian-statesman of the mid-nineteenth century, was a defender of the classical liberal society, meaning a society marked by constitutionally limited civil government and by private property. In 1857, he wrote a letter to an American, H. S. Randall, in which he discussed his doubts about pure democracy in general, and Jeffersonian democracy in particular. He made a number of predictions concerning the fate of private property under a rule of universal suffrage. Some of these predictions have come true in the United States; they did so during the New Deal of the 1930's. Other remarks seem more appropriate in describing his beloved England, especially since the 1930's.

The fundamental issue, he argued, is the question of *self-restraint*, or as I have put it elsewhere in this book, self-government. He despaired at the ability of the poorer members of society to refrain from using their numerical superiority at the ballot box to extort the property of richer men. Because of the difficulty in obtaining copies of the book in which this letter appeared, I have decided to reproduce it in full, except for a brief introductory paragraph, in which Macaulay thanked Randall for his gift of some books on the history of colonial New York State, and a concluding paragraph on Thomas Jefferson. The doubts raised by Macaulay are with us still, and will continue to be problems for stable political orders for as long as: 1) all men can vote; 2) some men have little property; 3) the Christian teachings against envy, covetousness, and theft are not universally honored. (I have taken the liberty of breaking this letter into paragraphs; the original constitutes the longest sustained paragraph I have ever come across.) Macaulay wrote:

You are surprised to learn that I have not a high opinion of Mr. Jefferson, and I am surprised at your surprise. I am certain that I never wrote a line, and that I never, in Parliament, in conversation, or even on the hustings — a place where it is the fashion to court the populace — uttered a word indicating an opinion that the supreme authority in a state ought to

---

20. Karl Marx, "On the Jewish Question" (1843), in T. B. Bottomore (ed.), *Karl Marx: Early Writings* (New York: McGraw-Hill, 1964), pp. 11-12.

be entrusted to the majority of citizens by the head; in other words, to the poorest and most ignorant part of society. I have long been convinced that institutions purely democratic must, sooner or later, destroy liberty or civilization, or both.

In Europe, where the population is dense, the effect of such institutions would be almost instantaneous. What happened lately in France is an example. In 1848 a pure democracy was established there. During a short time there was reason to expect a general spoilation, a national bankruptcy, a new partition of the soil, a maximum of prices, a ruinous load of taxation laid on the rich for the purpose of supporting the poor in idleness. Such a system would, in twenty years, have made France as poor and barbarous as the France of the Carlovingians. Happily, the danger was averted; and now there is a despotism, a silent tribune [Emperor Louis Napoleon Bonaparte, supposedly the nephew of the more famous Bonaparte—G.N.], an enslaved press. Liberty is gone, but civilization has been saved. I have not the smallest doubt that if we had a purely democratic government here the effect would be the same. Either the poor would plunder the rich, and civilization would perish; or order and prosperity would be saved by a strong military government, and liberty would perish.

You may think that your country enjoys an exemption from these evils. I will frankly own to you that I am of a very different opinion. Your fate I believe to be certain, though it is deferred by a physical cause. As long as you have a boundless extent of fertile and unoccupied land, your laboring population will be far more at ease than the laboring population of the Old World, and, while that is the case, the Jefferson politics may continue to exist without causing any fatal calamity. But the time will come when New England will be as thickly populated as old England. Wages will be as low, and will fluctuate as much with you as with us. You will have your Manchesters and Birminghams, and in those Manchesters and Birminghams hundreds of thousands of artisans will assuredly be out of work. Then your institutions will be fairly brought to the test. Distress everywhere makes the laborer mutinous and discontented, and inclines him to listen with eagerness to agitators who tell him that it is a monstrous iniquity that one man should have a million, while another can not get a full meal.

In bad years there is plenty of grumbling here, and sometimes a little rioting. But it matters little. For here the sufferers are not the rulers. The supreme power is in the hands of a class, numerous indeed, but select; of an educated class; of a class which is, and knows itself to be, deeply interested in the security of property and the maintenance of order. Accordingly, the malcontents are firmly yet gently restrained. The bad time is got over without robbing the wealthy to relieve the indigent. The springs of national prosperity soon begin to flow again; work is plentiful, wages rise, and all is tranquility and cheerfulness. I have seen England pass three or four times through such critical seasons as I have described. Through such seasons the United States will have to pass in the course of the next century, if not of this. How will you pass through them? I heartily wish you a good deliverance. But my reason and my wishes are at war, and I can not help foreboding the worst.

It is quite plain that your Government will never be able to restrain a distressed and discontented majority. For with you the majority is the Government, and has the rich, who are always a minority, always at its mercy. The day will come when in the State of New York a multitude of people, none of whom has had more than half a breakfast, or expects to have more than half a dinner, will choose a Legislature. Is it possible to doubt what sort of Legislature will be chosen? On one side is a statesman preaching patience, respect for vested rights, strict observance of public faith. On the other is a demagogue ranting about the tyranny of capitalists and usurers, and asking why any body should be permitted to drink Champagne and to ride in a carriage, while thousands of honest folks are in want of necessaries. Which of the two candidates is likely to be preferred by a working-man who hears his children cry for more bread?

I seriously apprehend that you will, in some such season of adversity as I have described, do things which will prevent prosperity from returning; that you will act like people who should in a year of scarcity devour all the seed-corn, and thus make the next a year not of scarcity but of famine. There will be, I fear, spoilation. The spoilation will increase the distress. The distress will produce fresh spoilation.

Your Constitution is all sail and no anchor. As I said before, when a society has entered on this downward progress, either civilization or liberty must perish. Either some Caesar or Napoleon will seize the reins of government with a strong hand, or your republic will be as fearfully plundered and laid waste by barbarians in the twentieth century as the Roman Empire was in the fifth; with this difference, that the Huns and Vandals who ravaged the Roman Empire came from without, and that your Huns and Vandals will have been engendered within your own country by your own institutions. [21]

This is an eloquent statement. It is easy enough to pick apart some of his specific arguments. For example, the territory of the United States is still predominantly either rural or wilderness, with a very thin population per square mile. The myth of "open spaces" as a factor in reducing class warfare in the U.S. is just that, a myth [22] (and

---

21. G. Otto Trevelyan (ed.), *The Life and Letters of Lord Macaulay* (New York: Harper & Brothers, 1875), II, pp. 408-10.

22. The American historian whose name is generally associated with this theory is Frederick Jackson Turner, a highly influential teacher at the University of Wisconsin and Harvard in the late nineteenth century, and a man who wrote almost

certainly as far as God was concerned when He promised the Israelites even more population growth in an already "overpopulated" nation). Overpopulation theories always paint pictures of starving masses, but in the decade following Macaulay's letter and continuing into the last decade of the nineteenth century, population in the United States doubled, filling the Eastern seaboard with immigrants who did not speak English, and who had little or no formal education, yet economic output quadrupled in this same era, doubling per capita income and lowering prices by 60 percent.[23] The question of per capita wealth does not hinge primarily on population growth as such, just as the Hebrews were informed by God. Population growth is a blessing. The relevant factors are such things as the time-orientation of the society, its commitment to biblical law, and its rate of per capita investment. The important question is: What is a society's capital base, which includes above all men's education and ethics?

In this respect, Macaulay misjudged the political life of his own nation, for it was England that first capitulated to the politics of envy, of mass democracy, not the United States. When, on August 10, 1911, the House of Lords voted to abolish its veto power over the House of Commons, under threat of the creation of hundreds of new Liberal Party peerages by the King, the handwriting was on the wall. When, the next day, the Commons passed the Payment of Members Bill, the wall itself collapsed.[24] No longer would members be required to raise their own funds to serve as politicians. The era of the professional politician had arrived in England.

But Macaulay's warning about the ability of the statesman to withstand the rhetoric of the "tax and spend" demagogue was valid. The history of the twentieth century points to the grim reality of the impotence of any institutional arrangements or formal constitutional

---

nothing. See Ray Allen Billington (ed.), *Frontier and Section: Selected Essays of Frederick Jackson Turner* (Englewood Cliffs, New Jersey: Prentice-Hall, 1961). For critical evaluations, see Richard Hofstadter and Seymour Martin Lipset (eds.), *Turner and the Sociology of the Frontier* (New York: Basic Books, 1968).

23. Milton Friedman and Anna Jacobson Schwartz, A *Monetary History of the United States, 1867-1960* (Princeton University Press and the National Bureau of Economic Research, 1963), charts 3, 8 (pp. 30, 94-95). Population data: *Historical Statistics of the United States, Colonial Times to 1957* (Washington, D.C.: Bureau of Commerce, 1960), p. 7, Series A 1-3.

24. Barbara Tuchman, *The Proud Tower: A Portrait of the World Before the War, 1890-1914* (New York: Macmillan, 1966), ch. 7: "The Transfer of Power."

restraints, in and of themselves, to reverse the spread of the ideology of socialism. Compulsory wealth redistribution is almost universally accepted in nation after nation, irrespective of the political history of any given society. Furthermore, it has not always been the property-less masses who have voted to impose socialistic policies; all too often the leadership has come from financially secure intellectuals.[25] Middle-class voters, simultaneously guilt-ridden and envious, have voted away their own economic futures unknowingly, always in the name of the poor, with the bills supposedly to be paid for by the rich. So Macaulay's concern about American institutional arrangements, as distinguished from British institutions, was misguided; both the British and the American systems capitulated in principle about the same time, from 1900 to the First World War, and both societies experienced increasing collectivism in the 1930's, in the political responses to the Great Depression. Since the Second World War, in fact, the British socialists have made far more gains than the American interventionists. But the substance of Macaulay's letter has been confirmed in several respects, and in no sense has the twentieth century proven him to be categorically incorrect. The drift toward socialism continues, despite intermittent political reversals.[26] Only when the major State programs for economic redistribution are actually repealed, either openly and directly, or through mass inflation (without a subsequent return to these programs after the inevitable deflationary collapse or the issuing of a new currency unit), will this drift be reversed.

Protection

All property is God's. He has established rules for the exchange, transmission, and development of this property. Theft is explicitly prohibited. God's law provides us with the case laws that enable us to define theft biblically. For example, it is *not* theft if a traveller picks an apple from a tree and eats it as he goes along the road (Deut. 23:24-25). Furthermore, it *is* theft if the owner of an agricultural property does not leave fallen fruit on the ground for gleaners (Deut.

---

25. Joseph A. Schumpeter, *Capitalism, Socialism, and Democracy* (New York: Harper & Bros., 1942), ch. 13; Ludwig von Mises, *The Anti-Capitalist Mentality*; F. A. Hayek (ed.), *Capitalism and the Historians* (University of Chicago Press, 1954), Pt. I.
26. Clarence Carson, *The World in the Grip of an Idea* (New Rochelle, New York: Arlington House, 1979). These essays also were published in the late 1970's in *The Freeman*, Foundation for Economic Education, Irvington, New York 10533.

24:19). The Bible is our standard of what constitutes theft, not Adam Smith or Karl Marx.

The civil government is required by God to serve as the protector of property. It must honor the laws of ownership that are set forth in the Bible. It should not prosecute a man who takes a few ears of corn from his neighbor's field. Christ and the disciples were not guilty of theft when they did so (Matt. 12:1). The civil government can legitimately compel a farm owner to respect the gleaning laws. But the civil government cannot legitimately say which persons have to be allowed into the field to glean. The owner of the property has that responsibility, just as Boaz did (Ruth 2:3-12).

This view of theft and protection is not in conformity to either modern socialism or modern libertarianism. In the first system (socialism), the State collects the tithe for itself, and many times God's tithe, to be used for purposes specified by bureaucratic and political bodies. In the second system (libertarianism), all coercion against private property is defined as theft, including taxation itself (in some libertarian systems).[27] Nevertheless, the Bible's standards are the valid ones, and the Bible is clear: *there is no absolute sovereignty in any person or institution.* Unquestionably, there are limits on the use of private property. But these limits are minimal. Given the biblical standards of theft, the civil government becomes a legitimate sovereign in the area of theft prevention and punishment — not the only institution, but one of them, and the one that has the lawful authority to impose economic sanctions against thieves.

R. H. Coase has stated emphatically: "A private-enterprise system cannot function properly unless property rights are created in resources, and, when this is done, someone wishing to use a resource has to pay the owner to obtain it."[28] The preservation of private ownership by the civil government against theft is, in and of itself, a foundation of capitalism. By *defining* the limits of ownership, and by *protecting* property from coercive attack from violent men and fraudulent practices, a godly civil government establishes the basis of economic growth and prosperity.

---

27. Perhaps the most systematic of the libertarian criticisms of all forms of taxation is Murray N. Rothbard's book, *Power and Market: Government and the Economy* (Menlo Park, California: Institute for Humane Studies, 1970).

28. R. H. Coase, "The Federal Communications Commission," *Journal of Law and Economics* (1959); reprinted in Eirik G. Furubotn and Svetozar Pejovich (eds.), *The Economics of Property Rights* (Cambridge, Massachusetts: Ballinger, 1974), p. 82.

One of the most important features of a private-property social order is *the reduction of uncertainty.* The market rewards forecasters (entrepreneurs) for their successful attempts to meet future consumer demand at competitive prices. This is the basis of the power of the consumers over the suppliers: the lure of profit. It also is a process through which less efficient (more wasteful) forecasters are steadily eliminated from the market, thereby increasing the stability of the market. Consumers can rely more readily on the free market for the future delivery of goods and services than they could dare to rely on a bureaucratic delivery system, with its guaranteed jobs for suppliers, its past-oriented rules, and its lack of risk-bearing. Uncertainty is reduced in society by the free, competitive market precisely because the market places such high rewards for *overcoming uncertainty,* namely, profits. The market's *flexibility* provides consumers with future *stability,* since the mistakes of producers tend to cancel out, and the more successful producers strengthen their position in the market.

Defining Property Rights

If the free market order rests on property rights, then what exactly are they? As with all definitions, the human mind, not to mention language, is imperfect. An absolutely rigorous definition is probably impossible. But one reasonable attempt has been made by Harold Demsetz: "Crucially involved is the notion that individuals have control over the use to which scarce resources (including ideas) can be put, and that this right of control is saleable or transferable. A private property right system requires the prior consent of 'owners' before their property can be affected by others. The role of the body politic in this system is twofold. Firstly, the government or courts must help decide which individuals possess what property rights and, therefore, who has the power to claim that his rights are affected by others. Secondly, property rights so assigned must be protected by the police power of the state or the owners must be allowed to protect property rights themselves. Presumably the best mix of public and private protection will depend on ethical and other considerations."[29] Unfortunately, the economics profession, in its self-professed moral neutrality, has not been able to come up with these ethical and other criteria, nor have economists shown exactly

---

29. Harold Demsetz, "Some Aspects of Property Rights," *Journal of Law and Economics,* IX (1966), p. 62.

how economics would relate to such criteria. (Biblical economists, not being morally neutral, are not equally hampered in answering these questions.)

Property, from this perspective, is basically a "bundle of rights." Again, citing Demsetz: "When a transaction is concluded in the marketplace, two bundles of property rights are exchanged. A bundle of rights often attaches to a physical commodity or service, but it is the value of the rights that determines the value of what is exchanged."[30] The control over such rights necessarily involves the right to *exclude* others from the value of the rights over time. It is here that the civil government must take special care: rights are not absolute, but they should be *sufficiently familiar* to acting men that these men can make *valid predictions* concerning the future — the future actions of competitors, as well as of the civil government. The *reduction of uncertainty* is of paramount importance. As Cheung writes: "The transfer of property rights among individual owners through contracting in the marketplace requires that the rights be exclusive. An exclusive property right grants its owner a *limited* authority to make a decision on resource use so as to derive income therefrom. To define this limit requires measurement and enforcement. Any property is multidimensional and exclusivity is frequently a matter of degree. But without some enforced or policed exclusivity to a right of action, the right to contract so as to exchange is absent."[31] The civil government must protect property.

The Market for Knowledge and Uncertainty

The establishment of property rights is therefore fundamental in any system of voluntary exchange. Men rely on the division of labor to increase their own economic output, and therefore their income. Of critical importance is the *exchange of information*, including the *exchange of uncertainty*. Those who want to buy more uncertainty, and therefore open up to themselves the opportunity for greater profit, are enabled to do so by purchasing higher-risk property from those who are willing to settle for a more guaranteed return.[32] Some peo-

---

30. Demsetz, "Toward a Theory of Property Rights," *American Economic Review* (1967); reprinted in *Economics of Property Rights*, p. 31.

31. S. Cheung, "The Structure of a Contract and the Theory of a Non-Exclusive Resource," *Journal of Law and Economics* (1970); reprinted in *ibid.*, p. 27.

32. I employ Frank Knight's distinction between *risk* and *uncertainty*. Risk is a statistically calculable class of future events, such as the deaths within a particular age group. Mortality tables used by life insurance firms are examples of statistical calcu-

ple want bonds, others want stocks, while still others want to speculate in commodities. Farmers may prefer to lock in a price for their
crops, and to concentrate their knowledge on raising more crops.
Some speculators who think they understand agricultural markets,
even if they know very little about the actual mechanics (or organics)
of farming, can contract with risk-avoiding farmers and assure them
of a specified future price for their crop. Those who want the risk can
buy it; those who want to avoid risk can sell it. This helps *reduce the
mistakes*—forecasting mistakes—in those societies that allow voluntary transactions in the marketplace. But a society which does not
take care to specify and enforce property rights cannot derive the full
benefits of the market in reducing uncertainty. Costs of ownership
remain needlessly high. Co-operation is reduced.

Man is not God. Man's knowledge is not God's exhaustive
knowledge. Man must seek wisdom and knowledge as one of his
tasks on earth (Prov. 1:1-7). He needs the *division of labor in knowledge*
more than he needs the division of labor in any other field, since wisdom is the thing above all which we are told to pursue. *The free market, more than any institutional arrangement in the history of man, facilitates
the division of labor in knowledge.*[33] Men are forced to recognize that
knowledge is never free of charge, and that other men put a high
price on certain kinds of knowledge. This, predictably, tends to encourage increased production of the high-valued knowledge.

The free market increases men's knowledge, but there must be
open *competition* for knowledge, and there must be *transferability* of
that knowledge. Competition concentrates or assembles knowledge
from all potential owners. The knowledge here is men's knowledge
of all the *potential uses* for a scarce resource, and all the *contractual arrangements* possible for implementing it. As Cheung states, the
"transferability of property rights ensures that the most valuable
knowledge will be utilized."[34] When society allows the competition of
potential contract participants to bid against each other, and it also
facilitates the owners' ability to transfer resources, it thereby reduces

---

lations of risk. In contrast, uncertainty is not subject to mathematical analysis in advance. Correctly forecasting uncertain future events—or at least events not deemed
as uncertain by one's competitors—is the source of all profits, Knight cogently
argued. Frank H. Knight, *Risk, Uncertainty and Profit* (New York: Harper Torchbooks, [1921] 1965).

33. F. A. Hayek, *Individualism and Economic Order* (University of Chicago Press,
1948), ch. 4: "The Use of Knowledge in Society."

34. Cheung, in *Economics of Property Rights*, p. 29.

the cost of enforcing the stipulated terms of the contract. Why? Because competing parties stand by to offer or accept similar terms of exchange. If one participant tries to cheat, others will step in and make legitimate offers. Thus, concludes Cheung, "competition *in the marketplace* reduces the costs of finding and pursuing the most valuable option in which a resource may be contacted for production."[35] This, of course, reduces waste. People can buy what they want with fewer resources, since all resources tend to be allocated to those uses most highly demanded by consumers. Producers know what other people want to buy, and those who want to buy gain power over suppliers precisely because the transactions are voluntary, and suppliers are seeking profit. To the extent that the State restricts the profitability of voluntary exchange, to that extent will buyers lose influence over suppliers, for the whole incentive structure is compromised. The State restricts the buyers' use of "economic carrots."

The words "mine" and "yours" are two of the most important words in any society. Biblical preaching has, over centuries, enabled men to appreciate the importance of these two words. When the differences between the two are honored in law, word, and deed, society benefits. Men can better co-operate with each other in peaceful transactions precisely because of the *predictability* provided by a social order which recognizes "mine" and "yours." This facilitates the division of labor. Demsetz has seen the importance of property rights from the perspective of *social co-operation.* "In the world of Robinson Crusoe property rights play no role. Property rights are an instrument of society and derive their significance from the fact that they help a man form those expectations which he can reasonably hold in his dealings with others. These expectations find expression in the laws, customs, and mores of a society. An owner of property rights possesses the consent of fellow men to allow him to act in particular ways."[36] Men can make contracts with each other, and enjoy the fruits of their decisions concerning the stewardship of God's resources. To return to a now-familiar theme, *property rights reduce the zones of uncertainty in life.*

Ownership as a Social Function

What is not understood by many is that private ownership necessarily involves social responsibilities. There can be no escape from

---

35. *Idem.*
36. *Ibid.*, p. 31.

the responsibilities of ownership. God always links power and responsibility.

Consider a scarce resource. Being scarce, it commands a price. (A non-scarce resource is any resource for which demand does not exceed supply at zero price.) Therefore, the person who owns it possesses wealth. What will he do with this wealth? Will he use the asset (money, for example) to invest? This makes the wealth available for a period of time to other people. Will he spend the money on a consumer good? Then he pays for it and necessarily forfeits the income that he might have received had he invested the money. Will he give it away? Then he forfeits the use of the investment income or the psychic income that the consumer good would have produced.

Who establishes the price of the asset? Consumers do. They make subjective evaluations of what any asset is worth, and their competitive bids in the marketplace establish the price of a particular asset. Producers compete against producers to sell to consumers, who in turn compete against each other. Producers cannot sell assets at prices higher than consumers are willing and able to pay. Thus, consumers determine what is going to be produced. Entrepreneurs act as their middlemen, buying up producer goods and using them over time to meet *expected* consumer demand. If they are successful in their guesses, they will reap profits. If they are incorrect, they will reap losses. But there is no escape from *consumers' sovereignty*[37] apart from the intervention of the civil government with some sort of coercive protection scheme.

This means that every person who owns an asset which commands a price must act as the agent of consumers (including himself), or pay the price of failing to serve their needs. If consumers want to see assets used in a particular way, and an asset owner refuses to sell, then *he pays a price*. He cannot ignore consumer demand at zero price to himself. Consumers or their servants (entrepreneurial middlemen) make bids for ownership, as revealed by a market price for the asset. Those present owners who refuse to take the offered price thereby forfeit all the uses to which they might otherwise have put the money. There is no escape from this required

---

37. The phrase "consumers' sovereignty" was coined by William H. Hutt as early as 1934: *Individual Freedom: Selected Works of William H. Hutt*, edited by Svetozar Pejovich and David Klingaman (Westport, Connecticut: Greenwood Press, 1975), p. 185, and footnote 1 on page 203.

payment. The owner who says, "I'll use it my way," is saying, "I'll pay for my decision." He turns his back on the money or goods offered by consumers for his property.

Thus, ownership is a social function. Men must act as *stewards for the consuming public*, or else pay the price. There is no such thing as a free (gratuitous) lunch. There is also no such thing as cost-free ownership of scarce economic resources. The existence of free markets — institutional arrangements for open, competitive bidding — enables consumers to price all economic assets according to their subjective evaluations. Free markets lead to accurate *objective* evaluations (prices) of the collective decisions of potential buyers. Free markets aid consumers in establishing their will over producers. Producers are free agents, but they are not cost-free agents.

There are two ways to impose your will on another person: reward and penalty, the carrot and the stick. The stick relies on coercion. Coercion is a legal monopoly of the civil government. Thus, consumers are to rely on the carrot approach. "Do it my way," they assert, "or suffer the consequences." What are the consequences? Forfeited income.

The market is not some autonomous institution which thwarts the "little guy." It is an institution which promotes the interests of every asset-owning participant. It provides consumers with the ultimate institutional carrot: a legal order which allows them to make competitive bids to the owners of the resources that they want to buy. The market is a *social institution* which places daily inescapable burdens of ownership on every resource owner.[39] As Mises writes: "Ownership of the means of production is not a privilege, but a social liability. Capitalists and landowners are compelled to employ their property for the best possible satisfaction of the consumers. If they are slow and inept in the performance of their duties, they are penalized by losses. If they do not learn their lesson and do not reform their conduct of affairs, they lose their wealth. No investment is safe forever. He who does not use his property in serving the consumers in the most efficient way is doomed to failure. There is no room left for people who would like to enjoy their fortunes in idleness and thoughtlessness."[40]

---

38. North, *Dominion Covenant: Genesis*, ch. 23: "The Entrepreneurial Function."

39. Gary North, *An Introduction to Christian Economics* (Nutley, New Jersey: Craig Press, 1973), ch. 28: "Ownership: Free But Not Cheap."

40. Ludwig von Mises, *Human Action: A Treatise on Economics* (3rd ed.; Chicago: Regnery, 1966), pp. 311-12.

Future-Orientation

In a society in which the rights of private property are honored, men can make decisions concerning their assets that will influence future generations in a conscious, calculating way. Familistic capital is protected by the prohibition against theft. Men's time perspectives can then focus on the long-term prospects of their capital, just as Abraham's vision did. Which system of property management tends to be more concerned with the future, private ownership or communal ownership? Demsetz addresses himself to this issue, and he concludes that private ownership tends to be far more future-oriented. By communal ownership, he means "a right which can be exercised by all members of the community."[41] He points to a phenomenon made famous by biologist Garrett Hardin, the "tragedy of the commons,"[42] although he does not use this terminology. "Suppose that land is communally owned. Every person has the right to hunt, till, or mine the land. This form of ownership fails to concentrate the cost associated with any person's exercise of his communal right on that person. If a person seeks to maximize the value of his communal rights, he will to tend to overhunt and overwork the land because some of the costs of his doing so are borne by others. The stock of game and the richness of the soil will be diminished too quickly."[43] People may agree to reduce the demands they are making, as individuals, on the land, but the *costs of negotiating* are high, and so are the *costs of policing* the agreement.

"If a single person owns the land," says Demsetz, "he will attempt to maximize its present value by taking into account alternative future time streams of benefits and costs and selecting that one which he believes will maximize the present value of his privately owned rights. We all know that this means that he will attempt to take into account the supply-and-demand conditions that he thinks will exist after his death. It is very difficult to see how the existing

---

41. Demsetz, "Toward a Theory of Property Rights," in *Economics of Property Rights, op. cit.*, p. 37.

42. Garrett Hardin, "The Tragedy of the Commons," *Science* (13 Dec. 1968); reprinted in Garrett de Bell (ed.), *The Environmental Handbook* (New York: Ballentine, 1970). Hardin calls for more government control over pollution and resource depletion. In contrast, C. R. Batten calls for less government control and greater attention to defining private property rights: Batten, "The Tragedy of the Commons," *The Freeman* (Oct. 1970).

43. Demsetz, in *Economics of Property Rights*, p. 38.

communal owners can reach an agreement that takes account of these costs."[44] Then Demsetz offers a stunning insight into the social function of an owner of a private property right: the *owner as broker between generations*. "In effect, an owner of a private right to use land acts as a broker whose wealth depends on how well he takes into account the competing claims of the present and future. But with communal rights there is no broker, and the claims of the present generation will be given an uneconomically large weight in determining the intensity with which the land is worked. Future generations might desire to pay present generations enough to change the present intensity of land usage. But they have no living agent to place their claims on the market."[45]

By its very nature and time perspective, *familistic capital is privately owned capital.* Privately owned capital necessarily involves the defense of private property. *The stewardship of resources should be supervised by the most intensely committed social unit, the family.* It is not the only legitimate institution of ownership,[46] but it is unquestionably the most universally recognized ownership institution historically, and it is the social unit to which God originally announced the dominion covenant. By establishing a tight (though imperfect) relationship between *costs* and *benefits*, private property rights encourage men to count the costs of their actions. The counting of costs is a biblical requirement (Luke 14:28-30). If a man overworks his soil, he or his heirs will pay the price. If his animals overgraze the land, he or his heirs will suffer reduced income later. He cannot pass on his costs so easily to those outside his family, which therefore encourages him to examine the effects, including long-run effects, of his present decisions. He seeks a profit—an excess of income over outgo—and he cannot ignore costs. He will waste fewer of God's resources because of the profit incentive, compared to the communal ownership or State ownership systems, where each man is offered direct incentives to waste the common asset while profiting personally from the immediate use of the asset. There can be commitment to the goals of other social units besides the family, but no institution historically

---

44. *Idem.*
45. *Ibid.*, pp. 38-39.
46. The corporation is another important institution for holding property, but corporate shares of ownership are held by heads of households primarily, or by agents of heads of households: banks, retirement funds, mutual funds, etc. Thus, these are *delegated* sovereignties.

has commanded the intense loyalty of men that the family has commanded. When devising a system of incentives, we should stick with the Bible and "go with the winner," which is the family. Familistic capital is *private* capital.

Communal Property and Nomads

Those within the Christian tradition who have been committed to socialism have pointed to the communal property of the early church as an example to be followed by all Christians. Several comments are in order. First, communal property in the early church was strictly voluntary (Acts 5:4). Second, property was shared in common (Acts 4:32), but for a reason: Christ's prediction of the coming destruction of Jerusalem (Luke 21:20-24). By selling fixed property, such as homes, the early church members made it easier to heed Christ's warning and flee the city during the crisis. They could convert their fixed capital assets into mobile capital, thereby helping to preserve the value of their capital. This prophecy concerning Jerusalem was fulfilled in 69 and 70 A.D., when the Romans surrounded the city and starved out the inhabitants.[47] The Christians fled to Pella, church legend has it, before the final siege of Jerusalem. The early church abandoned private property temporarily, but there is no indication that communal property was regarded as morally binding. It was a temporary response to a particular set of circumstances: Christ's prophecy and Rome's tyranny. The early church in Jerusalem (and *only* in Jerusalem) prepared to flee by selling fixed property and pooling the funds. They became, in effect, *temporary nomads*, for they intended to flee when the time came. As nomads, they adopted transportable property and more communal property ownership. There is no indication that this nomadic system of ownership was ever regarded as a permanent policy within the church.

The nomad is not a builder of civilization. His geographical perspective is too short run. He comes and goes, never staying to establish roots, whether personal or agricultural. The nomadic family concerns itself primarily with *transportable assets*. Weapons and household utensils are prized, and nomadic law protects them. Both kinds of articles require raw materials, human ingenuity, and time to pro-

---

47. David Chilton, *Paradise Restored: A Biblical Theology of Dominion* (Tyler, Texas: Reconstruction Press, 1985), ch. 10: "The Great Tribulation," and Appendix B of Chilton's book, which reprints sections from Josephus' *The Wars of the Jews*.

duce. But far less concern will be placed on defining and policing property rights in land. Demsetz writes: "Property rights in land among such people would require costs for several years during which no sizable output is obtained. Since to provide for sustenance these people must move to a new land, a property right to be of value to them must be associated with a portable object. Among these people it is common to find property rights to the crops, which, after harvest, are portable, but not to the land. The more advanced agriculturally based primitive societies are able to remain with particular land for longer periods, and here we generally observe property rights to the land as well as to the crops."[48]

A godly society will seek to defend the property rights of ever-multiplying kinds of goods and services, and an increasing market value of more and more formerly ignored goods is made possible by rising productivity. *Civilization can be measured by an increase in the kinds of private property recognized and developed by members of a particular society.* As societies advance, they will be marked by this extension of protection to new products, new technologies, and new transactions.

Human Rights and Property Rights

One of the most successful slogans of socialists in the twentieth century has been this one: "We're in favor of human rights over property rights." One of America's most beloved Presidents, the feisty and extremely well-read Teddy Roosevelt, used a variation of this slogan in the early years of the twentieth century: "In every civilized society, property rights must be carefully safeguarded. Ordinarily and in the great majority of cases, human rights and property rights are fundamentally and in the long run, identical; but when it clearly appears that there is a real conflict between them, human rights must have the upper hand; for property belongs to man and not man to property."[49]

Allen and Alchian's analysis strikes at the heart of such a contrast: "Exclusivity of control constitutes a basic component of the private-property economic system. We emphasize that property rights are *not* rights *of property*; they are rights *of people* to [the] use of goods. In sum, two basic elements of private property are *exclusivity*

---

48. Demsetz, in *Economics of Property Rights*, p. 37n.
49. Racine, Wisconsin, *Daily Journal* (April 23, 1910), "Roosevelt's Address on Citizenship"; cited in R. J. Rushdoony, *Politics of Guilt and Pity* (Fairfax, Virginia: Thoburn Press, [1970] 1978), p. 179.

of rights and *voluntary transferability* or exchangeability of rights. It is silly to speak of a contrast or conflict between human rights and property rights. Property rights *are* human rights to the use of economic goods."[50]

We can legitimately speak of a misuse of property by an individual. If my factory blows smoke on your house and wears off the paint, I have invaded your sphere of responsibility. I have attacked your property. I have assaulted your sense of justice. When men come to agree, through custom or law, that certain space is to be protected and honored, another man cannot legitimately invade that space for his own personal profit, except with the consent of the owner. But this is not a case of "property rights vs. human rights"; it is a case of a conflict between human rights — a dispute between people concerning the lawful use of privately owned property.

Pollution and Economic Competition

There are inevitably problems to be settled in human society, areas that need more research, more understanding. Even theoretically, the defender of the free market has difficulties in defining property rights, or an invasion of property rights. For example, free market defenders argue that when the State taxes one quarter of the income of a particular piece of property, it has in effect confiscated one quarter of that property.[51] Consider, then, this problem (raised by Demsetz).[52] If my factory blows smoke on your property, you expect restitution, or a cessation of smoke production, since it lowers the value of your property. Pollution-control equipment can be defended in terms of this view of property rights. However, if my factory is located a thousand miles away, or across the ocean, and my improvements in methods of production drive out of business a factory in your area, which happens to employ half the town, the market value of your home may drop even more than if my factory were spewing smoke into your neighborhood. Few defenders of the free market would insist that I owe restitution to anyone who has the value of his house wiped out in this manner. Yet the value of your house may be down 25%. Have I really confiscated 25% of your

50. Alchian and Allen, *University Economics*, p. 142.
51. Thomas Sowell, *Knowledge and Decisions* (New York: Basic Books, 1980), p. 39.
52. Demsetz, "The Exchange and Enforcement of Property Rights," *Journal of Law and Economics*, VII (1964), pp. 25-26.

house? Is the argument which is levelled at the tax collector equally applicable to my distant factory? Competition, confiscation, and co-operation are sometimes very difficult concepts to distinguish—not always, or even usually, but sometimes.

The Bible provides us with an example of "spillover effects" and what to do about them. If a man starts a fire on his property, and the fire spreads to his neighbor's property, the man who started the fire is responsible for compensating his neighbor for the latter's losses (Ex. 22:6). Obviously, this invasion of property is *physical*, rather than merely competitive and economic in nature, and therefore the fire-starter is liable. The destruction of property in this instance is physical and immediate; the victim actually loses part of his crop. But what about noise pollution, where the man's house is not burned, but its market value drops as a result of his neighbor's noisy factory? This would seem to be covered by the case-law on fire, since sound waves are physical phenomena, just as sparks are. But when the loss is exclusively economic, *without physical invasion*, the Bible is silent: there is no law that would require the successful innovator to compensate those who lost money because of the introduction of new production techniques or new products. Alchian's analysis would seem to apply: "Although private property rights protect private property from physical changes chosen by other people, no immunity is implied for the exchange value of one's property."[53]

Is it fair, then, to equate the economic effects of the State's collection of taxes and the industrialist's pollution? It depends on the level of taxation. If the State attempts to extract taxes greater than 10% of income, thereby equating its sovereignty with God's sovereignty (the tithe), then the answer is yes, the two should be equated. Both forms of economic redistribution rest on *illegitimate violence*. The tax collector extracts money or goods from the citizen upon threat of imprisonment or outright confiscation of capital assets. Thus, when the

---

53. Armen Alchian, "Some Economics of Property Rights," *Il Politico* (1965); reprinted in Alchian, *Economic Forces at Work* (Indianapolis, Indiana: Liberty Press, 1977), p. 131. His conclusion, however, that my making pornographic pictures and selling them must be free from legal restraint follows only if you assume that 1) there are no absolute standards of morality, 2) no God, and 3) no social consequences for immoral behavior—in short, no consequences imposed on many members of society by God's judgment. Most economists erroneously make all three assumptions. When we speak of the legitimacy of innovation, we must always have in mind this qualification: ". . . assuming the innovation or transaction is not singled out by the Bible as being defined by God as perverse, and also illegal."

State taxes, say, 50% of a present and future stream of income, the present capital value of the asset producing the stream of income is reduced by nearly 50%.[54] (Since some benefits may flow from the State's laws, such as protection from violence or fraud, the economic loss is not necessarily 100% of the tax.) The economic effect is almost the same as if the State had taken almost half the land, or almost half the shares of stock or bonds.[55]

Taxation: Investment vs. Consumption

This is why the modern welfare State is so destructive. By confiscating up to 100% of a person's income (in late twentieth-century England and Sweden, for example),[56] the tax collectors have wiped out billions and billions of dollars worth of capital assets, and lowered the public's willingness to invest more in productive capital. Money flows into other kinds of investments in a welfare State, such as expensive automobiles (that can be used without paying taxes on the psychological income received), beach homes, gold, jewelry, art objects, mistresses, and other forms of user-tax-free, user-satisfying capital.

---

54. Meaning, "reduced from what it would otherwise have been."

55. The economic effect is not precisely the same. It is generally easier for a special-interest group to get tax policies changed than it is for members of the group to get the State to return all the property which had been confiscated from each of them, especially if the confiscated property has been sold in the meantime to other private buyers, who will fight any such legislation. The longer the period after the confiscation, the more difficult it is to get the law changed. Thus, when the State confiscates 50% of the property's income in the form of taxes, this probably does not produce a full 50% drop in the market value of the property, whereas a confiscation of 50% of the property does involve a loss of 50%, unless the new owner does something with the property which enhances the value of the contiguous property which the original owner still owns.

56. In 1975, British citizens in the highest tax brackets paid up to 83% of all "earned" income, and 98% of "unearned" (investment) income. The tax authorities actually assessed Mick Jagger, the leader of the "Rolling Stones" rock music group, 101% of his income (since they have property taxes and capital taxes in addition to income taxes), but settled for 94%. He fled the country to become a resident of France, which had established far lower negotiable tax rates for rich immigrants from high-tax countries. "Taxing the Talent Out of England," *U.S. News and World Report* (Sept. 8, 1975). It was estimated in 1977 that as many as 100,000 British executives, middle managers, and entrepreneurs had left England to escape confiscatory taxation during the previous three years. Britain's "revenue loss" was estimated to be a billion pounds in 1976 alone. Bruce Bartlett, "Taxes in Great Britain," *The Libertarian Review* (June 1981), p. 26. In the 1970's, Sweden's world-famous film director, Ingmar Bergman, emigrated when the tax authorities taxed him over 100% of his previous year's income.

The *Wall Street Journal* has provided a classic example of how the State's existing tax policies discourage investment. Say that a very rich man wants to invest a million dollars. He takes the money and invests in a new business — 80% of which fail within the first five years. Let us say that he thinks the business will make him 10% on his money in the second year of operation, but nothing in the first year (a reasonable presumption). Let us also say that his estimations are rewarded. At the end of the second year, he has back $100,000 profit for his small corporation. Here is what happens to his corporation in New York City. "Of the hundred thousand dollars in profit, the city clears away roughly $5,700, leaving $94,300. The state clears away about 10 percent of that, leaving $84,870. The IRS, levying at progressive rates, snatches $38,000, leaving $46,870. Our good rich person then pays himself a dividend. Being rich, our man is of course in the highest personal income-tax brackets, and after paying 4.3 percent to the city ($2,015) has $44,855 left. The state clips him for 15 percent of that ($6,728) and leaves him $38,127. Uncle Sam 'nicks' him for 70 percent of that, which is $26,689, leaving him with $11,438. Thus, on the investment of 1 million dollars in capital and two years of hard work in assembling the enterprise that is risky to begin with, this lucky fellow who turned a profit of $100,000 has $11,438 to spend. He has given up two years on his yacht to gain $5,719 in annual income."[57] Now, it may not have been quite this bad.[58] But the point is clear, despite the slight exaggeration of the *Wall Street Journal* essay: the higher the tax level, the less people are going to invest in risky, future-oriented, employment-producing capital assets.

Paul Craig Roberts has described a very real decision facing a rich man in the late 1970's: "Take the case of a person facing the 70 percent tax rate on investment income. He can choose to invest $50,000 at a 10 percent rate of return, which would bring him $5,000 per year of additional income before taxes. Or he can choose to spend $50,000 on a Rolls Royce. Since the after-tax value of $5,000

---

57. *Wall Street Journal* editorial; cited in George Gilder, *Wealth and Poverty*, p. 174.

58. Federal tax laws in the United States during that period allowed deductions from taxable income for taxes paid at the state and local level. Donald Regan, the Secretary of the Treasury under President Reagan, announced immediately after Reagan's successful bid for a second term of office (November 1984) that the Treasury was proposing a new Federal tax rule which would deny the deductibility of local taxes from Federally taxable income.

is only $1,500, he can enjoy a fine motor car by giving up only that amount. Britain's 98% tax rate on 'unearned' (investment) income has reduced the cost of the Rolls in terms of foregone income to only $100 a year. The profusion of Roll Royces seen in England today is mistaken as a sign of prosperity."[59] The pre-1980 tax policies of England steadily wiped out the capital base of the nation — sacrificing future productivity for present luxury. Given the fact that a Rolls Royce generally appreciates with inflation, and also because the newly rich are always coming into the market, and given the tax-deductibility of interest payments in the United States in 1985, the rich man can make more after-tax money by buying a Rolls on credit, driving it several years, and paying off the debt in depreciated money — and meanwhile enjoying a tax break on the interest payments to the bank that loaned him the money to buy the Rolls. The price of a Rolls appreciated from 1977, when Roberts wrote his essay, until the recession of 1981, four years later. This is *present-oriented investing* with a vengeance, and it is a direct, predictable result of envy-inspired confiscatory taxation rates. With tax rates at modern levels, and with theological rebellion loose in the land, we actually find that the *systematic decadence of the rich* — cocaine parties, sexual deviation, perverse art forms — can in fact be interpreted as a form of *tax-free income.*[60] After all, pleasure as a result of spending is taxed only mildly (sales taxes), if at all. Better to spend now, says the present-oriented man, than to invest for the future. *Eat, drink, and be merry, for tomorrow we go broke, and can then apply for unemployment benefits and food stamps.*

The modern welfare State has imposed tax burdens on the wage-earning, middle class citizenry that are systematically decapitalizing the modern world. The envy-dominated legislatures and government-financed economic research centers are destroying the capital base of future generations. Economic growth throughout the West began to slow down, 1970-85, as a result of these tax policies. Capital is not being replaced. Investors all over the world were involved in housing speculation during the 1970's, where there were direct benefits (living in a nicer home), and in the United States, at

---

59. Roberts, "The Economic Case for Kemp-Roth," *Wall Street Journal* (August 1, 1978); cited in *ibid.*, p. 173. Because of reductions in tax rates in the highest tax brackets in both nations since 1978, the example is somewhat exaggerated.

60. One of the most comprehensive reports on decadence in the United States appeared in the final issue of the now-defunct magazine, *New Times* (Jan. 8, 1979). The entire issue was devoted to the topic.

least, there were also major tax benefits (interest-payment deductions from taxable income, as well as depreciation benefits for investment homes, despite the appreciation in value of these investment homes).

The State vs. Human Rights

So the answer to the original question — "Are taxes the equivalent of capital confiscation?" — is yes, they are. Taxes are no longer simply the means of supporting the civil government's protection of private property (which enhances the value of capital by protecting it). Taxes today are envy-dominated, based on a theology of salvation by statist law. *The State is a messianic institution in the modern world, and it is a destroyer of capital.* The Moloch State consumes the economic future of its worshippers, and the economic future of its worshippers' heirs. The State, like the polluting factory, is a coercive, capital-destroying agent in the economy. But the polluting factory may provide productive employment for local residents, and it provides the consumers with lower-priced goods (lower priced than if the factory had to pay for pollution-control equipment). The State, in contrast, employs only bureaucrats, and uses its funds generally to subsidize the improvident members of society (some of whom may be quite rich[61]), capturing them in a web of promised benefits, and destroying their incentive to work for the benefit of consumers. The very poor also suffer a reduction of their opportunities to obtain the work skills they need to advance themselves in modern economic society.[62] The confiscatory State is a far greater threat to property and freedom than some local factory which pollutes the air or water.

The modern State is a threat to human rights, for it is a threat to property rights. The modern State is a destroyer of human rights, for it is a destroyer of property rights. Guilt-ridden intellectuals, politicians, and sons of the rich have promoted an ideology of wealth redistribution that destroys capital, and therefore destroys human aspirations. They have used the misleading slogan, "human rights

---

61. By "improvident," I mean "one who wastes his capital, or the capital entrusted to him by others." This certainly applies to senior executives of major industrial companies that apply to the Federal government for financial aid, tariffs, and other stolen economic goods.

62. George Gilder's book shows how this system works to enslave people in the United States. The work of P. T. Bauer has contributed to our understanding of similar disincentives in underdeveloped nations. See especially Bauer's book, *Dissent on Development* (Cambridge, Massachusetts: Harvard University Press, 1972).

above property rights," to destroy both human rights and property rights. They have adopted as their commandment, "Thou shalt not steal, except by majority vote." The result, increasingly, is the *decapitalization* of the formerly Christian West.

Conclusion

The biblical doctrine of ownership is a doctrine of stewardship. God's property is to be carefully developed and improved by His stewards.[63] The servants have chosen to ignore God, and they have also chosen to ignore His commandment against theft. Modern man has adopted a new theology, the ownership of property by the State. The State, as the sovereign owner, delegates to its servants the right to administer the property, but the State gets its cut, its tithe. The tithe principle is built into the creation; the only question is this: *Who gets the tithe?* The State is collecting its tithe. As Thomas Sowell has summarized it: "Win, and the State wins with you; lose, and you lose alone." This is the rule for the rich and the middle class, in any case. *The modern State is a thief.* When Samuel warned the nation of Israel against selecting a king to rule over them, he tried to scare them by telling them that the king would extract a tithe of 10% (I Sam. 8:15-17). The greatest bureaucratic dynasty of the ancient world, Egypt, took 20% as its tithe (Gen. 47:26). There is not a Western industrial State that extracts as little as Egypt took. In fact, in most instances, substituting a tax rate of one-fifth of a nation's productivity would constitute a tax *reduction* of at least 50%.

Private property reduces uncertainty. It gives men an incentive to produce. It expands men's time horizons to unborn generations. It encourages economic growth by enabling innovators and workers to capture the value of their increased productivity. It encourages thrift. Being familistic in nature, it promotes the central institution of dominion. It allows the transfer of information, the transfer of uncertainty, and the transfer of capital to those who are willing and able to bear the economic responsibilities of ownership. *The protection of private property is one of the cornerstones of civilization.* The civil govern-

---

63. Though the idea will horrify socialists and egalitarians, the best way to assess the value of an improvement of any property is to compare its price today with its price before the improvement was made. If someone spent a great deal of money to improve a property, but these improvements did not produce a market price greater than the money invested, then that invested wealth was probably misallocated. It might have been better spent elsewhere.

ment is to protect private property, not steal it.

We have seen that private property is basic to God's program of dominion. It is crucial to the success of the Sinai strategy. The dominion covenant requires it. Thieves are not to be allowed to gain access to other men's lawful tools of dominion. They are not to appropriate other men's property except by voluntary contract. This includes thieves who use the ballot box as their weapon. The Bible does not teach, "Thou shalt not steal, except by majority vote."

This commandment parallels the third commandment, which prohibits magic: the unlawful use of the Lord's name. The thief and the profane person are linked together ethically in their rebellion, for they both seek to attain power and wealth apart from God's law. They substitute autonomous behavior — magic and theft — for ethical conformity to God's law. They seek power rather than long-term dominion. The ethical aspect of the covenant is clearly revealed in this eighth commandment; the anti-magical aspect is revealed more clearly in the third commandment.

The rise of the messianic State has threatened civilization. It is the greatest single danger today to the preservation and expansion of familistic capital. The envy-dominated ideologies of wealth distribution through coercion — Marxism, socialism, Keynesianism, and the "social gospel" — have captured the minds of the intellectuals and political leaders. Unless this process is reversed, these anti-biblical doctrines will decapitalize the modern world.

9

THE VALUE OF A NAME

Thou shalt not bear false witness against thy neighbor (Ex. 20:16).

The importance of the biblical concept of "name" can be seen in God's response to the builders of the tower of Babel, when they sought to "make a name" for themselves, i.e., to define themselves and their place in the universe apart from God's revelation concerning 1) Himself, 2) the creation, and 3) His sustaining providence.

Because the family's name is so important in a godly commonwealth, the Bible provides laws regulating the *family's name and reputation*. There was a law in the Hebrew commonwealth penalizing bastardy (Deut. 23:2), and this law reinforced the general prohibition against sexual activity outside of marriage (Deut. 22:21). It was unlawful for a newly married man to bring an unsubstantiated charge of non-virginity against a daughter of Israel (Deut. 22:19). The preservation of a man's name through children born to his widow and his brother was the basis of the Levirate marriage (Deut. 25:5-6).

A name in Old Testament times represented *power*—either magical power or ethics-based dominion power. Very early in the Genesis account, men of God began to call upon His name (Gen. 4:26). Abram, upon entering the land of Canaan, built an altar to God. He moved again, building a second altar unto God, "and called upon the name of the LORD" (Gen. 12:8b). This was in response to God's original command to Abram to leave his country: "And I will make of thee a great nation, and I will bless thee, and make thy name great, and thou shalt be a blessing" (Gen. 12:2). God changed Abram's name to Abraham—"father of nations"—(Gen. 17:5), and He changed Jacob's name to Israel (Gen. 32:27-29): the major transition point in each of their lives. A new name emphasized the magnitude of each of these turning points.

In the New Testament, the name of Jesus Christ must be invoked to enter into salvation. Peter's speech at Pentecost makes this clear. Citing Joel 2:32, Peter proclaimed: "And it shall come to pass, that whosoever shall call on the name of the Lord shall be saved" (Acts 2:21). Baptism is performed in the name of Jesus Christ (Acts 2:38). Peter healed the lame man in the name of Jesus Christ (Acts 3:6), but he attributed the man's healing to his faith in Christ's name (Acts 3:16). In a ringing affirmation of the centrality of Christ's name, Peter announced: "Neither is there salvation in any other: for there is none other name under heaven given among men, whereby we must be saved" (Acts 4:12). *To invoke the name of one's god is to invoke the power of that god.* This is equally true concerning the God of the Bible.

When we are adopted into the family of God (John 1:12), as when Israel was referred to by God as His son (Ex. 4:22), we take on *God's family name.* We are called by his name, even by the world. It was at Antioch, a pagan city, that the word "Christians" was first applied to the disciples of Christ (Acts 11:26). *God honors His own name.* The adoption by God of the sinner, who bears the name of Satan before his adoption, transfers to him a new family name. The confrontation between Christ and the Pharisees in John 8 focused on the claim of the Pharisees to be the sons of Abraham, and Christ challenged them defiantly: "Ye are of your father the devil, and the lusts of your father ye will do. He was a murderer from the beginning, and abode not in the truth, because there is no truth in him. When he speaketh a lie, he speaketh of his own: for he is a liar, and the father of it" (John 8:44). We should not mistake the nature of Jesus' accusation: He was calling them spiritual bastards, and bastards had no place in the congregational worship of Israel (Deut. 23:2).[1] *Like father, like son*: here was Jesus' challenge to His enemies. The Pharisees, Christ affirmed, were claiming the name of Abraham illegitimately, for they themselves were illegitimate sons.

Character and Reputation

It should not be difficult to understand the reason for the inclusion of the prohibition against false witness in the summary of God's law which is provided by the ten commandments. *Bearing false witness*

---

1. Those who prefer to avoid direct confrontations with God-hating men like to think of Jesus as "sweet Jesus, meek and mild." They pretend that Jesus spent His ministry avoiding conflicts. They think of Him as the original Caspar Milquetoast. This is certainly not the way the Pharisees thought of Him, for good reason.

against an individual is the same as bearing false witness against his family name. It is bearing false witness against the man's historical position in the plan of God. *It misrepresents God's plan for the ages.* It strikes at the key institution, the family, for it misrepresents the individual's family name. For example, when a new husband brought the accusation of non-virginity against his bride, he had to prove it in court. If he could not prove it, he had to pay a fine of one hundred shekels of silver — an immense sum — to her father, "because he hath brought up an evil name upon a daughter of Israel" (Deut. 22:19). The father's reputation could be harmed by the bad reputation of his daughter, and so could the reputation of the covenanted nation of Israel. This reputation was protected by law from false accusations.

In a godly social order, a man's name is one of his most vital assets. When we speak of "a man's name," we really mean his *reputation*. His reputation as an honest person, or as a competent workman, or whatever his calling may be, must be protected by law. *To impugn his name is to impugn his character.* A man's character, for good or evil, must be respected.

This preservation of a man's reputation is not a matter of being polite. Christ was hardly being polite to the Pharisees when he called them sons of someone other than Abraham, namely, the bastard sons of Satan. In fact, it is one sign of a godly social order that men recognize churls for what they are, and the sign of an unjust social order when they are not called what they are. Thus, Isaiah pointed to this aspect of a future reign of justice: "The vile person shall be no more called liberal, nor the churl said to be bountiful. For the vile person will speak villany, and his heart will work iniquity, to practice hypocrisy, and to utter error against the LORD, to make empty the soul of the hungry, and he will cause the drink of the thirsty to fail" (Isa. 32:5-6). The American slang expression, "calling a spade a spade," reflects this concern for honest witness. It includes calling the churl a churl. A man's reputation is to be protected, including his reputation for evil, if he is still evil. Anything else lends itself to "confidence games" by "con men." We are asked to have confidence in someone who does not deserve it. The con man steals from the unwary by means of a false reputation. He cultivates this false reputation, even as the Pharisees of Christ's day cultivated a false reputation. The so-called "polite culture" is a culture which is not guided by the law regarding false witness.

We forget that names were descriptive in Bible times. "Abram," for instance, means "exalted father." As I mentioned earlier, "Abraham" means "father of nations" or "father of a multitude." This naming process worked negatively as well. The evil man in Judges 9:26 is named Gaal ("Loathsome") the son of Ebed ("the slave"). It is unlikely that his parents gave him this name at his birth. Perhaps Samuel (or whoever wrote Judges) gave him that name for theological reasons. Similarly, in I Chronicles 8:34, the son of Jonathan is given as Meribaal ("Baal is advocate"). This was apparently his original name, given in the early days when the Lord was called by the term Baal ("husband, lord").[2] Later, when the word Baal came to have exclusively negative connotations, writers changed Meribaal's name to Mephibosheth ("shameful to mention"), the name by which he is known in II Samuel 4:4. Mephibosheth was not a shameful character, but the sound of his name came to be obnoxious in the ears of godly Israelites. In another case, the son of Saul who rebelled against David, Ishbaal ("man of Baal," or "man of the Lord": I Chron. 8:33), is called Ishbosheth ("man of shame"). Here the change is probably not due to the offense in the sound of the name, but because of the sinful actions of the man himself.[3]

A similar social phenomenon is found in contemporary China. Steven Mosher's fine book on the rural Chinese points this out. "Another result of life-long encounters on village paths is an effortlessly acquired and altogether exhaustive fund of knowledge of each fellow denizen's finances and possessions, history and hopes, strengths and weaknesses, allies and enemies. One sign of this intimate communal familiarity lies in the revealing nicknames which Chinese everywhere assign to one another, and which I found to be uncannily accurate appraisals of a person's appearance and character. The best are truly inspired sobriquets. One brigade [Communist] Party secretary surnamed Wang is known to everyone in his village as Toad Wang, which is precisely the image evoked by his squat body and flat, powerful head, as well as by a distasteful deviousness he is known for. Then there is Cherrystone Shen, a tightfisted peddler whom, as many of his neighbors have discovered, it is next to impossible to get the best of in a deal. Some handles are

---

2. The change is indicated in Hosea 2:16-17, when the Divine Husband states that "thou shalt call me Ishi ["my man, my husband"]; and shalt call me no more Baali. For I will take away the names of Baalim out of her mouth, and they shall no more be remembered by their name."

3. I am indebted to James Jordan for these examples.

obvious choices, like Big Head Yan for a man whose head is unusually large and dome-like, or Wine Rice Su for a villager who is well known for his habit of scooping only a finger of'steamed rice into his bowl and then filling it up to the brim with rice liquor. Others ring unpleasantly, even cruelly, to Western ears, for instance the nickname of one Sandhead brigade official who has a severe speech impediment. He is called Cripple Mouth Lin. But when I asked Comrade Lin, as I carefully addressed him, if his seemingly disparraging appellation had ever made him angry or uncomfortable, he was perplexed. 'Why should it have?' he answered mildly. 'After all, my mouth *is* crippled.' As he well knew, his nickname carried no hint of taunt or blame, but was simply the public recognition of the obvious fact of an infirmity. More generally, these names stem from the down-to-earth unpretentiousness of Chinese life, where people are seen — and indentified — as what they are."[4]

Brand-Name Identification

When we recognize the link between *reputation* and *performance*, and where the civil magistrate enforces this link by penalizing the false witness, we can understand the economic importance of brand names. Very early in man's history, this link between name and workmanship was established. For example, the two craftsmen who helped supervise the construction of God's tent, the Tabernacle, Aholiab ("a father's tent") and Bezaleel ("the shadow of God"), are mentioned repeatedly in Exodus 31-38 as master craftsmen. They had reputations for competence. God specially called Bezaleel, filling him with His own spirit — in wisdom, understanding, knowledge, "and in all manner of workmanship" — that he might perform this important task in Israel's history (Ex. 31:1-5). Throughout the history of Israel, their names were associated with fine craftsmanship.

When a craftsman knows that people recognize his work, or at least his name, he has a direct economic incentive to maintain this tradition. It takes great skill, and possibly many years of struggle in the competitive marketplace, for a craftsman or a producer to develop a sense of positive name-identification among his potential clientele. People learn, over many years in some instances, that a particular individual produces quality products that can be relied

4. Steven W. Mosher, *Broken Earth: The Rural Chinese* (New York: Free Press, 1983), p. 33.

upon to deliver long-term service. It may take years for buyers to discover this about a man's products, since it takes time to test them in actual use. Buyers invest time and energy, not to mention money, in their search for bargains. This information is expensive. Mistakes are easy to make. The "school of hard knocks" can be a high-tuition institution for slow learners. Thus, when a product line becomes recognized as a reliable, valuable one, the producer has an incentive not to tamper with quality, since he is now the recipient of *consumer loyalty* for his products. The recognition and acceptance given to his products by the buying public is an important *capital asset*. Like any capital asset, its value can plummet if the buyers begin to change their buying habits. He has an incentive to keep them from changing their buying habits.

This is not to say that name-brand identification cannot be used for short-term gains at the expense of long-term gains. We are all familiar with this scenario: a firm which has developed a reputation for producing high quality goods is taken over by an outside company. The new managers decide to reduce costs by cutting the quality of inputs. The public may not initially recognize that quality debasement is going on. It takes time and experience to convince them that such a change in policy has been made by top management. They may conclude that their recent bad experience with a particular product is not representative of the product line in general, since the firm has such a respected name. They may not trust their own judgment. But eventually, buyers learn that the old reliability is no longer available. At that point, they may choose to switch loyalties, or remain buyers only by inducements such as price reductions by the seller. The firm can obtain short-term profits — an excess of revenues over costs — by reducing quality, but only by risking the loss of the positive name identification that the firm previously enjoyed. In other words, this sort of short-run profit comes through a form of *capital depletion*.

Specialization and Marketing

In ancient history, the family which enjoyed economic surpluses (meaning an excess of production over actual expenditures or consumption) was in a position to seek buyers for its products or services. The family could begin to increase its output by specializing. Specialization increases the division of labor, and hence it increases output per unit of resource input. As the buying public began to differentiate one product or service from competing products or services, specialized sellers could begin to invest greater quantities of capital in the enterprise. These family businesses could be more confident of selling into a stable market, since product or service loyalty among buyers was beginning to develop. The *high costs* to consumers of shopping around, of searching for alternative product or service substitutes, make name-brand identification a convenient *economic shorthand.* This is as true today as it was in the ancient world.

As certain families, especially those engaged in craft production, found ways of differentiating their products from those of their competitors, they could convert this recognition in the marketplace into money or bartered goods. Perhaps a family head possessed a unique skill, or special knowledge of marketing. Others may have become known for their sense of honor. These family traditions became capital assets. The *family name,* which could be stamped on many products, became an early form of *familistic capital.* This was especially true among artists. With greater name identification, consumers found it less expensive to identify desirable products. This helped to extend market transactions, for consumers could make more purchases because of the savings that resulted from the better information to consumers as a result of name-brand identification.

This analysis is a form of "hypothetical history." We cannot find ancient family budget records that say, "Today, we saved 10% of our monthly budget because we reduced our search costs." We know that certain craftsmen gained reputations for excellence. We then analyze this fact from the point of view of economics. We know that people want to reduce their costs of searching for bargains. We know that in the Hebrew commonwealth, the preservation of the family name was of paramount importance. Such a concern always has economic implications. We can conclude that buyers understood that producers would want to maintain their names' good reputations. Thus, buyers could adopt the "short cut" of substituting the producer's name for an involved testing of the product or an expensive search for information.

The wider the reputation of a seller, the wider is his market. When a product's reputation is high, additional marketing expenditures may be reduced without reducing sales. This makes international trade less expensive, just as it makes domestic trade less expensive. But in foreign trade, reputation for quality counts for more, since foreigners may have great difficulty in returning a defective product to the producer for repair or a refund. The local buyer may find it relatively inexpensive to confront the seller directly, since his transportation costs are low. Foreigners, especially in the ancient world, are not the beneficiaries of many of the advantages that domestic buyers possess. They are not citizens of the country where the producer dwells. In the ancient world, this made it almost impossible for foreign buyers to gain justice in another nation's legal system, since foreigners had no legal rights, not being part of the civic religion. Thus, the reputation of the producer, or the importer-trader, was important in establishing foreign markets for the products of a nation's citizens.

What we can readily understand is that a close relationship between morality and the family name, between a sense of craftsmanship and the family name, or between both morality and craftsmanship and an identifying mark on the product, must have made it easier for a *nation* to gain an international reputation. Foreigners would learn of the high quality products produced by the citizens of some foreign culture. The reputation of that nation would be enhanced. This was true of Israel's laws:

Behold, I have taught you statutes and judgments, even as the LORD my God commanded me, that ye should do so in the land whither ye go to possess it. Keep therefore and do them; for this is your wisdom and your understanding in the sight of the nations, which shall hear all these statutes, and say, Surely this great nation is a wise and understanding people (Deut. 4:5-6).

What is true of a law-order is also true for products. When consumers can more readily identify products that satisfy them, the efficiency of the market is greatly enhanced. *The division of labor is limited by the extent of the market,* Adam Smith wrote in Chapter 3 of *Wealth of Nations* (1776), and by increasing brand-name identification, producers thereby contribute to extending the market. Men become familiar with buying in the marketplace, which is important in the transition between a primitive society, with its low division of labor, to a modern society. *Brand names transmit knowledge* in an effective, rapid, and summary fashion, and knowledge is what the Bible commends again and again. Brand names help consumers to *economize on knowledge*, which is the most important and valuable of all commodities (Prov. 3:13-20).[5]

Slander and Theft

The prohibition against bearing false witness is *theocentric*. Men are to give an honest account of God, God's work, and God's plan for history. The commandment requires men to adhere to the God-interpreted facts of history. The existence of this theocentric commandment against distorting the truth concerning God has created a unique property right: *the right to a name*. A man is entitled to his good name. *Slander is therefore a form of theft.* The civil government has an obligation to defend the right of an individual to use a particular name, both personal and corporate, both familial and institutional. The civil government must also defend that name against false witnesses. In doing so, the civil authorities thereby reduce consumers' search costs, for the property right to a name, trademark, or other identifying mark encourages men to build up their capital by establishing good reputations for themselves. This helps to increase the sale of quality products, or price-competitive products, and it also reduces search costs for the consumers. Buyers can make decisions more effectively (less wastefully) because of the availability of brand names.

Another neglected aspect of brand names is that a brand name makes possible scientific testing by independent research organizations. Brands establish an identifiable subclass of goods (a particular product line) which can then be compared scientifically by means of random selection from this and other competing products in that same class. The performance of a randomly selected product from an identifiable company can be compared with the performance of other randomly selected products that are produced by competitors. The results of these tests may be purchased by consumers. This helps consumers to make cost-effective decisions about which products to purchase.

If potential competitors were allowed to adopt identical identify-

---

5. By far the finest book on the economics of knowledge is Thomas Sowell, *Knowledge and Decisions* (New York: Basic Books, 1980). Also useful is the specialized study by the legal theorist, Henry Manne, *Insider Trading and the Stock Market* (New York: Free Press, 1966). A bit narrow in focus, but important in dealing with the question of knowledge and the stock market, is the symposium edited by Manne, *Economic Policy and the Regulation of Corporate Securities* (Washington, D.C.: American Enterprise Institute, 1969), especially the essay by Harold Demsetz, "Perfect Competition, Regulation, and the Stock Market." Cf. Frederick G. Klein and John A. Prestbo, *News and the Market* (Chicago: Regnery, 1974).

ing marks of successful products, including even the name of the competitor's firm, the consumer would find his ability to make cost-effective choices dramatically reduced, and the successful producer would be robbed of a capital asset, namely, his position in the market as a recognizable seller of desirable, familiar products. The costs of knowledge would rise dramatically. The consumer would be poorer, for his knowledge of name-brand product lines, gathered over months or years of reading or comparing brands, would be wiped out. The protection of a name by the civil government is basic to the efficient functioning of a free market society.

It was the fusion of *identifiable product lines* with *free pricing* (open competition) which made possible modern economic life. By speeding up consumers' decision-making — by lowering the costs of making decisions, in other words — brand-name identification has dramatically increased per capita wealth. Consumers not only can make more rapid decisions about buying, as a result of their past experience, but advertising also reduces the time and trouble associated with bargaining. *The wider the market for information, the narrower the zones of ignorance on the part of buyers and sellers.* The buyer knows more concerning the comparative offers of other sellers, while the seller knows more about the offers of competing buyers. Well-publicized prices for specific brands therefore reduce the need for "hard bargaining" between the buyer and seller — bargaining that all too often involves lying, cheating, misrepresentation, and special advantages to one party in the transaction over the other (an advantage based on better knowledge concerning market alternatives).[6]

The prohibition against an evil report should remind us of the proclivity of rebellious men to listen to evil, false reports, and then to spread such reports to others. The spread of lies within a rebellious, envious culture is far easier (less costly) than the spread of the truth. Men who are in rebellion against God have a vested interest in falsehood about God (Rom. 1:18-22) and therefore also about their fellow man. *There is greater demand for false rumors than there is for the truth.* Men delight in twisting the revelation of God concerning Him-

---

6. Hard bargaining is not innately evil, but it is fraught with ethical dangers. By reducing the need for hard bargaining — itself essentially an exercise in competitive knowledge, buyer vs. seller (although force of will is also important) — the wide knowledge of economic alternatives conveyed by a free market pricing system helps reduce men's temptations in economic affairs. Reducing the cost of knowledge reduces conflicts.

self and His creation. There are too many volunteer agents (gossips), and the market for false rumors is wider and more easily accessible than the market for truth, with its greater precision and its comparative lack of rebellion-filled excitement. False rumors are like mistresses: more exciting initially than wives, but more deadly. This is why Proverbs compares false knowledge with harlotry (Prov. 7:6-23), and compares wisdom with the honest woman crying in the streets, ignored by the inhabitants of the city (Prov. 1:20-33).

Because men are evil, the transmission of false reports against the just citizens is subsidized. This subsidy by the ungodly—their preference for falsehood—reduces the per capita wealth of a society, for decisions made in terms of false information are far less likely to produce beneficial results at the lowest possible costs.

Advertising

Advertising is not well understood by social commentators. There has been a great deal of criticism aimed at advertising in general and the advertising industry in particular.[7] Many sorts of economic evils are laid at the door of advertising, especially the creation of new wants—wants that become "needs" in the minds of the masses. This is an odd criticism, coming as it does from educated people. What was the university, or the inventor's laboratory, other than a means of creating hitherto unappreciated opportunities ("wants") for those who had not previously considered them? How can we imagine the operation of the famed institution, "the marketplace of ideas," apart from men's quest for better arguments, more effective presentations, and improved communications?

Property Rights in a Name

Christian commentators have failed to recognize the biblical foundation of advertising. *All advertising stems from the commandment*

---

7. Criticism of advertising has been a constant theme in the writings of John Kenneth Gailbraith. Cf. *The Affluent Society* (Boston: Houghton Mifflin, 1958), pp. 155-58; *The New Industrial State* (2nd ed.; Boston: Houghton Mifflin, 1971), pp. 203-9, 273-74. He comments: "The educational and scientific estate and the larger intellectual community tend to view this effort [modern advertising] with disdain" (p. 293). For a self-professed Christian's similar disdain, see Ronald Sider, *Rich Christians in an Age of Hunger* (Downers Grove, Illinois: Inter-Varsity Press, 1977), pp. 46-50. This book had gone through eight printings by 1980, three years after its original publication. I cite it, not because it is the only neo-evangelical book to take such a position, but because it is the representative book.

prohibiting false witness. This commandment, as we have seen, establishes a situation analogous to a *property right in a man's name.* This name can become a means of transmitting information to consumers. The name "Rembrandt" on a painting conveys certain information concerning the quality of the painting. The name "Coca-Cola" conveys information concerning the taste of a soft drink. (When the company changed the drink's formula in 1985, it suffered immediate losses. It was pressured by consumers to reintroduce the discontinued drink within three months.)

What the critics object to is the misuse of this property right. There are many failings of the advertising industry that are singled out. But are they really significant? Here are some of the typical complaints. "The industry creates unnecessary desires for consumer goods in the minds of the public." (In other words, advertising conveys knowledge of opportunities that potential purchasers might have overlooked.) "The industry manipulates buyers." (The same way these same advertising firms manipulate voters who elect politicians who will establish national policies, not just sell car wax. Should we therefore abolish democracy?) "The buyers are helpless to resist these manipulations." (Just as the buyers must be helpless to decide for themselves the better political candidate. Should we therefore abolish democracy?) "The industry sells dreams, not reality, sizzle rather than steak." (What else do national political party platforms sell except dreams, and how close to subsequent reality are the pre-election promises of politicians? Should we therefore abolish democracy?) "Advertising misleads buyers continually." (Apparently the competition of advertising presentations cannot offset such misleading information.) "Advertising reduces human freedom to act rationally." (Multiple opportunities apparently are bad for human freedom.)

The reality of advertising is simple enough: like any tool of motivation and communication, it can be misused, fraudulently used, tastelessly used, and illegally used. When a company promises something tangible (as distinguished from dreams and fantasies which no one really takes seriously), and then fails to deliver, the advertiser has violated the prohibition against false witness. He has promised that which cannot be delivered as promised. He has said that a particular brand offers a certain set of benefits, and it offers no such benefits. That is fraud, and it is illegal. Victims can sue in court. Prosecuting attorneys can bring charges in the name of the victims.

The point should be clear: any property right, or human skill, or tool can be misused. What is more important is to decide *who will have the right to use the tool or technique,* under what circumstances, under what penalties, and most important of all, *who will decide what is legitimate?* No one has stated the problems more intelligently than Thomas Sowell: "The broad sweep of knowledge needed for decision making is brought to bear through various systems of coordination of the scattered fragmentary information possessed by individuals in organizations. . . . The most basic decision is *who* makes the decision, under what constraints, and subject to what feedback mechanisms. This is fundamentally different from the approach which seeks better decisions by replacing 'the bad guys' with 'the good guys' — that is, by relying on differential rectitude and differential ingenuity rather than on a structure of incentives geared to the normal range of human propensities."[8] In other words, two issues — *the carrot and the stick,* and who has the *authority* to establish when to use the carrot and the stick — are far more important issues than the appointment of hoped-for moral giants to positions of high authority. How to co-ordinate knowledge? How to determine which facts are the economically relevant facts? How to devise an incentive system to encourage people to seek the proper facts and use this knowledge efficiently in order to satisfy consumer demand? These are the relevant questions.

Motivation

Advertising provides a means of communicating knowledge in an effective, motivating way. Let me offer an example from my own business. When I first began publishing my bi-weekly economic newsletter, *Remnant Review,* I wrote a promotion letter which was mailed to a specially targeted audience that was familiar with my name and my previous economic work. I received sufficient subscription income to pay for the mailing, and even show a profit. This same letter was reprinted (at zero cost to me) in a local newspaper with a circulation of over 100,000 — 50 times larger than the select group I mailed to originally. Total response: zero. Name-identification made much of the difference.[9] Because some people knew

---

8. Sowell, *Knowledge and Decisions,* p. 17.

9. Another difference: people do not expect to be asked to buy something when they read what appears to be an information article. They read ads in order to be sold. Thus, the mental switch from "information mode" to "buying mode" is not automatic. It is an expensive switch to make, unless the ad has been specifically designed to activate this switching process.

who I was, they were willing to risk their money and subscribe. I communicated in an effective way to one group, but not to the other. *Motivation* and *name-identification* are closely linked.

What about pictures of rugged cowboys (one might say "worn-out cowboys") that sell cigarettes? Marlboro has used "Marlboro Country" ads for two decades to gain and retain a large share of the cigarette market in the United States. Is this somehow immoral? Consider what went before. Marlboro originally catered to women and had a red filter tip. This approach in the 1950's was a resounding flop. The company dropped it in 1954. The second approach was a resounding success. Was either approach innately immoral (setting aside the question of whether cigarettes as such are somehow immoral)? Has the public been misled in the latter case, but not in the former? Or are buyers somehow pleased to smoke "he-man" cigarettes rather than "women's" cigarettes? Apparently, they are unwilling (or were) to buy red filter tipped cigarettes that attempted to sell to women. But did red filter tips convey "true" information about femininity? Was the early Marlboro cigarette more a women's cigarette than a man's? Or were the advertisers simply trying to position the cigarette in the market by a subtle (or not too subtle) appeal to the buyers' imagination? Is it wrong to give a consumer a sense of belonging to a "special breed" of men, even when nobody believes it? And if it is wrong, why do buyers return, year after year, to the companies that offer them illusions — harmless illusions — that buyers respond to? What possible benefit would the consumer or the seller derive from an endless series of ads that announce: "This product is basically the same as all the others, but we want you to buy ours, since we like our present employment opportunities." How exciting would that be, even though most of us know that such a disclaimer is essentially true, and that competition keeps most of the products within any given price range basically comparable (though not identical)?

The point which cannot be avoided is this: the very competitive structure which provides incentives for one company to improve a product, and for others to follow this lead, is heavily dependent on advertising to create the *desire to buy* in the minds of the readers or viewers. The advertising system, so widely criticized, is itself one foundation of the competitive system that makes "miracles" available to the public at competitive prices. The "evils of advertising," meaning effective, motivating advertising, are absolutely fundamental to free market sales. The *voluntarism* that lies at the heart of the market makes necessary the conveying of information concerning new opportunities in *effective packaging*. Sellers cannot force buyers to buy. [10]

Write a newspaper column about a new book, unless it is a book review in a major publication that caters to the book-buying public, and few sales will result. Publish a well-designed ad for the same book in the same newspaper or magazine, and sales could be considerable. Why the difference? Critics of advertising ignore the obvious: *people read ads with minds open to motivation*; they seldom read newspaper columns in such a way.

Then there is the filtering process of the mind. Men *screen out* vastly more data than they *notice*, let alone *absorb*, or even less, *act upon*. Habit screens out new opportunities. So do many other mental processes that we do not understand yet. Some way to "punch through" the mental veil of indifference must be found. This is what advertising is all about. It is not economically sufficient merely to inform people concerning opportunities; advertising must motivate them to act. We are not hypothetical Greek rationalists, who always do the right thing if we have sufficient knowledge. We are not saved by knowledge, nor are we exclusively (or even mainly) motivated by sheer intellectual awareness. We are motivated by other aspects of human personality: fear, greed, joy, hope, love, humor, imagination, respect, and the desire to be the first person on the block to own one. We are motivated by altruism, too, but you will receive far more donations to "save the children" if you include a picture of a waif and include a brief description of the waif's plight. People respond to real-life situations, or perceived real-life situations. They respond to emotions, to empathy, to the concrete — not to the abstract. They are not so ready to respond to statistical summaries of disaster-laden foreign nations. They want stories and photographs.

The Non-Primacy of the Intellect

The intellectual's favorite myth, *the primacy of the intellect*, is seldom taken seriously by advertisers, because advertisers know that human beings are multifaceted creatures, not just austere, pristine

---

10. The ability of consumers to resist the persuasion of advertisers is admired by Galbraith: "The power to influence the individual consumer is not, of course, plenary. It operates within limits of cost. . . . That the power to manage the individual consumer is imperfect must be emphasized." Galbraith, *Economics and the Public Purpose* (Boston: Houghton Mifflin, 1973), p. 138. The title of the chapter, however, tells the story: "Persuasion and Power."

intellects. If you want to help the real-life victims of those endless disasters, and you need money to help them, you had better be prepared to abandon the doctrine of the primacy of the intellect. You will use advertising techniques that have been successful in selling soap, as well as selling political candidates, if you want to communicate your program to the over-saturated, numbed potential donor. Jerry Huntsinger, one of the most successful direct-mail fund raisers in the world, says that once the recipient opens the envelope (and it is not easy to get him to open it), he will put it down or throw it away if you have not caught his interest within *five seconds*. This is the grim statistical reality of fund-raising appeals, and no chanting of the primacy of the intellect can overcome *this* discovery of the intellect, namely, the statistical results of direct-mail appeals for funds.

Thus, to judge the legitimacy of advertising strictly in terms of the myth of the primacy of the intellect, is to misjudge the validity of advertising. If some statistically significant (meaning profit-generating) portion of the buying public is responding to a "manipulative" advertising campaign, the proper response is not to call the State in to ban the campaign, but rather to allow the predictable free-market response, namely, for other sellers to enter the market with a similar "manipulative" campaign. Just as the answer to a "manipulative" defense attorney's presentation is an equally "manipulative" prosecuting attorney's presentation, so the answer for "manipulative" advertising is open entry to a competing advertising campaign. The important issue is not the presence of supposed manipulative elements in advertising, but rather *the open entry of competitors into the marketplace*. The only known alternative is a statist nightmare of regulatory activities by entrenched, monopolistic bureaucrats. This price is too high.

Conclusion

The free market social order is the product historically of Christian preaching and Christian institutions. By fostering respect for the family name, Christianity reaffirmed the Hebrew tradition of respect for truth. This created an atmosphere favorable to advertising, since producers are permitted to capture the capital value of a good reputation. Advertising in turn extended information to a much wider market. Costs of decision-making dropped, the market expanded, and the division of labor increased, thereby lowering the costs of production.

Information costs are inescapable. Men are not omniscient. The Bible warns men against the sin of presumption, the sin of seeking to be God. A godly society recognizes that information is not a free (gratuitous) good. It recognizes the need for establishing institutions that enhance the spread of *accurate, motivating,* and *self-correcting* knowledge. The West has overcome this cost barrier more effectively than any society in history precisely because the West has honored the laws protecting property, including the property right in one's name or company mark. The transmission of more accurate information through advertising, independent testing, and brand-name recognition has created the modern marketplace, with its relative lack of "hard bargaining" between buyers and sellers.

The modern market transfers the competitive bargaining process to a far more fair and beneficial system: buyers vs. buyers, and sellers vs. sellers. The better the participants' knowledge of market alternatives, the less benefit one bargainer (buyer or seller) has over the other (seller or buyer). Better information protects the weaker party in any economic exchange. The face-to-face hard bargaining which characterizes the Middle Eastern bazaar or other trading areas takes *too much time* to conduct transactions, and it puts too great a premium on *monopolistic psychological manipulation.* The average buyer or seller is protected by a broadly based ("impersonal")[11] free market, with its highly developed systems for transmitting accurate knowledge concerning available economic alternatives.

A man's reputation is to be protected, for good or evil, whether in a court of law or in the court of public opinion. Whether he is righteous or evil, efficient or incompetent, his reputation should reflect his true condition. The jury, the history book, and the free market are all institutions that *render judgment.* They must render righteous, accurate judgment. Rendering judgment is basic to the ninth commandment, and parallels the fourth commandment's sabbatical day of judgment by God. Evil men seek continuity not by establishing a righteous family name but instead by means of crime and false testimony. The result is a lack of rest for any society which refuses to judge men by God's standard. Where there is *no true judgment,* there can be *no rest* — none for the wicked, but more to the point, none for the societies that refuse to punish the wicked.

---

11. On the proper and improper use of the word "impersonal" as it relates to the operations of the free market, see North, *The Dominion Covenant: Genesis* (Tyler, Texas: Institute for Christian Economics, 1982), pp. 9-11.

10

COVETOUSNESS AND CONFLICT

Thou shalt not covet thy neighbour's house, thou shalt not covet they neighbour's wife, nor his manservant, nor his maidservant, nor his ox, nor his ass, nor anything that is thy neighbour's (Ex. 20:17).

Covetousness, biblically speaking, refers to an illicit craving of another person's possession, including his station in life. It can also involve the actual theft of someone else's property, either by force or by fraud (Josh. 7:21; Mic. 2:2). The Westminster Larger Catechism (1646) devotes only a few lines to the tenth commandment, having covered outright theft in the eighth commandment: "The sins forbidden in the tenth commandment are, discontentment with our own estate; envying and grieving at the good of our neighbour, together with all inordinate motions and affections to any thing that is his" (Answer 148). The Westminster Assembly understood the *centrality of envy in all covetousness*: the desire to hurt the person who is better off, as a result of grieving because of another's success or benefits. Nevertheless, covetousness involves more than envy.

The term "envy" has several connotations. First, in American slang, it is used harmlessly. Upon learning of another person's job promotion, or success in some area, the speaker may say, "I sure envy your good luck." The speaker is not saying that he wishes that the other person were not successful. He is saying only that he *appreciates* the magnitude of the other person's success, and that he would like to be equally successful. Generations of Christian preaching against the sin of covetousness have produced a harmless usage for the term.

A second connotation would better be described by the modern usage of the English word *jealousy*. When a person says that another person is envious, he really means that the other person is jealous. The other person is said to desire someone else's property or station in life. The other person's advantage is understood to be transferable, and the envious person would like to see the transfer. He wants to prosper at the expense of the one who has the advantage.[1]

A third definition is better. *Envy is the desire to see a successful person brought low, even when, should the person be brought low, the envious person does not benefit directly.* Perhaps the envied person is famous. His fame cannot be transferred to the envious person, yet the envious person delights when the famous person suffers a crisis. Or perhaps the envied person is beautiful. An envious woman secretly delights when the other woman is burned, or scarred, or in some way is disfigured. This description of envy was the basis of a little-known novel by L. P. Hartley, *Facial Justice,* which is discussed by Helmut Schoeck in his classic study, *Envy: A Theory of Social Behavior* (1966).[2] This is what the Westminster Catechism means when it speaks of the envious person's grieving at the good of a neighbor. Envy in this sense is *resentment.*

Trade

There is a problem in dealing with the biblical concept of covetousness. The tenth commandment groups together several forms of coveted property: a neighbor's wife, manservant, maidservant, and work animals. The problem here is *trade.* How can men come together and trade if they are not desirous of purchasing each other's goods? Not every exchange is preceded by an announcement, "goods for sale." Sometimes men see an item that belongs to another, and they approach the potential seller to offer an exchange. Obviously, when men decide to sell, they are acknowledging that they prefer to own the goods being offered by someone else.

The sale of a wife is obviously illegal. A man is not permitted to lust after another man's wife. No exchange here is legitimate. But why should the same prohibition restrict the exchange of, say, gold for work animals? Why should it be immoral to offer to buy the services of work animals on a permanent basis? True, the manservant or maidservant may be permanently associated with a particular family. The permanent slave in the Old Testament voluntarily de-

---

1. Clearly, this usage does not refer to the meaning of jealousy in the Bible, where God is spoken of as a jealous God.

2. L. P. Hartley, *Facial Justice* (Garden City, New York: Doubleday, 1960); Helmut Schoeck, *Envy: A Theory of Social Behavior,* translated by Michael Glenny and Betty Ross (New York: Harcourt, Brace & World, [1966] 1970), pp. 149-55, 197, 373.

cided to undergo the pierced ear ritual (the shedding of blood) in order to become part of a family (Deut. 15:16-17). He was unsalable. But other servants could be sold. Why, then, the prohibition against coveting these others?

Since bargains are made constantly, including the sale of Esau's birthright, which Jacob unquestionably desired, what sense can we make of the commandment? The passage in Micah throws light on the usage of the Hebrew word for coveting. Covetousness involves *uncontrolled lusting*, a desire that can be satisfied only by possessing the other man's property. It is the kind of lusting that is involved in adultery, where the desire cannot legitimately be fulfilled, yet it persists. It is the desire that results in lawlessness when it is thwarted, the desire which cannot take "no" for an answer. "Woe unto them that devise iniquity, and work evil upon their beds! When the morning is light, they practice it, because it is in the power of their hand. And they covet fields, and take them by violence; and houses, and take them away: so they oppress a man and his house, even a man and his heritage" (Mic. 2:1-2). It is the kind of desire that resulted in Ahab's unlawful confiscation of Naboth's vineyard (I Ki. 21). The man with power uses that power, despite the protection given to the original owner by the biblical laws regarding property.

The prohibition against covetousness therefore does not deal primarily with envy, meaning envy in the sense of resentment. The covetous person really *is* intent upon obtaining the other man's property. *Covetousness*, in the biblical view, is an illicit form of *jealousy*. The attack against the other man's property is not motivated by a desire only to tear down his property, but to confiscate it.

The covetous person resents his own station in life. Someone else possesses what he wants. He is dissatisfied with the role he is playing in God's plan for the ages. It is this resentment against one's station in life which Paul condemns (I Cor. 7:21-22). One person desires another's good looks, prestige, or worldly possessions. He feels thwarted by his own limitations, and therefore thwarted by his environment. God has thwarted his personal development, the covetous man is asserting. The Bible teaches that the other person is working out his salvation or damnation before God. His property must be respected. Nevertheless, the covetous man thinks that he can appropriate for himself the fruits of the other man's labor, as if those fruits were unrelated to that man's personal responsibility before God as a steward.

Downward Social Mobility

Another aspect of this jealousy is overlooked by most commentators. *Covetousness can also be directed downward*, toward those who have fewer goods, and therefore fewer responsibilities. This can be seen in the social phenomenon known as the *drop-out mentality*. In the late 1960's, for example, the sons and daughters of the middle classes and the wealthy were on the road, all over the world. They adopted the dress codes of poor people, wearing the faded blue denim jeans of field hands.[3] They would even bleach their new, dark blue jeans, to give them an instant fade.[4] Blue jeans became so associated with Western culture that they commanded a high price — a black market price — in Iron Curtain nations, especially the Soviet Union. Young people adopted the life style of nomads — unwashed drifters who refuse to face the responsibilities of dominion. Those with wealth and responsible callings became "primitive," in an attempt to escape the burdens associated with economic stewardship. They wanted others to take the risks and bear the responsibilities.

The Bible prohibits men from escaping lawful callings, unless they are upgrading their responsibilities. A slave is authorized to take his freedom, if and when it is voluntarily offered by his master, either free of charge or by sale (I Cor. 7:21). The idea is to extend God's rule into every area of life, and men are not to turn their backs on this task simply because a particular calling looks as though it would involve too much responsibility. *It is important for each person involved to evaluate his own capabilities accurately, and then to match those capabilities with his calling before God — his highest, most productive calling.* God calls men to be imitators of His son, Jesus Christ, to conform themselves to Christ's image (I Cor. 15:49). They are to work out the salvation that God gives them, and they are to do this with fear and trembling (Phil. 2:12). This kind of steady improvement involves *upward mobility*: spiritual improvement, at the very least, but also economic and social mobility. The individual may not see himself advancing economically, but over generations, the spiritual heirs of a

---

3. The original blue jeans were sold by the Levi Strauss Company during the gold rush days in California in the 1850's. Hence the almost generic name, "Levis." The pants were marketed as being especially durable, a desirable feature in the opinion of gold miners.

4. The 1970's brought a fusion of symbols: "designer" jeans. These were blue denim jeans that bore the name of famous rich people or famous designers, and brought three or four times the price of a pair of normal blue jeans.

man will advance. The wealth of the wicked is laid up for the just (Prov. 13:22). Upward mobility must be in terms of God's calling — service to God — and not simply in terms of amassing wealth (I Tim. 6:6-10). We are to imitate godly examples (I Cor. 11:1), but we are not to worry about "keeping up with the Joneses" in a purely material sense.

Political Covetousness

The commandment against covetousness refers to an individual who looks longingly at his neighbor's property. *The beginning of covetousness is clearly the human heart* (Jas. 3:14-16). Men want goods that they have neither earned nor inherited. Their relationships with their neighbors cannot possibly be in conformity to God's law when such feelings are present in their hearts. The fact that one man possesses goods that are confiscatable in the eyes of his neighbor will disrupt their relationship. The possessor will be seen by the covetous man as an illegitimate owner, someone who has no right, under God, to maintain control over his possessions.

The commandment has implications beyond the local neighborhood. *When covetousness becomes widespread, the next step is political coercion.* The very usage of the words, "to covet," implies violence. The covetous man will not limit his attempt to gain control of another man's property to an offer to purchase. Like Ahab, who was determined to gain control of Naboth's vineyard when Naboth refused to sell, the covetous man seeks to coerce his neighbor. When this cannot be done with the connivance of the police — outright oppression or theft — then he seeks to gain control of the civil government. Covetous men can join forces and encourage the civil government to adopt policies of wealth redistribution. The *monopoly of legal violence* possessed by the civil government can then be turned against property owners. Those within the civil government can gain control over people's assets. They can then use them personally, or inside a government bureau, or distribute them to political special-interest groups. Political covetousness is a manifestation of *unrestrained desire* and the *threat of violence.* When the civil government becomes an instrument of covetousness, its monopoly of violence increases the danger of theft. A new commandment is adopted: "Thou shalt not covet, except by majority vote." What private citizen can effectively defend his property against unjust magistrates? Naboth died in his attempt to keep that which was his by law — God's law.

The misuse of the civil government in this way is doubly evil. First, it violates the principle of responsible stewardship. Second, it misuses the office of magistrate. *The spread of covetousness cannot be restrained by the magistrate when the structure of civil government is deeply influenced by political covetousness.* The old warning against putting the foxes in charge of the chicken coop is accurate: when the State becomes the agent of widespread covetousness, the whole society is threatened. *Waves of power struggles ensue, for each special-interest group recognizes that it must gain control of the primary agency of wealth redistribution.* The more power is offered to the controllers by means of statist coercive mechanisms, the more ferocious is the struggle to gain access to the seats of power. Central planning rewards ruthlessness. Hayek has spoken plainly concerning the awful implications of unlimited State power: *the worst get on top.* These two paragraphs are among the most important in the history of political theory.

But while for the mass of the citizens of the totalitarian state it is often unselfish devotion to an ideal, although one that is repellent to us, which makes them approve and even perform such deeds, this cannot be pleaded for those who guide its policy. To be a useful assistant in the running of a totalitarian state, it is not enough that a man should be prepared to accept specious justification of vile deeds; he must himself be prepared actively to break every moral rule he has ever known if this seems necessary to achieve the end set for him. Since it is the supreme leader who alone determines the ends, his instruments must have no moral convictions of their own. They must, above all, be unreservedly committed to the person of the leader; but next to this the most important thing is that they should be completely unprincipled and literally capable of everything. They must have no ideals of their own which they want to realize; no ideas about right or wrong which might interfere with the intentions of the leader. There is thus in the positions of power little to attract those who hold moral beliefs of the kind which in the past have guided the European peoples, little which could compensate for the distastefulness of many of the particular tasks, and little opportunity to gratify any more idealistic desires, to recompense for the undeniable risk, the sacrifice of most of the pleasures of private life and of personal independence which the posts of great responsibility involve. The only tastes which are satisfied are the taste for power as such and the pleasure of being obeyed and of being part of a well-functioning and immensely powerful machine to which everything else must give way.

Yet while there is little that is likely to induce men who are good by our standards to aspire to leading positions in the totalitarian machine, and much to deter them, there will be special opportunities for the ruthless and unscrupulous. There will be jobs to be done about the badness of which taken by themselves nobody has any doubt, but which have to be executed with the same expertness and efficiency as any others. And as there will be need for actions which are bad in themselves, and which all those still influenced by traditional morals will be reluctant to perform, the readiness to do bad things becomes a part to promotion and power. The positions in a totalitarian society in which it is necessary to practice cruelty and intimidation, deliberate deception and spying, are numerous. Neither the Gestapo nor the administration of a concentration camp, neither the Ministry of Propaganda nor the S.A. or S.S. (or their Italian or Russian counterparts), are suitable places for the exercise of humanitarian feelings. Yet it is through positions like these that the road to the highest positions in the totalitarian state leads.[5]

Hayek's book was intended to demonstrate how totalitarian societies develop out of the attempt of socialist planners to mold the economy into a centrally directed framework. He argued that in theory, nothing must deviate from the central economic plan, since human freedom will thwart any such plan. Thus, the power to redistribute wealth in accordance to some preconceived statist program eventually destroys human freedom and therefore thwarts personal responsibility to act as a steward under God. *Covetousness, when legislated, becomes a major foundation of totalitarianism.*

Hayek's little book evoked outraged cries of "foul!" from the statist intellectuals when it first appeared. Herbert Finer's *Road to Reaction* is perhaps the best example. But year by year, decade by decade, *The Road to Serfdom* has grown in stature, until it is now considered a classic. It stays in print, and has served as the financial backbone of the University of Chicago Press' paperback division. Twentieth-century voters and politicians have not yet been blessed with the moral courage to act in terms of Hayek's arguments against the centrally planned economy, but those intellectuals who even bother to worry about the problem of human liberty in relation to the economy have steadily begun to take Hayek seriously on this point. Four decades after the *Road to Serfdom* first appeared, the humanists who write scholarly books have at last begun to catch up with the wisdom of the average book buyer who made *Road to Serfdom* a bestseller in 1944. (It even appeared in the *Reader's Digest* in 1944 as a condensed book.)

---

5. F. A. Hayek, *The Road to Serfdom* (University of Chicago Press, 1944), pp. 150-51.

Beyond the Tithe

The civil government is to be restrained by biblical law. The warning of Samuel against the establishment of a human kingship stands as a classic statement of what earthly kingdoms involve. The king will draft sons to serve in his armed forces. He will conscript daughters to serve as cooks and confectioners. He will confiscate the best agricultural land. He will impose a tithe on the flocks. In short, the king will collect a tithe for himself (I Sam. 8:11-19). The Hebrew State, Samuel promised, will be such a burden on them that they will cry out to God to deliver them, but He will not do it (v. 18). By denying God and His law-order, the Hebrews placed themselves under the sovereignty of man, and this sovereignty was centralized in the civil government. It is an ungodly State which demands tax payments as large as ten percent, God's tithe, let alone a State which requires more than God's tithe. Such a State has elevated itself to the position of a god. It is a false god. It is demonic.

Civil governments since World War I have found that a "mere ten percent" is not sufficient to finance massive programs of domestic and international wealth redistribution. Virtually all modern Western civil governments impose taxes of over 40% — national, regional, and local—which is twice that imposed by the tyrannical bureaucracy of Egypt (Gen. 47:23-24). The allocations for welfare programs—wealth redistribution — are generally double the combined allocations for national defense and the law enforcement system. What we have seen in the twentieth century is the creation of a universal system of *legislated covetousness.* Biblical law has been ignored, even as Christians have ignored the principle of the tithe. (Deuteronomy 26 is an exposition of the tenth commandment, and it ties this commandment directly to the tithe.) Steadily, political freedoms have been removed; the after-tax income of the citizenry has been reduced systematically, leaving men with fewer resources to use in stewardship programs of voluntary charity. The civil government has steadily supplanted churches and voluntary associations as the primary agent of charity—a compulsory charity which is in fact a form of State-operated serfdom. The difference is this: the non-working servants (welfare recipients) are controlled by the State, and the working servants who support them are also controlled by the State. *Massive, unrelenting political covetousness has led to universal enslavement.*

Social Co-operation

When men do not trust their neighbors, it becomes expensive for them to co-operate in projects that would otherwise be mutually beneficial to them. They hesitate to share their goals, feelings, and economic expectations with each other. After all, if a man is known to be economically successful in a covetous society, he faces the threat of theft, either by individuals or bureaucrats. He faces the hostility of his associates. He faces others on a regular basis who are determined to confiscate what he has. The obvious response is to conceal one's success from others. But this also means concealing one's economic expectations. *Planning becomes clothed in secrecy.* The planning agency of the family limits its goals. Disputes between families increase, since families cannot easily co-operate under such circumstances. The future is a topic of discussion only in vague terms, except in the privacy of family economic planning councils. The social division of labor is thwarted, and the future-orientation of communities is drastically reduced, since men refuse to discuss plans openly.[6]

The commentators are conspicuously vague about the precise meaning of covetousness. They link it with theft, especially Ahab's theft of Naboth's vineyard. They link it with envy in the sense of resentment. But one insight that Charles Hodge offered, which was followed by Herman Hoeksema, is this: above all, covetousness is *discontent with one's position in life.* Hodge wrote: "Thou shalt not inordinately desire what thou hast not; and especially what belongs to thy neighbor. It includes the positive command to be contented with the allotments of Providence; and the negative injunction not to repine, or complain on account of the dealings of God with us, or to envy the lot or possessions of others." Hodge did not have in mind any otherworldly or mystical rejection of property. As he said in the next section: "The command to be contented does not imply indifference, and it does not enjoin slothfulness. A cheerful and contented disposition is perfectly compatible with a due appreciation of the good things of this world, and diligence in the use of all proper

---

6. What Schoeck writes concerning envy applies equally well to legislated covetousness: "Ubiquitous envy, fear of it and those who harbour it, cuts off such people from any kind of communal action directed towards the future. Every man is for himself, every man is thrown back upon his own resources. All striving, all preparation and planning for the future can be undertaken only by socially fragmented, secretive beings." Helmut Schoeck, *Envy,* p. 50.

means to improve our condition in life."[7] He cited Philippians 4:11: "I have learned, in whatsoever state I am, therewith to be content." He could have continued quoting Paul's words: "I know both how to be abased, and I know how to abound: every where and in all things I am instructed both to be full and to be hungry, both to abound and to suffer need. I can do all things through Christ which strengtheneth me" (Phil. 4:12-13). *Any external condition is acceptable to the man who is content with his present role in God's plan for the ages.* But having little is usually the condition against which men rebel. Paul is clear on this point: "But godliness with contentment is great gain. For we brought nothing into this world, and it is certain we can carry nothing out. And having food and raiment let us be therewith content" (I Tim. 6:6-8). The rich have many temptations (I Tim. 6:9-10).

Hodge saw the other aspect of covetousness: *envy.* Again, I think this aspect is overemphasized in explaining this verse, although the fact that commentators have focused on it in the past testifies to the importance of Christian preaching against envy, even though in the context of the tenth commandment it is not completely appropriate. Hodge's words show that he fully understood the meaning of envy as *resentment,* and that he distinguished this aspect of envy from covetousness as the desire to confiscate another man's property for one's own use. "The second form of evil condemned by this commandment is envy. This is something more than an inordinate desire of unpossessed good. It includes regret that others should have what we do not enjoy; a feeling of hatred and malignity towards those more favoured than ourselves; and a desire to deprive them of their advantages. This is a real cancer of the soul; producing torture and eating out all right feelings. There are, of course, all degrees of this sin, from the secret satisfaction experienced at the misfortunes of others, or the unexpressed desire that evil may assail them or that they may be reduced to the same level with ourselves, to the Satanic hatred of the happy because of their happiness, and the determination, if possible, to render them miserable. There is more of this dreadful spirit in the human heart than we are willing to acknowledge. Montesquieu says that every man has a secret satisfaction in the misfortunes even of his dearest friends. As envy is the antithesis of love, it is of all sins that most opposed to the nature of God, and more effectually

---

7. Charles Hodge, *Systematic Theology,* 3 vols. (Grand Rapids, Michigan: Eerdmans, [1872] 1960), III, p. 468.

than any other excludes us from his fellowship."[8] It is clear that Hodge regarded envy as the most dangerous of all the sins. *It was this kind of preaching, generation after generation, which made possible the economic development of the Protestant West.* It is the absence of such preaching in the twentieth century that has damaged the economic institutions of Western capitalism — the source of the West's productivity.

Hoeksema also identified covetousness as *discontent.* "The sin of covetousness is the desire to possess anything apart from God, against His will; anything that he does not give me and that evidently He does not want me to have. . . . If the sin of covetousness could be rooted out of society, most of our economic problems would be solved. Covetousness is the root of all the sinful unrest in society. The same is true of international life and relationships; if the sin of covetousness were not so deeply rooted in the heart of the depraved man, most wars, if not all, would be eliminated. Take covetousness away, and there would be no reason for men to fly at one another's throats, and you could hardly conceive of the possibility of war. . . . Positively, this means, of course, that the tenth commandment enjoins us to be content with what we have. Christian contentment is perfect satisfaction with what one has, for the sake of God in Christ Jesus our Lord, and that, too, in the midst of a corrupt and covetous world."[9]

Hoeksema is correct: discontent is the heart of sin's problem, beginning with Satan's discontent with God's sovereignty. Discontent is an aspect of all sin, for if men were contented with righteousness and the fruits of righteousness, they would not rebel against God. Covetousness is a specific form of discontent: the desire to possess another's goods at all cost, including the other man's loss. As Matthew Poole, the Puritan commentator, wrote in the seventeenth century: covetousness is the "inward and deliberate purpose and desire of a deceitful or violent taking away of another man's goods; but this is forbidden in the eighth commandment."[10] Theft is forbidden; covetousness is the *inward desire* that leads to theft or fraud. It is the evil desire which overwhelms the law's restraint on the sinner, the desire to have another man's property, whether or not the other man bene-

---

8. *Ibid.*, III, pp. 464-65.
9. Herman Hoeksema, *The Triple Knowledge: An Exposition of the Heidelberg Catechism*, 3 vols. (Grand Rapids, Michigan: Reformed Free Publishing Association, 1972), III, pp. 427-28.
10. Matthew Poole, *Commentary on the Whole Bible*, 3 vols. (London: Banner of Truth Trust, [1683] 1968), I, p. 160.

fits from the transaction. Voluntary exchange offers the other man an opportunity. He may not have known of the opportunity. He may not have known of a person's willingness to part with some resource in order to obtain what he, the owner, possesses. It is not immoral to offer another person an opportunity, unless the opportunity is innately immoral (such as offering to buy his wife's favors). *Covetousness is the lawless desire to take the other man's property, whether or not he finds the transaction beneficial.* When covetousness is common, men lose faith in their neighbors, in the social and political structure which protects private property, and in the benefits offered by the division of labor. Covetousness threatens the very fabric of society.

The tenth commandment was given to us so that we might enjoy the fruits of *social peace* and *social co-operation*. This is equally true of the earlier commandments. The law-order of the Bible is a means of *reducing conflict* and *extending the division of labor*. Greater efficiency becomes possible through the division of labor. Whatever contributes to social peace thereby tends to increase per capita productivity, and therefore per capita income. People have an economic incentive to co-operate. The prohibition against covetousness increases social co-operation by reducing its costs. In other words, more co-operation is demanded because its price drops. One of the social institutions that results from such a prohibition is the free market. It, too, is an institution which furthers social co-operation.

It is significant that the prohibition against covetousness begins with the mind of man. There is no means of enforcing any civil law against thoughts, but God's law applies to men's thoughts. Since the very concept of covetousness involves the threat of violence and oppression, the *outworkings of covetousness* can be controlled by civil law, assuming the civil government has not been corrupted by a philosophy of universal legislated covetousness. The costs of policing the visible manifestations of covetousness are high. By focusing on the hearts of men, the Bible reduces the costs of law enforcement.

Men are to be taught from an early age that covetousness is a sin against God. These instruction costs are to be borne initially by the family (Deut. 6:7). By making men aware of God's hostility to covetousness, teachers of the law reduce the need for heavy taxation, either for law enforcement against visible, coercive oppressors, or for programs of legislated covetousness, i.e., "social welfare" programs. By helping to increase the social division of labor, the *internalization of the law against covetousness* helps to increase per capita output, also reducing thereby the proportion of income going to support law enforcement. The society is blessed in two ways: reduced crime (including the crime of statist wealth redistribution programs) and increased output per capita. *Men wind up with more wealth after taxes. They increase their opportunities for responsible action before God and men.*

The Modern Welfare State[11]

The twentieth century, since the outbreak of World War I, has abandoned the tenth commandment. Divorce and remarriage of the sinful partner are common events. Men covet their neighbors' wives. They covet their neighbors' goods. (Coveting a man's goods is certainly less of a threat to the integrity of his family unit than the coveting of his wife.) The rise of massive taxation, including the inflation tax, has led to the spread of covetous political programs. The graduated income tax, with its increasingly burdensome rates of taxation for those with higher income, has been proclaimed in the name of social justice, even Christian social justice.[12] Nevertheless, the combination of graduated income taxation, the psychology of debt (and even tax deductions for interest payments in the United States), and the control of money by the State and its licensed agents, the banks, has led to ruinous taxation of the middle classes.[13] Men are tempted to vote for more wealth redistribution programs, and then they are tempted to pay for them by means of monetary inflation. This enables both individuals and the State to repay loans with depreciated money. "A little inflation" seems to be beneficial in the early years, since it fosters an economic boom.[14] It involves the destruction of the creditors' interests, but who cares about creditors?

---

11. The phrase "welfare State" first attained prominence in 1949, writes historian Sidney Fine, and has come to be associated in the United States with the administration of President Harry Truman, 1945-53: Sidney Fine, *Laissez Faire and the General Welfare State: A Study of Conflict in American Thought, 1865-1901* (Ann Arbor: University of Michigan Ann Arbor Paperback, [1956] 1964), Preface.

12. John C. Bennett, who taught ethics at Union Theological Seminary in New York, and who served as president of that institution, writes concerning needed social reforms: "The third reform is changes in the tax system that would close loopholes for the rich and in many ways bring about a more equal distribution of wealth. The adoption of the idea of a progressive income tax was in itself an early breakthrough of great importance." Bennett, *The Radical Imperative: From Theology to Social Ethics* (Philadelphia: Westminster Press, 1975), p. 153.

13. James Dale Davidson, *The Squeeze* (New York: Summit Books, 1980).

14. Ludwig von Mises, *Human Action: A Treatise on Economics* (3rd ed.; Chicago: Regnery, 1966), ch. 20.

Yet most middle-class citizens are *creditors*. When they vote, they may not fully understand this, failing to grasp its implications for their economic futures, but they are creditors nonetheless. They hold *paper certificates of ownership for future payments of paper money*. They buy mortgages, they invest in pension programs, they buy cash-value life insurance, and they buy annuities. Worst of all, at least before the public catches on, they own long-term bonds, especially government bonds. The economist, Franz Pick, has called government bonds "certificates of guaranteed confiscation." The result is the *universal expropriation* of these classes of investors when mass inflation strikes. Everyone is pushed into higher income levels, which means that people are forced to pay a higher percentage of their nominal (meaning their paper money-denominated) incomes to the State. The result of these three features of economic life — graduated income taxes, universal debt, and fiat money — is the eventual destruction of the middle class. Yet it has been the middle class (and the parents and grandparents of the late twentieth century's middle class) that voted for these programs of legislated covetousness. They set a trap for the rich, and inflation subsequently made *them* nominally rich. God will not be mocked.

Christian Socialism

Those Christians who will look back upon the twentieth century in some future era will marvel at the unwillingness of Christian intellectuals to challenge the economic policies of the welfare State. Worse: Christian intellectuals all too often defend such policies, or even call for an expansion of them.[15] Future generations will not understand why programs of legislated covetousness were not decried as violations of the tenth commandment. They will be astounded to learn that spiritual leaders in every nation not only approved of such policies, but actively sought to have them enacted into law. The ethics of anti-biblical humanism has permeated the thinking of twentieth-century Christians, so that the opposition to compulsory wealth redistribution programs generally has not come from Chris-

---

15. See, for example, Ronald J. Sider, *Rich Christians in an Age of Hunger: A Biblical Study* (2nd ed.; Downers Grove, Illinois: InterVarsity, 1984). For a refutation, see David Chilton, *Productive Christians in an Age of Guilt-Manipulators: A Biblical Response to Ronald J. Sider* (3rd ed.; Tyler, Texas: Institute for Christian Economics, 1985). See also the essay by John Gladwin, in Robert Clouse (ed.), *Wealth and Poverty: Four Christian Views of Economics* (Downers Grove, Illinois: InterVarsity, 1984), and my response to his essay.

tian leaders, but has come from humanists who are defenders of nineteenth-century economic liberalism—a perspective which itself was a secularized and Darwinian version of biblical social ethics.[16]

What has been called "the climate of opinion" in any given era is a most powerful social force. This is why it is imperative that Christians develop and preach a systematically biblical social program. Because Christians have neglected this critically important task, the secularists have taken the lead in setting the climate of social opinion. This climate of opinion has subsequently influenced the thinking of Christian intellectual leaders. The competing conclusions of the god of humanism, autonomous man, have become the standards for Christian thinkers and policy-makers.

Not all Christian scholars are socialists, of course, but it is a widely held opinion that any social and economic framework is acceptable to Christians. Those Christians who believe that any economic framework is acceptable (except one based explicitly on biblical law, of course), just so long as Christians have the right to preach the gospel of personal salvation, are faced with a problem: By what standard can a Christian legitimately conclude that all economic frameworks are acceptable to Christ? Furthermore, *if any and all social and economic frameworks are legitimate before God, then in what way can the preaching of the gospel influence the social institutions of the day?* How can they be reformed? And if they do not need reform, how is it that rebellious, sinful men have succeeded in creating social institutions that are not in need of reconstruction? How, in short, can Christians avoid constructing a social order on the shifting sands of warring humanist philosophies, special-interest groups, power-seekers, and contradictory social and political programs? Is the Bible irrelevant to social institutions?

Conclusion

Social peace is a major goal of biblical law—the social peace demanded by the prophet Isaiah: "They shall not hurt nor destroy in all my holy mountain: for the earth shall be full of the knowledge of the LORD, as the waters cover the sea" (Isa. 11:9). *The juridical foundation of such peace is biblical law.* The ten commandments serve as the basis of long-term, God-blessed social peace.

---

16. Gary North, *The Dominion Covenant: Genesis* (Tyler, Texas: Institute for Christian Economics, 1982), Appendix B: "The Evolutionists' Defense of the Market."

One important aspect of biblical social peace is the absence of covetousness—in the hearts of men, in the relationships between neighbors, and in the legislation of civil governments. A covetous person's discontent with his station in life makes it impossible for him to have personal peace. This lack of personal peace spreads to society as a whole when covetousness becomes universalized through the political process. Where political covetousness reigns, there can be no social peace. There also cannot be personal freedom.

The covetous person disrupts social peace, just as the satanic magician and thief do. The sinner covets that which he has not lawfully earned or lawfully inherited. Nevertheless, he wants the other man's patrimony or inheritance. He may not steal it outright, but he lusts after it.

The tenth commandment is framed in terms of neighboring families. It implies that peace must begin at home. The peace-breaker begins locally. The covetous man wants the other person's house, wife, and goods. He cannot lawfully have all of these, and even the goods must be bargained for. The jubilee year in Israel guaranteed that the house would eventually return to the lawful family heirs (Lev. 25), and the law against adultery protected the wife. The eighth commandment protected the goods, although they could be exchanged. The lawful heirs will inherit. The tenth commandment therefore parallels the fifth, which is also concerned with the question of legitimacy and inheritance, although the seventh and eighth commandments also add their force to the tenth.

The dominion covenant requires men to obey God's laws of inheritance. To gain social peace, these laws must be honored. The lack of social peace in the modern world testifies to the unwillingness of men, as mandated through political institutions, to respect God's laws of inheritance. The modern world has institutionalized covetousness politically.

CONCLUSION

Ye shall therefore keep my statutes, and my judgments: which if a man do, he shall live in them: I am the LORD your God (Lev. 18:5).

The ten commandments set forth *God's laws of life.* They do not provide life, but they set forth the standards of life. This is why Jesus Christ came to earth to fulfill the terms of the law, not to annul them (Matt. 5:17-19).[1] Without His willingness and ability to live out these laws, in time and on earth, God would not grant eternal life, or even temporary earthly life, to any law-breaker.

These laws were presented to the Israelites by God in the form of a covenant treaty.[2] Men inescapably live in terms of covenants: either before God or before Satan, and always with each other. Thus, these laws of life are necessarily covenantal laws, both social and personal, both general and particular.[3] What are the covenantal goals of God's laws of life in society? *Social peace and economic blessings,* "peace and prosperity." There is no other way to interpret Deuteronomy 28:1-14: the list of external and internal blessings is comprehensive. Furthermore, the list of cursings is long and threatening: Deuteronomy 28:15-68. What we need to understand is that God's law is intended to create conditions leading to peace, harmony, and wealth.

The ten commandments also lay down the religious, legal, and economic foundations that are necessary for the creation and long-term maintenance of a free market economy. In other words, observ-

---

1. For a detailed consideration of Christ's words in Matthew 5:17-19, see Greg. L. Bahnsen, *Theonomy in Christian Ethics* (2nd ed.; Phillipsburg, New Jersey: Presbyterian & Reformed, 1984), ch. 2.

2. Meredith G. Kline, *The Structure of Biblical Authority* (rev. ed.; Grand Rapids, Michigan: Eerdmans, 1975), pp. 113-71.

3. James B. Jordan, *The Law of the Covenant: An Exposition of Exodus 21-23* (Tyler, Texas: Institute for Christian Economics, 1984), ch. 1.

ance of the basic principles of the ten commandments is both *necessary and sufficient* for the creation of a capitalist economy. (Humanistic free market economists reject the first assertion—"necessary"—since they want a free market without God, while "Christian" socialist theologians reject the second—sufficient—since they want God without a free market.) Whenever the ten commandments are enforced by all agencies of human government, men will gain freedom. Economic freedom of contract and freedom from excessive taxation and bureaucratic interference produce that social order which we call the market society. This is why the Christian West was the first society to create national and regional economies called capitalistic. This is why long-term economic growth has come only in the West, and in those nations that trade with the West and have imitated some of its institutional and legal arrangements, most notably Japan. But if the goal of the Bible is social peace under God's covenants, and if the free market economy has been not only the logical result of the ten commandments but also the historic product of Christianity, then a controversial conclusion follows: *biblical social order and free market capitalism are a "package deal."* Societies cannot attain the kind of long-term, compounding expansion which is required by the dominion covenant without the social, moral, and legal foundations that are established by law in the ten commandments. Humanistic free market economists refuse to believe this, and so do "Christian" socialists.

The Ten Commandments and Capitalism

The ten commandments as a unified whole offer mankind the moral basis of a progressive society. I am not arguing that it is only the eighth commandment, with its prohibition against theft, which sets forth such a view of private ownership. All ten commandments have provided mankind with the faith which has produced Western prosperity:

> God as the sovereign owner of the creation
> Faith in the healing power of God's law
> Personal stewardship before God and other men
> Legal responsibility for one's actions
> Faith in *predictable*, permanent laws
> Faith in economic cause and effect
> Faith in ethical power over magical power
> Faith in work rather than luck

Faith in the productiveness of rest
Faith in the covenantal family (family name)
Optimism concerning the future (linear history)
The possibility of compound economic growth
Defense of the private ownership of both the means of
  production and the fruits of production
The sanctity of covenants and the analogous and derivative
  legitimacy of contracts
Social co-operation through private contracts
Contentedness as a way of life
The illegitimacy of covetousness and envy
The legitimacy of civil government as a monopolistic agent
  of law enforcement, but not wealth redistribution
Penalties against violence and verbal assault
Penalties against slander and theft
Salvation by grace, not law (or legislation)

We compare these premises with the underlying premises of backward societies, and we find almost a perfect reverse image. The society of Satan also has first principles. A list of the major "tenets of backwardness" is provided by P. T. Bauer, a specialist in developmental economics, and a devout Roman Catholic: "Examples of significant attitudes, beliefs and modes of conduct unfavourable to material progress include lack of interest in material advance, combined with resignation in the face of poverty; lack of initiative, self-reliance and a sense of personal responsibility for the economic future of oneself and one's family; high leisure preference, together with a lassitude often found in tropical climates; relatively high prestige of passive or contemplative life compared to active life; the prestige of mysticism and of renunciation of the world compared to acquisition and achievement; acceptance of a preordained, unchanging and unchangeable universe; emphasis on performance of duties and acceptance of obligations, rather than on achievement of results, or assertion or even a recognition of personal rights; lack of sustained curiosity, experimentation and interest in change; belief in the efficacy of supernatural and occult forces and of their influence over one's destiny; insistence on the unity of the organic universe, and on the need to live with nature rather than conquer it or harness it to man's needs, an attitude of which reluctance to take animal life is a corollary; belief in personal reincarnation, which reduces the significance of effort in the course of the present life; recognized status of beggary, together with a lack of stigma in the acceptance of charity; opposition to women's work outside the household."[4]

Haters of the West

When I cited this passage in an essay defending free market capitalism, "radical Christian" Art Gish was outraged: "It troubles me then that North expresses an elitist, if not racist, view that Western values are superior to Third World values, that the Third World is poor because of its ignorance. This is not only arrogant; it is also unbiblical."[5] This, of course, is a total misrepresentation of my views. I do not believe that ignorance is the Third World's problem. The Third World's problems are religious: *moral perversity*, a long history of *demonism*, and outright *paganism* — including especially *socialistic paganism*. But I can well understand why Gish is troubled by my analysis; he himself has adopted the "more-poverty-per-capita program" of the Third World and zero-growth pagans. When he is confronted with the economic curses God has poured out on such pagans, he is troubled. (He should be terrified.)

Having criticized my arrogance — and when it comes to pagan societies and pagan world views, there is no question about it: I am arrogant about the superiority of Christianity — Gish then gets to the point: "I wonder why North quotes Bauer's long list of attitudes which are opposed to capitalistic development. He seems unaware of the extent to which Jesus and the biblical prophets stand condemned by that list. I wish North could see the demonic and destructive nature of Western values. . . . I am shocked that North would suggest that we go to the Third World and preach 'the culture of the West.' I thought we were to preach Jesus and him crucified. Or is capitalistic affluence the same as the way of the cross? Apparently,

---

4. P. T. Bauer, *Dissent on Development: Studies and debates in development economics* (Cambridge, Massachusetts: Harvard Univerrsity Press, 1972), pp. 78-79.

5. Art Gish, "A Decentralist Response," in Robert Clouse (ed.), *Wealth and Poverty: Four Christian Views on Economics* (Downers Grove, Illinois: InterVarsity Press, 1984), p. 78. It occurs to me: Was Moses arrogant and unbiblical when he instructed the Israelites to kill every Canaanite in the land (Deut. 7:2; 20:16-17)? Was he an "elitist" or (horror of horrors) a racist? No; he was a God-fearing man who sought to obey God, who commanded them to kill them all. It sounds like a "superior attitude" to me. Of course, Christians have been given no comparable military command in New Testament times, but I am trying to deal with the attitude of superiority — *a superiority based on our possession of the law of God*. That attitude is something Christians must have when dealing with all pagans. God has given us the tools of dominion.

North believes thrift, education, development and responsibility will save. I don't. I believe the biblical vision stands in fundamental opposition to 'the culture of the West.' "[6]

Mr. Gish is certainly forthright. He is unafraid of aligning himself with the culture of the Third World. He is not neutral in the slightest. *He hates Western civilization.* He recognizes that the West was originally the civilization of capitalism, and that large sections of it are still capitalistic, *and therefore he hates it.* He refuses to admit that the culture of the West, prior to its secularization in the eighteenth and nineteenth centuries, was the product of Christianity. He also refuses to admit that the poverty of the Third World is the product of its anti-Christian background. In an orgy of guilt, he calls us to adopt the poverty-stricken life style of Third World paganism in the name of Jesus.

It is remarkable that self-styled "radical Christians" are surprised to learn that God hates ethical rebellion, and that He brings earthly judgments against pagan societies. The God of the Bible sends ethical rebels to the eternal miseries of the lake of fire (Rev. 20:14). What is earthly poverty, sickness, and political oppression compared to eternal judgment? It makes me wonder if these "radical Christian" critics of capitalism and the West believe in a God who sends people to eternal punishment. It even makes me wonder if they believe in the God of the Bible. I will go so far as to say that if they continue to argue that God will not, does not, and has not allowed the West's wealth to come to demon-worshipping, socialistic, pagan Third World nations, that they will eventually also deny that God sends people to hell and subsequently to the eternal lake of fire. Eventually, these "radical Christians" will become fully consistent and deny the God of the Bible. It may take a decade or two, or it may take less, but this is where they are headed, if they continue to think of the West as the cause of Third World poverty rather than the Third World's moral rebellion against the ten commandments and the God who authored them.

Embittered by Guilt

Gish's problem is the problem he shares with a whole generation of Western intellectuals: too much reliance on endless criticism and too much guilt. This attitude is beginning to paralyze the West.

6. *Ibid.*, pp. 78-79.

Revel's comments are on target: "Not only do democracies today blame themselves for sins they have not committed, but they have formed a habit of judging themselves by ideals so inaccessible that the defendants are automatically guilty. It follows that a civilization that feels guilty for everything it is and does and thinks will lack the energy and conviction to defend itself when its existence is threatened. Drilling into a civilization that it deserves defending only if it can incarnate absolute justice is tantamount to urging that it let itself die or be enslaved."[7] This guilt-induced self-flagellation is made even easier for humanism-influenced "radical Christians," for self-flagellation has been characteristic of Anabaptist groups from the beginning, as have both pacifism and defeatism. By failing to understand and rest upon the doctrines of definitive sanctification and progressive sanctification, they have become guilt-ridden and impotent. Definitive sanctification teaches that Jesus' perfect moral life is imputed to His followers at the point of their conversion. Progressive sanctification teaches that converted people are required by God to work out their salvation with fear and trembling *in terms of biblical law*, even though they are imperfect in and of themselves. Their imperfect work is accounted righteous because of their definitive sanctification. It builds up over time, until the day of final judgment and final sanctification.[8]

But "radical Christians" do not understand these doctrines. They are visibly overwhelmed with guilt concerning their own ineffectiveness, and the ineffectiveness of "Christianity" in not putting a stop to the "moral evil" of capitalism. They have also been overwhelmed by the seeming impossibility of godly dominion. After all, we live in a sinful world. *We* are sinful. So how can we—pitiful, guilt-ridden worms that we are—take dominion? Aren't we sinful perpetrators of injustice? Aren't we the sinful religious accomplices of the evil elite which rules (and profits from) the greedy and corrupt capitalist system? Oh, let us escape to the communal farm, where the morally polluted efficiency of mass-producing, price-competitive industrialism is kept out of our sight (even though we benefit from it 24 hours a day)! Oh, let us refuse to fight in wars to defend our miserable freedoms, even if the Communists should invade. (This is the paci-

---

7. Jean-François Revel, *How Democracies Perish* (Garden City, New York: Doubleday, 1984), p. 10.

8. Gary North, *Unconditional Surrender: God's Program for Victory* (2nd ed.; Tyler, Texas: Geneva Divinity School Press, 1983), pp. 43-47.

fist recommendation of Ron Sider and Richard Taylor, even though, as they admit, "hundreds of thousands, perhaps even millions, might die" as a result of nonviolent resistance.[9]) Oh, let us be delivered from this corrupt and capitalist world! Oh, oh, oh.

Above all, *they crave escape.* This is why they are progressively impotent. This is why their movement is doomed intellectually and doomed historically. These people will be bypassed, either by dominion-oriented Christians or power-oriented humanists, but they *will* be by-passed. They will not determine any civil government's policy. They will be able only to wring their hands on the sidelines of life, telling everyone how guilty they feel and how guilty we ought to feel for not joining them on the sidelines. At most, they will cheer on the statist politicians every time the latter try to pass a tax increase for the higher income brackets. This is the politics aptly described by Rushdoony as the politics of guilt and pity.[10]

Capitalism's "Christian" Critics

There have been two major intellectual movements within twentieth-century Christianity that have been utterly hostile to capitalism: the social gospel movement and the "radical Christianity" or "liberation theology" movement. The first was prominent from the late nineteenth century through the 1950's. The second group came into prominence in the late 1960's and especially in the 1970's. (Art Gish is a representative of the second group.) Both groups hate capitalism with all their hearts—not just the secular version of nineteenth- and twentieth-century capitalism, but every manifestation of capitalism in history. They hate the premises of capitalism. Yet these premises are essentially biblical, derived from the ten commandments. Thus, *the critics of "capitalism in general" are inescapably also haters of the law of God.* This is my conclusion, based on long years of study, both of the economics of the Bible and the published manifestos of the "Christian" socialists.

With the failure of socialist economies to "deliver the goods," the underlying *religious presuppositions* of capitalism's critics—including the "secular" critics—have become clearer. In the nineteenth century, capitalism's critics heralded socialism as the next stage in the

---

9. Ronald J. Sider and Richard K. Taylor, *Nuclear Holocaust and Christian Hope* (Downers Grove, Illinois: InterVarsity Press, 1982), p. 281.

10. R. J. Rushdoony, *Politics of Guilt and Pity* (Fairfax, Virginia: Thoburn Press, [1970] 1978).

economic progress of mankind. Capitalism was more efficient and productive than ancient slavery or medieval feudalism, Marx and others readily admitted, [11] but they believed that socialism would escalate the rate of progress and per capita wealth. That vision is now dead, outside of Western universities; it lies buried in the ashes of the socialist experiments of the twentieth century.

The promoters of secular evolutionary socialism were confident people. They believed that they would eventually be victorious. The social gospel movement picked up this humanistic optimism. It was therefore future-oriented and optimistic. Its members confronted capitalism as if they were in the vanguard of the next stage of human history. They believed in the State, and they sought to transfer power to the State, especially national government. They saw themselves as social revolutionaries — nice, well-meaning, well-fed, humanitarian, and above all *risk-free* revolutionaries of the sanctuary. The sanctuary was just that for them: a place of refuge. But it was to serve as headquarters for a co-ordinated program (they hoped) of social transformation.

A good example of this satanic misuse of the sanctuary is provided by Nathaniel Weyl, in a footnote in his book on Karl Marx. In the 1940's, he reports, "when I was the leader of the radical movement on the Columbia University campus, I was invited to become an honorary member of the Atheists' Club at adjacent Union Theological Seminary. I asked rather naively how an honorable man could accept an appointment to the ministry if he didn't believe in God. The reply was that the pulpit provided a captive audience, a position of authority and a regular salary — all most useful to socialist and Communist propagandists. I declined the invitation."[12] This is the humanists' strategy that I have called "capturing the robes."[13]

That older optimistic socialism, both secular and "Christian," is pretty well gone today. Its optimism was drained by the experiences of power. The European socialist economies are becoming basket cases. In the United States, the hard realities of the Presidency of

---

11. See especially the summary of the economic revolution of modern capitalism in Part I of the *Communist Manifesto*. Karl Marx and Frederick Engels, "Manifesto of the Communist Party" (1848), in Marx and Engels, *Selected Works*, 3 vols. (Moscow: Progress Publishers, [1969] 1977), I, pp. 109-10.

12. Nathaniel Weyl, *Karl Marx: Racist* (New Rochelle, New York: Arlington House, 1979), p. 67.

13. Gary North, *Backward, Christian Soldiers?* (Tyler, Texas: Institute for Christian Economics, 1984), ch. 7.

Lyndon Johnson—crass, calculating, coercive, and above all, *unstylish*—removed much of their hope in the older faith. Furthermore, the rise of alternative theologies undermined the older theological liberalism: politically pessimistic (Reinhold) Niebuhrism, non-rational Barthianism, and New Age transcendentalism. The spiritual odyssey of Harvard theology professor Harvey Cox is representative, though somewhat flamboyant: from outright secular humanism (old liberal-style rationalism) to irrationalism to liberation theology.[14] Cox was the leading theological weather vane of the decade, 1965-75, and every four years, he switched positions.

In place of the old secular socialism has arisen a new critique of capitalism. Capitalism is evil, we are now informed by the critics, because it is too growth-oriented. Economic growth is a liability.[15] More than this: *economic growth is a sin.* We find the "simple life style" people advocating *on principle* a reduced division of labor and lower per capita income, especially for rich nations—that is, the nations in which guilty readers can afford to buy mass-produced, low-cost paperback diatribes and monthly magazines.

Paralleling the transformation of the secular socialists, the church has produced "radical Christianity," sometimes known as "liberation theology." In some senses, these are two different movements. The latter movement tends to be more Marxist; the former is more likely to be made up of Anabaptist pacifists. Sometimes their memberships overlap. The more hard-core liberation theologians tend to be Roman Catholic. The radical Christians are usually Protestants: neo-evangelicals, sometimes Reformed (seminary professors and younger seminary graduates), and especially Anabaptists.

We find so-called radical Christians (who are openly the spiritual heirs of the radical Anabaptist sects of the sixteenth century) espousing the "small is beautiful" philosophy of "neo-Gandhian" E. F. Schumacher, author of *Buddhist Economics*, as well as *Small Is Beautiful*. Schumacher's recommended economic system is consistent with his religious presuppositions; the "radical Christians" are either

---

14. Harvey Cox, *The Secular City: Secularization and Urbanization in Theological Perspective* (New York: Macmillan, 1965); *The Feast of Fools: A Theological Essay on Festivity and Fantasy* (Cambridge, Massachusetts: Harvard University Press, 1969); *The Seduction of the Spirit: The Use and Misuse of People's Religion* (New York: Simon & Schuster, 1973).

15. E. J. Mishan, *The Costs of Economic Growth* (New York: Praeger, 1967); Mishan, *The Economic Growth Debate: An Assessment* (London: George Allen & Unwin, 1977).

inconsistent with theirs (Christianity), or else they are consistent with their *true* presuppositions (anti-Christianity), but dishonest in revealing publicly their true commitment. In any case, what the critics of capitalism — *all the critics of capitalism* — hate is the thought of a literal, comprehensive application of the ten commandments in society.

A Two-God Theology

These "radical Christians" are invariably implicit defenders of some version of the "two-god" theory which Marcion and other early church heretics promoted. They contrast the views of Jesus with the views of Moses. *They hate Old Testament law with a passion.* They argue that there is some fundamental dualism between the Old Testament and the New Testament. They reject the Old Testament and proclaim the New Testament — a New Testament which is now conveniently stripped of its Old Testament foundations. (In this sense, they are not significantly different from modern pietists, dispensationalists, and conservative antinomians, who also assume a radical dualism between the Old and New Testaments.) Then, in the name of this "pure and undefiled" New Testament, they attack anyone who dares to appeal to passages in the Old Testament that sanction private ownership and individual responsibility. (The Old Testament, it seems, is only to be used when you are looking for passages that support modern socialist revolutionism or modern pacifism. Incredibly, some "radical Christians" support both.) "Why is it that conservative Christians have such difficulty with the New Testament?" asks Gish. "They either ignore it, as North does, or try to explain it away."[16] My relevant but incomplete response would be to throw back this contrast: Why do "radical Christians" — who are also generally pacifists — have such difficulty with the Old Testament? Why do they ignore it, as Gish does, or try to explain it away?

But the significant answer to Gish's rhetorical questions is to point out that the difference between Jesus and Moses was a *difference in historical circumstances*: Moses was waiting for the younger generation of Israelites to become a military force (so hated by the "radical Christians"). He was waiting to invade Canaan militarily. God had instructed Moses to destroy the Canaanites and establish Israel's kingdom in the conquered territory. In contrast, Jesus established a new set of tactics, since the Holy Spirit would come at last and lead

---

16. *Wealth and Poverty*, p. 77.

God's people out of the narrow geographical confines of Palestine and into confrontation — religious confrontation, not military confrontation — with the world.

Jesus, like Moses, was preparing His people for a *fight*. It is a fight which involves self-discipline. As was true in Moses' day, it involves multiple covenantal organizations: church, state, and family. Initially, He called on poor men to begin the fight. But Jesus has always called His followers, whether rich or poor, to victory. He has called them *to exercise dominion in terms of His Father's law*. This long-term strategy of dominion has never changed. Redeemed mankind's fulfillment of the dominion covenant is to produce a unique society, simultaneously a garden and a city. This new civilization will operate in terms of God's law, by means of God's grace.

The possibility of such a society is rejected by "radical Christians." The hatred of God's law by "radical Christians" — from the late medieval peasant and artisan rebellions[17] to the Evangelicals for Social Action — is so total that they assert as forever binding the Christian life style of rural Israel in A.D. 30. But this has never been the Bible's perpetually normative social order. What Jesus was talking about was precisely what Moses was also talking about: *a strategy of long-term dominion* — in economics, in politics, in law, in public health, and everywhere else. This strategy remains the same throughout history. There was a shift in both tactics and geography with the coming of the church, but not a change in strategy. What Jesus was offering was *comprehensive redemption*.[18]

Liberalism: From Power to Impotence

The social gospel's advocates saw correctly that Jesus was a revolutionary, in the sense that He offered a program for comprehensive social change. He did exactly that. But they incorrectly modeled His revolution along the lines of the Fabian socialist movement in Britain.[19] They saw that He was an advocate of economic

---

17. Norman Cohn, *The Pursuit of the Millennium: Revolutionary messianism in medieval and Reformation Europe and its bearing on modern totalitarian movements* (New York: Harper Torchbooks, 1961); Igor Shafarevich, *The Socialist Phenemonon* (New York: Harper & Row, [1975] 1980), ch. 2.

18. Gary North, "Comprehensive Redemption: A Theology for Social Action," *The Journal of Christian Reconstruction*, VIII (Summer 1981).

19. On Fabianism, see Margaret Patricia McCarren, *Fabianism in the Political Life of Britain, 1919-1931* (Chicago: Heritage Foundation, 1954); Rose L. Martin, *Fabian Freeway: High Road to Socialism in the U.S.A., 1884-1966* (Boston: Western Islands,

growth and development, an advocate of external progress. They simply rewrote His program to fit their model of evolutionary socialism. But the failure of socialist policies to produce economic progress has necessitated a change in strategy for the advocates of statist social change.

Today the spiritual heirs of the social gospel movement — "radical Christians" — are calling for the same old sectarian Anabaptist revolutions: either some version of common-ownership communalism "down on the farm," or else the expansion of power of the State to redistribute wealth by compulsion. What makes their present appeal unique in our day is that both scenarios are defended by a call for this revolution in the name of a *vision of poverty*, which is the one thing that socialism always produces in abundance. They defend their vision in the name of the "simple life style" — a life style without a high division of labor, mass production, price competition, computers, automobiles, jet planes, and similar high-technology tools of dominion. Richard K. Taylor (who co-authored the InterVarsity Press book with Ronald Sider on why we should disarm the United States of *all* weapons, unilaterally if necessary) wrote an article in *the other side* (July-Aug. 1974), a journal of "radical Christianity," entitled, "the imperative of economic de-development." (The editors at *the other side* did not use capital letters in the old days.) Taylor concluded: "It is imperative that we *de*-develop the American economy, while encouraging the growth of the poorer nations' economies to a level of ecologically sound adequacy, in which basic needs for food, clothing, housing, and medical care are met." Question: Who will decide for Third World national leaders precisely what "ecologically sound adequacy" is? Who will tell them, "Stop, you've had enough!" when they reach these predetermined levels? Who will determine just how much State-enforced "de-development" America needs? And over whose dead body? *Here is a proposal guaranteed to produce social war, endless envy and resentment, and eternal confrontations.* In short, here is a proposal which will make Satan proud of his success in turning men's eyes away from the ten commandments.

"When I get to dreaming about this," Taylor says, "I see Christians leading a movement of tremendous significance. I see Billy Graham walking from one crusade to another rather than flying in a

---

1966), which was based on the voluminous research in McCarren's unpublished manuscript, The Fabian Transmission Belt.

jet. I see him cutting his wardrobe to one suit, and hear him preaching on Mark 10:23 and I Timothy 6:7-10. I see the church going back to the Gospel ideal of humble poverty." What I see is a bunch of presently well-fed, pampered, and tenured social utopians out in a field during the day, trying to feed themselves without tools, and spending the evening writing their economic manifestos on papyrus with their goose quills and ink. "Radical Christianity" is anything but a movement of "tremendous significance." It is a temporary phenomenon of guilt-ridden, public school-educated, socialism-peddling, suicidal, retreatist *poverts*.[20] They are self-consciously *advocates of impotence* — zero-growth impotence. As a movement, they will undoubtedly achieve their goal. They are going nowhere, for they are low-capital nomads without a known destination. The "radical Christianity" of the neo-Anabaptists is a classic contemporary manifestation of *escapist religion*.[21] They propose programs that inescapably produce social conflict, but always in the name of social peace and social justice. They propose programs that lead inescapably to cultural impotence, but always in the name of relevance and importance. If they had any serious economic ideas or any likelihood of becoming influential leaders politically or even intellectually, we would call them wolves is sheep's clothing. They are goats in sheep's clothing.

These "radical Christians" serve the political left in the same capacity that the old fundamentalists[22] and pietists have long served the humanist establishment: as *dogmatists of social impotence*. They are as hostile to the Christian reconstructionists' vision of capitalist Christianity as the old fundamentalists were hostile to the social gospel's vision of socialist Christianity. Both groups come up with the same answer: *the Bible offers no economic blueprints*. They are equally incorrect in this assertion.

The Ten Commandments and Western Development

What the ten commandments provide is a strategy. It is neither a power strategy nor an escape strategy. It is a *dominion strategy*. It is a strategy *for not staying poor*, either individually or socially. It is a

---

20. "Povert" [PAHvurt]. Noun. "A person who promotes poverty as a way of life for everyone, but with everyone else starting first." The term was coined by Rev. Lewis Bulkeley. Let us hope it gains a wide circulation.

21. Gary North, *Moses and Pharaoh: Dominion Religion vs. Power Religion* (Tyler, Texas: Institute for Christian Economics, 1985), Introduction.

22. Gary North, *Backward, Christian Soldiers?*, ch. 4: "Fundamentalism: Old and New."

strategy which was first delivered by God to a rabble of ex-slaves who were about to begin a 40-year wandering in a wilderness, precisely because they rejected God's strategy. It is a strategy based on covenantal *subordination under God*, both personally and corporately, and calls for *dominion over creation*, both personally and corporately. A radical theologian of the "old liberalism," John C. Raines, has recognized this impulse in John Calvin: "Calvin understood the Christian life not as 'a vessel filled with God' but as an active 'tool and instrument' of the Divine initiative. But this is precisely our point. Active toward the world, the Christian knows himself as utterly passive and obedient toward God, whose Will it is his sole task to discover and obey."[23] Unlike Raines, Christians find God's will in the ten commandments.

The ten commandments, wherever respected, have produced remarkable economic growth and social progress. This includes the much-maligned Middle Ages, a name given to Christian Europe by Enlightenment humanists who wanted to revive the civilization of pagan antiquity. The medieval era was a period of remarkable technological change and economic growth.[24] The earlier transitional period to the late medieval era (1100 A.D. to 1500 A.D.), called the "Dark Ages" (400 A.D. to 1100 A.D.), came as a result of the collapse of Roman civilization. It was a period of economic growth, though irregular. Economic historian Robert Latouche remarks that it is incorrect to assume that the Christian world had contracted by comparison to the ancient world, because we always look at the Mediterranean world of Augustus and compare it to northern Europe eight hundred years later. The point is, northern Europe improved its economic position under Christianity compared with what it had been in classical times.[25] He also notes that some of this early stagnation was the product of pessimistic millennialism: "By continuing to prophesy that the end of the world was approaching, it created an atmosphere of indifference to the natural and physical sciences which promoted worldly well-being and happiness, and which in the tenth century

---

23. John C. Raines, "From Passive to Active Man: Reflections on the Revolution in Consciousness in Modern Man," in John C. Raines and Thomas Dean (eds.), *Marxism and Radical Religion: Essays Toward a Revolutionary Humanism* (Philadelphia: Temple University Press, 1970), p. 114.

24. Lynn White, Jr., *Medieval Technology and Social Change* (2nd ed.; New York: Oxford University Press, 1966).

25. Robert Latouche, *The Birth of the Western Economy: Economic Aspects of the Dark Ages* (New York: Harper Torchbooks, [1956] 1966), p. 306.

were still suspected of being inspired by the devil."[26]

There was extensive worldwide commerce during the "Dark Ages," including European visits to North America, up until about the year 1000. This fall-off in trade was probably the result of the breakdown in security for the Indian tribes in North America,[27] not the result of a breakdown of the European economy. After 1000 A.D., the European economy began to experience accelerated growth.

Furthermore, the progress of medieval civilization was not limited to economics and technology. The Papal Revolution of 1076-1150 created the legal foundations of Western civilization.[28] In that same period, Christians invented the university.[29] A great revival of learning took place after the year 1100.[30] The triumphs in architecture, most notably the great cathedrals but also the castle fortresses, are not denied by anyone. The later Middle Ages have been properly described as an age of ambition.[31]

The coming of the Protestant Reformation in the sixteenth century transformed European thought and culture, politics and economics. There is little doubt that Max Weber's thesis that the Protestant ethic led to the creation of a spirit of capitalism and entrepreneurship is correct.[32] Without Christianity, but especially Protestantism, there would never have been modern science, as the voluminous (and generally ignored) researches of French historian Pierre Duhem and American scholar Stanley Jaki have demonstrated.[33] An enormous body of scholarly literature has built up which indicates the close relationship between the rise of Calvinism-Puritanism and

---

26. *Ibid.*, p. 304.

27. Barry Fell, *Saga America* (New York: Times Books, 1980), p. 385.

28. Harold J. Berman, *Law and Revolution: The Formation of the Western Legal Tradition* (Cambridge, Massachusetts: Harvard University Press, 1983).

29. Charles Homer Haskins, *The Rise of the Universities* (Ithaca, New York: Cornell University Press, [1923] 1965).

30. Christopher Brooke, *The Twelfth Century Renaissance* (New York: Harcourt, Brace & World, 1970).

31. F. R. H. Du Boulay, *An Age of Ambition: English Society in the Late Middle Ages* (New York: Viking, 1970).

32. Attempts to refute Weber have been numerous, but even after eighty years, the bulk of his thesis holds up well to specific criticisms. See Gary North, "Weber's 'Protestant Ethic' Hypothesis," *The Journal of Christian Reconstruction*, III (Summer 1976). A good general introduction to the question is collection by S. N. Eisenstadt (ed.), *The Protestant Ethic and Modernization* (New York: Basic Books, 1968).

33. Stanley Jaki, *The Road to Science and the Ways to God* (University of Chicago Press, 1978); *Science and Creation: From eternal cycles to an oscillating universe* (Edinburgh: Scottish Academic Press, [1974] 1980).

the rise of modern science.[34]

The Christian world view created the foundations of Western civilization — foundations that are now being eroded by humanism. The antinomian (anti-biblical law) pietist tradition of withdrawal, non-involvement, and internal "spirituality" could not withstand this erosion process.[35] When Christians lose faith in four essential biblical doctrines — the sovereignty of God, the victory of God's people in time and on earth, the law of God, and the self-sufficiency of the infallible Bible — they find themselves nearly defenseless (intellectually, institutionally, and culturally) against their rivals in every area of life.[36] When Christians refuse to take the offensive, they become like the Israelites of Moses' generation: nomads without an earthly future.

The Restoration of Biblical Law

How should Christians begin to take the offensive? By means of biblical law. In other words, we must put to good use the grace of God which has been shown to us in Christ. *We are to live by grace, in terms of biblical law.* We judge ourselves by our fruits, and we judge our fruits in terms of their conformity to God's law. The ten commandments are the starting point today, just as they were in 1445 B.C., and just as they have been at all points in between. What I have tried to demonstrate in this book is that in the field of economics, there is no doubt: the ten commandments still apply. More than this: without the principles laid down by the ten commandments, there is no hope for the economic future of man.

A God-blessed economic future is a future based on *personal self-government under God*, as evaluated by each individual (self-evaluation) and others (market evaluation) in terms of God's revealed law. Economic justice, like economic progress, is not based on the reign of the king, the politician, or the bureaucrat. Above all, it is *familistic responsibility* which is the dominant force in economic life. Economic progress ultimately requires future-orientation and

---

34. For a survey and analysis of a portion of this literature, see E. L. Hebden Taylor, "The Role of Puritan-Calvinism in the Rise of Modern Science," *The Journal of Christian Reconstruction,* VI (Summer 1979); Charles Dykes, "Medieval Speculation, Puritanism, and Modern Science," *ibid.*

35. *Christianity and Civilization,* 1 (1982): "The Failure of the American Baptist Culture." Published by the Geneva Divinity School, Tyler, Texas.

36. Gary North and David Chilton, "Apologetics and Strategy," *Christianity and Civilization,* 3 (1983).

faith in a providential world of cosmic personalism — faith in the existence of economic order, faith in economic cause and effect. It was this confidence which created the Western economy, and only this faith can sustain it.

Humanism is losing its self-confidence, and is doomed. The question is, *is humanism doomed historically?* The Bible teaches that it *is* doomed historically, for Satan is doomed historically, despite the familiar eschatological teachings of the "pessimillennialists." His defeat at Calvary *definitively* established his defeat in history. Nevertheless, history requires action. To establish the visible cultural manifestation of Christ's historic triumph, Christians must first learn the truth of an old political slogan: "You can't beat something with nothing." Humanism's visible failures today will not automatically lead to some sort of Christian "victory by default." There is no Christian "kingdom by default." Christians cannot win by default because men are *born* into Satan's kingdom (original sin). Sinners must be actively pursued — by God's Holy Spirit and by those who bring the gospel message. If Christians were passive in terms of personal evangelism, Satan's kingdom would *remain* unchecked and unchallenged. The same is true of *cultural evangelism* by Christians: *no activism — no victory.* Once Adam sinned, had Christ's death not atoned for man's sin, Satan could have remained passive and have been historically victorious. Satan would have won by default, had it not been for Calvary. Christ's activism conquered Satan; analogously, Christians' activism will conquer Satan's troops, both human and angelic. Ethics, not power, is the critical factor. Biblical law, not State power or magical power, is decisive.

What I am arguing is simple: *there are no civilizational vacuums.* There are no tie scores in the competition to build an external kingdom, whether Satan's or God's. Unless Christianity positively wins, Satan positively wins. Christianity, if it is not accompanied by a program of comprehensive Christian reconstruction, cannot triumph historically. "You can't build something with nothing." There should be no doubt in any *orthodox* Christian's mind that in the field of economics, the basis of such reconstruction is faith in, and obedience to, the ten commandments.

Appendix A

THE ECONOMIC IMPLICATIONS OF THE SABBATH

Six days may work be done; but in the seventh is the sabbath of rest, holy to the LORD: whosoever doeth any work in the sabbath day, he shall surely be put to death (Ex. 31:15).

Six days shall work be done, but on the seventh day there shall be to you an holy day, a sabbath of rest to the LORD: whosoever doeth work therein shall be put to death (Ex. 35:2).

One man esteemeth one day above another: another esteemeth every day alike. Let every man be fully persuaded in his own mind (Rom. 14:5).

I see no way to avoid interpreting the Old Testament sabbath in terms of the explanatory case-law provided in Exodus 31:15 and Exodus 35:2. If we take these words at face value — and I see no way not to and still remain faithful to the text — then we must come to grips with the rigorous nature of the Old Testament sabbath. There were almost certainly exceptions to this universal prohibition against work, such as milking cows (in effect, giving rest to them) or serving as a law-enforcement officer, but the universal condemnation of working at one's occupation on the sabbath bore the strongest of all sanctions: the death penalty.

I also see no way to avoid interpreting the New Testament Lord's day in terms of Paul's injunction that every man should make up his own mind concerning the equality of, or special nature of, any particular day. More than this: if Paul's words are not to be interpreted as referring to the sabbath (along with other Hebrew days of celebration or fasting), then the death penalty still has to be imposed by the civil government on anyone who fails to observe the New Testament Lord's day as identical to the Old Testament sabbath.

Our explanation of how the sabbath functioned in Israel, and how it should (or should not) be observed today, must be governed by the words of Exodus 31:15 and Exodus 35:2. In short, if we argue that the death penalty is no longer to be imposed on people who work on the Lord's day (as I do), then we must present a case that the requirements of the Old Testament sabbath have been fulfilled by Christ and are now annulled, and that God has substituted new rules to govern the Lord's day (which is what I attempt to do in this appendix). On the other hand, if someone denies that there has been a fundamental break between the Old Testament sabbath and the New Testament Lord's day, then he must demonstrate exegetically how it can be that the God-ordained death penalty has been abolished, but the moral and even ecclesiastical requirements concerning the observation of the Lord's day have remained essentially the same.

Why did God regard a violation of His sabbath as a capital crime? We have seen the answer in Chapter 4: *violating the sabbath involves a denial of the mandatory nature of rest for mankind.* Such a violation involves the assertion of *autonomy* on the part of man. Such an assertion brings spiritual and eternal death. But why did God wait until after the Exodus to announce that working on the sabbath is a capital crime? Probably because He wanted Israel first to understand what it meant to live under the domination of a self-proclaimed god-man who did not allow God's people to rest. In the recapitulation of the ten commandments in Deuteronomy, God gave them a different reason for honoring the sabbath: they had been in bondage to Egypt, and God had delivered them from this bondage (Deut. 5:15). He brought death to Egypt's firstborn; He would do the same to them if they failed to honor His covenant with them.

A key question then has to be considered: Why in New Testament times has the church never advocated such a harsh penalty? I hope to answer this question at the end of this appendix. The fundamental answer is that there has been a shift in the locus of sovereignty for sabbath enforcement: from civil government and ecclesiastical government to self-government (the individual conscience).

We have come at last to the really difficult issues, the issues of applied theology. We must consider these preliminary issues:

I. What was the Old Testament Sabbath?
   A. What were men supposed to do on the O.T. sabbath?
   B. What were the economic implications of the Mosaic sabbath, especially with respect to the division of labor?

II. Is the New Testament Lord's day essentially the same as
the O.T. sabbath?
  A. Is there N.T. evidence of a shift: sabbath to Lord's day?
  B. Is the Lord's day legally enforceable by the State today,
     as it was in the Old Testament?
  C. What are the economic implications of the Lord's day
     —again, especially with respect to the division of labor?

Once we have a general idea of the answers to these questions,
we can go on to other issues, such as the Old Testament's rescheduling of the Passover, and the possibility of rescheduling the New
Testament Lord's day for people employed in unique occupations;
the priestly exemptions from sabbath observance and their relationship to rescheduled worship in New Testament times; sabbath enforcement and the creation of a one-world State; proper leisure activities in New Testament times; and several other topics. But first,
we need to understand better both the Old Testament sabbath and
the New Testament's doctrine of the Lord's day.

I. Old Testament Sabbath

The Bible gives us almost no information about the activities of
faithful Hebrews on the sabbath. We know something about what
people did not do, but nothing for certain concerning what they did
do, except on special sabbaths like the Passover, the day of atonement, and so forth.

The experience with the manna in the wilderness, before the law
was given in a completed form to Moses, indicates that there was to
be no cooking in Israel on the sabbath. The cakes made from the
manna were to be cooked the day before the sabbath (Ex. 16:23).
After they arrived in Canaan, this law may have been relaxed. The
Bible does not say.

They were not to engage in commercial activity (Neh. 13:15-18).
We know that evil men did not appreciate the sabbath, since they
wanted to cheat buyers seven days a week (Amos 8:5). The man who
gathered sticks on the sabbath was executed at God's explicit command (Num. 15:32-36). There is certainly the possibility that a stick-
gatherer might be gathering sticks as a commercial venture.
Jeremiah warned the people:

Thus said the LORD; Take heed to yourselves, and bear no burden on
the sabbath day, nor bring it in by the gates of Jerusalem; Neither carry

forth a burden out of your houses on the sabbath day, neither do ye any work, but hallow ye the sabbath day, as I commanded your fathers. But they obeyed not, neither inclined their ear, but made their neck stiff, that they might not hear, nor receive instruction. And it shall come to pass, if ye diligently hearken unto me, saith the Lord, to bring in no burden through the gates of this city on the sabbath day, but hallow the sabbath day, to do no work therein; Then shall there enter into the gates of this city kings and princes sitting upon the throne of David, riding in chariots and on horses, they, and their princes, the men of Judah, and the inhabitants of Jerusalem: and this city shall remain for ever. And they shall come from the cities of Judah, and from the places about Jerusalem, and from the land of Benjamin, and from the plain, and from the mountains, and from the south, bringing burnt offerings and sacrifices, and meat offerings, and incense, and bring sacrifices of praise, unto the house of the Lord. But if ye will not hearken unto me to hallow the sabbath day, and not to bear a burden, even entering in at the gates of Jerusalem on the sabbath day; then will I kindle a fire in the gates thereof, and it shall devour the palaces of Jerusalem, and it shall not be quenched (Jer. 17:21-27).

Kindling a fire on the sabbath was forbidden (Ex. 35:3). If this law was disobeyed, God promised to kindle a fire in the gates of the city, meaning the seat of judgment. The gates, as the place of entry into the city, would be destroyed. The city would fall to a conqueror. God was serious about their not starting fires on the sabbath. His promised judgment — fire in the gates — reflected His rigorous standards in this regard.

A. What Were They Supposed to Do?

But what, specifically, were men required to do on the sabbath? They may have celebrated together at some form of formal worship service. The "holy convocations" described in Leviticus 23:3 may have constituted weekly sabbath worship services, although it is not absolutely clear that these services were conducted outside the home. "Six days shall work be done: but the seventh day is the sabbath of rest, an holy convocation; ye shall do no work therein: it is the sabbath of the LORD in all your dwellings" (Lev. 23:3). Israel's various seasonal feasts (holy convocations) are subsequently described in Leviticus 23, and these were unquestionably public feasts. Thus, it can be argued that the local Levitical priests who resided in each community called the weekly convocations together in some sort of public meeting place. But this is not absolutely clear from the text, and the specific details of these public worship services are nowhere described in the Old Testament.

A. T. Lincoln has fairly described our present state of knowledge concerning the celebration of the Hebrew sabbath in Old Testament times: "The sabbath was not a day of total inactivity but was meant to provide rest and refreshment from the regular work of the six other days. It is true that this rest provided opportunity for devotion to the worship of God, that the Sabbath was called a 'holy convocation' (Lev. 23:2-3), that an additional burnt offering was required on every Sabbath (Num. 28:9, 10), and that since it was done from obedience to God the resting itself could be considered an act of worship, but cultic worship was not a major focus of the Sabbath institution for Israel as this is reflected in the Old Testament."[1] This is my concern: to discern the *major focus* of the Old Testament sabbath. It was *rest*, not worship.

The Hebrews were supposed to delight themselves in God. In the oft-quoted words of Isaiah: "If thou turn thy foot from the sabbath, from doing thy pleasure on my holy day; and call the sabbath a delight, the holy of the Lord, honourable; and thou shalt honour him, not doing thine own ways, nor finding thine own pleasure, nor speaking [thine own] words: Then shalt thou delight thyself in the Lord; and I will cause thee to ride upon the high places of the earth, and feed thee with the heritage of Jacob thy father: for the mouth of the Lord hath spoken it" (Isa. 58:13-14). They were to acknowledge the God-centered nature of creation.

What did it mean, "doing thy pleasure"? We are not told, except in reference to commercial activities and the common household chores of cooking, gathering sticks, and carrying burdens in and out. Idle talk was forbidden. But what kind of talk, specifically, constituted idle talk, "speaking [thine own] words"? We are not told. As far as the written record indicates, neither were they.

The law said nothing about the legality, or even propriety, of the following activities: napping in the afternoon, walking in a garden (park), listening to music, going for a (non-commercial) swim, floating in a small boat, and having sexual relations with one's spouse. In short, there are no guidelines in the law concerning the

---

1. A. T. Lincoln, "From Sabbath to Lord's Day: A Biblical and Theological Perspective," in D. A. Carson (ed.), *From Sabbath to Lord's Day: A Biblical, Historical, and Theological Investigation* (Grand Rapids, Michigan: Zondervan Academe, 1982), p. 352.

limits of recreation and the beginning of work or "thy pleasure."

Recreation (Re-Creation)

When we think back to the garden of Eden, we are confronted with the obvious possibility of a walk through the garden, God's gift to man. This is a form of recreation. To forbid recreation in post-Edenic times seems ludicrous, yet certain problems arise as soon as we admit the legitimacy of recreation but deny the legitimacy of commercial activity.

Consider the rich man. He owns a large garden, a lake, and a boat. He chooses to spend his day of rest walking through his garden, going for a swim, and sailing. Has he broken God's law? Then consider the poor man. He owns no garden, but he has access to a nearby profit-seeking park. (In this book, I choose to avoid the question of the morality of tax-supported public parks. It is a relevant question, however.) There is a profit-seeking lake or swimming pool nearby. A firm will rent him a boat on Sunday afternoon. If the ban against profit-seeking activities includes recreation activities, then the poor man is limited. He cannot afford to buy the tools of recreation, yet he is also prohibited from renting them.

We cannot escape this problem. We must ask ourselves at least five questions. First, must we ban recreation on the Lord's day for all people, rich and poor, in order to avoid economic discrimination? Second, must we ban the poor or middle-class citizens from the delights of publicly provided recreation? Third, must we ban rentals of recreation services and implements on the day of rest? Fourth, must we see to it that the State confiscates funds through coercion in order to create "free" recreation services for the poor and middle-class citizens? Or fifth, may we look upon sabbatical recreation capital of the rich man as a legitimate covenantal blessing which poorer men do not enjoy, and should not enjoy until God showers similar economic blessings on them?

There is also a sixth possibility. What if the rich invite the poor in to enjoy their wealth? What if the rich donate money to the church, or some other private charity, in order to create recreation facilities? This could be regarded as a weekly version of the "tithe of celebration" (Deut. 14:26-29). Rich men could celebrate the sabbath by inviting all men in to enjoy the fruits of their labor. Charity-supported agencies might offer access to gardens, lakes, and so forth. Labor is donated: lifeguards, physicians, police protection, lost children booths, and so forth. Instead of profit-seeking labor, we find works of mercy.

In a predominantly rural society, most people could enjoy the sight of their fields. They could go for a stroll in the "garden." In an urban society, people can go for a stroll to view front lawns. They can visit friends for a chat. But then we are back to another bothersome question: What constitutes idle talk? Talk about families? Talk about sports events? Talk about politics? Talk about the stock market? We are not told. *Conscience* must be our guide. But conscience is difficult to put into concrete legislative proposals. In fact, it is because men have not universally defined "idle talk," that they resort to the language of conscience or circumstance.

If we take the Old Testament legislation seriously, we are faced with a conclusion that tends to alienate the guilt-manipulated and socialism-influenced Christian: the rich were allowed to enjoy recreation activities that were legally prohibited to the poor, who were not allowed to lease or rent such recreation implements or opportunities on the sabbath. It might be argued that the law allowed a man to buy a "seven days a week" ticket to recreation opportunities, but if someone had to collect tickets on the sabbath, or in some way monitor his profit-seeking operation on the sabbath, then any judge who understood basic economics would have shut down the operation as a sham, an attempt to escape the clear-cut prohibition on commercial activities on the sabbath. It paid to be rich on the sabbath. (Of course, it normally pays to be rich on the other six days of the week, too.)

Carrying burdens in and out of doors was illegal (Jer. 17:22). Profit-seeking work was illegal. But leisure is a consumer good. It must be paid for by forfeited income — income not earned during the leisure period. Leisure could be "stored up" in effect. It was legitimate to enjoy leisure on the sabbath, but only that kind which could be "stored up" in the form of capital goods: private gardens, private lakes, and so forth.

"Works of Mercy" in Rural Society

Israel was a rural society. Certain daily chores are works of necessity on a farm, such as milking and caring for the animals. But what was done with the milk? Was it thrown away? Was it saved only for other animals? Was it given to the poor? If it was sold at a profit, then milking constituted profit-seeking activity, i.e., engaging in trade. Such sabbath violations would have been difficult to detect.

What about the use of such sabbath-produced milk by the family? This is an important question. If personal family use of the economic output of sabbatical "acts of mercy" (to the cows) is legitimate, then the definition of what constitutes profit-seeking must be narrowed. Engaging in commercial trade would be prohibited, but engaging in intra-household trade would not; one family member milks the cow, another cooks the food, another washes the dishes, and so forth. From the point of view of human action — exchanging one set of conditions for another set — the intra-family exchange seems to be equally profit-seeking, but perhaps not from the point of view of Old Testament sabbath legislation. The milk could be sold the next day. Wouldn't this constitute a violation of the sabbath? It certainly appears that way. But to consume the milk directly thereby increases the family's consumption as surely as the income gained from the sale of the milk would increase it. What is the economic difference, in terms of family income? More to the point, what is the biblical difference, in terms of the specific application of the law of the sabbath?

The strict sabbatarian would have to argue that the milk should be given away. Such a person is a defender of what Lewis Bulkeley has called "the marathon sabbath." But is it the sabbath which God required of His Old Testament saints, let alone His New Testament saints? Unquestionably, the Old Testament did not prohibit output of effort as such; cows deserved to be milked, as an act of mercy, an act of *giving rest* (Ex. 23:12). But what about *income* which was the by-product (i.e., unintended product) of such merciful labor? Should it have been given to the poor, or to household animals, but kept away from human family members? Or is giving food to one's own family itself an act of mercy?

If giving milk to one's own family or domestic animals is an act of mercy, then it is an act of mercy which has unintended economic consequences, namely, an increase of consumption which is not paid for by increased output (more milking) or more thrift (reduced consumption) during the days preceding the sabbath. Feeding one's family or animals with milk produced by sabbath milking would then be understood as being fundamentally different from gathering sticks for a fire on the sabbath, for sticks had to be gathered during the workweek and stored up for use on the sabbath. But wouldn't this "anti-stick-gathering" requirement have applied equally to milking, even though milk in this instance was a by-product of acts of mercy? A strict sabbatarian would clearly have to insist that milk which is produced as a by-product of an act of mercy be given to the poor, or spilled on the ground, in order to make certain that such merciful work remained exclusively merciful and not an excuse for profit-seeking (cost-reducing) sabbath violations.

Then there is the question of full pay for "normal" works of mercy or necessity performed by professionals, including people who are paid by the civil government: police, firemen, military forces, etc. Should those who perform such services on the sabbath be paid for that day's work? Christ defended the right of a man to pull a beast of burden out of a ditch, but does this imply that individuals can legitimately operate "beast-retrieval" companies at a profit on the sabbath? Thomas Gouge, a contemporary of Owen and Baxter in seventeenth-century England, praised as shining examples several Christian physicians who refused payment for Sunday labor.[2] More than this: Should the civil government make it illegal for people to receive payment for emergency services? And if it does, won't this reduce the number of emergency services offered, and thereby render it more dangerous to suffer an emergency on Sundays? These are questions that strict sabbatarians must eventually deal with.

B. The Division of Labor in Rural Israel

Modern mass production, with its capital-intensive mechanization, is characterized by a high division of labor. Until the late-nineteenth century, agricultural societies were characterized by a comparatively low division of labor. In such societies, production is initially for the family unit. Surplus goods can be traded or sold, but there is not much surplus. Men work primarily for home consumption.

The workweek is scheduled in terms of the needs of the family. Wives can bake extra loaves on the day before the sabbath without disrupting normal production and distribution patterns. Husbands can cut extra wood for the fire on any day of the week. In ancient Israel, people structured their workweek's rhythm in terms of the sabbath. This did not involve a major interruption of supplies of needed goods and services. Where men are not continually serving each other through production for a market, but where they serve

2. On Gouge, see Richard Schlatter, *The Social Ideas of Religious Leaders, 1660-1688* (London: Oxford University Press, 1940), pp. 129, 137.

themselves and their families directly through labor, it is far easier to restructure the workweek to honor special feast days or sabbaths. A rural family can schedule its activities to include a day of rest.

In a rural society, it is also far easier to identify commercial activities, since there are fewer of them than in a modern, mass-production society. It is therefore easier to identify sabbath violations. A face-to-face society which is dominated by family and tribal ties offers men the opportunity to observe the daily affairs of their neighbors. While families might have hidden certain kinds of indoor commercial labor, it would have been difficult in ancient Israel to conceal agricultural labor in the fields.

Another important aspect of rural societies is *the relative absence of 24-hour-a-day capital equipment*, whether public or private. Power generation, telecommunications, repair services, hospitals, and similar services have only been commonplace to rural areas in the twentieth century, and then only in industrial societies, or in urban areas of industrializing societies. The continuing dependence of urban society on such services stands in stark contrast to the traditional rural community, which has a lower division of labor, and which is far more self-sufficient. The interruption of "vital services" in a modern city could bring paralysis and breakdown. In a traditional rural community, such an interruption could not take place, since such "vital services" are not normally available. In other words, services that are vital to a modern urban community are not vital in a traditional rural society. Only in modern rural societies that are fully integrated into urban society through the market and shared public utilities will such services be regarded as vital. The economic rhythm of a traditional rural society is far different from a modern industrial society. Traditional rural societies are not characterized by an extensive, even life-sustaining, division of labor.

The economy of Israel was not highly integrated. In the cities, civil rulers were influenced heavily by the Levites. Profit-seeking activities on the sabbath would have been difficult in cities whose civil rulers were highly influenced by sabbath law-enforcing priests. The cities of ancient Israel did not become dependent on a market order characterized by a high division of labor. I am arguing that God's sabbath requirements necessarily prohibited the creation of such an interdependent society. It is my contention that the annulment of the Old Testament sabbath laws by Jesus Christ was a necessary (though not sufficient) precursor to modern civilization.

If strict sabbatarians believe that I am incorrect in this conclusion, then they have an obligation to show how the authorities today
would be able to differentiate between what constitutes an illegitimate sabbath violation and one which is acceptable. It should be
clear that the enforcement of strict sabbath legislation in a traditional agricultural society will produce *economic effects* far different
from those produced by such enforcement in a modern industrial
economy. Similarly, the economic effects of sabbath *violations* are
different in the two types of society. Since the *effects* are different,
shouldn't the *penalty* be different? But the Old Testament did not
offer any alternative penalties. It required execution of all sabbath
violators — no "ifs, ands, or buts."

Did the Mosaic law implicitly allow the authorities to redefine a
sabbath violation in terms of regional settings? Did an act of sabbatical defiance in a rural society become acceptable behavior in an urban setting because of its differing economic effects? Is an act which
seems to be visibly (physiologically) the same but which produces
different consequences in different environments really the same
act? Or is it different? And if the act *is* different, should it be rede-
fined, even though physiologically it is the same act?

If the Mosaic law did implicitly allow the authorities to redefine
sabbath violations into non-violations according to differing economic effects, then what are the distinguishing criteria that officials,
whether ecclesiastical or civil, should adopt in order to determine
which acts are legitimate, under which circumstances, and where?
On the other hand, if the Mosaic law never did permit such redefini-
tions of a sabbath violation — and I do not believe that it did — then
how could the Old Testament economy (meaning the Old Testament
system as well as the Old Testament economic order) ever have pro-
gressed into the modern industrial West? (For more detailed arguments along these lines, see below: "Mass Production and Worldwide Trade.")

II. New Testament Lord's Day

The various New Testament accounts of Christ's activities on the
Hebrew sabbath provide us with evidence concerning the true
nature of the Old Testament sabbath. Works of healing were basic to
that sabbath, not as exceptional acts, but as acts that were integral to
sabbath observance. Christ healed the withered hand of one man on
the sabbath (Matt. 12:10-13). He also healed the crippled man who

had been waiting for healing near the pool of Bethesda. Again, this was on the sabbath (John 5:1-17). He replied to those Jews who were critical of His action: "My father worketh hitherto, and I work" (John 5:17). They were to *give* rest. His general principle was this: "The son of man is Lord even of the sabbath" (Matt. 12:8). Again, "It is lawful to do well on the sabbath days" (Matt. 12:12b). (The King James English conveys the wrong message. The Greek is better translated to "do good," not "do well."[3] Salesmen do well; servants do good.)

What is meant by Christ's use of the word "work" in John 5:17? Work as a charitable service is in view, not work in one's profit-seeking vocation. The Old Testament sabbath was a break from the ordinary routine of profit-seeking labor, meaning one's calling. *Those activities associated with a man's income-producing occupation were to be avoided.*

Blameless Profanation

Nevertheless, there were exceptions to this rule. The obvious Old Testament exception was the routine labor of a priest. Christ replied to His critics: "Or have ye not read in the law, how that on the sabbath days the priests in the temple profane the sabbath, and are blameless" (Matt. 12:5). We are not told specifically which activities of the priests profaned the sabbath. They had to sacrifice two yearling lambs every sabbath, along with meal and drink offerings. Also, they had to maintain continual burnt offerings (Num. 28:9-10). Jesus said that they actually profaned the sabbath. This is a strong word to use. It could also be translated "desecrate."[4] They violated the requirements of the sabbath in the temple itself. Nevertheless, they were held blameless before God. The importance of their labor in the sight of God made them blameless. They were following a *higher command*. They were offering the blood sacrifices that were required by God to cover the sins of His people.

The context of Jesus' remarks on the profaning of the sabbath is important. He and His disciples had been criticized for having walked through cornfields on the sabbath, plucking ears to eat. This was not theft, according to Old Testament law; travellers had legal access to

---

3. Walter Bauer, *A Greek-English Lexicon of the New Testament and Other Early Christian Literature*, trans. by William F. Arndt and F. Wilbur Gingrich (2nd ed.; Chicago: University of Chicago Press, 1979), p. 401: *"kalose,* [3]."

4. *Ibid.*, p. 138: *"bebeilao."*

a handful of the fruit of the ground (Deut. 23:23-25). Jesus was not criticized for having taken the corn. He was criticized for having taken the corn *on the sabbath.*

What was Christ's answer? He pointed to David's taking of the showbread from the temple on the sabbath (Matt. 12:3-4). Here was a far more culpable act, for it was not lawful for David or his followers to eat the showbread, since it was reserved for the priests (v. 4). Yet it was necessary that they be fed. They were godly men involved in an important work. The priest himself had suggested that David take the hallowed bread (I Sam. 21:21-24). Yet God commanded that this showbread be set before Him at all times (Ex. 25:30; Num. 4:7). *But the needs of men were more important in this instance,* a fact recognized by the priest. On the one hand, the priest had to offer sacrifices. On the other hand, David had to flee from the wrath of Saul. Both requirements were cases of necessity. But the priest told David to eat the showbread. How, then, could the priests of Jesus' day legitimately criticize Him?

Jesus' healing of the man with the withered hand was a work of mercy. Traditional Christian sabbatarianism has always made exceptions of these two works, *necessity* and *mercy.* But necessity and mercy impose even greater pressures on men's actions than merely offering exceptions to the sabbath requirement against labor. Necessity and mercy require *positive action.* This is acknowledged by the Westminster Confession of Faith (1646), a pro-sabbatarian document, which forbids men to think "about their worldly employments and recreations," and *requires* them to take up "the whole time, in the public and private exercises of His worship, and in the duties of necessity and mercy."[5]

The priests of the Old Testament profaned the sabbath, yet they were blameless. The office of priest, coupled with a mandatory assignment from God, permitted the profaning of the sabbath. Indeed, it *requires* it. Yet David was not a priest, nor were his men. This points to the truth of Christ's words, that the "Son of man is Lord even of the sabbath day" (Matt. 12:8). In His incarnation, as the son of man, Christ ruled the sabbath. The account in Mark is even clearer: "The sabbath was made for man, and not man for the sabbath" (2:27-28). When human life and health are at stake, the sabbath may be profaned without blame. It *must* be profaned. When an

---

5. *Westminster Confession of Faith,* XXI: VIII.

assignment by God to a priest is in question, the sabbath may be profaned without blame. Again, it *must* be profaned. But then we face some very difficult questions: How can we tell when human health and life are at stake? Who is the true priest? What is a God-given assignment?

A. Transformation: The Lord's Day

In the New Testament, the first day of the week is called the Lord's day (Rev. 1:10), but it is *never* called the sabbath. Unquestionably, there was a shift from the seventh day of the week to the first. The evidence also points to a shift from sundown-to-sundown celebration to a sunrise-to-sunrise celebration. These are very important changes. They involve a radical break with the Hebrew sabbath. F. N. Lee, in his defense of the New Testament sabbath, argues explicitly that *the entire system of Mosaic sabbaths and holy days was abolished by Christ.* He cites Paul's epistle to the Colossians: "Let no man therefore judge you in meat, or in drink, or in respect of an holyday, or of the new moon, or of the sabbath [days]" (2:16). (The last word, "days," was added by the King James translators; it should read simply, "sabbaths.") Lee concludes:

Now these ceremonial sabbaths, listed in Leviticus 23 together with the Israelite Sinaitic weekly sabbath, are all called "feasts" of holy convocation or "holy days"; and all involve the keeping of a "sabbath" day or a "day of holy convocation" on which "no servile work is to be done," or a "day of solemn rest." They were all a shadow of the things to come, namely the benefits of the New Testament in Christ; and they were all blotted out and nailed to His cross. . . . So Paul means exactly what he says. It is useless to argue (as S.D. Adventists do) that St. Paul here means the *ceremonial* sabbaths by his words "or the sabbath (days)," for St. Paul has just a few words beforehand (in the very same verse) dealt with such ceremonial sabbaths under the blanket term "*holy day*" — the same term (*heortai*) used in the Septuagint of Lev. 23 to refer to *all* the (Sinaitic) sabbaths — both the ceremonial sabbaths *and* the "weekly" sabbath of Israel, Lev. 23:2-3. . . . If it is argued that Paul means (only) the *ceremonial* sabbaths in Col. 2:16 where he refers to "the sabbath day(s)," then *which* days is he referring to under the blanket term "holy days" just mentioned previously in the very same verse? The two can hardly be synonymous, for Paul would then be repeating himself, saying in effect: "Let no man therefore judge you . . . in respect of a ceremonial sabbath or a new moon or a ceremonial sabbath," when the latter phrase would simply be idle repetition.[6]

6. F. N. Lee, *The Covenantal Sabbath* (London: Lord's Day Observance Society, 1972), pp. 28-29.

Lee argues that the day of rest, or sabbath, is part of God's moral law, and therefore it is still in effect. But the Old Testament sabbath is gone. In other words, *the theological justification for switching to the first day of the week is that the older sabbath is absolutely abolished, and a new one is morally binding.* There was a total break at Calvary with the Mosaic law's sabbath.

There seems to be no exegetical way to escape Lee's treatment of Colossians 2:16. Paul was not speaking of ceremonial sabbaths, but the *Mosaic* sabbath. It is gone forever. The fact that the church celebrates a new day should testify to this theological fact. But then a crucial question has to be answered: How much of the *Mosaic legislation* has been abolished along with the day of the week and the hours of the day? A clean break has been established with respect to the day of the week. On what basis, then, can the church recommend that the Old Testament sabbath law be enforced by the civil government? The testimony of almost 2,000 years of church history provides at least a partial answer: the church has *not* committed itself to a full-scale revival of the Mosaic sabbath legislation.

The principle of interpretation which is supposed to govern Christian orthodoxy is that Christ came to establish, confirm, and declare the Old Testament law (Matt. 5:17-18).[7] Only if we find an explicit abandonment of an Old Testament law in the New Testament, because of the historic fulfillment of the Old Testament shadow, can we legitimately abandon a detail of the Mosaic law.

In the case of the Mosaic sabbath, Paul provides us with full justification for just this sort of abandonment. We no longer enforce the Mosaic provisions, because the Mosaic sabbath ended at Calvary. We have a new day of rest, and we dare not arbitrarily select some of the Old Testament sabbath definitions, restraints, and legal sanctions *without taking them all.* But we have no exegetical grounds for taking them all, since the very change in the day of celebration, not to mention Paul's explicit teaching regarding the locus of responsibility for enforcement (the conscience), testifies to the break with the past.

The biblical account of what constitutes a week unquestionably establishes as definitive six days of work and a day of rest or feasting. God's originally creative week was a six-one pattern, while Adam's

---

7. Greg L. Bahnsen, *Theonomy in Christian Ethics* (2nd ed.; Nutley, New Jersey: Craig Press, 1984), ch. 2.

subordinately re-creative week was supposed to be a one-six pattern, with God's pronouncement of judgment against Satan coming at the end of the seventh day, or possibly at the beginning of the next day (evening). Adam's rebellion led to a curse: God's imposition on man of a God-imitating six-one pattern, with rest to come only at the end of man's week.

Jesus Christ, by redeeming His people, annulled the six-one pattern of the cursed week. He did not restore the original (pre-Fall) pattern of one-six, since He changed the day on which the Lord's day is celebrated to the day after the Hebrew sabbath—what Christian commentators for at least 1,800 years have called the eighth day. Therefore, He established a *one-six-one* pattern—rest, work, and judgment. This judgment comes on the day of the Lord, the archetypal Lord's day. This is why the Lord's day is celebrated in New Testament times on the day following the Hebrews' seventh-day sabbath: it points to the *final judgment* and the *inauguration of a new week*, the full manifestation of the New Heaven and the New Earth. The first day of redeemed man's week is now the eighth day after the initiation of God's work, not the seventh day after. It represents a *re-creation*, a new week which re-establishes a one-six pattern, but which also implies the one-six-one pattern as a herald of the total regeneration and re-creation of all things. The shift to the eighth day testifies to Christ's new creation.

Conscience: The New Locus of Enforcement

Paul was concerned with the souls and consciences of his readers. The Colossians passage mentions meat, drink, holy days, and sabbaths. He was doing his best to convince his readers that there had been a definitive break from Old Testament law with respect to these four features of Hebrew life. He knew that Judaizers were criticizing the Christian Hebrews for their abandonment of these external tests of faith, and he did not want his readers to feel guilty. No one could legitimately judge them with respect to these four issues. No one could turn to the Mosaic law and confront them with the Mosaic rules, instructions, and regulations regarding meat, drink, holy days, and sabbaths. This did not mean that the old rules were evil. It meant that the Judaizers had no right to criticize Christians for no longer adhering to the old forms. New applications of the Old Testament's general principles in these four areas are now binding in New Testament times.

Paul repeated this same teaching to the church at Rome. In Romans 14, Paul covers much the same ground. Those who are weak in the faith are not to be distressed by rigid theological criticism. Paul observes that there are debates within the churches concerning the proper foods and the proper holy days. Judgment of each other should not go on in these areas of disputation. Men must *decide for themselves* which foods to eat or which days to celebrate.

For one believeth that he may eat all things: another, who is weak, eateth herbs. Let not him that eateth despise him that eateth not; and let not him which eateth not judge him that eateth: for God hath received him. Who art thou that judgest another man's servant? To his own master he standeth or falleth. Yea, he shall be holden up: for God is able to make him stand. One man esteemeth one day above another: another esteemeth every day alike. Let every man be fully persuaded in his own mind. He that regardeth the day, regardeth it unto the Lord; and he that regardeth not the day, to the Lord he doth not regard it. He that eateth, eateth to the Lord, for he giveth God thanks. For none of us liveth to himself, and no man dieth to himself. For whether we live, we live unto the Lord; and whether we die, we die unto the Lord: whether we live therefore, or die, we are the Lord's. For to this end Christ both died, and rose, and revived, that he might be Lord both of the dead and the living. But why dost thou judge thy brother? Or why dost thou set at nought thy brother? For we shall all stand before the judgment seat of Christ. For it is written, As I live, saith the Lord, every knee shall bow to me, and every tongue shall confess to God. So then every one of us shall give account of himself to God. Let us not therefore judge one another any more: but judge this rather, that no man put a stumbling block or an occasion to fall in his brother's way (Rom. 14:2-13).

The Lord's day, the first day of the week, has been set apart by Christ for His church as a day of worship, fellowship, and communion. This, above all, is the church's testimony to the day of rest. Members are required to attend a worship service with their fellow believers. "And let us consider one another to provoke unto love and good works: Not forsaking the assembling of ourselves together, as the manner of some is . . ." (Heb. 10:24-25a). We must not forsake other members. We are to help each other.

Some members may view all days the same. So be it. Good men have taken this position historically. Zwingli was one of them.[8] But Zwingli attended church on Sunday, since he would not forsake the

---

8. Lee, *Covenantal Sabbath*, p. x.

brethren. The pattern of one day in seven for rest from one's normal labors is formalized in the worship services themselves. We need not badger each other about the specifics of Old Testament law regarding the Lord's day, Paul said, because no one should judge another on this matter. Participation in the required church service or fellowship, which has been on the first day of the week since the day of Christ's resurrection, is sufficient testimony.

Worship: A New Testament Emphasis

Perhaps strict sabbatarians are unwilling to take Paul's words at face value. Yet the ironic aspect of strict sabbatarianism is this: without the definitive break with the Mosaic sabbath, the sabbatarian's emphasis on Sunday *worship* reduces his case's biblical support. How can the sabbatarian consistently argue for full continuity of the Lord's day with the Old Testament sabbath, when the Old Testament sabbath was primarily a day of *rest* rather than a day of worship? The New Testament Lord's day focuses on the worship requirements, not the rest requirements.

The Old Testament sabbath was *primarily* a day of rest, of cessation from profit-seeking labor. Sabbath worship, if it is mentioned at all, is only mentioned indirectly (Lev. 23:3). There were no prohibitions against recreation. There were only prohibitions against labor. The modern sabbatarian's emphasis on the Lord's day primarily as a day of worship must be drawn from a handful of references in the New Testament that show that the church met on resurrection day to worship. It is possible to make a case against doing "thy pleasure" on the *sabbath* by appealing to the Old Testament, but it is not possible to make a case for the *Lord's day* as a day primarily devoted to *worship* by appealing to the Old Testament.

To define the sabbath primarily in terms of corporate worship, rather than primarily as a day on which no commercial trade is permitted, raises some exceedingly difficult questions for strict sabbatarians. First, if honoring the first day of the week requires that sabbath violations be prohibited by civil law, then the law is being enforced on all people in a particular society. If this is what the New Testament requires, then any sabbath-enforcing society is thereby admitted to be *covenanted under God*. This is an inescapable relationship: State-enforced sabbath laws and the existence of a covenant. (There are many defenders of various sabbath laws who categorically deny that any New Testament society is ever covenanted under God as Israel was. This is especially true in the American South, where "blue laws" that prohibit certain businesses from operating on Sunday, or that prohibit certain products from being sold in supermar-kets on Sunday, are voted into law time after time by covenant-denying Southern Baptists, Methodists, and Church of Christ members. I cannot explain this; I only report it.)

Second, there is the problem of the Lord's day as primarily a day of worship. If the Old Testament's sabbath-enforcing civil law is still binding in New Testament times, and if the Lord's day is understood as predominantly a day of worship (as the Westminster Confession and most pastors assert), then *the civil magistrate ought to enforce compulsory worship on all members of a (covenanted) society upon threat of death.*

The New England Puritans went at least part of the way down this path. They legislated compulsory worship, and they banished sabbath violators from Massachusetts and Connecticut in the early years. Even this half-hearted attempt to imitate the Old Testament only lasted a few years. There were more and more church absentees, until by the middle of the seventeenth century, the churches of New England could not have held the whole population, had everyone decided to visit on some Sunday morning.[9] Eventually, "blue laws" replaced the threat of banishment for failure to attend church in New England.

Modern sabbatarians have refused to become consistent. They do not pressure the civil government to establish a death penalty for Lord's day desecrations, and they certainly avoid the obvious conclusion concerning the Lord's day as a day of worship, namely, compulsory church attendance, enforced by the civil government.

The New Testament Church's Celebration

What Paul was asserting should be clear to anyone who reads Romans 14. Not only do those outside the church have varying opinions concerning a day of rest, or special holidays; even those inside the church have varying opinions. We see in the twentieth century

---

9. Carl Bridenbaugh writes: "A consideration of the number and seating capacities of village meeting houses and churches demonstrates the sheer physical impossibility of crowding the entire village populations into their houses of worship. At no time after 1650 does it seem possible for the churches of Boston to have contained anywhere near a majority of the inhabitants; in 1690 little more than a quarter of them could have attended church simultaneously had they been so disposed." Bridenbaugh, *Cities in the Wilderness: The First Century of Urban Life in America, 1625-1725* (New York: Capricorn, [1938] 1964), p. 106.

that the same situation still exists. The debates went on in the Reformation, too. The Old Testament sabbath laws were *absolute in the sanction* involved — the death penalty — and they were *negative in effect*. They told men what not to do, one day in seven. The New Testament's emphasis shifted on the day of resurrection. The first day of the week is now a day of communion between God and His church. It involves a positive, loving corporate celebration. It involves preaching (Acts 20:7-12), singing (Matt. 26:30; Col. 3:16), praying (I Cor. 14:15), and a communion feast (I Cor. 11).

The testimony of the church is that there is indeed a very special day of celebration, of feasting and sharing the blessings of salvation. If the early church in Israel had wanted rest more than the experience of true communion, it would have met for communion on the Hebrew sabbath, since the Roman authorities acknowledged the right of the priests to require a day of rest. But the early church broke with rest on the first day of the week in order to celebrate communion on the evening of that first day. They rested on the Hebrew sabbath, worked on the Lord's day, and gathered together in the evening. They rested — assuming they did rest, which seems reasonable — on a day different from the day of worship, at least in Israel. In gentile cities in the Empire, they probably could not rest even one day in seven. But they celebrated on Sunday evening after work.[10]

The historical circumstances of the early church necessitated compromises with the sabbath principle. Had there been no break from the Old Testament requirement of a full day of rest one day in seven, the church would have been bottled up in Israel, since the Roman Empire did not honor the rest principle. Had the legal obligation of resting on the sabbath been the binding obligation, then the early church, dwelling in Israel, would have had to take two days off: the Hebrews' day (legally binding) and the Lord's day (religiously binding). But this would have violated the more important pattern of one day of rest and six days of labor.[11] The church, in short, was forced to break with the Hebrew sabbath. God, in His grace, abolished the Hebrew sabbath on the day of resurrection, so

---

10. "It is certain that the eucharist was at first an evening meal. The name (*deipnon*) implies this." Wilfrid Stott, in Roger T. Beckwith and Wilfrid Stott, *The Christian Sunday: A Biblical and Historical Study* (Grand Rapids, Michigan: Baker Book House, 1980), p. 89.

11. I am defining "merciful labor" as that activity which *gives rest* to others, both animals and humans. I argue in this appendix that it is morally and legally valid to *sell* merciful labor on the Lord's day.

that members could rest on the seventh day (Saturday) and celebrate on the evening of the first day, which was a working day in Israel. They could do this in good conscience precisely because they knew that God honored their faith. Like the priests who sacrificed on the sabbath, profaning it blamelessly, the early Christians worked on the Lord's day, profaning it, but it was not held against them.

This is not to say that the ideal situation is not the Lord's day as a day of rest *and* worship, universally recognized, universally respected, except in cases of emergency or merciful labor. But Paul was careful to warn the church at Rome that it should not burden its new members with rigorous regulations concerning a special day of the week. Yes, they were to commune together. But whatever they did on the Lord's day—and in Rome, most of them must have worked—they were to do it in faith. The sabbath ideal is to grow out of respect for the principle of resurrection, the basis of man's release from sin and eternal death. The institutional church sets the pattern with its special day of worship, which can be made binding on members (Heb. 10:25). But it cannot legitimately force its members to honor the one-six pattern of rest. That pattern is built into Christ's kingdom, but Paul makes it clear that the *conscience* is to guide men to this conclusion, not compulsion. In fact, he was writing against one man's criticizing another—moral compulsion. If moral compulsion is forbidden, then how much more ecclesiastical compulsion? And how much more than this, compulsion by the civil government?

The Early Church Fathers on Rest vs. Worship

This distinction between Sabbath rest and Lord's day worship was unquestionably made by the early church fathers. Until the fourth century, church fathers generally condemned the "idleness" of the Jewish sabbath, and commanded church members to devote Sunday to worship and acts of mercy. Bauckham comments: "For Tertullian, the meaning of the Sabbath commandment for Christians was 'that we still more ought to observe a sabbath from all servile work always, and not only every seventh day, but through all time.'[12] It is entirely clear that for all these writers the literal commandment to rest one day in seven was a temporary ordinance for Israel alone. The Christian fulfills the commandment by devoting all his time to God. The rationale for this interpretation depended, of

---

12. Tertullian, *An Answer to the Jews*, ch. IV.

course, on a wholly 'religious' understanding of the commandment; no writer of the period betrays any thought of its being a provision for needed physical rest. The Jewish form of observance was therefore 'idleness.' The commandment was really about devotion to God. . . . This was the basic principle from which the Fathers argued that literal Sabbath observance was not required of Christians."[13] In short, "It must be stressed that, outside Jewish Christianity, all second-century references to the Sabbath commandment either endorse the metaphorical interpretation or reject the literal interpretation as Judaistic or do both."[14] The church fathers were so adamant about this distinction that they condemned mere abstention from normal work as idle. "The Fathers could see no value in inactivity and hardly ever recognized in the Sabbath commandment provision for necessary physical relaxation."[15] He cites the Syriac *Didascalia* (*c.* 250?): "Daily and hourly, whenever you are not in church, devote yourselves to your work."[16]

In the fourth century, Christians often began to imitate Jewish customs. Again, citing Bauckham: "This Judaizing tendency was a grass roots tendency that the authorities of the church opposed. The Council of Laodicea (A.D. 380), for example, legislated against a series of Judaizing practices including resting on the Sabbath (canon 29). It seems that while the popular tendency was to imitate the Jewish practice, the authorities often responded by insisting on a specifically Christian kind of Sabbath observance sharply distinguished from the Jewish kind. The Sabbath was not to be observed in 'idleness,' imitating the Jews, but as a day of Christian worship when the *New Testament* Scriptures were read and as a commemoration of God's creation of the world *through Christ*."[17] It was Constantine, in 321, who first legislated Sunday rest. He specified Sunday as "the most honourable day of the Sun." He may have done so to promote sun worship, as well as to placate Christians.[18] As soon as the State got involved in sabbath legislation, there was theological confusion and compromise.

---

13. Bauckham, "Sabbath and Sunday in the Post-Apostolic Church," in Carson (ed.), *From Sabbath to Lord's Day,* pp. 266-67.

14. *Ibid.*, p. 269.

15. *Ibid.*, p. 282.

16. *Ibid.*, p. 286.

17. *Ibid.*, pp. 261-62.

18. *Ibid.*, pp. 280-81.

B. Civil Government

What is the proper "sabbatarian" role today of the civil government? One very distinct possibility is this: the civil government should declare null and void any labor contract that requires a person to work seven days a week as a condition of employment. This is a contract against conscience, comparable to requiring a woman to commit illicit sexual acts as a condition of employment. Businesses would be compelled to honor the desires of employees to take one day off per week—and that day would probably be the first day of the week. The compulsion here is essentially *negative:* the State may prohibit economic coercion against people's consciences, when their consciences are based on an explicit statement of the word of God.[19] The Bible is quite explicit about resting one day in seven. Nevertheless, Paul acknowledges that some men may not see this, and that apart from required church attendance, they should not be molested or made to feel guilty.

The Bible teaches us about Christian maturity. The Old Testament's death penalty for sabbath violators was stark and entirely negative. Men were not to be governed primarily by conscience in questions regarding the sabbath. They were to be governed by fear. They were told what could *not* be done. They were treated as children. But with the coming of Christ, and the victory He sustained at Calvary, His people have been given *positive requirements concerning worship* on His day. They are to meet corporately to celebrate and worship (as they may have been required to do in the Old Testament: Lev. 23:3). Overnight, the disciples were given a new vision. Overnight, the compulsion of the civil government regarding the Lord's day ended. Overnight, the sabbath became primarily a positive requirement of corporate worship, without the civil penalty of execution for working on the sabbath. Overnight, the question of a day of rest on the Lord's day became a matter of conscience. It had to; the Jewish leaders were not about to make the Christian equivalent of the sabbath compulsory as a day of rest.

As the theological insight of men improves over time, they will come to recognize the implications of God's creation week (six-one)

---

19. In the summer of 1985, the U.S. Supreme Court overturned state legislation that made it illegal for employers to compel individuals to work on Sunday as a condition of employment. Thus, the Supreme Court has made illegal the one type of Lord's day legislation that the New Testament implicitly sanctions.

and covenant man's re-creative week (one-six). They will recognize the necessity of a day of rest—a moral, physical, and economic necessity. When they do, they will make economic decisions and social decisions that will *indirectly* pressure recalcitrants into honoring the Lord's day. For instance, if Christians refuse to go out to shop on Sunday, there will be no economic incentive to keep stores open on Sunday, except to sell to non-Christians. If most people in a society are eventually converted, or at least honor the Lord's day externally, then there will be almost no economic incentive to remain open on Sunday. But a person's *conscience* is the guide in New Testament times, not civil compulsion.

Because the day of the Lord is now a day of communion, they will try to see to it that they get time off for Sunday worship whenever possible. They will not work as professional football players. They will not pay money to go to professional football games. They will not watch professional football games on television, nor will they buy the products advertised during Sunday sports events—at least, not *because* they are advertised during Sunday sports events. Christians will increasingly honor that day as a day of *worship for almost all*, and therefore of a day of *cessation of income-producing labor for almost all*. The new Christian sabbath—cessation from normal work—is a *by-product* of worship on the Lord's day. Christians will do their best to schedule their jobs to give themselves a day of rest. And as more and more people do this, more and more occupations will find it economically profitable to honor the desires of their maturing Christian employees. Sunday will become most people's day of rest, including professional athletes. Only those occupations that serve the needs of resting people—public utilities, emergency services, and (in my view) restaurants (where wives get a break from the normal workweek)—will still be profitable on Sunday.

The State in New Testament times is to leave men free to act positively; its role is to suppress lawless acts of violence and fraud. It is not to make men positively good; it is to *restrain them* from committing *evil, public acts*. When the God-revealed emphasis of the sabbath changed from a day of no work to a day on which God mandates corporate worship, the State's role also changed.[20] Conscience now is to

---

20. I am not arguing here that there was unquestionably no public, corporate aspect of sabbath-worship in the Old Testament, but only that whatever the nature of this corporate worship may have been, the specifics of such worship services did not receive any attention in the Old Testament. There is no mention of tithes being

lead men in the decision to rest on the first day of the week or another day, or not rest at all. The State is not to force men to decide. The State is not to be trusted to tell men to take positive steps toward righteousness, such as worship. If God tells men to do something positive (such as worship Him publicly on a particular day and in specific ways), the State must remove itself from the arena of human decision. This is not because societies are not covenanted by God, but because they *are*.

Admitted Changes

The church has admitted the following changes in the day of rest: 1) the seventh day to first (eighth) day; 2) the abandonment of sundown-to-sundown timing; and 3) the abolition of the death penalty imposed by the civil government. A fourth change may be involved in the addition of required church attendance (communion and worship) to what was previously primarily a day of rest. (This is not a major change *if* Leviticus 23:3 did involve weekly public worship.) Unquestionably, the church has modified its concept of what constitutes legitimate labor, which we will consider in greater detail in Section C.

These alterations are of monumental importance. They represent a sharp break with the Mosaic law. To maintain that such modifications are theologically valid, the church needs New Testament evidence of an *announced break*. It needs New Testament revelation that specifies that such a discontinuous transformation has been announced by God through His prophets. If the church is unwilling to take seriously the radical break announced by Paul in Colossians and Romans — the abolition of the Mosaic sabbath — then it has only a few scattered references to first-day worship to defend its position. Yet the church has hesitated to use these Pauline teachings to justify the break, since they are so radical in nature. Protestant churches that have clung to at least a watered-down version of the Puritan sabbath — itself a watered-down version of the Mosaic sabbath, since the Puritans did not execute Lord's day violators — have used the

---

collected on sabbath-day meetings, or psalms being sung, or a communion meal being shared, or lectures from a Levite. Such events may have taken place, but there is no direct evidence. In the New Testament, such events are mentioned as taking place in corporate worship on the Lord's day. Thus, I *am* arguing that there is a change of *emphasis* in the New Testament, and the specifics of biblical revelation testify to this change.

Old Testament passages as guides for modern Lord's day-keeping. They have not wanted to admit that such a sharp break with the Mosaic sabbath has been announced, since the New Testament offers no specific guidelines for rest on the Lord's day. Furthermore, the New Testament spells out the requirement of weekly corporate worship, and it mentions a communion meal, celebrated in the evening.

Churches have refused to admit that the kind of rest we choose for the Lord's day is a matter of *conscience discipline* rather than church discipline. They have not been content to point to the sabbath of Genesis 2:2-3 as a creation sabbath, the one-six pattern for man's week. They have selectively and arbitrarily quoted *some* aspects of the Mosaic sabbath — but always without the death penalty — as if there were exegetical justification for part of the Mosaic law to be brought into the New Testament era, but not the required Mosaic sanction against sabbath desecration. They often call for some kind of sanctions by the civil government — sanctions never mentioned or contemplated in the Mosaic law — but not the death penalty, which is the sanction specifically required by the Mosaic law. To say that the interpretational principles of modern sabbatarian exegetes are muddled is putting it mildly. It is another case of *smorgasbord religion*: taking this or that aspect of biblical revelation, while leaving others alone, all according to personal taste, familiarity, "reasonableness," and church tradition.

This is not to say that all Mosaic guidelines to what we should not be doing on the day of rest are permanently abolished. The guidelines are there: avoidance of household chores, no profit-seeking commercial ventures, and no idle talk. It is not the guidelines that have been abolished; it is the *locus of the sanctioning agency* which has changed. The *conscience*, not the civil government, is the earthly locus of Lord's day enforcement in New Testament times. It is the individual conscience, not the institutional church, which makes the decision concerning what constitutes idle talk, or a postponable household chore, or the lawful limits of recreation. Pressure can come from sermons, or from patient instruction from the elders. Christians are to be educated concerning the Lord's day principle. They are not to be coerced.

No Compulsion

Paul warns us, in the area of diet and the Lord's day, that different views exist, and that *discussions are not to resort to compulsion, social or institutional, in order to settle the issues.* Ostracism is not valid. But refusing *on Sunday* to eat in a restaurant operated by a "Lord's day-violator" *is* valid, since the potential meal-buyer has decided that such activities as the purchase of a meal on the Lord's day is against his conscience. He is not seeking to punish the "Lord's day violator"; he is seeking to do the Lord's work in his own life.

The church should not be fearful of the weaknesses of human conscience in the areas of the *Lord's day* and *diet.* (Actually, the church is quite willing to allow personal choice in the case of diet, but it resists the authority of conscience in the question of the Lord's day.) If the church is to avoid bothering people in these two areas of life, how much more the civil government! Furthermore, it is incorrect to argue that since the State can legitimately establish pure food and drug standards, it (or the church) can therefore legitimately establish sabbath restrictions. Commentators should not make the mistake of equating restrictions against *eating* certain ritually prohibited foods with the question of restrictions against *the sale of* chemically or biologically adulterated food. The State is empowered to restrict the sale of adulterated, dangerous products, not on the basis of the dietary laws, but on the basis of the *quarantine* (Lev. 13, 14): *a negative sanction against violence* — namely, the violence of microbes or poisons against unsuspecting buyers. The State may not tell people what they must eat, but only what they must not *sell*, because of injuries that such adulterated food can produce in the victims — injuries that can be proven in a court of law to have resulted from the product in question.

The New Testament does mark off certain areas of life and calls them, in effect, either things indifferent or things that are not a matter of compulsion. A thing indifferent, for example, is circumcision. "Circumcision is nothing, and uncircumcision is nothing, but keeping the commandments of God" (I Cor. 7:19). Yet it is possible to make a case against circumcision, since the resurrection of Christ has made unnecessary the flow of blood in New Testament times: the sacrifices, the firstborn offerings (eighth-day separation from the dams), and circumcisions (the eighth-day marring of male infants). But Paul does not ask us to make an issue of circumcision or noncircumcision. He wants us to avoid confrontations in this area. The confrontations are divisive in this area, and not worth the trouble they cause. If a medical case were straightforward in favoring circumcision (which it is not in the late twentieth century[21]), the question of circumcision could become important again, but not for narrowly theological reasons. The same is true of diet. Most Christians understand this in the case of circumcision and diet. They do not understand it in the case of the Lord's day. They refuse to take Paul's words literally in Romans 14:5.

It must also be pointed out that we are dealing here with *specific injunctions* in the New Testament. The proper exegetical principle is this: *Mosaic law is still to be enforced, by the church or the State or both, unless there is a specific injunction to the contrary in the New Testament.* To place the locus of enforcement concerning Lord's day violations in the human conscience is not a general New Testament principle of social, political, or legal action with respect to Old Testament laws and sanctions. The Bible does not call for a society operated in terms of man-invented sanctions. The reign of conscience is not to become the reign of anarchy. The Bible does not establish antinomianism as a New Testament principle. But in *certain specified instances*, New Testament writers have removed the locus of enforcement from the church and State, placing it in the conscience. There are not many of these instances, either, but the Lord's day appears to be one of them.

C. Economic Implications of the Lord's Day

We know that the man caught gathering sticks on the sabbath was tried by God and executed at God's direct command (Num. 15:32-36). This was what was required by Exodus 35:3. The death penalty was *indissolubly* integral to the Mosaic laws governing the sabbath. The fact that the church historically has acted as though the death penalty has been officially removed by God from His law testifies to the church's confusion concerning biblical exegesis and

---

21. "The Committee on Fetus and Newborn of the American Academy of Pediatrics stated in 1971 that there are no valid medical indications for circumcision in the neonatal period. . . . There is no absolute medical indication for routine circumcision of the newborn. . . . A program of education leading to continuing good personal hygiene would offer all of the advantages of routine circumcision without the attendant surgical risk. Therefore, circumcision of the male neonate cannot be considered an essential component of adequate total health care." Ad Hoc Task Force on Circumcision, reporting its findings in *Pediatrics*, Vol. 56 (October 1975), pp. 610-11. Cf. Editorial, *British Medical Journal* (May 5, 1979), pp. 1163-64. For a summary of many medical arguments against circumcision, as well as bibliographical references, see Paul Zimmer, "Modern Ritualistic Surgery: A Laymen's View of Nonritual Neonatal Circumcision," *Clinical Pediatrics* (June 1977), pp. 503-6.

the rule of God's law. Those who proclaim their allegiance to the Mosaic view of the sabbath have to come to grips with the Numbers 15 passage. They must integrate this passage into their understanding of society and economics. I am limiting my enquiry to the question of economics, although the Mosaic sabbath affected far more than just the realm of economics. I here reproduce (with some minor modifications) a section from my essay on the sabbath which was first published in R. J. Rushdoony's *Institutes of Biblical Law* (pp. 831-36).

*　　*　　*　　*　　*　　*

The gathering of sticks is a fine example of Hebrew case law as applied in the light of a general requirement of the Decalogue. It shows, perhaps, better than any other instance, the economic implications of the fourth commandment for the Hebrew nation. Consider the economic implications. What was involved in the gathering of sticks? Sticks could be used for at least four purposes:

1. *Heating* the home
2. *Lighting* the home
3. *Cooking* the meals
4. *Selling* the sticks for uses 1-3

As far as actual use of sticks was concerned, the case-law application in Numbers 15 applied more to the daily life of Hebrew women than it did to the men of the family. It is more often the man and his work which are the focus of modern sabbatarian concern, but this was not necessarily the case in a rural, pre-industrial community. The gathering of sticks was more likely to be the task of children; women were to use the sticks for household tasks, once gathered. Men were to reap the benefits of both the gathering and actual use of the sticks, but in general they would not have much to do with the actual handling of sticks. There could be a few exceptions, of course, but one exception seems to be far more likely, namely, that of the *professional stick-gatherer.* His work would be most in demand on the sabbath, precisely the day on which the prohibition against work was enforced. A woman who failed to gather sticks earlier in the week could buy some from a professional.

We are not told that the man in Numbers 15 was such a professional, but the severity of the punishment clearly would have made it far more dangerous for such a class of professionals to have come into existence. There was a need for a harsh penalty, men and women being what they are. There is always a delight in violating God's commandments if one is a sinner; if that violation also brings with it certain superficial benefits above and beyond the mere pleasure of defiance, so much the better. Sabbath prohibitions involved heavy costs for the obedient; enforcement of the sabbath required stiff penalties, thus burdening violators with high costs in the form of high risk.

What were the costs of the sabbath? For the man, it was the forfeiture of all income—monetary (less likely in a rural society), psychological, or physical property—for that day. But women also paid. They had to gather all sticks earlier in the week. This meant more work during the week, either in longer days, or by increasing the intensity of the working day, or both. Had the working day not been lengthened or intensified, then other tasks which it was desirable to accomplish would have to have been foregone, and that, as any wife knows, also involves costs (especially if a husband or a mother-in-law notices the failure in question). There would always be a temptation to forgo the gathering of sticks during the week, especially if a professional would come by with a load of wood on the sabbath for a reasonably cheap price. If his price was less than the woman's estimation of the costs involved in gathering the wood earlier in the week, she would set aside funds for a sabbath transaction.

By imposing a rigorous and permanent form of punishment on the violator—death by stoning—the community was able to force up the price of the sticks; risks would be so high that few professionals could survive. How many women could or would pay the costs? It would be cheaper to buy them earlier or to gather them earlier in the week. Stick-gathering was made an unlikely source of profitable employment on the sabbath. Since the market for sticks on the sabbath was restricted because of the high prices for the sticks (due to the risks involved), the opportunities for temptation were thereby reduced to a minimum. It did not pay many people, net after deduction of risk expenses, to violate the sabbath, and it was very expensive to hire someone to violate it.

To the degree that the penalties are weakened in a case like this, to that degree it becomes *a matter of conscience* as to whether or not someone violates the sabbath or pays someone else to do it. Conscience then stands without the protection of higher economic costs to keep a man acting in a holy fashion. In the mid-twentieth century, rest on Sunday is based primarily on Christian tradition and labor union negotiations; where these restraints are absent, conscience is the only barrier against the violation of the Old Testament application of the sabbath principle. Men who value leisure less than other forms of income will tend to seek out employment on the sabbath.

Hiring Others to Sin for Us

If we accept the principle that it is wrong for us to hire another person to commit a crime for our benefit and his profit, then certain implications follow. Sabbath violations were capital crimes. If strict sabbatarians regard Old Testament provisions as binding on Christians, then it is as wrong to hire a man to violate the sabbath as it is to hire someone from Murder, Inc. to kill a neighbor. The execution of the crime and the guilt of the hiring party are in both cases equal. Capital crimes are major ones. *If the Hebrew sabbath is legally binding today, then its implications and applications are equally binding.*

I have heard Christian people charge their fellow Christians with a violation of the "sabbath" (Lord's day) because the latter have gone out to a restaurant to eat after church services are over. This violation supposedly also holds for those who purchase food in a supermarket on Sunday. Why should this be a violation? Clearly, only on the grounds that it is a violation of the Lord's day to encourage another's violation of the Lord's day by paying him to remain open for business. *If* the standards of the Hebrew sabbath are still morally binding today, then entering a place of business on the Lord's day *is* morally a capital crime, and an abomination in the sight of God. Therefore, pastors and elders must tell their flock to refrain from entering into trade of any sort on the Lord's day.[22]

If a man wishes to take seriously the standards even of the Westminster Confession of Faith (a pre-industrial document, it

---

22. I have worshipped in churches that sold books to worshippers on Sunday, but refused to accept payment until later in the week. To have taken money for the books, the pastors believed, would have violated the sabbath. But the book buyer incurred a debt. He had to pay off this debt later on. What is the difference between this transaction and the purchase of gasoline by means of a credit card? Sabbatarians recognize that credit card purchases are economic transactions, as surely as cash payment purchases are. They would prohibit credit card gasoline purchases on Sunday just as firmly as they would prohibit cash payment purchases. Again, sabbatarians have not thought through the economic implications of the sabbath.

should be pointed out) in all of its pre-industrial rigor, then he should encourage his elders to enforce the provisions. Of course, the provisions of the Confession do not even approach the requirements of Numbers 15, Exodus 31:15, and Exodus 35:2-3, i.e., the true biblical standards in the eyes of a consistent sabbatarian, but at least they are something. If the creeds are valid in their 1646 interpretation, then 1646 standards of enforcement ought to be applied. If such standards are not applied, then it is a clear admission that *the church no longer recognizes as valid the 1646 definition of the sabbath.*

Buying Fuel

Let us pursue the charge against the "restauranteers" with rigor. Those same people who make the charge pride themselves on their Lord's day observance because *they* do not go out to restaurants on the Lord's day. *They* do not shop in supermarkets. *They* have stored up provisions to eat at home. Prior shopping is quite proper, if one is a sabbatarian, for it is of the very essence of Lord's day-keeping that one store up provisions in advance of the Lord's day. But the Old Testament required more than the mere storing up of food. The passage we have referred to, Numbers 15, makes it explicit that not only food but the *fuel* was to be stored up in advance; fuel for heating the home, cooking the meals, and lighting the room had to be procured in advance. It was a capital offense in the eyes of a righteous and holy God to gather sticks — fuel — on His sabbath.

The modern Puritan-Scottish sabbatarian thinks that his is the way of the holy covenant of God simply because he buys his food early, and cooks it on Sunday, while he regards his brother in Christ as sinning because the latter eats at a restaurant on Sunday. But under the provisions of Numbers 15, both crimes appear to be equally subject to death, for both the restaurant-goer and the meal-cooker have paid *specialized fuel producers* to work on the Lord's day. There is this difference, however: the man who enters the restaurant is not self-righteous about his supposed keeping of the Lord's day, and he has made no charges against his fellow Christians. He would seem to have violated the sabbath provisions of Numbers 15, but that is the extent of his guilt. The modern sabbatarians I have met too often violate the Lord's day and the commandment against gossip, or at least they indulge in the "judgment of the raised eyebrow and clicking tongue." They neglect Christ's warning: "Judge not, that ye be not judged. For with what ye judge, ye shall be judged . . ."

(Matt. 7:1, 2a).

The very architecture of our churches is a standing testimony to the unwillingness of contemporary Christians to accept the economic implications of the Lord's day. We fill our buildings with all sorts of electrical appliances; we heat and cool the rooms to a comfortable 75 degrees, winter and summer. We often pride ourselves on the efficiency of modern technology, forgetting that people must go to work and operate the machines that provide the power — the fuel — for our gadgets. These workers are committing sabbatarian capital crimes each Sunday, and every Christian sabbatarian who uses these gadgets, apart from some legitimate emergency, implicitly sends people to hell every Sunday, morning and evening, as he sits in the comfort of his air-conditioned church. If the sabbatarian creeds are correct, then sabbatarians are weekly condemning others to the flames of eternal torment, just so that they can sit in 75-degree comfort.

Naturally, sabbatarians can always defend a 75-degree temperature in the name of "works of necessity." Freezing churches would drive away unbelievers in winter; stifling churches would do so in the summer. Possibly this argument is legitimate, if this *really* is the reason we heat our churches. Or perhaps our bodies really could not stand what our Puritan forefathers went through to establish Reformed worship in America; perhaps we could not bear churches so cold that communion bread would sometimes freeze solid. Possibly we would die if our present technological comforts were to be taken away from us (as pessimists have asserted may be a prospect in the near future). But if mere comfort is our defense of our power-consuming central heating systems, then we are not giving much thought to our sabbatarian creeds. It has become altogether too fashionable to adapt the interpretation of the Lord's day to each new technological breakthrough; sabbatarians cling religiously to standards written centuries ago, while violating the terms of those creeds regularly. It is schizophrenic. The wording of the creeds should be altered, or else sabbatarians should alter their easy acceptance of a radically non-sabbatarian technology.[23]

---

23. The development of a cost-effective program of solar power, with each household supplied with electrical power generated from the home's roof, is quite likely. It is technologically feasible today, though not yet economical. There are some indications, as of 1985, that several firms have designed what could in the future become cost-effective home power systems. This will make it possible for homes, and possibly even churches, to "unplug" from the public utilities, thereby escaping condem-

McCheyne's Accusations

This plea should not be regarded as something new. It was made by one of the strictest and most consistent sabbatarians in the history of the post-Reformation Protestant church, the Scotsman, Robert Murray McCheyne. He minced no words in his condemnation of his fellow Christians: "Do you not know, and all the sophistry of hell cannot disprove it, that the same God who said, 'Thou shalt not kill,' said also, 'Remember the Sabbath day to keep it holy'? The murderer who is dragged to the gibbet, and the polished Sabbath-breaker are one in the sight of God."[24]

Andrew Bonar has preserved McCheyne's teachings on the sabbath question in his *Memoirs of McCheyne*, and any self-proclaimed strict sabbatarian would do well to ponder what McCheyne wrote. If the standards of Numbers 15 made no provision for exemptions of specific professions,[25] and if these standards are still morally and legally binding in New Testament times, how can a man who proclaims the sabbath escape the thrust of McCheyne's words? McCheyne saw clearly what the industrial revolution would mean. In 1841, he challenged the right of the railways to run on Sunday, but he was not followed by most of his sabbatarian countrymen in Scotland. They chose, as sabbatarians ever since have chosen, to turn their backs on the implications of their creed, while vainly proclaiming the moral validity of that creed. McCheyne has a word for those who today enjoy having others work on the Lord's day to provide them with fuel at reasonable prices: "Guilty men who, under Satan, are leading on the deep, dark phalanx of Sabbath-breakers, yours is a solemn position. You are *robbers*. You rob God of His holy day. You are *murderers*. You murder the souls of your servants. God said,

---

nation. But this still does not answer the ethical question: What kind of sabbath-defying technologies were instrumental in the coming of solar power? Without the industrial age, could such a sabbath-honoring technology have come into production? Another problem: the homes will probably remain "plugged in" to the local electrical utility company. The power generated during the day will be sold to the power company, to serve as at least a partial credit for the power purchased that night. In effect, sabbatarians will be tempted to become sellers of sabbath-gathered "sticks." The moral and economic questions will still be with the solar-powered age of the future.

24. R. M. McCheyne, "I Love the Lord's Day" (1841), in Andrew Bonar (ed.), *Memoirs and Remains of Robert Murray McCheyne* (Edinburgh: Banner of Truth Trust, [1844] 1973), p. 599. This is a reprint of the 1892 edition.

25. I argue later in this appendix that there were probably exemptions in specific cases: "Rescheduling Worship."

'Thou shalt not do any work, thou, nor thy servant;' but you compel your servants to break God's law, and to sell their souls for gain. You are *sinners against the light.* . . . You are *traitors to your country.* . . . Was it not Sabbath-breaking that made God cast away Israel? . . . And yet you would bring the same curse on Scotland now. You are *moral suicides,* stabbing your own souls, proclaiming to the world that you are not the Lord's people, and hurrying on your souls to meet the Sabbath-breaker's doom."[26]

Sabbatarians should heed McCheyne's warning. Those who stand in pride because of their sabbatarian position ought to consider the implications of that position. God will not be mocked! When the provisions of the Westminster Confession of Faith are rigorously enforced, then the sabbath debate can take on some meaning other than the playing of theological games. Then, and only then, will the issues be drawn clearly and honestly.

Enforcement Should Begin at the Top

When the elders of the church *begin at home* to follow the sabbatarian standards of the Old Testament, and when they impose such standards on their recalcitrant wives who enjoy their stoves, their hot running water, and their air-conditioning systems, then non-sabbatarians will be impressed. Let them turn off their electrical appliances, or purchase 24-hour power generators (no "lighting fires," please), or install solar-powered cells on their roofs, in order to provide the power. Let them turn off the natural gas, or else purchase butane in advance. Let them cease phoning their friends for "Christian fellowship," so that the lines might be kept open for truly emergency calls. Let them stop using the public mails on Friday, Saturday, and Sunday, so that mail carriers and sorters will not have to miss their observance of the Lord's day. Let them, in short, shut their eyes to the offenses of others until the church, as a disciplinary force, begins to enforce more rigorous requirements on all the membership, *starting at the top of the hierarchy* and working down from there. Let all self-righteousness be abandoned until the full implications of the economics of sabbath-keeping are faced squarely by the church's leadership. Until then, the debate over the sabbath will remain an embarrassment to Christ's church.

Rethinking the sabbath question will involve a rethinking of the

---

26. *Ibid.*, p. 600. See also his "Letter on Sabbath Railways," (1841), pp. 602-5.

whole of Western industrial civilization. It will certainly involve the questioning of the last two centuries of rapid economic growth. Strict sabbatarians should at least be aware of the possible effects of their proposals. If the world should be conformed to Christian standards of biblical law, and if the standards of the Hebrew sabbath practice are, in fact, still the rule for the Christian dispensation, how would these standards be imposed on the population at large? Would it not make impossible our modern version of industrial, specialized society? In other words, if such standards had been enforced for the past two centuries, could this civilization, which most modern Christians accept as far as its technological conveniences are concerned, have come into existence? How much of our economically profitable, efficient, "sabbath-desecrating" technology would we have been forced to prohibit by civil law? The costs, I suspect, would be considerable. It is time for strict sabbatarians to count those costs.

*   *   *   *   *   *

Fire has served as man's major technical tool of dominion, and has been challenged as a primary tool only in the twentieth century, first by electricity and then by the electronic computer.[27] Lewis Mumford has discussed the three-fold uses of fire: light, power, and heat. His essentially evolutionistic interpretation could easily be reworked to conform to biblical imagery. "The first artificially overcame the dark, in an environment filled with nocturnal predators; the second enabled man to change the face of nature, for the first time in a decisive way, by burning over the forest; while the third maintained his internal body temperature and transformed animal flesh and starchy plants into easily digestible food. *Let there be light!* With these words, the story of man properly begins."[28] Thus, fire has been basic to the dominion covenant from the beginning. That the kindling of a sabbath fire was prohibited in the Old Testament is understandable; it is the very essence of work. To kindle a fire, or to gather sticks for a fire, would have symbolized man's autonomy in the dominion process, the essence of lawlessness. Furthermore, as symbolic of God's glory cloud, fire unquestionably served the Hebrews as a reminder of God's power, in addition to being a pri-

---

27. Jeremy Rifkin, *Algeny* (New York: Viking, 1983), ch. 1.
28. Lewis Mumford, *Interpretations and Forecasts: 1922-1972* (New York: Harcourt Brace Jovanovich, 1973), p. 425.

mary economic tool. Kindling a fire on the sabbath therefore was illegal for more than one reason.

"Strange Fire"

There was a fifth use of sticks on the sabbath: lighting a fire, or expanding the intensity of a fire, as a religious testimony. Exodus 35:3 prohibits the kindling of a fire on the sabbath. This seems to mean *starting* a fire.

The priests of Israel kept a fire burning constantly on the altar (Ex. 29:25; Lev. 1-7). When Nadab and Abihu, the sons of Aaron, offered strange fire on the altar, God sent a fire and consumed them (Lev. 10:1-2). It is possible, therefore, to regard the kindling of a fire on the sabbath as an assertion of sacramental rebellion. For this reason, it has been argued, there was a death penalty for kindling any new fire on the sabbath — an assertion of autonomy from the sacrificial system of Israel.[29] This line of argumentation was pursued by at least one sabbatarian Puritan scholar in the seventeenth century, George Walker.[30]

One possible piece of evidence for this position is that the Hebrews were not sure what to do with the stick-gatherer in Numbers 15. The law was clear: violators must be executed. Why didn't they know what to do with him? Why did they seek God's specific pronouncement (Num. 15:34-36)? Doesn't this indicate that they were not sure what to do with him because they had not actually caught him *kindling* a fire, meaning indulging in a ritual trespass of starting a strange fire? He was working, but he had not kindled a fire. Why didn't they execute him, if merely working on the sabbath was a capital crime? Wasn't their hesitation based on their confusion concerning an *unstated* warning against strange fire, a confusion which would not have been present if Exodus 35:2 referred to all labor? Gathering sticks was labor, but they nevertheless enquired of the Lord. Doesn't this imply that they did not suppose that God required the death penalty for working in general — the mere *gathering* of sticks — but that He required it for lighting a fire, something they

---

29. This is the approach to the sabbath question taken by James B. Jordan: *Sabbath Breaking and the Death Penalty: An Alternate View* (forthcoming).

30. George Walker, *The Doctrine of the Holy Weekly Sabbath* (London, 1641), pp. 121-22; cited by James T. Dennison, Jr., *The Market Day of the Soul: The Puritan Doctrine of the Sabbath in England, 1532-1700* (Lanham, New York: University Press of America, 1983), p. 111.

had not seen him do?

My answer is *no*, it was not any confusion associated with an un-stated but implied warning against false ritual which led them to en-quire of God. It was a much more basic problem: confusion over the specific transgression. But before I present my reasoning, I first need to point out the obvious: *Exodus 35:3 does not speak of strange fire*. It speaks only of fire. The "strange fire" interpretation is roundabout and hypothetical, although biblically possible. It relies on *an exclus-ively symbolic interpretation of otherwise plain words*. I prefer to interpret the passage as *primarily economic* but with implicit symbolic overtones.

It should be clear why a few interpreters have appealed to strange fire as the frame of reference for the imposition of the death penalty for sabbath violations: it gets them out of an embarrassing exegetical problem. With the permanent extinguishing of the temple's fire by the Romans in 70 A.D., the biblical law against kindl-ing a fire on the sabbath ceased to be symbolically relevant. Thus, if the altar's fire was the sole reference point in the discussion of the death penalty for sabbath-breaking—that is, if the death penalty which is required by Exodus 35:2 is to be interpreted exclusively in terms of 35:3, the prohibition against starting fires—then the death penalty cannot sensibly be imposed in New Testament times. This enables the commentators to escape from a highly embarrassing problem, namely, the requirement of the death penalty for working on the sabbath in New Testament times. But this line of reasoning immediately backfires on any "strict sabbatarian."

If "strange fire" was the sole reference point for the death penalty for sabbath breakers, then what penalty is to be applied today? Ex-communication alone? Are we to interpret Exodus 31:14—the cut-ting off of the sabbath-breaker from the people—as excommunica-tion rather than execution? If this "cutting off" is not the execution demanded by Exodus 31:15—and I argue that it did mean execution for sabbath violators—then an inescapable conclusion results: *the civil government has no legitimate sanctions to apply against sabbath-breakers in New Testament times.* The only civil sanction specified is execution (35:2), but if this was only for a ritualistic trespass, then there was nothing for the civil government of Israel to do about non-ritual violations. Certainly there is nothing specified for the civil govern-ment to do about a now meaningless practice in New Testament times. First, the fires of the temple are long extinguished. Second, hardly anyone in industrial societies gathers sticks to light fires. This highly anti-sabbatarian conclusion concerning civil sanctions is not likely to appeal to modern sabbatarians. Yet so far, this line of reasoning is the only one which any scholar has used in response to my arguments regarding the termination of institutional sanctions against sabbath violators.[31]

Let us return to the problem of why the Hebrews enquired of God about what to do with the stick-gatherer. Why were they unable to decide what to do with him? The text says that it was not declared to them what should be done (Num. 15:34). I interpret this to mean that *as a case-law application* under *either* interpretive scheme — either as a work transgression or as a sacramental transgression — it was not clear to them whether stick-gathering constituted a capital crime. God then said that it did. But the text does not tell us which interpretation governed. Either type of violation constituted a capital crime: false worship or sabbath work. If stick-gathering was the latter type of violation (and I think it was), we then need to ask: What constituted unlawful labor on the sabbath? My answer: 1) commercial labor was prohibited on the sabbath (Ex. 31:15; 35:2), and 2) no household labor that could be done beforehand — e.g., kindling a new fire — was permitted (35:3).

Nehemiah 13

What about Nehemiah 13? Here we find a specific case of sabbath-breaking by foreign merchants from Tyre who came into Jerusalem to buy and sell on the sabbath (v. 16). Nehemiah locked the doors of the city on the evening of the sabbath to keep them out (v. 19), but they clustered around the wall. "Then I testified against them, and said unto them, Why lodge ye about the wall? If ye do so again, I will lay hands on you. From that time forth came they no more on the sabbath" (v. 21).

He could have had them executed, in terms of biblical law, but he warned them first. As foreigners, they may not have understood the specifics of the law, and because biblical law had not been enforced in the land for so long, the general public may not have understood the nature of the penalty. In this respect, modern strict sabbatarians are not much different from the people of Nehemiah's day; they proclaim the continuing application of the Old Testament's sabbatarian

---

31. I have submitted this appendix and Chapter 4 to four Reformed scholars so far, and James Jordan is the only one who was willing to comment on it. I trust that the "silent three" will remain equally silent when the book is published, even if they disagree with my arguments. When men are asked for counsel and refuse to provide it, they should remain decently silent after the damage is done.

standards, but they have forgotten about the death penalty. By threatening to lay hands on them, Nehemiah warned them that the full rigor of God's sanctions would be imposed. For good reason, they ceased their violation of the sabbath. This does not testify to a reduced penalty; on the contrary, it shows how great a threat was involved. Once they understood that the civil government was serious about adhering to Exodus 31:15 and 35:2, they ceased selling goods in the city.

The question of strange fire was not raised by Nehemiah. The issue was buying and selling on the sabbath. While stick-gathering could have involved some aspect of outright sacramental rebellion, it didn't need to in order to call down the death penalty on violators. As far as the Hebrews were informed by God, either working on the sabbath or the kindling of a fire could result in execution. The subtleties of biblical theology or symbolism were of no real concern to them. They simply had to avoid working and also avoid kindling a fire.

Mass Production and International Trade

Consider the modern metallurgy industry and its consumption of "sticks." It takes enormous quantities of power to produce steel or aluminum. Power is expensive, and grew more expensive in the 1970's. The cost of shutting down a steel mill for one day and then starting it up again the next day would make the production of steel economically prohibitive. It could be done technically, of course, at some astronomical cost. It would be like the proverbial textbook example of growing bananas at the North Pole. Technically, it can be done; economically, it would involve massive losses — waste of scarce economic resources. Such waste is not tolerated by a free market. Steel could not be manufactured under such conditions. The cost of power which is required to reheat a steel plant, not to mention the man-hours wasted in supervising such a wasteful operation, would force steel manufacturers out of business.

If the civil government enforced the Puritan-Scottish interpretation of the Mosaic law against Lord's day violations on the steel industry, there would soon be almost no domestic steel being manufactured. At that point, buyers of steel would begin to pay foreign manufacturers for their steel — manufacturers who do not honor the Mosaic sabbath. This would place the Lord's day-honoring nation at the mercy of foreign manufacturers. The "Lord's day-desecrating" foreign firms would be rewarded for their violation; the Lord's day-honoring domestic manufacturers would risk going bankrupt. Furthermore, since the supply of steel would be reduced worldwide, as a result of the bankruptcy of the domestic firms, the cost of steel would rise, thereby penalizing marginal purchasers and users of steel who could no longer afford to buy.

The only way to make steel available domestically apart from rewarding the foreign Lord's day violators would be to erect tariffs against foreign steel. This would force up the national price of steel to levels that would permit the production of six-day-per-week steel, meaning very expensive and specialized steel. The middle class and lower class would be effectively cut off from the enjoyment of many products made of steel. In a modern economy, this could produce a breakdown of the division of labor. It could produce an economic collapse, a return to low-productivity subsistence agriculture.

There is no way that steel can be produced that would not involve profits from Lord's day production. If the civil government required all profits (let alone total revenues) from the seventh day of production to be paid as a fine, or paid to the poor, then the price of steel would rise. The income from the other six days would have to cover the losses of the seventh day. The six-day-per-week revenue limitation would make the nation's steel mills uncompetitive in world markets. Again, tariff barriers would have to be placed on imported steel, and the nation in question would find its foreign markets for steel wiped out. The world consumers of steel would turn to the steel produced by "Lord's day-desecrators."

The International Division of Labor

The modern economy involves the whole world in the international division of labor. Manufacturers of literally thousands of products have been drawn into a worldwide market. Transportation costs have dropped steadily in the modern world, so those products which once satisfied only local needs are now facing competition from similar products produced abroad. Also, products that once stayed in a local district can now be sold abroad. The pressures of world competition force all manufacturers to respect world market prices.

In Israel in Moses' day, a predominantly agricultural and tribal society did not involve itself in extensive world trade. There was trade, or course, but this trade was centered on the major cities and port cities. Consider an undeveloped rural economy. Transportation costs effectively insulate interior rural communities from the benefits and competition of world markets. Trade is overwhelmingly aimed at high-value, low-volume products bought and used by the rich, the powerful, and the well-connected. The division of labor is minimal, and output-per-unit-of-resource-input is low. Per capita productivity is low, and therefore per capita income is low.

The Puritan-Scottish interpretation of the Mosaic sabbath laws could be enforced in ancient Israel without wiping out whole segments of the economy only because per capita income was low, economic expectations were low, and the international market for goods did not affect most of the products in use in rural areas. More than this: if the Puritan-Scottish view of the Mosaic sabbath laws had remained in force, the sabbath-honoring economies of the world would probably still be predominantly rural, characterized by a minimal division of labor. The rhythm of the one-six week is suitable only for rural societies, *if* that rhythm is mandatory on *all* citizens on the *same* day.

Do we want to argue that God has determined that the low division of labor of rural life is a moral requirement forever? Do we want to argue that God has created limits on the development of world trade in the form of a rigid sabbath code which forces all men within a covenantally faithful society into an identical one-six weekly pattern?

As far as I am able to determine, questions like these have not been dealt with by defenders of a New Testament version of the Mosaic sabbath. Only because those who defend such a view of the Lord's day have seldom been in positions of formulating or enforcing national economic policy, have they been able to avoid the hard reality of sabbatarianism. They have not thought through the economic implications of their position.

When I raised some of these questions in the appendix that appeared in *Institutes of Biblical Law* in 1973, I expected to see strict sabbatarians respond, to propose answers, or at least modifications in their position that would enable them to avoid the obvious implications of their position. So far, I have waited twelve years to receive a single letter or see a single refutation in print. Rushdoony's book has been read by many influential theologians and Christian leaders,[32]

---

32. What is rather amazing is how few copies *Institutes of Biblical Law* has sold, in comparison to its influence. It has unquestionably begun to reshape the thinking of numerous conservative Christian leaders, yet as of early 1985, it had sold under 18,000 copies in twelve years. Its press runs have always been small — sometimes as

and critics have attacked its overall thesis concerning the New Testament applicability of Old Testament laws, but sabbatarians have systematically, conscientiously avoided going into print with objections to my appendix on the Lord's day. The debate has not yet begun.

The Puritan Sabbath

The sabbatarian heritage is unquestionably a legacy of the Puritans. It is just about the only theological legacy of the Puritans which still exercises widespread intellectual influence within the Protestant community. It does not exert widespread practical influence, because few people honor the Puritan vision of the sabbath, even though they may honor it verbally.

The Westminster Confession of Faith, a uniquely Puritan document, states that "This Sabbath is then kept holy unto the Lord, when men, after a due preparing of their hearts, and ordering of their common affairs before-hand, do not only observe an holy rest, all the day, from their own works, words, and thoughts about their worldly employments and recreations, but also are taken up, the whole time, in the public and private exercises of His worship, and in the duties of necessity and mercy" (Chap. XXI:VIII). The Larger Catechism amplifies these words: "The Sabbath or Lord's day is to be sanctified by an holy resting all the day, not only from such works as are at all times sinful, but even from such worldly employments and recreations as are on other days lawful . . ." (A. 117).

We lack a detailed historical study of the Puritan view of recreation. I have never seen even a scholarly article on the topic. I would never advise a doctoral student to adopt such a dissertation topic. The reason should be clear: *The Puritans had no doctrine of recreation.* It was a topic utterly foreign to them. It is exceedingly difficult to take seriously their view of holy rest when they had no doctrine of worldly rest.

The Puritan Obsession

There is a popular picture of the Puritans which says that they were a dour bunch, that they never laughed, or wrote poetry, or wrote plays, or created great works of art, or in any way delighted in

---

few as 1,000 copies. Any historian who looks back at its sales figures, and who then tries to evaluate its influence in relation to these figures, will have a difficult time explaining its impact.

the recreations of life. It has become popular in recent years to dismiss this picture of the Puritans as a myth. It is not a myth. It is rooted in reality—at least the reality of the documentary record.

I spent several years working with the primary sources of the colonial American Puritans, especially their sermons and legislative records. If someone were to tell me that the Puritans were a fun-loving lot because of their fondness for taverns, I would reply: "How do you know they enjoyed taverns?" There is only one reasonable reply: "Because I read all the laws they passed regulating them." In every town and in the records of the Massachusetts Bay Colony, a recurring legislative concern was the control of taverns: hours they could be open, the kinds of games that could be played in them (they were obsessed with the evils of shuffleboard, and the laws repeatedly took notice of this notorious deviant behavior), restricting access to taverns by apprentices, and so forth. The legislators did their best to minimize the operations of these dens of iniquity.

What about Puritan poetry? There was Milton, whose reputation as a Puritan is somewhat questionable (though I think on the whole he was in the Puritan camp). There was no one else of comparable reputation. Anne Bradstreet, the poetess of North Andover, Massachusetts, had a collection of her poems published without her knowledge in England in 1650, and twenty-eight years later, a larger collection was published in Boston. By this time, she had been dead for six years.[33] The other great colonial Puritan poet was Edward Taylor, who forbade his heirs to publish any of his poems, and which did not see publication until 1939. His manuscript book was not even discovered in the Yale University Library until 1937.[34] Not until 1968 was a full-length edition of seventeenth-century American poetry published. Meserole's comments are appropriate: "In New England particularly, there were strictures against too consummate an attention to poetry. 'A little recreation,' asserted Cotton Mather, was a good thing, and one should not contemplate an unpoetical life. But to turn one's mind and energies wholly to the composition of verse was to prostitute one's calling, to risk opprobrium, and most important, to lose sight of the proper balance God envisioned for man on earth. The sheer quantity of verse that has come down to us proves that these strictures were not completely heeded. It is similarly clear

---

33. Hudson T. Meserole, "Anne Bradstreet," in Meserole (ed.), *Seventeenth-Century American Poetry* (Garden City, New York: Anchor, 1968), p. 3.
34. *Ibid.*, p. 119.

that these strictures had their effect not only in the nature and intent of much of the surviving verse but also in the sparse numbers of poems printed in America before 1725."[35]

There were the two poems by Michael Wigglesworth, *The Day of Doom* (1662) and *God's Controversy With New-England* (1662). No copy of the first printing of 1,800 copies of *Day of Doom* survives; Meserole says that they were literally read to pieces. These two heavy dirges were obsessed with death and judgment. They were wildly popular in New England, and probably had a great deal to do with the shift in perspective in New England sermons from a more optimistic post-millennialism to a new pessimistic sermon form called the Jeremiad by Perry Miller.[36] These were formula sermons of imminent judgment that were as predictable as they were ineffective in achieving their goal: repentance and the "affirming of the covenant" by the second and third generations.[37]

There were no Puritan playrights, no Puritan sculptors, no Puritan painters, no Puritan composers of merit. They were, from start to finish, *craftsmen*, not artists. They were the theologians of artisanship, of diligence in the calling, of self-discipline and lifelong exertions to achieve middle-class output. They achieved their economic goals as no similar group in man's history ever has. They subdued a howling wilderness in New England, a land of insects, rocky soil, fierce winters, and no minerals of value, a land of which it could truly be said it was devoid of milk and honey. As a substitute, its trees had sap for maple syrup, but New England was a "promised land" of *freedom* rather than raw materials. They swapped their way into wealth. "From Puritan to yankee" is a constant theme in history books, for good reason: it was a real transformation.

From beginning to end, they were obsessed with one sin. It was not sexual debauchery, it was not drunkenness, it was not theft or murder or any of the other ten commandments. It was the sin of

35. *Ibid.*, p. xviii.
36. Perry Miller, *The New England Mind: From Colony to Province* (Cambridge, Massachusetts: Harvard University Press, 1953), ch. 2.
37. I can remember staggering out of the microfilm reading room in graduate school, after having suffered half a dozen of these forty- to eighty-page exercises in congregational flagellation. There is no doubt in my mind: young Ben Franklin was right when he fled Boston to the lighter climate of Philadelphia in the 1720's; anyone with any sense would have fled after 1662. It is one thing to admire the Puritans' ability to work all week and suffer five or six hours of these sermons on Sunday. It would be something else again to have to put up with what they suffered.

idleness which obsessed them. In their sermons, their laws, and their pious diaries, they were obsessed with the fear that they were not working hard enough to please God. They did not believe that they could work their way into heaven, but they took seriously the dominion covenant—took it more seriously than any Christian group before or since. It was through work and thrift that they believed they could turn the wilderness into a paradise. Their efforts helped to prepare the religious soil for the industrial revolution a century later, long after Christians had abandoned their Calvinist theology. The Methodists of the late eighteenth century were the true spiritual heirs of the Puritans, for they too adopted a theology of work and thrift. The legacy of Puritanism even bears their name: the Puritan work ethic.

One thing they never learned to do gracefully was to rest. They did not understand how they could rest and please God. They had no developed theology of lawful recreation. They worked from sunrise to sunset six days a week. The men sneaked out to a tavern occasionally, and felt so guilty about it that for decades they elected and re-elected magistrates who kept writing unenforced laws regulating their beloved taverns. They had no systematic theology of leisure. They could not deal with the prosperity which their great efforts produced.[38] They remind me of the medieval Benedictine monasteries that also could not deal with the wealth they produced, and so suffered periods of recurring internal reform every few centuries.

The Marathon Sabbath

This obsession with work colored their view of the sabbath. The *Directory for the Publick Worship of God* published by the Westminster Assembly specifies concerning Sunday activities: "That what time is vacant, between or after the solemn meetings of the congregation in publick, be spent in reading, meditation, repetition of sermons; especially by calling their families to an account of what they have heard, and catechising of them, holy conferences, prayer for a blessing upon the public ordinances, singing of psalms, visiting the sick, relieving the poor, and such like duties of piety, charity, and mercy,

---

38. Miller writes: ". . . the Jeremiad could make sense out of existence as long as adversity was to be overcome, but in the moment of victory it was confused. . . . It flourished in dread of success; were reality ever to come up to its expectations, a new convention would be required, and this would presuppose a revolution in mind and society." Miller, *From Colony to Province*, p. 33.

accounting the sabbath a delight." To which the modern reader replies: "You've got to be kidding! A delight? An ordeal beyond measure after the pressures of a Puritan workweek."

James T. Dennison's polemical defense of the Puritan sabbath (published in the guise of a master's thesis in history) is a detailed account of the debates concerning the sabbath of this period. Summarizing William Gouge's tract, *The Sabbaths Sanctification* (1641), Dennison writes: "Duties of mercy consist in those which concern man's soul and those which concern man's body. Ministering to the soul includes: instructing the ignorant; establishing those who are weak in the faith; resolving doubts of the downcast; comforting the troubled; informing those in error; reproving the sinner; and building one another up in the Lord. Ministering to the body includes: visiting the sick and imprisoned; relieving the need; rescuing those in danger; and giving all other succor necessary."[39] This is in addition to works of necessity: preparing food, washing the body, putting on clothing, putting out fires in houses, closing up flood breaches, fighting in wars, releasing animals in danger. He admits that not all sabbatarians took the following strict sabbatarian positions (though some did): no baking or cooking, walking, any kind of work, or gathering sticks for a fire.[40] Thus, we can appreciate Dennison's summary statement: "It is apparent that the Puritan Sabbath was not a day of idleness. There was as much activity, if not more, on the Lord's day as on any other day of the week."[41]

The question arises: When did these people rest? The answer: they seldom did. When they did, they had no developed theology to tell them when they had rested too much. So out of desperation, they avoided rest like the plague.

By the early eighteenth century, Puritanism was fading. Newer religious movements arose that were capable of dealing with success — success that came from the Puritan work ethic. The second and third generations of Puritan heirs failed to affirm the covenant, join the church, and take up the "redeemed man's burden" of endless labor. Puritanism literally worked itself to death.

Nevertheless, the forms of the Jeremiad were retained. In the 1730's, ministers were still using its outline, even though it was even less relevant as a formal exercise than it had been eight decades

---

39. Dennison, *Market Day of the Soul*, p. 113.
40. *Ibid.*, p. 110.
41. *Ibid.*, p. 113.

earlier.[42] Social and literary forms sometimes survive long after the cultural environment which gave birth to them has disappeared. Even longer lived has been the Puritan rhetoric of sabbath-keeping, a rhetoric which is still maintained by a handful of Calvinist churches whose members have never observed the detailed positive requirements for *hard, merciful work* that Puritan sabbatarian doctrine established, and who would transfer membership from any church which would actually enforce these requirements, and vote out of office any politician who might attempt to legislate them.

The Puritan view of the sabbath (though not its practice) has been maintained unbroken only by the more rigorous Presbyterians in the Scottish tradition. This tradition goes back to the seventeenth century. In Aberdeen, Scotland, in the 1640's, shops were shut on Thursdays, Saturday afternoons, and of course all day Sunday. On Sundays, the highways were watched to identify absentees. In April of 1646, at the height of critical negotiations between Charles I, the Scots, and English representatives of Parliament, Balmerino, who was travelling to Newark with an urgent message from London, stopped when he was 13 miles from his destination in order not to travel on the sabbath.[43] The Scottish-Puritan doctrine of the sabbath unquestionably had powerful effects on its adherents—effects that would today be regarded as near-pathological by those who claim that they are still faithfully upholding that very sabbatarian view.

General Preaching Creates Specific Guilt

In *Presbyterion,* a journal published by Covenant Theological Seminary, Robert G. Rayburn offers a standard essay on the sabbath. He defends the idea of a day of rest, and his familiar line of argumentation is that of the Presbyterian elder in the Scottish tradition. There is nothing unique about the essay, and nothing uniquely wrong with it. It is traditionally wrong, familiarly wrong, but not uniquely wrong. It is no different from a thousand other essays on the topic over the last three centuries.

What needs to be pointed out is that in a 15-page essay, he devotes less than two pages to the section: "Practical Questions Concerning Sabbath Observance." This, too, is typical. It is traditionally the practical questions that the sabbatarians have avoided dealing

---

42. Miller, *Colony,* p. 484.
43. Christopher Hill, *Society and Puritanism in Pre-Revolutionary England* (2nd ed.; New York: Schoecken, 1967), p. 183.

with for the last century. From the day the Scots faced the question of Sunday railroads, the commentators (McCheyne excepted) have mumbled. When it comes to public utilities — water, gas, electricity — they do not even mumble. They are stony silent.

Rayburn offers several reasons for the sabbath, all of which are traditional and correct: the dependence of man on God; the glorification of God through worship, especially corporate worship; the biological need for rest in the weekly rhythm. He says that Christ observed the sabbath, and He used it for works of mercy. Equally predictably and equally traditionally, he rejects the clear meaning of Paul's words in Colossians 2:16-17 concerning new moons and sabbaths, arguing that Paul was really concerned about a "teaching which was a mixture of Jewish ritualism and an Oriental Gnostic-type philosophy." He therefore concludes: "So this passage, as well as two others which do not use the word 'sabbath' but speak of observing days (Rom 14:5 and Gal 4:11), obviously do not refer to the observance of the first day of the week as the Lord's Day, the Christian's sabbath, for Paul observed the first day himself and directed others to observe it by setting aside their offerings to the Lord (I Cor 16:2). He was instructing believers not to attach special significance and sacredness to Jewish religious festivals and thus to pass judgment on those who failed to observe them, but rather to rejoice in their wonderful new-found liberty in Christ. As for the observance of the first day as the Lord's Day or Christian Sabbath, all Christians, Jew and Gentile, kept it."[44]

Where should I begin? If this is the meaning of these passages, then why do churches refuse to insist that the civil government execute sabbath-breakers, as required by Exodus 31:15 and 35:2? If the locus of sovereignty of enforcement has not shifted to the individual conscience, then on what basis do New Testament commentators assert (implicitly or explicitly) that the civil government is no longer the responsible agent of enforcement? Why has the church remained silent about the death penalty for two millennia? After two thousand years, the silence has become deafening. Second, it is not true, as Bacchiocchi's dissertation (p. 79, note 4, above) makes clear, that all Christians, Jew and gentile alike, worshipped on the first day of the week in Paul's day. Third, just because Paul insisted on corporate worship does not explain why the day of the Lord is to be a day of rest. It only shows that

---

44. Robert G. Rayburn, "Should Christians Celebrate the Sabbath Day?" *Presbyterion*, X (Spring-Fall 1984) pp. 83, 84.

corporate weekly worship is required by New Testament law. Paul emphasized this because there was no *equally clear-cut* requirement for sabbath worship in the Old Testament.

What does Rayburn say is required? We must glorify Him by not making Sunday a day of doing our own personal desires and pleasures. No definitions, no examples, no study of what is restful or fun, what is allowed and prohibited. In short, he burdens his readers (should they take him seriously) with a *mountain of guilt*. They are told to be faithful to God, but they are not told *how*. This, too, is traditional.

We must make the day a day of rest, he says. But rest really doesn't mean rest; it means . . . ? (Marathon sabbath? What?) "Resting on the Sabbath does not mean staying in bed all day or even most of the day, although some rest for the body is certainly appropriate." But, we should be moved to inquire: *What amount of time in bed is appropriate?* He does not say. In short, here is another pile of guilt for the reader. How about a one-hour nap? A two-hour nap? Why all this babble about staying in bed all day? Who on earth ever recommended staying in bed all day? This is a serious article and a serious topic, yet what we are given is exaggeration and hyperbole rather than specific, God-required guidelines. *This is all that we ever get from sabbatarian commentators*. This is all we have been given for 400 years. We grow tired. *We want rest from guilt*. We want specifics. When will they give us rest?

Then comes the usual refrain: *evil restaurants*. "Since the obedient believer is to observe the Sabbath as a holy day of rest, he must *be careful not to interfere with others having the same privilege*. He must not keep others working that he might not need to work. The waitress or cook at the restaurant and the attendant at the filling station have the right to rest also."[45] Restaurants on Sunday: the modern Calvinist's equivalent of taverns in seventeenth-century New England.

This essay is neither better nor worse than a century of similar essays, which stream endlessly from the pens and typewriters and word processors of those who simply will not take seriously the problems of economics and their relationship to the Bible. They just hammer away at the helpless readers, who, if they have adopted "strict sabbatarianism, twentieth-century style," desperately need specific, God-required guidelines. Neither do the commentators confront Exodus 31:15 and 35:2. They refuse to deal with the prob-

---

45. *Ibid.*, p. 86.

lems of public utilities, yet they criticize those who attend restaurants. It is clear why: *they* do not attend restaurants on Sunday, and
their wives unquestionably do use the services of public utilities on
Sunday. It is exegesis based on personal convenience and tradition.
Such exegesis is productive of nothing except guilt, and perhaps a
late reaction against sabbatarian precepts because of the lack of
guidelines. The exegesis never progresses, because it never gets sufficiently *explicit* in its applications. It still sounds as though it was
written in 1825 — and even then, such exegesis was running into difficulties with respect to the industrial revolution.

Preliminary Conclusion

The New Testament Lord's day is not the same as the Old Testament sabbath. The shift in the day of the week, from Seventhday
(Saturday) to Firstday (Sunday), which is in fact the Eighthday, indicates that there are fundamentally new aspects of the Lord's day.
This shift enables us to understand better Paul's warning of a shift in
the locus of enforcement of the "day of rest" principle: from the ecclesiastical and civil governments to the conscience of the individual,
meaning the head of the household.

By attempting to impose the workweek rhythms of the sabbath-
honoring Old Testament rural society onto a modern industrial
economy, the civil government would destroy modern civilization.
This fact has been "honored in the breach" by most magistrates and
church officials for several centuries, but sabbatarian theologians
have yet to present a coherent biblical case that would morally justify
this "aversion of the eyes" of civil and ecclesiastical governments.
Church leaders see what is going on, yet they remain silent.

Another question needs to be dealt with. It is one thing to say
that the conscience governs the selection and enforcement of the day
of rest. It is something else to say that the church may not enforce
the day of church attendance. The New Testament's emphasis on the
Lord's day as a day of worship may have eliminated the role of the
civil government in enforcing public rest, but what about the institutional church's unquestioned right to name the day of public worship
for its members, and to establish times for worship? Does the church
have an obligation to provide alternative times of worship for
members who, because of specialized occupations, decide to honor
the rest principle by resting on a day other than the first day of the
week?

Rescheduling Worship

It is not normal in a Christian nation to find that most occupations of necessity involve labor on seven consecutive days. In fact, most of them are five-day occupations, leaving time for goofing off Saturday (that terrible Roman word for Seventhday), to watch televised sporting events all day in violation of God's one-six pattern for the workweek. But a few members are called to occupations that require Sunday work at least occasionally. And, by the grace of God, most pastors say nothing if the practice does not get out of hand.

Rescheduling Passover

We find a parallel in the case of the Israelite who was not able to celebrate the Passover in the specified month, the first month of the year.

Speak unto the children of Israel, saying, If any man of you or of your posterity shall be unclean by reason of a dead body, or be in a journey afar off, yet he shall keep the passover unto the LORD. The fourteenth day of the second month at even[ing] they shall keep it, and eat it with unleavened bread and bitter herbs (Num. 9:10-11).

Why would any man be on a journey? What would a Hebrew be doing outside the nation? He might be on some sort of a foreign policy mission, serving as an ambassador of the king. He might have been an evangelist. More likely, he would have been a merchant. His occupation kept him away from Jerusalem in this important month. For those who had a legitimate excuse, the Passover could be celebrated in the second month of the year. Not many people would have had a legitimate excuse. This was no license for missing the Passover feast. "But the man that is clean, and is not in a journey, and forbeareth to keep the passover, even the same soul shall be cut off from among his people: because he brought not the offering of the LORD in the appointed season, that man shall bear his sin" (Num. 9:13). The penalty was excommunication from the congregation. The first-month Passover was normally binding, but those on journeys were exempted.

The law of God provided a means of satisfying the requirement of the Passover in certain instances when, through no fault of the individual, it was impossible or unlawful for him to enter into the celebration. The Old Testament law was not perfectionist in nature. It acknowledged the problems men face in complying with its terms. The law was neither perfectionist nor antinomian. Within the framework of the law, there is no temptation facing man which is insurmountable; God offers a way of escape (I Cor. 10:13).

The normal requirement was that each family should celebrate the Passover on the fourteenth day of the first month of the year. There was an *institutional arrangement* which enabled each man to fulfill the terms of the covenantal celebration. This should convince us that the celebration of the New Testament version of the Passover, namely, the weekly communion feast, normally takes place on the day of rest, but this should not be absolute in every instance.

Worldwide Trade: Passover vs. Dominion?

The question then arises: What if the Hebrew were on a distant journey? What if he couldn't return to Jerusalem even for the second Passover? If the journey were limited to the Middle East, there could be time available to return. But what if the Hebrew were visiting North America on a trading mission? They did journey this far in the days of Solomon, although conventional historians refuse to face the evidence.[46] A remarkable piece of evidence for just such a journey is the Los Lunas stone near Los Lunas,[47] New Mexico. The alphabet used was a North Canaanite script which was in use as early as 1200 B.C., and would have been no later than 800 B.C.[48] Here is what the inscription says:

I am Yahweh your God that brought you out of the lands of Egypt.

You shall not have any other gods beside me.

You shall not make for yourself any graven image.

You shall not take the name of Yahweh in vain.

Remember the day of the Sabbath, to keep it holy.

Honor your father and your mother, so that your days may be long on the land which Yahweh your God is giving to you.

---

46. Barry Fell, *Bronze Age America* (Boston: Little, Brown, 1982).

47. This is the correct name, despite the normal Spanish usage of the article "los" as masculine and "as" suffixes as feminine.

48. This estimation was made by someone who was not familiar with, or who chose to ignore, Velikovsky's reconstructed chronology. But it needs to be understood that after 750 B.C., Velikovsky's dating corresponds closely with the conventional dating of the ancient world. Thus, the late conventional date of 800 B.C. would be placed by Velikovsky's dating in roughly the same era. In short, the inscription was made no later than the era of the prophet Isaiah.

You shall not murder.

You shall not commit adultery.

You shall not steal.

You shall not testify against your neighbor as a false witness.

You shall not covet your neighbor's wife, nor anything of your neighbor's.[49]

Here we have evidence of a worldwide trading system. Barry Fell's revolutionary books demonstrate how early this trading system existed, especially his book, *Bronze Age America* (1982). There is no doubt that the Hebrews were involved in this trade. What could a distant Hebrew trader have done about Passover? The Bible does not say, but it seems clear that he would occasionally have missed a Passover celebration. There is no specific release provided in the law, but to have required Passover for every Hebrew, regardless of circumstances, would have restricted the spread of Hebrew culture and trade. The ten commandments would have been far less likely to have wound up on a rock in New Mexico. Thus, we have to speculate about the rule of God's law as applied by the priests. Was the "dominion mandate" or dominion covenant to be sacrificed on the altar of formal adherence to ritual requirements? Was the celebration of the Passover more important than the subduing of the earth? Should we not conclude that the laws associated with Passover were flexibly applied in cases where Hebrews had legitimate, world-subduing reasons to be absent from the festival?

The same problem faces modern keepers of the sabbath or Lord's day. What should the pastor do in cases where a church member must work on the traditional day of rest to keep his job, because of the nature of that job? Wouldn't the best approach be to go to the member and see whether he is taking another day for his rest? After all, the early church took Seventhday off in Israel, since it was the law of the land. Would it not be proper for the member to do the same? The priests of the Mosaic era must have taken other days off, family by family. Should we not regard modern laborers as priests? "But ye are a chosen generation, a royal priesthood, an holy nation, a

---

49. Jay Stonebreaker, "A Decipherment of the Los Lunas Decalogue Inscription," *The Epigraphic Society Occasional Publications*, Vol. 10, Pt. 1 (1982), pp. 80-81. Several of the papers in this issue deal with Los Lunas. Address: 6625 Bamburgh Dr., San Diego, CA 92117. For a photograph of the stone, see Barry Fell, *Saga America* (New York: Times Books, 1980), p. 167.

peculiar people . . ." (I Pet. 2:9a). No doubt, most priests rested on the national sabbath day in Israel. No doubt, most Christians rest on the Lord's day. Would it not be proper to acknowledge the legitimate exceptions — profanations of the Lord's day that are blameless?

Rural Life Forever?

We have to ask ourselves this fundamental question: *Did God establish the self-sufficient rural society as His perpetual societal standard?* Is this standard still morally binding on Christian cultures? The Mosaic sabbath was specifically created as a means of preserving an economy that adhered to a six-one rhythm of the workweek. Even the most seemingly trivial violation of the pattern, namely, stick-gathering, was to be punished by death. It is difficult for us to imagine the smooth operation of a modern industrial economy within the stated framework of Numbers 15. But the law was not perfectionist. It did allow exceptions with respect to Passover. It is likely that similar exemptions existed for other celebrations for Hebrews with unique occupations. But there is no list of exceptional occupations in the Old Testament which proves that such exceptions did exist, other than for the priesthood itself. It should be clear that anyone appealing to the elders for an exemption would have had to prove his case, namely, that his occupation unquestionably required seven-day operations.

It is true that automation is steadily reducing the number of people who must be employed on any given day, but engineers and emergency servicemen must be there to keep the equipment running. The moral issue of using services that require only a few men to violate the Lord's day, simply because there has been a change in technology, is still a question of right and wrong. In any case, could such a technology ever have developed, had Sunday workers been prohibited from the very beginning in the light and power industry?

What the strict sabbatarian is calling for is a drastically reduced material standard of living one day per week, an alteration of modern life styles so radical that its consequences for the economy can barely be contemplated. The Puritan-Scottish interpretation of the Mosaic standard is undeniably rigorous: no cooked meals, no restaurants, no television, no radio, no newspapers delivered on Sunday or Monday morning (Sunday production),[50] no hot water

---

50. In Athens, Georgia, a university town, the Sunday newspaper in the 1950's was delivered on Saturday night, and there was no Monday morning newspaper, James Jordan informs me.

for showers or shaving (unless produced by wood heat, solar power, or bottled gas), no commercial recreation centers, no air conditioning (unless powered by home diesel electrical generators or solar cells), no gasoline stations open (except one or two stations on a rotating basis, and only for servicing emergency vehicles or aiding legitimate travellers in an emergency — state-certified legitimate travellers), no supermarkets open for business, and endless forms to fill out in any commercial operation in order to justify the emergency nature of the sale, with fines and warnings for buyers and sellers for first violations, and death for repeated violations.

It should be understood that these conclusions are *minimal* ones; a strict sabbatarian civilization, if it is to remain true to its professed faith, would have to impose these restrictions, and it might very well find other wide-ranging applications of the sabbath principle. That contemporary sabbatarians, or even most of the sabbatarians since 1825, have refused to discuss the comprehensive specific proposals that follow from their position, has led to confusion on the part of church members. That anything so minimal as not going to a restaurant on Sunday has become the "litmus test" of strict sabbatarianism indicates just how misleading modern sabbatarianism has become. Closing all restaurants on Sunday would be the mere beginning, not the end, of civil legislation in a sabbatarian commonwealth.

A Proposal for Lord's Day Reform

What I am proposing is a consideration of the possibility that the Old Testament did make provisions for *an alternate sabbath observance schedule for people whose professions, by their very economic nature, require seven-day operations.* If so, then the New Testament Lord's day should also make provision for an alternate day of rest-worship for certain individuals. When some employees must work on the day of normal worship, the church could make another day of the week available for rest and worship. In our era, it would probably be Saturday, when the whole family is at home. If several churches with similar theological views made a single service available for their Lord's day workers, the fact that few members per congregation are in need of the alternative day would not be a pressing institutional problem. A few members from several congregations could meet to partake of the Lord's supper in the evening. In short, *the churches should make institutional provisions for those who are required from time to time to work on the day of rest.*

Certain professionals, such as policemen and firemen, are already granted a kind of unofficial "Lord's day-desecration voucher." They are not brought before the elders for working on Sundays. They are also paid by the civil government for their Lord's day-desecration activities. But this is an unofficial exemption. Sabbatarian churches (as far as I have been able to determine) make no official institutional alterations for these members to celebrate communion. These members are simply ignored. Elders "shrug off" the whole problem. Why not face the problem, and rethink the whole question of legitimate employment on the Lord's day, and legitimate communion meals on other days of the week?

Admittedly, corporations and small firms should see to it that no one employee is stuck permanently with Sunday (Firstday) assignments. This assignment should be rotated, so as not to disrupt men's worship on a permanent basis. But labor on the Lord's day is not automatically to be regarded as Lord's day desecration.

Priestly Exemptions

There is always the standard solution to the general problem posed by the steel industry example: the "works of necessity" argument. Perhaps this really is the right approach. The sabbatarian argues that steel is vital to the economy. Such an argument certainly seems reasonable. Then, since there appears to be no way to produce steel on any basis except seven days per week, the steel industry should receive a special dispensation from the church and the State which allows it to go on producing. While the Lord's day is profaned, the profaners are held guiltless. The owners (share-holding investors), managers, and laborers are treated as Christ said that God treated the priests in the temple. They are held innocent. Those associated with steel production have become "honorary priests." They are laboring in a vital industry, so this constitutes an assignment from God, comparable to God's assignment to his priests in Moses' day. They become exempt from the Lord's day prohibitions.

The church or State which takes this position has decided to become involved in endless appeals from industries that want to be reclassified as "priestly" in nature: vital to the economy *and* also innately seven-day operations because of the nature of the markets they face. What predictable, legal criteria would the State use to determine such questions? What constitutes a vital industry? Which industries, now just starting out, will (and should) be *allowed* by the civil magistrates to *become* vital? Which industries used to be vital, but are no longer vital? Public utilities? (What about cable television service?) The healing professions? (What about cosmetic plastic surgery?) Should they be allowed to charge a fee for "emergency service"? What is an emergency service?

Having somehow solved the problem of providing legal definitions of vital services and products, the State's authorities would then have to decide what market pressures really face these industries. Are they really required to operate seven days a week? They may say that they are, but are they? What criteria should be used by civil magistrates to determine the true state of affairs? Which factors determine the economics of any particular profession or industry and its market? Foreign competitors (including competitors across the county line, or state line)? Consumers' buying habits (including consumers across the county line or state line)?

The One-World State

Perhaps most important, how can we grant such a decision-making authority to the civil government without seeing the creation of a vast, arbitrary, powerful bureaucracy? These questions concerning "works of necessity and mercy" and "true state of market competition" are enormously complex. They cannot even be decided on a local basis, given the worldwide division of labor. They cannot even be decided nationally. They have to be decided by a one-world State — a State that has the power to enforce its decisions.

The Mosaic sabbath was to be enforced in Israel, whatever its exemptions for specific occupations, despite tribal practices or preferences. With the breaking of the old wineskins of Israel's economy (taken in the broader sense of "economy"), the church that would impose the Mosaic sabbath laws now faces an enormously more difficult and complex task. How can it define the problem areas? How can it enforce its decisions internationally? And if solutions can be found to these questions, there is always the critical one remaining: How can a one-world State enforce the Mosaic sabbath without becoming top-heavy, imperial in nature, and a threat to the very idea of decentralized Christian institutions? How can the Mosaic sabbath be enforced in international markets without destroying the legal basis of freedom, namely, predictable law enforced by an impartial civil government?

Will sabbatarians now argue that nations have to come to an

agreement on the nature of the semi-priestly offices (e.g., steel workers, physicians, public utility workers) and the nature of the markets facing them? But what if one or more nations will not agree? If there is no enforcement mechanism internationally, will sabbatarians then argue that each nation must decide for itself, in terms of a hypothetical "national conscience"? And once they admit this exception, what is to prevent further extensions of this "conscience" exemption: to the states or provinces, to the counties, to the cities? What about to the churches? And finally, we find ourselves right back where the Apostle Paul began in Romans 14:5, namely, with the conscience of the individual Christian.

If sabbatarians refuse to allow conscience to decide, then the exegetical war will be carried right back up the chain of appeal: to denominational authorities, to the cities, counties, states or provinces, nations, and finally to the one-world State. Each level of government attempts to impose its view of the Lord's day on those below it. But the Mosaic law does not tell men what to *do* on the sabbath, and the New Testament does not tell men *how* to rest. Will we need a world State to enforce laws against idle talk (Isa. 58:13)? What will constitute, or should constitute, lawful recreation? Is walking through a garden lawful? How about running through a garden? How about running after a ball in a meadow in front of paying spectators? On worldwide television? And if some nation's rulers decide that playing football (soccer) on worldwide television is immoral, then watching it is equally immoral. Will they set up jamming stations to keep out the satellite broadcasts? (Operating State-owned or State-licensed jamming stations will unquestionably be classified as a sabbatical work of necessity.)

Leisure

We do not know for certain how Adam and Eve spent their first sabbath, although it seems likely that they ate of the forbidden fruit on this day. We do not know how they spent their second sabbath, though it probably was outside the garden. We do not know how the sabbath operated from Adam and Eve until the Hebrews experienced the manna that would not come on the seventh day. We do not know how the Hebrews spent their sabbaths. We know a little about what they were not to do, but nothing for certain about what they did.

We know what the early Christians did on the Lord's day: they worked for a living. At the end of the day, they went to a meeting and ate the Lord's Supper.

We have sufficient revelation to know that the *normal* pattern of the week is to rest one day and work for six. Must we always work six days? The Mosaic law said yes, in general, but it also established other feast days and days off. There are problems of applying God's word to specific cases.

These were precisely the problems faced by new Christians in Romans 14:5. They are our problems, too. Which days off are legitimate? Which day should men take off during the week? None? One (Sunday or Saturday)? Two (Saturday and Sunday)? Three (Saturday, Sunday, and Monday, given the trade unions' pressure to create three-day holidays whenever an American national holiday rolls around)? What is the answer? What is the incontrovertible, conscience-binding answer that all Christians must respect, since it is so clear exegetically and historically? Which is the morally and legally binding day for rest?

The answer is not so easy to produce. Sunday (the Roman name for Firstday) is the common day of worship and therefore *preferable*, although the early church could not always adhere to it as the day of rest. But some members will have to work on Sunday, at least part of the day. In practice, the churches tend to acknowledge this economic reality, so long as the individual shows up one Sunday out of three or four. Why make exceptions at all? Why not get every member to quit his job if it requires Sunday labor? Because the church officials are more realistic when they count the tithes than when they write their sabbatarian tracts. They do not want trouble. They acknowledge in practice what their tracts deny: men do have legitimate callings that appear to be seven-day operations by economic necessity. Cows need milking, and churches need their tithes.

This raises the question of legitimate leisure. What should men do for leisure? Also — a question virtually never discussed by sabbatarians — what kinds of leisure are legitimate on the other six days of the week? God's law gives no indication that the six days of labor in a normal week were to involve leisure activities. With the exception of national (nonweekly) sabbaths, and the various feast periods (Deut. 14:23-29), men were told to work six days a week. Yet it is obvious that people cannot long sustain a life of zero leisure six days a week — not if they are to maintain their productivity. They sleep, they eat, and they chat. They teach their children (Deut. 6:7). Presumably, families enjoy some hours of leisure during the day. But the Bible says nothing about such leisure, or when it is legitimate to enjoy it during the week or during the day. It leaves this decision to the individual conscience, within the framework of family schedules and occupational requirements. If idle talk — "speaking thine own words" (Isa. 58:13) — is prohibited on the Lord's day, then is it legitimate on the other six days? If doing "thy pleasure" is prohibited on the Lord's day, then is it legitimate on other days? Or are these things prohibited generally, but *especially* on the Lord's day?

Should we cancel all Sunday-delivered and Monday morning newspapers? Sunday papers are read on Sunday. If delivered before sunrise, perhaps they could be set aside for reading on Monday, but Monday morning papers are produced on Sunday. Should Christians subscribe only to afternoon papers to avoid this problem?

Bishop J. C. Ryle had answers, or at least strong opinions, in regard to lawful and unlawful leisure on the Lord's day. "When I speak of *private Sabbath desecration*, I mean that reckless, thoughtless, secular way of spending Sunday, which every one who looks around him must know is common. How many make the Lord's Day a day for giving dinner parties — a day for looking over their accounts and making up their books — a day for reading newspapers or novels — a day for talking politics and idle gossip — a day, in short, for anything rather than the things of God. . . . When I speak of *public desecration of the Sabbath*, I mean these many open, unblushing practices, which meet the eye on Sundays in the neighbourhood of large towns. I refer to the practice of keeping shops open, and buying and selling on Sundays. I refer especially to Sunday trains, Sunday steamboats, and excursions to sea and country, and the opening of places of public amusement; and to the daring efforts which many are making in the present day, to desecrate the Lord's Day, regardless of its Divine authority."[51] (Sabbatarians have always had problems with large towns.)

This is quite a list of desecrations. But let us add some more. What about watching television on the Lord's day? Not allowed? Then what if we could make videotape recordings on the Lord's day with our electronically controlled videotape tape machines (with automatic timers)? Not even then, by the consistent logic of sabbatarianism, for men and women must labor at power-generating sta-

---

51. John Charles Ryle, *Lord's Day or the Christian Sabbath* (London: Lord's Day Observance Society, n. d.), pp. 17-18. He wrote in the late nineteenth century.

tions and television stations in order to deliver the programs to our lifeless videotape machines.

What about listening to music? With a church choir, it is obviously legitimate. What about classical music? At the park? Aren't the performers working? What if they are offering their services voluntarily? What if they are amateurs? Possibly legitimate. What if they are professionals who are paid on other days of the week to practice, but who then play on Sunday? Who pays them? The city? This is socialism. A private corporation? This is business (advertising). A charitable organization? Possibly valid.

What about listening to a radio broadcast of classical music? Not if you use public power or public airwaves. Then again, is classical music really valid? Should we regard it as Christian? Would we allow listening to folk music as a Lord's day activity? After all, is folk music or popular music any less secular than Wagner or Beethoven? Choirs sing words, and words are a form of preaching. Choir music is therefore valid on Sunday — music performed "in his sanctuary" (Ps. 150:1); all other music, delivered anywhere but in church, is either suspect or outright illegal, given the Mosaic law.

How do we settle these issues by means of legislation? How do we create an enforcing bureaucracy to police such activities without jeopardizing freedom? How can sabbatarian expositors go on writing tracts without providing plausible biblical answers to these practical, inevitable legal questions? How, in short, can we legitimately remove these questions from the area of human conscience and transfer their enforcing to an agency of institutional government, other than the family, where the father's conscience *may possibly* be given legitimate authority over other people? If men must struggle intellectually and morally to discover concrete answers to Lord's day questions for their own lives, businesses, and families, then how can we expect the institutional church or the civil government to come to recognizably valid, freedom-protecting conclusions? In short, *how will we design institutional restraints on the bureaucrats?*

Additional Questions

There are other questions that need practical answers. A corporation or business may permit people employed by it to take a day off each week, yet the firm remains open seven days a week. The example of a restaurant is useful here. The restaurant may remain open on Sunday, helping to make a day of rest available to housewives.

Some of the employees must work on Sunday, but their labor makes it easier for families to enjoy a meal together without putting burdens on the wives. Most of the employees are given another day off. They take a day of rest on a day other than Sunday, just as members of the early church did.

Is a Business a Person?

Here are some fundamental questions. If the firm splits working schedules for Sunday laborers, allowing them to attend morning or evening worship services, has it profaned the Lord's day blamefully or blamelessly? If workers take another day off, has the firm forced its employees to violate the Lord's day? If so, then everyone who spends money in that restaurant on Sunday is as guilty as the proprietor and the employees. Second, is the firm to be treated as a person? Must a firm remain closed one day each week, even when employees are given alternate days of rest?

The problem exists, especially in an urban, industrial society, because of the high division of labor and high specialization of production. Companies serve the needs of large numbers of people. The rhythm of rural, subsistence farming can be more easily geared to a six-day workweek than the rhythm of an industrial society. *The workweek's rhythm in an industrial society is necessarily flatter*, since its members are far more dependent upon the availability, moment by moment, of services of other citizens than is the case in a low division of labor rural society. Urban dwellers do not produce many goods for their own personal use; they produce specialized services or goods for sale. If we can legitimately buy natural gas or electricity from a public utility in order to cook our Sunday meal, then why is it illegitimate to buy a meal at a restaurant? Either both acts are blameful violations of the Lord's day, or neither, assuming that the selling firm does not require seven days of consecutive labor from individual employees.

Cooking on the Lord's Day

The Mosaic sabbath in the wilderness seems to have required the baking of manna on the sixth day; they ate cold cakes on the sabbath. Will strict sabbatarians call for the death penalty of anyone cooking on the Lord's day? If not, why not?

The issue of cooking on the Lord's day is a difficult one. The Hebrew women probably cooked their manna cakes on the sixth day during the period they spent in the wilderness. We are not told specifically in the Mosaic law that cooking was permanently abolished on the seventh day. At the same time, the experience in the wilderness was to have given them indications concerning the cooking schedule preferred by God, and that schedule involved storing up cooked food the day before the sabbath, just as it involved storing up extra firewood.

When we come to the New Testament, we face a more difficult problem. The Lord's day should be timed from dawn to dawn. The communion meal in the first-century church was an evening meal. Must we conclude that this communion meal, the central weekly event in the life of the corporate church, prohibited the eating of freshly cooked food? Does the Sunday evening meal have to be cooked on Saturday night or even earlier on Saturday? Would we not expect the wives in the early church to have prepared their best meal of the week for this night? On the other hand, is the Lord's day to become a day of cooking competition? In modern churches, the existence of Sunday evening church suppers stands as a testimony to sabbatarian confusion.

Meals, whether cooked or leftovers, leave messes behind. What are wives to do, leave the crumbs lying on the table for the benefit of rodents and insects? But if they clean up the table and kitchen in their households, haven't they violated the Lord's day? If so, is this a case of Lord's day desecration comparable to the desecration of the priests, that is, blameless? May they use hot water to wash dishes? Can they legitimately (blamelessly) draw such hot water out of the tap? If so, someone is on duty at the local public utility company, serving the needs of the Lord's day-desecrating wives. It takes power to heat water. It also takes a water company to deliver water that is to be heated.

The modern church has given no systematic thought to these issues. The Protestant churches have their Sunday evening covered dish suppers, and no one goes away feeling guilty about having cooked on the Lord's day or having eaten cooked food on the Lord's day. But the ethical question still remains: Is cooking on the Lord's day a sin?

Evading the Problems

These are relevant issues. The fact that they are not discussed seriously by modern defenders of the Puritan-Scottish sabbath is an indication of the political impotence of those who defend it. They write their booklets, preach their sermons, and occasionally force a nonsabbatarian pastor or elder out of the denomination, but they do not address their tracts to those who make decisions, or who might possibly make decisions in the future, in the world of business and government. Their tracts and booklets fail to speak to these issues. They are written as if we were still in the deserts of Palestine, as if paper and ink were not produced for international markets, as if the steel in printing presses could be produced in a six-day workweek. These men are rather like the ecologists of the late 1960's who decried pollution and then climbed into their automobiles to be driven to airports, where they flew on mass-polluting jet planes in order to give their emotion-laden speeches — at a profit, of course.

The writers of sabbatarian tracts would better spend their time in dealing with the real questions, *the questions of conscience*. What are the guidelines that pastors should use in counselling guilt-ridden congregation members who realize that they have ignored the one-six pattern of covenant man's week? How should pastors and elders teach the Lord's day, in order not to pressure excessively those who have not fully understood the implications in their own lives of the Lord's day, but who still need instruction? *How can leaders deal with ignorance without violating consciences?* This is the focus of Romans 14:5. Here is where we need tracts, books, and seminars.

Sabbatarian Debates in England

After this appendix was typeset, I went on vacation. In a Church of England book store in London, I discovered a copy of John Wigley's *The Rise and Fall of the Victorian Sunday,* published by Manchester University Press in 1980. This book is a scholarly survey of the debate over sabbatarianism from Puritan days until this century, but with its focus on the nineteenth century. I decided to add a summary of this little-known history to this appendix.

What I learned from the book is that many of the issues that I had raised in this appendix had been discussed at length throughout the period, 1550-1900, and in many cases, the debates had been taken to Parliament for reconciliation. Parliament never seemed to be able to reconcile them. Thus, the seemingly hypothetical arguments found in my theoretical discussion of various sabbath issues were far from hypothetical in English history.

Wigley's book presents evidence that the most decisive changes in English attitudes and manners took place between 1780 and 1830, the period of the early industrial revolution. Wigley cites several authorities, including Charles Dickens, to this effect (p. 1). Each social group had different values and manners, and all were subject to changes in the nineteenth century (p. 2). He argues that English sabbatarianism was the primary influence on the Victorian sabbath, and that it was an integral aspect of English life and history.

The sabbath debates began long before 1780. Sunday amusements were prohibited by law by the Sunday Observance Act of 1677, which was passed not in the Cromwell era but over a decade and a half into the Restoration era of Charles II. A century later, in 1780, Anglican evangelicals were able to pressure Parliament to pass an Act which made it illegal on Sunday to charge admission to places of entertainment (p. 3). They wrote in a loophole for themselves, however, which was to be taken advantage of by their opponents a century later: religious organizations were allowed to charge a fee.

Elizabethan and Puritan England

In the mid-sixteenth century, the Church of England had no clear-cut teaching with respect to the sabbath. In 1569, Queen Elizabeth authorized certain sports on Sunday: archery, leaping, running, wrestling, and oddest of all, hammer throwing. In 1574, she authorized other sports, but forbade them during church services. Bear-baiting and bull-baiting were prohibited (p. 14). A 1580 law against Sunday plays in London pushed plays into Southwark (p. 15), an early indication of the problem faced by all strictly local sabbatarian legislation: geographical escape. Then, in 1595, Nicholas Bownde published his strongly sabbatarian book, *The True Doctrine of the Sabbath*: no saints days during the week, and no recreations on Sunday. Controversy increased from that time until the Puritan Revolution of the 1640's.

In 1618, James I issued his *Book of Sports*, in which he reaffirmed the legality of Elizabethan Sunday sports. His recommended Sunday was recreation-oriented. The English Calvinists, following Bownde rather than Calvin, were outraged. Many non-Calvinists in the Church of England shared their views. Restrictions on Sunday travel were passed in 1625 and 1627 (p. 19). The debate accelerated after 1633, when Arminian Archbishop Laud promulgated Charles I's rewrite of his father's *Book of Sports*, and required it to be read in the churches. Essentially, the debate was between the "marathon sabbath" Puritans and the "recreation sabbath" traditionalists.

During the Puritan era, 1642-1660, the Parliament abolished all remaining saints' days and holy days, along with Christmas and Easter, and substituted the second Tuesday every month as a holiday for apprentices. Why there was a legitimate exception to "six days shalt thou labor" was not explained. This was the Act of 1647.

The problem of technology arose in this era. What about occupations that seem to be seven-day operations? "In 1657 two Acts forbade between them milling, cloth-making, tallow-melting, baking, brewing, soap-boiling and distilling—trades in which natural contingencies, market pressures and technical considerations made it difficult to avoid Sunday work" (p. 23). But as the author says, Parliament met on Sundays during emergencies. Furthermore, Cromwell was no sabbatarian.

The debates continued. The rival opinions concerning the proper administration of the sabbath proved to be irreconcilable. Many of the same disagreements persist today. "Even before the Civil War disputes about the commandment's meaning had raised disconcerting issues of principle. If the Fourth Commandment no longer applied in its full and original force, did the other nine? If it applied to all men, was a servant right to disobey his master's order to work on the Sabbath? Who should judge in such cases? Now extremists claimed that the Sabbath should be kept from sunset on Friday till sunset on Saturday, mystics believed that Sabbath-keeping destroyed true spiritual religion, the Quakers taught that there should be no distinction of days and the Diggers began to cultivate St George's Hill on a Sunday. No less a person than Milton thought that the only true guide and authority in such matters was the individual's conscience" (p. 24). The question arises: How can society find rest from these interminable disagreements? How can church and State be governed by God and be blessed by God if God-fearing people have discovered no way, at least so far, to come to an agreement about these issues?

The Traditional Sabbath

The Puritan era and its legislation lapsed in 1660, when Charles II came to the throne, but sabbatarian pressures continued. The Sunday Observance Act of 1677 was the king's attempt to forestall a more rigorous bill being considered by the House of Commons. It prohibited all Sunday labor except for emergencies and charity, and prohibited all retail trade, except for the general sale of milk and meat for inns and other restaurants. It severely restricted Sunday travel (p. 25). Opposition began almost immediately, for sabbatarian ideas were beginning to lose their popularity. The Act was more closely enforced in rural areas; in the cities, retail sales were overlooked where custom allowed, except during worship services.

What about honoring the sabbath in the home? Would it be a feast day or a fast day? Different groups took differing positions. Some upper class members ate uncooked meals, banished secular reading, newspapers, horseback riding, needlework, and painting on Sunday. Others used the day for huge feasts, toured the kennels and gardens, and ate a light supper, thereby allowing servants to attend the evening meeting (p. 83). For most Englishmen, it became traditional to have the best meal of the week on Sunday. The middle classes followed this tradition, but generally avoided recreation. There the matter rested — with regional tradition as the primary guide — for a hundred years.

In the 1780's, sabbatarianism had a revival (p. 26). In the 1790's, sabbatarianism was set in contrast to the anti-sabbath 10-day week of the French Revolution. Loyalty to Britain and sabbatarianism became linked (p. 27). William Wilberforce, who was later to take up the cause of abolitionism, in the late 1780's became a moderate sabbatarian. Parliament reacted negatively to these views in the 1790's, loosening some of the old requirements of the 1677 law, legalizing bakers' work from 9 A.M. to 1 P.M. Sundays, when they could sell puddings and meat pies (the poor man's Sunday dinner). In a very real sense, the home sabbath made itself felt in the marketplace; the law was revised in order to favor an easier celebration of the home feast. Parliament rejected several attempts over the next 30 years to outlaw Sunday newspapers (p. 27).

In the 1820's, the sabbatarians emerged as a determined group with a strong sense of mission (p. 30). Rev. Daniel Wilson preached a series of sabbatarian sermons in 1827. In 1831, he helped found the Lord's Day Observance Society (LDOS), which still exists. (It published F. N. Lee's dissertation, *The Covenantal Sabbath*, in 1972.) In the 1830's, Sir Andrew Agnew, a one-issue member of Parliament, introduced a sabbatarian bill four times, and it was defeated each time. It is interesting that the bill exempted the labor of servants in households. The fourth commandment, he argued, gave masters complete religious and civil authority over their servants (p. 38). Wigley comments: "The Sabbatarians' distinction between 'private' and 'public' behaviour enabled them to avoid a fundamental challenge to the rights of property. They defended the right of the private property owner to use his servants, his horses and his grounds without any interference; but claimed the right to regulate that which was corporately or nationally owned, such as railways and the Post Office" (p. 46). This represents a continuing compromise, or at least confusion, among sabbatarians. Is the civil government the enforcer inside the family? If not, then the sabbath principle is not primary but secondary to the rights of private property, at least in this one area. But if the State can impose no sanctions here, why is it allowed to in "public" property, meaning private property outside the household?

By the 1840's, the 1677 law was close to a dead letter. Fines were small, the authorities preferred not to enforce it, and prosecutions brought by individual citizens did not often lead to convictions (p. 53).

Urban, Industrial Society

The 1830's and 1840's were years of rapid development of railroads. The sabbatarians organized politically to keep trains from running on Sundays. Some rail companies tried to honor their wishes. The Liverpool & Manchester restricted Sunday operations and actually inaugurated a scheme whereby sabbatarian shareholders could donate to charity that portion of corporate profits that were generated by Sunday traffic. The North Eastern adopted a similar practice. Most companies restricted traffic during worship hours. Demand was small, so this was reasonable. All refused total closure, however (p. 54). This did not satisfy the sabbatarians.

The Post Office Act of 1838 enabled the Postmaster General to compel trains to operate a Sunday mail train, and firms added passenger cars in order to gain some revenues. In 1846, the final attempt to prohibit Sunday rail traffic was introduced into Parliament. It failed (p. 57).

The Post Office in 1847 announced its intention to send mail through London on Sundays. The Lord's Day Observance Society began a campaign to reverse this decision, and also to cease Sunday collecting and delivering of the mail. Eventually, Sunday mail delivery ceased, as a result of trade union pressures, long after the sabbatarians had ceased to be a political factor, but the movement of the mail went on. Some Post Office employees, then as now, had to work on Sundays.

Other sabbatarian societies were formed in this period: the Evangelical Alliance and the Wesleyan Methodists. John Henderson, a Glasgow merchant, began a national essay contest on the benefits of sabbath observance. Other groups followed his lead, and a tradition of annual prizes was begun. Wigley says that these contests and the publication of the essays transformed the controversy. What had been primarily a debate over religion became a debate over practical benefits of the sabbath. The essays did not ask for legislative action; they advocated total abstention from Sunday amusements (p. 65). These essays were generally non-theological in nature; they were practical. Understandably, the LDOS took no part in promoting them.

In 1851, the Great Exhibition opened. This monumental exhibition of the wonders of mid-century technology transformed the thinking of a generation. In 1852, a private company took it over as a business venture, and the firm announced its intention to open it on Sunday afternoons. This created a huge wave of protest. Tracts aimed at every sector of society poured off the presses, with different arguments for each class. The government inserted into the firm's charter the language of the 1780 Act, that no money payment could be collected. This was a victory for the sabbatarians.

There was a loophole in the 1780 Act which was exploited in the late 1860's. The Act exempted religious organizations from restrictions on taking in money. One anti-sabbatarian, Baxter Langley, organized his followers into a "free unsectarian church," registered it under the Toleration Act of 1688, and began selling reserved seats to Sunday evening lectures. The government could not prosecute the group successfully (p. 125).

In 1855, working men protested a Sunday trading bill which would have permitted open shops. A crowd of 150,000 turned out on Sunday, June 24, to protest the support that Chartist radicals were giving to the bill. The shops remained closed.

The next crisis was provoked by a radical M.P., Sir Joshua Walmsley, who in 1855 and 1856 introduced legislation to allow the British Museum to open on Sundays. It was supposed to be an alternative to Sunday drinking. Sabbatarians were outraged. The bills did not pass. Then Sir Benjamin Hall, Commissioner of Works, began promoting military band concerts in the parks. The sabbatarians were again outraged. This was national desecration. Prime Minister Palmerston later stopped the concerts (p. 70). So the theoretical question I have raised concerning music in the park is not hypothetical; it became a serious political issue.

The Middle Classes

Wigley argues that the appeal of sabbatarian ideals to middle class people gave it great strength. A new appeal, based on practical benefits rather than an appeal to the Bible, became increasingly prominent within sabbatarian circles. He calls this *social sabbatarianism*. "Social Sabbatarianism was of enormous importance. It moulded and enlivened the controversy for almost fifty years. It allowed the Sabbatarians to avoid authoritarianism and to champion the working classes. It allowed Nonconformists to assuage their consciences and to defend the civil observance of the Sabbath. It allowed M.P.'s to reconcile their *laissez-faire* principles with their religious values, for no legislation was called for, merely the defense of the *status quo*" (p. 72). But it was a departure from the earlier sabbatarianism, and on many occasions, defenders of a religious sabbath refused to join with social sabbatarians in "the great cause." As the pragmatic arguments weakened, especially as the century wore on and more leisure time was made available to workers, the religious sabbatarians recognized the epistemological weakness of social sabbatarianism. "Six days shalt thou labor" became five and a half, and in this century, five; Sunday amusements also appeared to be beneficial, so the pragmatic arguments no longer carried as much weight. But the religious sabbatarians had been pre-empted by 1900, and few people listened to them any longer.

The leisure of the high-capital late nineteenth century was not characteristic of the low-capital era of the late eighteenth. There is no doubt that the industrial revolution increased the number of working days in the late eighteenth century. For example, the Bank of England (the private central bank) steadily reduced the number of holidays from 46 in 1761 to 4 in 1836 (p. 74). The 12-hour, 6-day industrial workweek became the norm as the industrial revolution gathered strength. Sabbatarians could appeal to overwork as one reason for a legislated sabbath. But they steadfastly refused to promote a law which would prohibit masters from working servants on Sundays. The theological justification: acts of mercy and necessity (p. 78). This was an exemption for rural lords at the competitive expense of the industrial managers.

Wigley presents the interesting case of W. H. Smith, the Christian founder of the giant book store chain. Smith invoked the "acts of necessity and mercy" exemption when he decided to publish the names of the dead and wounded during the Crimean War in 1855. On the other hand, he refrained from walking outdoors on a visit to Canada, to avoid giving the impression of being a sightseer. On the other hand, he complained when his Sunday evening bath was late, blaming the assertive attitudes of Canadian hotel workers (p. 78). Convenience, predictably, triumphed over theology.

What about the Sunday operation of profit-seeking public utilities? This is not a hypothetical example. In the 1840's, some private water companies had left parts of London without water on Sundays (p. 82).

In the 1870's, numerous secular organizations formed lecture societies. Libraries began to remain open on Sundays. So did free art galleries (p. 131). The sabbatarians opposed all such violations. In 1884, Herbert Spencer, the evolutionist and defender of pure *laissez-faire*, remarked that a dispute over the opening of a reading room on Sunday could split a mechanics' institute (p. 1).

By the late 1880's, sabbatarians had generally lost public support. In 1896, the government finally voted to allow the opening of the British museums and national galleries on Sundays (p. 147). There was no opposition from the churches or the denominational newspapers. The twentieth century, especially after World War I, saw the end of most relics of the 1677 and 1780 laws.

Wigley's summary of the problem is remarkably similar to my own discussion of the economic questions raised by the sabbath in an industrial civilization, especially with respect to the differing rhythms of the workweek. "Sabbatarianism was an inappropriate way to provide rest, for it applied a simple, essentially pre-industrial, religious prescription to a complex, essentially urban, social problem. Sabbatarians avoided the difficulties which a complete cessation of labour would have produced for themselves by requiring servants to work and applying the formula 'acts of necessity and mercy,' but failed to appreciate that society at large similarly needed the work of some railwaymen, shopkeepers and the like, whose work rhythm ran counter to that of the rest of the community. Sabbatarianism thus justified some Sunday work, but regarded the unjustified as sin for condemnation, rather than as a problem suitable for social reform" (p. 79).

Self-Imposed Irrelevance

It is also revealing that the LDOS refused in 1855 to enter into the political question of the half-Saturday movement, which would have required employers to provide the afternoon off. It merely established a committee to look into the subject, and they were not required to report back. One Presbyterian minister argued that anything less than six full days of work was generosity on the part of employers which went beyond God's justice (p. 80). So the sabbatarian commitment to one day off seemed to imply no rest for the other six days. When, then, would men receive time for recreation, which was banned on Sunday? The sabbatarians have never faced this issue. Their concern as sabbatarians is not with rest, and their concern as neo-Puritans is with work.

Frederick Peake, the LDOS's secretary, made the society's position clear in a statement in 1895, one which summarized three centuries of sabbatarianism. The issue is not rest. The issue is enforced religious behavior. "Anything [on Sundays] that is not distinctly religious is wrong. . . . We should hardly make it purely a question of 'rest.' We . . . seek the religious observance of the Lord's day as the primary thing, and the question of human rest . . . as a secondary matter arising out of that" (p. 153).

The Sunday school movement had been developed in the late eighteenth century in order to provide religious education for the children of the poor. But some sabbatarians objected when Sunday schools began teaching newly literate children to write, "arguing that it was not necessary to be able to write to understand the Bible, and writing was thus a secular employment, unfit for the Lord's day" (p. 81). The controversy gathered force in the early years of the nineteenth century. The Wesleyan Methodist Conference passed such an anti-writing measure in 1808. This controversy divided sabbatarians. In the 1840's, the sabbatarians had succeeded in most independent congregations in stamping out the practice (p. 82).

The LDOS became progressively more consistent and progressively out of touch with reality. It criticized Charles Spurgeon's allowing his sermons to be telegraphed to Cincinnati on Sunday mornings. It criticized book sales in church. (At least it did not have to deal with the issue of book deliveries on Sunday with payment coming on a work day; churches were not likely to extend credit in this era.) In 1892, the *Quarterly Paper* of the LDOS said that Salvation

Army bands "have done untold harm" (p. 141). The LDOS thereby forfeited the support of Nonconformist leaders. It also opposed the use of automatic vending machines in the 1880's, despite the fact that no labor was involved (p. 153). In short, the issue was not rest; the issue was the marathon sabbath—self-denial for God, not external convenience and rest. As the Society announced in response to a 1909 attempt to pass a pro-sabbatarian law that had been drafted by the National Hygenic League, "This determination to settle the whole matter on the basis not of Divine Law but of personal convenience, with a flavouring of humanitarian sentimentality . . . a most threatening danger" (p. 165).

What the LDOS and strict sabbatarians had accomplished in over a half century of non-cooperation with other "less rigorous" brethren and allies was to demonstrate the political irrelevance of their position. They had taken the "moral high ground"—so high that they were in the heavens and of little earthly use to the cause of restful Sundays. They had adopted the marathon sabbath position of certain segments the non-industrial seventeenth-century English Puritans, and had suffered the consequences.

Conclusion

Several questions should be raised. Did the failure of the Lord's Day Observance Society come because of their political intransigence? If so, was this intransigence biblically valid? Were the leaders correct in refusing to compromise with anything that was not "pure marathon sabbath"? Was the LDOS doomed at the end because of an increasingly secular society? Or was it doomed from the beginning because the "marathon sabbath" is neither biblical nor suitable in an urban civilization?

There really were public debates over the timing of the sabbath, the locus of sovereignty of enforcement (Milton's locus: conscience), travel on Sunday, feast day vs. fast day, "seven-day-per-week" technologies, railways, public utilities, defining "mercy and necessity," servants' labor on Sundays ("mercy and necessity" . . . for the masters), mail delivery and shipping, newspapers, museums, bakeries, and the appropriateness of cooking on Sunday. There were debates, but there were no definitive answers. Eventually, people grew tired of debates that could not be resolved, and the honoring of the sabbath became a matter of conscience. Milton's suggestion became a social reality.

The summary provided by Wigley is accurate, but it indicates the extent to which sabbatarianism brought Christians little credit in English history, even though a day of rest was universally acknowledged at least in principle to be a blessing. The marathon sabbath did not survive, and it is understandable why it didn't.

In the depression-stricken countryside of the 1880's no harvest work was done on Sundays, but the migrant Irish labourers were thought to be heathens because they sang and danced after returning from Mass. Protestant English farmers' children were taught to ' "remember that thou keep holy the Sabbath day." Of course the manservant and the maid-servant had to milk the cows, that was necessary work [but]'. . . Nobody ever read a newspaper or whistled a tune except hymns . . . on Sundays.' [Allison Uttley, *The Country Child* (Penguin ed., 1970), pp. 222, 206.] No wonder the Sabbatarians quoted the Fourth Commandment as given in Exodus and ignored the version in Deuteronomy (5: 14) 'that thy man servant and thy maid servant may rest as well as thou.'

The most characteristic feature of Sabbatarianism and of the Victorian Sunday which it produced was the attempt to proscribe Sunday amusement and recreation, and over the course of the century this had had different effects on each class. By encouraging church and Sunday school attendance, and drawing a picture of domestic comfort, the Sabbatarians had given the lower classes a standard at which to aim. But by doing so they had undermined the festal Sunday tradition in accordance with which the lower classes already cleaned and dressed themselves on Sundays. They wanted a day of abstention, whereas the workers kept a holiday, a feast not a fast.

The abstemious Sunday was better suited to those who spent their week in easy circumstances than to those who labored for their bread. The Sabbatarian standard and the Victorian Sunday were essentially middle class phenomena. They produced a day which had a funeral character, notorious for its symbols—the hushed voice, the half-drawn blind and the best clothes. When adopted by the lower classes these symbols produced the respectable poor. Neville Cardus, the (Manchester) *Guardian's* cricket correspondent, remembered William Attewell, in 1912 cricket professional at Shrewsbury School: 'Each Sabbath, after our mid-day meal, he put on a hard stiff collar. I recollect his struggles with it. "Cuss it," he would protest, "but ah mun do it; it's the Lord's day." ' (p. 185)

Conclusion

Questions concerning the proper form of Lord's day observance, not to mention the proper role of the institutional church and civil government in enforcing Lord's day observance, are extremely complex. This is one reason why Paul assigned to the individual conscience the task of sorting out these problems. They are too complex, and too disputed, for the institutions of government to apply sanctions. This was not the case in rural Israel, when the sabbath was primarily negative—refraining from normal, profit-seeking labor one day per week—and the civil government's role was also negative, namely, prohibiting commercial trade and restricting most of a family's daily routine. When the Lord's day became both a day of rest and a day of corporate worship, its emphasis changed, and the State's role in protecting the Lord's day was radically altered. When the sabbath day, or the Lord's day, became a day which *emphasizes* positive worship, the State ceased being a reliable agency of enforcement.

The Lord's day is essentially a day in which the normal routine of work is broken—a ritual testimony of a man's reliance upon God's grace rather than his own labor. It is a day of inactivity one day in seven with respect to one's source of income and to one's area of daily responsibility for labor. It is an admission that man is not sovereign, that man rests on God's creative work, that man cannot bring his work to completion apart from God, that man's efforts are limited, and that autonomous man cannot, even with a seven-day workweek, expect to prosper. It is a symbolic announcement that *man must rest in the grace of God*, and that he can rest one day per week in confidence that God honors His covenant with His people. It takes faith to honor the Lord's day—faith in the terms of the covenant, and faith in the ability of God to fulfill His part of the compact.

The Lord's day of rest-worship forces men to schedule their lives more efficiently, to take time for rest. It forces them to order their workweek carefully, buying in advance, storing up goods in preparation for the Lord's day. It forces wives to get their homes cleaned before the day of rest. It forces people, in short, to establish *budgets*, rather like the budgets necessitated by the requirement of the tithe. In this case, however, what is budgeted primarily is *time*, not money. A family's week is to have a God-honoring one-six rhythm.

The break from the normal work routine was required of the priests of Israel, but other responsibilities forced the priesthood as a whole to maintain seven-day operations. What was required of individual priests was not required of the priesthood as a whole. The corporate body of priests had to offer sacrifices daily; each individual priest could reschedule his workweek to permit him to rest on another day, if it was his day to offer sacrifices on the sabbath. *God distinguishes between organizations and the individuals who make up the organizations.* A six-day workweek was required of individual priests and their families, but not the priesthood as a unit.

Modern Christians are priests. They are sometimes assigned tasks on the Lord's day that are vital to the economic survival of the firm. The decision as to whether the seven-day workweek is really crucial to the economic survival of the firm is made in terms of several criteria: the decision of the owners; the decisions of employees and potential employees whether they are violating their consciences in working on the Lord's day; and the decisions of customers who decide whether they are violating the sabbath principle in spending their money on the products or services of the Lord's day-profaning company. We are not told how the priests of the Old Testament worked out the mid-week day of rest for those who had to offer sacrifices on the sabbath. We are not told exactly how the sorting out of the Lord's day issue would be done in modern, industrial, post-resurrection societies. Some men regard all days the same. Others regard one or more days as special. Each man should be convinced in his own mind (Rom. 14:5).

What we must understand is this: the fact that Paul now assigns to the individual human conscience the task of making the decisions concerning rest, leisure, and employment on the Lord's day does not mean that all days are the same during the week. Man's conscience must make the decision for man, but this does not mean that God's revelation is not clear regarding the special nature of the Lord's day. It does not mean that the one-six pattern is invalid in New Testament times. It means only that from an *institutional* standpoint, Paul removed the civil government and the church courts from the position of decision-makers. With respect to the day of rest-worship, the external sanction of the Old Testament economy, the death penalty, has been abolished. It has been abolished along with the duty of the civil government to impose sanctions on individuals or firms that choose to work on the Lord's day.

The fact that individual conscience is assigned the task of decoding the limits of the Lord's day activities has not subjectivised the reality of the sabbath principle of rest-worship. The sabbath principle of rest-worship is still intact. But God has determined that the complexity of Lord's day observance is too great for the church or State to enforce. The requirement of honoring one day in seven is still with us, but not all people see this, and hardly any group agrees concerning the exact ways in which any profit-seeking firm or individual must honor the sabbath principle. God will be the final judge, not the earthly institutions of government. There are objective standards, but they must be interpreted subjectively, person by person, in the New Testament era. We have been given specific revelation to this effect with respect to the sabbath, and we must honor this revelation.

It solves few if any concrete sabbatarian problems to read into Leviticus 23:3 an Old Testament sabbath version of the New Testament's requirement of positive worship on the Lord's day. The testimony of the Old Testament is clear: Seventhday was generally (and possibly even exclusively) a day of *rest*, except for a few priests in the temple. It is equally futile to read into Exodus 35:3 a highly symbolic and hypothetical interpretation concerning "strange fire." Clear texts should be used to interpret obscure texts. Even more to the point, clear texts should not be turned into obscure texts. Exodus 35:2 is clear: death for working on the sabbath. Exodus 35:3 is also clear: no kindling of fires. An apologetic for a hypothetical "less rigorously enforced Old Testament sabbath" which is then said to be in continuity with a church government-enforced and State government-enforced New Testament Lord's day — an apologetic based on "strange fire" — is clear to practically nobody, which is why we find no similar line of argumentation in the historic creeds. It also fails to explain the sharp discontinuity which was announced by Paul in Romans 14:5 and Colossians 3:16.

In short, if Paul's words are not taken at face value, a whole series of problems arises. Few churches have been willing to face these problems squarely over the last two hundred years, and none has been willing so far to deal forthrightly with the question of the death penalty in Exodus 35:2. There is no way, biblically speaking, to escape the necessity of imposing the death penalty on persistent sabbath violators, unless we interpret Romans 14 as having changed the locus of enforcement from the civil government to the individual conscience. If Paul was not speaking about the Old Testament sabbath in that passage, then Exodus 31:15 and 35:2 are still morally and legally binding, and Christians must forthrightly call for the civil government to abide by God's sabbatical standards, and to begin executing sabbath breakers.

Appendix B

COVENANTAL LAW AND COVENANTAL LOVE

But when the Pharisees had heard that he had put the Sadducees to silence, they gathered together. Then one of them, which was a lawyer, asked him a question, saying, Master, which is the great commandment in the law? Jesus said unto him, Thou shalt love the Lord thy God with all thy heart, and with all thy soul, and with all thy mind. This is the first and great commandment. And the second is like unto it, Thou shalt love thy neighbour as thyself. On these two commandments hang all the law and the prophets (Matt. 22:34-40).

The New Testament is a commentary on the Old Testament, in the light of the new revelation given by Christ and the Holy Spirit. We need to understand the New Testament by referring to the Old Testament, and we need to look at the New Testament in order to understand the Old Testament. It is not that the New Testament revelation is in opposition to the old. Jesus categorically denied such a possibility (Matt. 5:17-19).[1] What the New Testament does is to specify more clearly the *general principles* that undergird Old Testament law, and to specify which of the Old Testament's laws were fulfilled by Christ's life, death, and resurrection. Christ did not annul the *principles* of the law, but in certain cases He annulled the *ritual form* in which those principles had been set forth by God to His people.

Jesus and the Pharisees

We should not expect that Jesus would announce a revision of the Old Testament law's fundamental teachings. The Pharisees clearly did not expect Him to say that the law — meaning the ten commandments — is no longer applicable. Had they expected such a

---

1. Greg L. Bahnsen, *Theonomy in Christian Ethics* (2nd ed.; Phillipsburg, New Jersey: Presbyterian & Reformed, 1984), ch. 2.

statement, they would not have asked Him which one of the laws is most important. What the lawyer probably intended to do was to drag Jesus into a detailed, "Pharisaical" argument over which of the ten was most fundamental. Then, with the skills of a legal professional, the lawyer no doubt believed that he could make Jesus' answer look incomplete. "What about this other law? And what about still another law? Haven't you undercut the very law itself, etc. etc." In short, it was one more example of the Jewish leaders unsuccessfully trying to tie Jesus up in the details of the law. It was another "leading question."

Jesus invariably responded to their leading questions in such a way as to expose the spiritual rebellion of those who asked such questions. This is why they fell silent every time He answered one of their questions. In this instance, He shifted the discussion to the ultimate aspect of all biblical religion: the *theocentric* nature of all true worship. The greatest of the commandments is that commandment which demands that we worship God with every aspect of our being. He cited Deuteronomy 6:5 to prove His point.

He could have stopped right there. He had answered the lawyer's question. This is the greatest of the commandments. To have denied Jesus' answer, or quibbled with it in any way, the lawyer would have had to say that some other law is the all-encompassing law, of which this one is simply a partial derivative. But there is no such law. All the laws of the Bible are applications and extensions of this great theocentric principle. We must begin with acknowledging our absolute responsibility to worship God with everything we have as creatures — not just our goods, but with ourselves. Could the lawyer have appealed to one of the Old Testament sacrifices as more important? Hardly; they involve giving up only goods. But the biblical principle which Jesus sets forth here, which Paul illuminated in a different context, is this: "I beseech you therefore, brethren, by the mercies of God, that ye present your bodies a living sacrifice, holy, acceptable unto God, which is your reasonable service" (Rom. 12:1).

Nevertheless, Jesus went on. He gave the second greatest commandment: to love our neighbors as ourselves. This was Jesus' way of nailing down the argument. The lawyer was now in no position to respond, "Yes, but what about the specifics of the laws that Moses gave? What about our day-to-day dealings with men?" He might not have asked this. If he wanted to appeal to the crowd, however, he might have. "What about our obligations to man? What law gets our first attention?" Jesus' response headed off all such questions. The second principle is analogous to the first. Men are made in God's image. We should therefore love our fellow man. But how much love is proper? Certainly, not the love we show to God. We owe him everything. But a good test of how much we love another creature is to estimate how much we love ourselves. Jesus assumes that each man wants to do his best for himself. Men are always "looking out for Number One." So, He said, look out for your neighbor just as you look out for yourself. You are a man; he is a man; both of you deserve the same consideration, for both of you are made in God's image.

Love and the Law

The question related to the law. The answers spoke of love. Are these two in opposition? Obviously not. Jesus always dealt faithfully with the questions of his questioners. This is why they were always struck dumb. They were incapable of replying, precisely because Jesus' answers were flawless. There was never anything more to say without either agreeing with Him or winding up in opposition to the Old Testament. Therefore, when Jesus answered the lawyer's question concerning the greatest of the laws, He was saying clearly and unmistakably that all the laws of God are a working out of the principle of love — theocentric love first of all, and neighborly love second. If these laws are applications of the principle of love, then how can they be in opposition to love?

The lawyer recognized this. He did not reply. By focusing on the loving aspect of love, Jesus removed the question from the realm of legalistic debate. You love God with everything you are and have; *therefore*, you also must love your neighbor as yourself. But how do we love our neighbors? Clearly, by treating them as faithfully as we treat ourselves. By giving them the same "benefit of the doubt" in a dispute that we give ourselves. In short, this is the so-called *golden rule*: "Therefore all things whatsoever ye would that men should do unto you, do ye even so unto them: for this is the law and the prophets" (Matt. 7:12). This is the biblical version of the more common phrase (which is not found in the Bible): "Do unto others as you would have others do unto you."

The Sermon on the Mount

Jesus' sermon on the mount is a commentary on God's "sermon" on the mount to Moses. This is what modern Christians have failed to recognize. There is a deeply rooted tradition of interpreting Jesus' words as if they stood in opposition to the law which God delivered at Mount Sinai. This tradition is wrong. It is perhaps the most dangerous heresy in twentieth-century Christianity. It flies in the face of Jesus' warning: "Think not that I am come to destroy the law, or the prophets: I am come not to destroy, but to fulfil. For verily I say unto you, Till heaven and earth pass away, one jot or one tittle shall in no wise [way] pass from the law, till all be fulfilled. Whosoever therefore shall break one of these least commandments, and shall teach men so, he shall be called the least in the kingdom of heaven: but whosoever shall do and teach them, the same shall be called great in the kingdom of heaven. For I say unto you, That except your righteousness shall exceed the righteousness of the scribes and Pharisees, ye shall in no case enter into the kingdom of heaven" (Matt. 5:17-20).

Who were the scribes? They were the Jewish lawyers. In Mark's account of the lawyer's question to Jesus, it says that he was a scribe (Mark 12:28). This scribe apparently had not heard Jesus' original statement at the "Sermon on the Mount," or if he had, he had forgotten about it. Jesus did not vary His views. Doing righteously to other men is the essence of biblical law, for we do our righteous acts unto God (Matt. 25:34-40). His first answer to the lawyer did help to clarify the theocentric foundation of the law commanding neighborly love. But the Pharisees should have understood already that it was not a particular Old Testament law which was the focus of His ministry, but the *underlying principle of all God's laws*. This, in fact, was what *distinguished Jesus' teaching from the common culture's first principles*. The common doctrine in Israel was that men should love their friends and hate their enemies.

Ye have heard that it hath been said, Thou shalt love thy neighbour, and hate thine enemy. But I say unto you, Love your enemies, bless them that curse you, do good to them that hate you, and pray for them which despitefully use you, and persecute you. That ye may be the children of your Father which is in heaven: for he maketh the sun to rise on the evil and on the good, and sendeth rain on the just and on the unjust. For if ye love them which love you, what reward have ye? Do not even the publicans [tax collectors] do the same? And if ye salute your brethren only, what do ye more than others? Do not even the publicans do so? Be ye therefore perfect, even as your Father in heaven is perfect (Matt. 5:43-48).

Notice His frame of reference here. *Your* enemies. Those who use *you* despitefully. Jesus was not saying that the enemies of God should be allowed to escape the lawful punishment of their crimes against man and God. He was not repudiating the ten commandments, that He had affirmed categorically a few moments before (vv. 17-19). What He was saying is this: in your dealings with all men, treat them as you would treat your friends. If your friends violate God's law, you do not repudiate the law. If your friend commits murder, you do not allow that murder to go unpunished, if you have information that would convict him. To do so would be to become an accomplice to the crime. Jesus is taking this principle of law enforcement right to the heart of each man. If you yourself commit murder, you must turn yourself in to the civil authorities, just as you would turn in your worst enemy. *You must honor God's law.* Paul announced this principle forthrightly when he was in court: "For if I be an offender, or have committed any thing worthy of death, I refuse not to die" (Acts 25:11a). To refuse not to die is to love God, and to love the righteousness of God, more than you love your own life. This is the essence of conversion: "He that findeth his life shall lose it: and he that loseth his life for my sake shall find it" (Matt. 10:39).

The New Testament tells us to love our neighbors as ourselves. We are to deal with them in terms of God's law. We *owe* them such fair dealing. "Love worketh no ill to his neighbour; therefore love is the fulfilling of the law" (Rom. 13:10). But what is "ill"? It is unrighteous dealing. How do we test what is "ill" and what isn't? By the standard of the law of God. This is why love fulfills the law. It is not that love overcomes the law, or annuls the law, or abrogates the law. Love *fulfills* the law, just as Jesus Christ fulfilled the law. He did not go on to deal unlawfully with men. How could He? He was the *author* of the law. Nor should we go on to deal unlawfully with men.

Jesus was not denying the legitimacy of biblical law. On the contrary, He was *affirming* biblical law. We love God first; God commands us to keep His word; therefore, we must enforce the law on ourselves. We start with ourselves because we have more knowledge of ourselves and more responsibility over ourselves. This is the meaning of *progressive sanctification.* Jesus was not calling us to ignore biblical law; He was calling us to enforce it first on ourselves, before we enforce the same laws on others.

Judge not, that ye be not judged. For with what judgment ye judge, ye shall be judged: and with what measure ye mete, it shall be measured to you again. And why beholdest thou the mote that is in thy brother's eye, but considerest not the beam that is in thine own eye? Or how wilt thou say to thy brother, Let me pull out the mote out of thine eye; and behold, a beam is in thine own eye? Thou hypocrite, first cast out the beam out of thine own eye; and then shalt thou see clearly to cast out the mote out of thy brother's eye (Matt. 7:1-5).

Notice what He did *not* say. He did not say that it is all right to go through life with motes (small chips) in our eye. The eye is the most sensitive organ in the body. A mote in an eye could blind it, or seriously interfere with our vision. Jesus did not condone sin in any form. Sin is a horror; it jeopardizes our very existence. It should not be allowed to remain in your eye, and we are required by God to do what we can to help remove chips from our neighbors' eyes. We are to use biblical law to assist them. What Jesus was saying is that we need to be constantly on the lookout for motes in other people's eyes, so that *we can help them remove them.* But to accomplish this, we must first get rid of the beams in our own eyes. We must be able to go to the other person and tell him: "Look, I used to have a really bad beam in my eye, and it blinded me. But through the grace of God, I was able to remove it. I see that you're suffering from the same thing. Let me show you how God's word speaks to your minor problem, just as it spoke to my major one." In other words, "I've been there. I know what it is. *It leads to blindness and agony.*"

This is the approach of the most successful alcoholic rehabilitation program in history, Alcoholics Anonymous. When a man at last chooses to become sober, and is faced with a terrible craving to drink, he calls his sober friends who were former alcoholics. He goes to those who have suffered what he is suffering. He doesn't telephone his Aunt Tilly, who never touched a drink in her life, unless Aunt Tilly has a known prayer life which produces healings and near-miracles whenever she prays. Besides, he probably already asked Aunt Tilly to pray for him, and he still got drunk. So he calls the men who suffered from beams (Jim Beams?) and who successfully solved their problem.

There is a tendency in twentieth-century fundamentalism, evangelicalism, and pietism for law-hating, responsibility-avoiding Christian people to piously assert, "It is not our responsibility to judge. We must show mercy to everyone. We are sinners, too." This is the worst kind of hypocrisy. What they are *really* saying is that they judge not, because they do not want to be judged. They want perpetual mercy for their *continuing* sins, so they therefore avoid criticizing others. But this is evil. The goal of redeemed man's life is ethical perfection (Matt. 5:48). The means by which redeemed people *approach* this goal is *self-government under God's law*, what we also call progressive sanctification. We *want* to be judged by God's law. This is our affirmation of the sovereignty of God. We *want* the law of God to rule over every man's actions, every institution, throughout history. Such honoring of God's law is the basis of the dominion covenant. But to see God's law universally honored, we must do everything that we can to honor it in our own lives.

The "judge not" verse warns us not to judge others by any standard other than the one we want to be used in judging us. But the converse is equally true: once we have judged ourselves, and have disciplined ourselves in terms of God's standard, it is our moral obligation to begin to apply this same law to every area of life over which we have a God-given authority. This is why the Bible sets forth rigorous standards for becoming an elder or deacon (I Tim. 3). They must achieve self-discipline and then discipline over their families before they are allowed to discipline other church members. Similarly, if we are eligible to vote, we must get registered. If we are registered, we must take time to study the issues. Then we must vote accordingly. The "judge not" passage is not a license for pietistic retreat from the world. The context of the "Sermon on the Mount" shows clearly that *the "judge not" passage is a call to dominion*. It instructs us to begin with ourselves, so that we can then work to extend the principles and enforcement of God's principles to areas of life over which we have lawful authority.

Exercising Judgment

The "judge not" passage is a *positive command* by implication: a command to *judge righteously in terms of God's law*. We are called by God to exercise judgment. This is the inescapable reality of man (Gen. 1:28). Man judged in the garden, but he judged rebelliously. Redeemed men will eventually judge the angels (I Cor. 6:3). If we are never to judge on earth, then when will we get the ability? Will God grant the gift of good and godly judgment to men who have fled this responsibility all their lives?

If we do not exercise good judgment, then how can we fulfill the terms of the dominion covenant? The historic response of the "judge not" pietists — the defenders of the *escapist religion* — is to deny the existence of this covenant. But if Christians deny the existence of a law-covenant — if they deny that all men are under God's dominion covenant — and if they deny that there are eternal laws that serve as standards by which all men are required to perform, then how is the sinner to be confronted with the reality of his sin? If Christians are incapable of helping unregenerate men see their sins, and if they are therefore incapable of assisting newly regenerate men to overcome their newly perceived sins, then what happens to church discipline? The institutional answer of the pietists to this question has been *to deny the necessity of church discipline.* The consistent ones go so far as to deny the legitimacy of much of civil government, too. They deny the death penalty for capital crimes. Some of them do everything possible to promote the State as a substitute parent, but a parent without a rod of discipline. Others simply deny all civil law whatsoever — and therefore are compelled to deny the continuing authority of the Old Testament.[2]

The power-seeking religionists understand the centrality of judgment and discipline, but they have substituted the State in God's place. Thus, they seek to expand the centralized power of the State, and to extend the State's power over every area of life. They seek to worship their God, human power, by incorporating it into a political monopoly. They understand the fixed relationship between *sovereignty, power, and judgment.* As agents of collective mankind, they seek to become agents of the power State. They seek ever-increasing opportunities to exercise judgment.

This is why the power religionists always find allies with the escapist religionists. The escapist religionists point to the power of hu-

---

2. Mark McCulley, "Faith and Freedom: A Fifth View of Christian Economics," *Nomos,* II (Winter 1984). McCulley calls his anti-Old Testament, anti-civil government position the "economics of Christian exile." This is well-named. *Exile* is the essence of the escapist religion. He ends his article with a partial citation of John Wesley: "earn all you can; give all you can." He deliberately ignores Wesley's third principle, *save* all you can, which is the foundation of economic growth and linear development unto dominion. McCulley is hostile to such a view, for he understands the thrift principle well enough to see where it leads in principle, and where it has led in the past: to modern industrial capitalism. He does not hate capitalism, unlike so many of his Anabaptist colleagues; he hates growth-oriented industrial production. This is why he praises as followers of Jesus' New Testament ethic "Ballou, the Hopedale community, and a few 'come-outers' " in the post-Civil War Christian era. "Down on the farm" communalism has long been the final resting and retreating place for pacifist Anabaptists. The revolutionary Anabaptists have generally headed for the cities, in order to consolidate power.

manist man, who is ultimately satanic man, and they conclude that this power is an aspect of Satan's control over the earth until Jesus comes again. When these escapist religionists are confronted with the responsibilities associated with the dominion covenant, they recoil in horror. Dominion, in their eyes, is too much like autonomous man's power. To adopt such a view of Christianity would mean that they would have to become involved in a head-on, lifetime confrontation with Satan's earthly kingdom of power. They would have to begin to exercise judgment. They prefer to stay in the shadows of history in the name of a "higher spirituality" or a "higher calling" from God. They prefer to avoid the visible, *civilizational* confrontations. Thus, the power religionists can enlist the retreatists as allies in their war against covenantal religion.

The standard ploy of the theological liberals in the United States from the late nineteenth century until they consolidated ecclesiastical power in the 1920's and 1930's in the North, and in the 1950's and 1960's in the South, was to criticize all heresy trials — where they were going to be the victims — in the name of institutional peace and toleration. They directed this incomparably successful appeal to the weak-hearted souls in the churches. These people wanted institutional peace above all. Until the liberals gained complete control and shoved them aside, these conservative battle-avoiders had a majority in every major denomination. Decade by decade, the liberals quietly consolidated power: in seminaries, in colleges, and in the churches' various boards, especially the missions boards. When the theologically committed conservatives finally realized what had happened, it was too late. They could no longer gather theologically committed troops for a fight. The theology of a majority of the conservatives was "peace at any institutional price." So they paid the highest possible price: the capture of their churches by the opponents of biblical Christianity. In the churches with a strong hierarchy, the liberals eventually pushed out the orthodox pastors, with the exception of the Missouri Synod Lutherans.[3] In the decentralized associations, they simply isolated the orthodox men from the seats of power. This has always been the humanists' strategy. With only a few exceptions, it has worked superbly in this century. The archetype was the capture of the Presbyterian Church, U.S.A. (Northern).[4] This strategy

---

3. Kurt E. Marquart, *Anatomy of an Explosion: A Theological Analysis of the Missouri Synod Conflict* (Grand Rapids, Michigan: Baker Book House, 1977).

4. See Gary North, *Rotten Wood: The Capture of the Presbyterian Church, U.S.A.* (forthcoming).

has only recently begun to be reversed in the Southern Baptist Church.

Social Co-operation

When Christian men treat non-Christians as men deserving of the benefits of biblical law, they become evangelists. The benefits of the law become visible to covenantal outsiders. The law is to be a tool of evangelism (Deut. 4:6-8). But this program of evangelism requires God's people to keep the law (Deut. 4:9).

Because Jesus made it plain that all men are to be extended the *courtesy* of the law, as well as the *restraining authority* of the law, Christianity has become an international leaven. It has risen up in pagan cultures and has replaced many of the worst features of the old paganism. The Old Testament also required God's people to deal righteously with other men, but the empowering of the Holy Spirit and the church's first-century exodus out of Palestine universalized the declaration and manifestation of biblical law in a new way.

Consider the concept of the contract. When Christians are commanded to deal with non-Christians righteously, they are placed under the terms of God's revealed law. To the extent that they obey God's law, other people can make better predictions concerning the performance of Christians in voluntary associations. The law is an open book. It is easily read and understood. Children are to be taught the law (Deut. 6:7; 31:12). It is suitable for children, in other words. Thus, non-Christians should find it less risky to co-operate in economic ventures with Christians, *if Christians respect God's law.* By reducing the risk (uncertainty) of working with Christians, the law thereby *increases the non-Christians' demand for Christians to associate with.* The price of co-operation drops when uncertainty drops. As the price drops, more of the good is demanded. The "good" in question is the honest labor and insight of the covenant man. More people want it.

This is another impetus to Christian dominion. Christians become the people other men prefer to work with and deal with. Their opportunities for increasing their own authority are increased because of this added readiness of non-Christians to work with them. The unbeliever hopes to benefit personally from the relationship. This could be called the "Laban" strategy, or the "Potiphar" strategy: make it beneficial for the covenant-breakers to co-operate with the covenant-keepers.

This does not mean that Christians are to become "doormats."

They are not to become "pushovers." They are to honor the law, both when it benefits them personally and when it doesn't. There are times when enforcing the law decreases the unbeliever's capital or opportunities — sinful opportunities. In such cases, Christians are to abide by the law. The terms of God's covenant must govern the Christian's enforcement of the terms of a contract.

Honesty is the best policy, Ben Franklin said. He was correct. As men perceive that Christians are honest and can be trusted, honest men will seek them out. Those non-Christians who have been given the common grace of honesty will want to work with Christians, *if Christians honor the law of God*. This puts Christians in association with honest people, who are also following the best policy. This puts dishonest people at a competitive disadvantage, for Christians can take advantage of the increased productivity of the division of labor by working with honest non-Christians. Christians increase their authority and capital by associating with, and learning from, skilled honest people, whether Christian or non-Christian.[5] This is a major economic benefit of honoring the golden rule.

Antinomianism, Anarchy, and Tyranny

What I have argued throughout *The Dominion Covenant* is that biblical law is the ideal foundation for social order. Only to the degree that societies conform to the standards of biblical law can they experience the blessings promised by the law (Deut. 28:1-14). This does not mean that a society needs to become explicitly Christian, nor does it mean that all or a majority of its members must be regenerated by the Holy Spirit. It means only that the written standards of God's law be honored.

I have also argued that it is inconsistent for non-Christian societies to retain allegiance to the standards of biblical law. Over time, they will become more consistent with their covenant-breaking presuppositions. Special grace is therefore necessary in the long run to sustain a society's commitment to the standards of biblical law. Nevertheless, during that historical period in which the law's externals are honored in deed, and possibly even in word, the society in question will become the beneficiary of the external power that the law delivers. Examples in the Bible of such external power and

---

5. Gary North, "Competence, Common Grace, and Dominion," *Biblical Economics Today*, VIII (June/July 1985).

blessing are Egypt under Joseph's counsel, Nineveh after the preaching of Jonah, and Medo-Persia under Daniel's counsel. It is true that the law eventually brings death (Rom. 7), for it testifies to man's rebellion and curse, and this is why covenant-breaking societies cannot remain faithful to the externals of biblical law forever. They must either abandon God's law or be converted to the gospel.

We also find examples of Christian societies that steadily abandon the externals of biblical law, and in doing so, grow culturally impotent. Americans have lived in such a society for over a century. We find that those who should proclaim a dominion religion have become adherents of the escapist religion. Meanwhile, the most consistent and ruthless advocates of the power religion in the history of man, the Communists, threaten to overwhelm the West. The Christians have become subservient to one group of law-hating humanists, who in turn have proven to be no match ideologically or militarily for the consistent humanists behind the Iron Curtain. It appears to be a replay of Israel's experience in the era of the judges: when the nation began to worship the gods of the Philistines, God delivered them into the hands of the Philistines. They learned just what it is like to live under foreign gods.[6]

Christian leaders for a century have consistently denied the continuing validity of Old Testament social and political law. This has led Christians to abandon God's tool of dominion, His law. God delivered them into the hands of the progressive educators and Darwinists, the political salvationists and the welfare statists. Conservative Christians in dispensational churches, liberal Christians in mainline denominations, and Calvinist Christians inside tiny, invisible denominations have stood arm in arm theologically on the question of the authority of God's law today. It has no continuing authority today, they affirm. Such a doctrine has played into the hands of the humanists, who also affirm this doctrine.

In 1984, the increasingly liberal InterVarsity Press published a collection of four essays and responses, *Wealth and Poverty: Four Christian Views of Economics.* I was one of the participants, the defender of the free market approach. There was a socialist, a Keynesian, and a socialist who pretended to be a defender of voluntary communalism. His chapter was misleadingly labeled, "Decentralist Economics."

---

6. James B. Jordan, *Judges: God's War Against Humanism* (Tyler, Texas: Geneva Ministries, 1985), pp. 40-41.

This latter position is the only significant alternative to free market Christianity, either intellectually or theologically, within American evangelical circles. The popularity of Ron Sider's *Rich Christians in an Age of Hunger*, also published by InterVarsity Press, is indicative. (In Roman Catholic circles, especially in Latin America, Sider's brand of Christian socialism is regarded as soft-core and irrelevant; the liberation theologians there are Marxist revolutionaries. Sider was content merely to send the Nicaraguan Sandinistas money through his Jubilee Fund;[7] he is not yet willing to adopt their rhetoric. Too risky for a Baptist seminary professor. At least for now.)

Art Gish, the Sider surrogate in the published debate, was forthright in his moral outrage against capitalism and Western Civilization. (See "Haters of the West," above, pages 214-17.) Why does Gish hate Western Civilization and capitalism? Because he hates biblical law, and Western Civilization and capitalism are the social products historically of biblical law. He is a devout antinomian. "The answer to our problems is not biblical law but God's grace, the saving grace of Jesus Christ expressed in a new order, God's kingdom. The law cannot bring salvation. Neither will the capitalist doctrine of salvation by works lead to life."[8]

The startling aspect of this statement is that it has become the theological "coin of the realm" in Protestant circles. The reason why the old-time fundamentalists have been unable to counter Sider and his followers — the reason why tens of thousands of young Christians have been converted to their view of capitalism — is that the conservatives have adopted the same view of biblical law. Therefore, to counter Sider and the radicals, they have only conservative humanist arguments, and these do not have the emotional and rhetorical appeal for college students that warmed-over liberal rhetoric has. Furthermore, the students are in rebellion against their socially unconcerned and culturally impotent fundamentalist origins. So they respond positively to Sider and Gish because these "radical Christians" seem to be offering them relevance, but without breaking with the familiar "grace vs. law" theology they have brought with them to college or seminary. The old-time fundamentalists have lost the fight; they simply cannot compete with the radicals in terms of the "grace vs. law" theology.

---

7. *theOtherSide* (September 1979), p. 41.
8. Art Gish, "A Decentralist Response," in Robert Clouse (ed.), *Wealth and Poverty* (Downers Grove, Illinois: InterVarsity Press, 1984), p. 75.

Gish goes on: "In the New Covenant we are offered something much better, the grace of going beyond greed and revenge and therefore the need of law. . . . As Christians, our lives can be governed by God's love and grace instead of law."⁹ At last, he gets to the point. Well, not quite. He is not yet ready to go the whole distance. So he lays down the theological foundation of his unstated but inescapable conclusion: *the abolition of all government.* This has to be the conclusion, for without law there can be no government.

This conclusion is that same old demonic position which has accompanied radical revolutionaries and anarchism throughout history: the "truly free" man and the "truly free" society is lawless. He has no need of law. In short, the "new mankind" is perfect. There is no need for civil government. There is also no need for church government. The next step, historically, has always been taken by the radicals, though not normally until they set up a local "kingdom of the saints": there is no need for *family government.*

Gish is an Anabaptist. His theology is the theology of the Anabaptists. In the sixteenth century, Anabaptist revolutionaries began to terrorize Europe. They gathered mobs together, set up city-states, adopted free love (or polygamy for the rulers) and socialism. They tore down churches. They murdered opponents. And they did it all in terms of the freedom of the Holy Spirit. Igor Shafarevich, a Soviet dissenter, has written a chapter on this revolutionary heritage in his excellent book, *The Socialist Phenomenon* (Harper & Row, 1980). The chapter is titled, "The Socialism of the Heresies." David Chilton devotes an appendix to the same subject in his *Productive Christians in an Age of Guilt-Manipulators.* It summarizes Shafarevich and adds more historical data: "Socialism, the Anabaptist Heresy."

Where does such a theology lead? To tyranny. In the name of zero-law, the "saints" impose tyranny. Law is a means of self-government first, and a means of restricting tyranny secondarily. Biblical law, when enforced, restrains sin's public manifestations. Without it, men are left at the mercy of people who categorically deny the need for outward law because they have been "purified" by the Holy Spirit. Thus, the theory of anarchy and antinomianism invariably results in tyranny. This is why it is so misleading to label Gish's position "decentralist economics." It may appear to be decentralist, but it inescapably leads to tyranny by way of antinomianism.

---

9. *Idem.*

In condemning Gish, I am simultaneously condemning all forms of antinomianism, including the antinomianism of modern dispensationalism and modern pietism. The difference between the typical Baptist preacher's message and Gish's message is a matter of personal taste and financing. It is not a difference in theology. The Baptist minister might be fired if he started preaching sermons that sounded like Gish's chapter. Gish is already safely down on his communal farm (at least until its economic principles drive it into bankruptcy), and he has a constituency of faithful "poverts" who can survive financially and send him money because they are employed by free market institutions or government institutions that are financed by taxes collected from free market institutions. Gish can afford to pursue his Anabaptist heritage somewhat more faithfully than the typical antinomian pastor. In short, the difference between antinomian conservatism and antinomian liberation theology is more a matter of style and constituency than it is a matter of theology.

What is my thesis? Very simple: anyone who contrasts the love of God with the law of God is an implicit defender of tyranny.[10]

Conclusion

This is not the place to conduct an extended discussion of the relationship between grace and law. That topic has been covered in depth by Greg Bahnsen in *Theonomy in Christian Ethics* and in Part II of my book, *75 Bible Questions Your Instructors Pray You Won't Ask* (1984).[11] The issue here is the relationship between covenantal love and covenantal law. God saves His covenanted people by grace. This is an act of love. How does He do this? He looks at the *law-conforming* life, the *law-required* death, and *animal sacrifice-annulling* resurrection of Jesus Christ, and He counts Christ's righteousness as the righteousness of Christ's covenant people. He *imputes* Christ's righteousness to them *judicially* (definitive justification) and *morally* (definitive sanctification).[12] In short, God imputes definitively to the regenerate the absolute perfection of biblical law.

As men progressively work out their salvations with fear and trembling (Phil. 2:12b), they are to be guided by God's law, since

---

10. Greg L. Bahnsen, *By This Standard: The Authority of God's Law Today* (Tyler, Texas: Institute for Christian Economics, 1985), Part II.

11. Published by Spurgeon Press, P.O. Box 7999, Tyler, Texas 75711.

12. Gary North, *Unconditional Surrender: God's Program for Victory* (2nd ed.; Tyler, Texas: Geneva Divinity School Press, 1983), pp. 43-51.

God's imputation to them of Christ's perfect keeping of this law is the only foundation of their salvation. They are to *judge* their own acts, both internal (mental) and external, in terms of this standard. They are to judge the external acts of other people by this same standard. *What other standard could regenerate men possibly use?* We must constantly ask ourselves, and endlessly ask the critics of the New Testament authority of Old Testament law: By what *other* standard? If we love Christ, we will keep His commandments (John 14:15).

Only if Christ's commandments were different from the commandments God gave to Moses could we legitimately conclude that the love of Christ is different from the love of God. Only then could we conclude that obedience to Christ is different from obedience to God. But there can be no difference; the God who created everything is the divine Logos, who was incarnated as the perfect human, Jesus Christ (John 1). Thus, any attempt to create a dualism between God's Old Testament law and Christ's New Testament law is simultaneously an attempt to offer *a two-God theory of history*, with the Old Testament God different from a New Testament God. This was attempted by Marcion in the second century, and he was condemned as a heretic. An implicit two-God theory has been proclaimed for centuries by Christian mystics and Anabaptists, and also by modern fundamentalists and evangelicals. The results have been culturally disastrous: the *anti-dominion principle in action.*

There is no contradiction between the ten commandments and the sermon on the mount. God's love is manifested to us in the law, which is the law of life. There is grace in God's law.

Appendix C

SOCIAL ANTINOMIANISM

Antinomianism — the denial of the validity of the concrete application of Old Testament law in this era — has influenced modern
Christianity to such an extent that virtually no Christian seminary
even teaches a single course against it. Anglo-Israelite sects do pay
attention to biblical law, which is, I believe, the reason that Garner
Ted Armstrong's "The World Tomorrow" had such a huge radio audience and why he was more interesting than any orthodox Christian broadcasting in the late 1960's and early 1970's. He could comment successfully on the collapse of modern culture because he had
concrete alternatives to offer.

Social antinomianism makes itself manifest in many ways. In the
Reformed Protestant circles, the Dutch Calvinist movement associated with the name Herman Dooyeweerd was briefly influential in
this regard, 1965-75. Always searching for the "true Christian attitude," the radical young neo-Dooyeweerdians proclaimed almost
complete freedom from the restraining hand of concrete biblical law.
Thus, attitude is substituted for obedience to revealed law. The non-
Dooyeweerdian churchmen were unable to refute the radicals precisely because they held a similar, though less rigorous, antinomian
philosophy. Their instincts may have been conservative, but their
operating presuppositions did not allow them to challenge successfully
the young radicals. The leaders of the neo-Dooyeweerdians, located
primarily at the Free University of Amsterdam and the Institute for
Christian Studies in Toronto, combine a preference for government
intervention and orthodox Christian language. The following article
criticizes this combination. Troost's answer appeared in the same
issue (Oct. 1967) of the *International Reformed Bulletin*. It did not convince me. Similar terminology and identical antinomianism have
become universal in the "radical Christian" Anabaptist circles.*

---

*From this point on until "Troost's Response," this appendix is a reprint of my
original article in *International Reformed Bulletin*.

In the issue of the *International Reformed Bulletin* for Jan./April, 1966, an article written by A. Troost [TROWST, not TRUEST] appeared, "Property Rights and the Eighth Commandment." Troost, the article informs us, is a professor of social ethics at the Free University of Amsterdam, and as such he seems to be representative of an increasingly large number of Dutch Reformed scholars who claim to be building upon the foundation laid down by Herman Dooyeweerd. It is my belief that the basic implications of Troost's essay are ultimately antinomian, and for this reason it deserves an extended analysis.

The problem which faces the Christian scholar in the area of social philosophy is a very great one: he must make an attempt to outline policies for social reconstruction that are in accord with the biblical framework, and at the same time he must make use of a vast quantity of scholarship which has been produced by non-Christian thinkers. In other words, he must acknowledge that common grace has enlightened the unregenerate scholar to the extent that some of his endeavors may be useful to the Christian, but at the same time the Christian must sift and choose from this scholarship in the light of Reformed, biblical standards. Clearly, it is not a simple task, and some errors are bound to creep into the work of even the most careful Reformed thinker. Yet part of the heritage of the Reformation is the rejection of perfectionism, and the fact that some errors are inevitable does not relieve us of the task of working out the implications of our Christian position.

The Bible, in short, is absolutely fundamental in this work of social criticism. Without it, the Christian is left without a basic frame of reference by which he can evaluate the various proposals for social change. Bearing this in mind, the reader may be able to understand my hostile reaction to Troost's starting point: "As we saw in section 12, the Bible does not provide us with data, points of departure or premises from which to draw logical conclusions relevant to modern society's socio-economic problems, including property relations" (p. 32). The question immediately arises: By what standard are we to evaluate the validity of any particular political or social proposal? If, as Christians, we cannot approach the special revelation presented in the Bible in the hope of finding our standards for social action, then where are we to go? It is Troost's position (and the position of many of his fellow Calvinist scholars) that the Bible gives us no data, no concrete recommendations, by which we can judge political programs; the task of ushering in the Kingdom of God is apparently to be accomplished without the guidelines of special, concrete revelation.

Nevertheless, Troost can assert that "The message of the Bible reveals something to us!" What is it which the Bible reveals? It gives us the story of the coming kingdom, of "the re-establishment of all things, to the total reconciliation, liberation and renewal of life by the person and work of Jesus Christ through his cross and resurrection." Even more than this, "The cross and the resurrection promise to our practice of property relations a complete liberation from the powerful grip of the sins of injustice and lovelessness" (p. 32).

Apparently, there *are* standards of "injustice and lovelessness." What are they, the Christian must ask, and where do we find them? So far, all that we know is that the Bible cannot provide them, at least not in the socio-economic realm. Troost reaches an impasse at this point. He has proclaimed a vague pietism in the name of Reformed scholarship. Unless he can find concrete standards of judgment that are somehow self-evident and eternally valid apart from the Bible, he leaves us without any basis for decision-making.

In spite of the fact that he has eliminated the Bible from the realm of social affairs, he now refers back to the book of Acts: "These first Christians did not abolish property, nor yet the means of production (e.g., landed estates). No, they put ownership and property rights back into the place where they belong, back into their proper function. 'Not a man of them claimed any of his possessions as his own, but everything was held in common' (Acts 4:32) . . ." (p.33). Two preliminary observations should be made with regard to the interpretation of this passage. First, the decision to enter into such common ownership was voluntary, and anyone was permitted to hold his private property out of the common stock (Acts 5:4). Peter, in other words, proclaimed the right of private ownership as a perfectly legitimate Christian practice. Second, it is also relevant that the Christians in Jerusalem were expecting the fulfillment of the prophecy of the destruction of Jerusalem (Luke 21:20ff.), and any application of the early church's practice of common ownership should be interpreted in this light. In times of social catastrophe (and in times of the confiscation of property by the State), it may be a wise decision for Christians to hold some common property, especially property which is mobile and easily hidden. But is it a general law?

The real issue, however, goes much deeper than either of these two criticisms. Troost argues from this passage in the following manner: "Thus did the practice of this church confirm the preaching of the gospel with signs and powers. Property relations were set free from their natural self-willed self-assertion and employed for loving service of God and neighbor" (p. 33). Now what are we to conclude from all of this? The Bible, Troost has argued, does not give us any "data, points of departure or premises from which to draw logical conclusions relevant to modern society's socio-economic problems, including property relations." Nevertheless, we are now told that the early Christians "put ownership and property rights back in the place where they belong," and Troost obviously expects us to take this example seriously. But on his grounds — on the presuppositions upon which he began his analysis — why should we pay any attention to what the early church did? Troost wants us to make an application of the church's practice in today's world, but why should we, if the Bible is not relevant to present-day economic and social problems? Does he mean that we should create a society in which property is held in common (socialism) and yet at the same time believe that we are not living under socialism (since property, he says, was not "abolished")? The whole argument is vague, but it appears that this is Troost's conclusion. If it is not, then I do not understand what he is talking about.

He refers to the fact that the early church "did not abolish property, nor yet the means of production (e.g., landed estates)." Private property was preserved in the sense that it was not sold to the State, true enough. They sold some of their fixed assets to non-Christians and deposited the wealth in the common treasury. They also gave some of their other goods directly to the Christian community. But this means that in order to follow their example in our day, we must sell our goods to unbelievers, thus making ourselves perpetual wage-earners and salaried laborers. It means that as private individuals, we can no longer own fixed capital goods like land and especially machinery. We are to become, in other words, a sort of huge Christian co-operative movement, at best employed by each other, but more probably employed by the unregenerate world. And if we are not to draw such conclusions, then why did Troost bring up the subject in the first place? Either it is a concrete example to be followed, or else the whole incident is irrelevant. Again, we can admit that under social conditions comparable to those faced by the early church, something like this might be necessary, but as a prescription

for all eternity it seems silly, especially in light of the fact that Peter
did say that a total contribution to the common treasury was not required. Since Troost does not think that the Bible provides us with
concrete data concerning economic affairs, it does not seem logical
for him to bring up the matter at all. If he means simply that Christians should, on occasion, be willing to give up some of their private
wealth to the Christian community, then he has not said very much.

Troost then mentions the fact that "the New Testament is not socially revolutionary" in the eyes of some Christians. He says that the
New Testament, at least on its surface, "does not radically condemn
the situation in which its authors preached and wrote" (p. 33). It
even accepted slavery as an institution, as Paul's epistle to Philemon
indicates. Troost realizes that the New Testament is, in this practical
sense, profoundly conservative — it did not attack directly the social
fabric of Roman society. This disturbs him, and therefore he returns
to his old theme: "It would, however, be entirely at variance with the
spirit and intention of the gospel, with the Message, if from the
above we were logically to draw up socio-economic conclusions
which would then have to be applied in practical politics. Not a few
Christians perpetuate in this way an *economic* and *political conservatism.*
The same goes for progressivist-socialistic conclusions from biblical
'data' . . ." (p. 34). Common property in Acts 4:32 is somehow relevant today; conservative elements in the Bible are not. He reasserts
himself once again: "The biblical message of the kingdom of God
does not *directly* address itself to the betterment of human society
which includes, among other things, property relations. But, to be
sure, it does indeed affect them!" To be sure of *what*? *How* does it
affect them? In his answer, Troost arrives at a position of total antinomian mysticism: "In order to exercise our property rights in every-
day life in the right manner, and to handle our possessions before the
face of God in a way pleasing to him, nothing less is required than the
merciful intervention of God, from above, through the Holy Ghost.
Unless regenerated, common sense will change nothing. Renewal
must come from the top down; it will not come up by itself from the
bottom. Our natural reason can achieve nothing here" (p. 34).

Consider what Troost is saying. The Bible, he has said, does not
provide any concrete data — no applicable kind of special revelation
— in the area of economic and political affairs. Yet he is also saying
that "Our natural reason can achieve nothing here." Not only is there
no special revelation in social affairs, there is no general revelation

on which we can rely. And so we must sit quietly and wait for the mystical intervention of the Holy Spirit to guide us in all of our private community decisions; God has seen fit to leave us without any concrete standards in such matters. This, I am compelled to conclude is antinomianism. It is strangely like the mystical brand of Christianity that is called Penielism. I am unable to see how it is even remotely Reformed.

This does not mean that Troost has no recommendations for the contemporary world. Naturally, he does not derive them from the Bible, and apparently the "common sense" of the unregenerate world has given him no aid. In fact, he does not specify any source for his recommendations. Nevertheless, he is able to conclude that "It is part of our *religion* to engage whole-heartedly in the battle for a just distribution of income (nationally, but also internationally, through foreign aid), for just property relations, and for a just economic order. It is part of our religion because we are called to it by Him who gave his life for this world . . ." (p. 35). Unfortunately, he does not specify which sphere of life is involved here. Does he mean merely that the church should give private charity (a teaching made explicit by the Scriptures), or does he mean that as Christians we are obligated to promote the political projects of land redistribution and foreign aid sponsored by our civil governments? If he means simply private charity, then he is saying nothing new. If he means public projects of political coercion, then he must show us on what grounds such a conclusion is justified; certainly the Bible teaches no such doctrine, and even if it did, Troost does not accept the Bible's testimony in such matters.

He goes on: "The World Council of Churches itself is sponsoring a study on a large scale dealing with society and social problems, in connection with which a book is to appear entitled *The Theological Foundation of a Christian Social Ethics.* Unfortunately it appears to me that historic Reformation Christianity ('Calvinism') is not making much of a contribution to this study and reflection" (p. 36). Naturally, the World Council can engage in such activities; it is a humanistic organization which is not bound to work within the framework of limits established by the Bible. It has no difficulty in producing all the humanistic, secular documents that it wants to distribute. But given the presuppositions which Troost holds, that the Bible offers no concrete social proposals, and that "common sense" of the fallen world is equally helpless in aiding the thinker in his work, how could we possibly hope that "historic Reformation Christianity" would make any contribution? Troost denies the only two foundations upon which such contributions can be made: concrete special revelation on the one hand, or natural revelation granted by God in common grace. We are left without standards. Troost offers us a classic example of the truth proclaimed by the late C. S. Lewis: we castrate our men and then bid them to be fruitful.

Finally, we are told this truth by Troost: "However, it is plain, inevitable, and imperative that in our society more and more limitations be put on private property rights by social law and economic law, both in the domain of public law as well as in private community law such as internal industrial law" (p. 39). There is *absolutely nothing* in Troost's essay that would indicate that such a requirement is either plain, inevitable, or imperative. Troost does not seem to be aware of the fact that he is inserting conclusions made by modern, secular socialists and Marxists into his essay, and that he is doing it in the name of "historic Reformation Christianity." It is possible that he does not mean that socialistic legislation is increasingly imperative, although his language certainly implies this. The reason that it is not possible to say for certain what Troost means is that he stops at this point and refuses to elaborate! He gives no examples of concrete cases, and he offers us nothing to show where such limitations on private property are needed.

Troost has attempted to destroy the biblical foundations of conservatism (and, he meekly asserts, of socialism), yet he then proceeds to make what is inescapably a highly socialistic pronouncement in the name of Christianity. Worst of all, he then uses the "disclaimer" approach, so that he will not have to elaborate: he modestly says that he is unqualified to go on. "Here the theologian must stop, for we landed in the thick of concrete socio-economic problems. As a *theologian* I was allowed to go beyond sections 16 and 18 where I tried to sketch the task of the *church* and her *preaching* with respect to our subject. But now I too have come to the limit of my own competence; beyond this I am not qualified to speak" (p. 41). Troost is a professor of social ethics at the Free University of Amsterdam, and in this capacity he has denied the possibility of concrete biblical revelation in aiding us in our task of Christian social reconstruction. Yet beyond this, he says, he is not qualified to speak. He adds, of course, that we must promote some undefined "economic justice," increase foreign aid, and put even more restrictions on private property in an already frighteningly socialistic era. It is as if a professor of engineering were to tell his Dutch students that the dikes should be blown up, but in regard to any substitute for them, he protests that he is not qualified to speak.

He criticizes conservatives thusly: "One of the causes giving the church a conservative mentality — and the same holds for Christian social organizations — can be that her members keep on thinking in traditional, outdated concepts" (p. 39). But in destroying the only possible foundation for concrete Christian alternatives to such "outdated concepts" (i.e., concrete biblical revelation), Troost leaves the Christian world with nothing but mysticism. He offers us in the name of historic Reformed Christianity the whole amorphous, planless, interventionist ethic of the Dutch economy. It is a decision made on the basis of his personal preference, yet proclaimed in the name of God's kingdom; he denies, nevertheless, that those pronouncements can be based upon the special revelation of the Bible. In short, Troost's conception of Christian social ethics is without foundation, either from the point of view of the Scriptures (which he rejects as a source of data concerning social affairs) or from the point of view of modern economics and politics (which is based upon the logic of the unregenerate world, which he also rejects). Yet because this system is totally without a foundation, we are expected to accept it as "modern" and "Christian," and not part of some "traditional, outdated" world. Because it is without roots, we Christians are to call it our own.

The magnificent theoretical criticism of secular thought which Dooyeweerd began has been eroded away. Dooyeweerd cut the intellectual foundations from under all secular thinkers, but Troost and other Calvinists who stand with Troost are unwilling to replace their secular foundations with concrete scriptural examples and requirements. They have left themselves without any foundations at all. But even this is not quite true, since men cannot think or speak without some foundation. Troost and those who support him have brought back the teachings of the secular world (and, more specifically, the socialist secular world) in the name of Dooyeweerd. That such antinomianism in the social spheres can be considered a part of the Reformed heritage testifies to the loss of the Puritan vision in the modern world.

Troost's Response

In the issue of *International Reformed Bulletin* which published my critique of Troost's essay (October 1967), Troost was afforded an opportunity to reply. His response was titled, "A Plea for a Creation Ethic." I have waited long enough to respond to his attempt to escape my criticisms. The reason why I am bothering to respond at this late date is that I am trying to point out the flaws in a certain kind of approach to economics. Troost was never a significant figure in the debate, either in the U.S. or in Holland, but several of his arguments and slogans have appeared in recent "liberation theology" books, even though it is highly unlikely that any prominent liberation theologian has ever heard of Troost. It is the so-called "climate of opinion," especially left-wing neo-evangelical opinion, which is the focus of my concern. This climate change began to appear in the mid-1960's, and Troost was one small gust in the hurricane of error.

One thing annoys me exceedingly. I see Christian scholars who adopt phrases such as "creation law" or "creation ethics," yet they refuse to affirm their commitment to a literal six-day creation, with 24-hour days, hours being measured as we measure them today (give or take a few nanoseconds per day). In short, they wrap themselves in the language of biblical orthodoxy, and then they climb in bed with the evolutionists. They reject explicit biblical laws in the name of a vague "creation law," and then they reject the six-day creation in the name of some sort of vague age-day hypothesis, or "framework" hypothesis, or whatever the latest "creative evolution" buzzwords are in evangelical academic circles. They believe in neither the biblical doctrine of law nor the biblical doctrine of creation. They are, in short, hypocrites. We need to understand this from the beginning. They are compromisers. Their self-appointed task is to deceive the faithful.

Troost begins with the standard response: "In the preceding article of Mr. Gary North there is what appears to me to be a misunderstanding that is as serious as it is tragic." This is the old "misunderstanding ploy." Then he goes on to demonstrate that I understood him only too well.

He rejects my accusation that he is an antinomian. Then he appeals to his defense of the *cosmonomic idea* to prove that he is a good, law-abiding Dutch Calvinist Christian. In short, he appeals to his membership in the school of Herman Dooyeweerd, the Dutch Calvinist philosopher. This, he supposes, should relieve the fears of his Dutch audience. Understand that his reply was first published in the Dutch Christian newspaper which had run a translation of my critical essay. His essay and mine only later were published in the *International Reformed Bulletin*.

Dooyeweerd's Antinomianism

My response is straightforward: *Dooyeweerd was an antinomian, too.* This is why his thought was immediately adopted by a group of radical Christians who used his philosophical system to defend the idea of Christian medieval guild socialism, or worse. The "Toronto School" of neo-Dooyeweerdians was, from the mid-1960's onward until it began to fade in the early 1970's, at the center of an anti-capitalist revival. They broke new rhetorical ground that Ronald Sider and other non-Dutch liberation theologians later travelled over. These neo-Dooyeweerdians were subsequently superseded on campus by the neo-evangelicals, but they held very similar ideas. The heart of their critique against the West and the United States in particular was that the West was built in terms of free market competitive capitalism.

Dooyeweerd never publicly broke with his radical North American followers. Thus, they have been able to wrap themselves in the flag of the "cosmonomic idea" school of philosophy, for whatever that is worth. (Outside of very tiny Calvinist intellectual circles, primarily Dutch, it is worth nothing.) At best, this is not much of a protective covering, since from the beginning, Dooyeweerd's system was successful only as a negative critique of humanists who proclaimed neutrality. It was unquestionably a brilliant and detailed critique of this pretended autonomy, but Dooyeweerd was from the beginning a dedicated antinomian, meaning a critic of Old Testament law in New Testament times. He could build nothing positive precisely because his system is strictly a negative critique.[1] It is revealed as another brand of natural law-common ground philosophy whenever it is used to construct a positive program. Ironically, he and his disciples believed that they were forever destroying the intellectual foundations of all natural law, common ground philosophies.

I was privately arguing along these lines as early as 1965. Subsequently, Dooyeweerd's essay in the collection of essays edited by

---

1. H. Dooyeweerd, *A New Critique of Theoretical Thought*, 4 vols. (Philadelphia: Presbyterian & Reformed, 1953-58). Pronounced: DOUGH-yeh-vehrd.

E. R. Geehan, *Jerusalem and Athens: Critical Discussions on the Philosophy and Apologetics of Cornelius Van Til* (Presbyterian & Reformed, 1971), revealed just how hostile he was to biblical presuppositionalism. He replied to Van Til's criticism of his work as not going far enough in its confrontation with "natural law" doctrines. He, too, used the same old tactic: ". . . you have misunderstood what I mean . . ." (p. 74). No, Dr. Van Til understood precisely what Dooyeweerd meant—a magisterial accomplishment, given the frequently obscure nature of Dooyeweerd's verbiage. (I agree entirely with Nash's observation regarding Dooyeweerd: "Good thinking is never complimented by and should not be accompanied by poor communication."[2])

Dooyeweerd's system is a collection of philosophically empty "self-attesting" boxes (categories supposedly derived from logic, not the Bible) into which anyone can pour any content whatsoever. This is especially true of the political and economic categories. Nash is correct: "Apart from his presupposition that the cosmos is a divinely created world order, it might be objected that his law spheres are only fabrications of his own mind."[3] Most of his followers have poured socialism and antinomianism into these empty boxes. In fact, I contend that it was the very emptiness of Dooyeweerd's categories which attracted his followers—and his verbiage, which they have developed into an art. (Doubt me? Take a look at almost any book published in Canada by Wedge Books.)

Van Til put his finger on the problem when he wrote that "the entire transcendental method hangs in the air except for the fact that it rests upon the fullness and unity of truth accepted on the authority of Scripture."[4] Dooyeweerd's system hangs in the air because it does not *begin* with the presupposition of the necessity and adequacy of biblical revelation for all philosophical inquiry. In short, argued Van Til, either you start with the Bible as your standard, or you begin with man's mind as the standard. You will inescapably end up with whatever you began with presuppositionally. Dooyeweerd's whole system does not begin with the self-attesting authority of the Bible.

---

2. Ronald H. Nash, *Dooyeweerd and the Amsterdam Philosophy: A Christian Critique of Philosophical Thought* (Grand Rapids, Michigan: Zondervan, 1962), p. 105.

3. *Ibid.*, p. 104.

4. This criticism appeared in the little-known syllabus by Van Til, *Christianity in Conflict*, Volume II, Part 3, "Biblical Dimensionalism," a 59-page, single-spaced critique of Dooyeweerd and the Amsterdam school. Anyone who would like a photocopy of this essay can order it from Geneva Ministries, 708 Hamvasy, Tyler, Texas 75701: $10.

Therefore. . . .

Dooyeweerd was upset by this "therefore." Yet his response shows perfectly well how accurate Van Til's criticism had been. He categorically denied that any critique of humanism's presuppositions should begin with a confession of Christian presuppositions: ". . . this transcendental critique is obliged to *begin* with an inquiry into the inner nature and structure of the theoretical attitude of thought and experience *as such* and *not* with a confession of faith. In this first phase of the critical investigation such a confession would have been out of place" (p. 76). He begins with the autonomous mind of man. This is why Dooyeweerd was a scholastic in his methodology, despite his attempt to refute all medieval scholasticism by means of his critique. He shared humanism's methodological presuppositions concerning the obligation of good, rational men to begin debating without any reference to the Bible and the God who wrote it. Dooyeweerd's use of a non-biblical concept of the "heart" was the very heart of his humanism and antinomianism.[5] Van Til's response to Dooyeweerd's essay returns to his original theme, namely, that Dooyeweerd had given away the presuppositional case for biblical truth by his methodological starting point.

Troost argues that he had written his dissertation against the antinomianism of situation ethics. The question is: Did he simply substitute another brand of antinomianism? My answer was (and is), "Yes, he did." Either you affirm revealed biblical law as a permanent

---

5. It is not simply that Dooyeweerd's exposition is incomparably verbose and filled with jargon; it is that it is devoid of revelational content, including biblical law. But Van Til was not concerned about Dooyeweerd's implicit antinomianism; he was concerned about the lack of biblical content for Dooyeweerd's philosophical categories. Sadly, Van Til was himself almost as weak on the question of biblical law as Dooyeweerd was. He was not a theonomist, which is why he was always unwilling to promote publicly the writings of Rushdoony, and why he expressed reservations in private concerning Rushdoony's approach—and, by implication, the approach of the whole Christian Reconstruction movement. Rushdoony was taking Van Til's presuppositionalism into areas that made Van Til nervous; Van Til carefully avoided topics outside of traditional apologetics. Christian Reconstruction did not exist in a finished outline in 1971, when *Jerusalem and Athens* was published; not until Rushdoony's *Institutes of Biblical Law* appeared in 1973 did the capstone of the system appear. Van Til was always enthusiastic about Greg Bahnsen's apologetics, but he remained judiciously silent about Bahnsen's *Theonomy in Christian Ethics* (1977). Van Til's writings were necessary for the creation of the Reconstruction movement (presuppositionalism), but not sufficient (biblical law). In this sense, the Reconstructionists have criticized Van Til in much the same way as Van Til criticized Dooyeweerd: he did not go far enough in his adherence to biblical revelation.

standard,[6] or you affirm humanistic laws, of whatever variety. It is this radical dichotomy which humanists, dispensationalists, and Dooyeweerdians prefer not to accept. It is their common ground.

Troost's Jargon

The heart, mind, and soul of the Dooyeweerdian brand of humanism can be seen in the following paragraph in Troost's response. Be prepared for the usual incoherent jargon; Dooyeweerdians are incapable of writing, either in English of Dutch, without this jargon. It serves them as "ink" serves the escaping squid: a cover which hides them from their attackers.

> As for so-called social ethics, let me explain it in the following way: The question of what justice is in the concrete case and of what love to my neighbor means, cannot any longer be viewed as a metaphysical 'given' — as all forms of idealistic ethics suggests. However, the content of justice and love in the concrete case hic et nunc is not found literally in the Bible as a recipe for all time. But here the biblical-a[p]riori of faith in the divine creation order must *function* in the philosophical and social investigation. In so far as this has in broad lines and outline form led to preliminary results in the philosophy of the cosmonomic idea, this philosophy has shown that in the concrete giving of form to justice and love cultural-historical basic possibilities and the regulating function of faith always play roles in a normative way (p. 54).

Got that? Let me assist you. First, there are Troost's "pre-theoretical presuppositions":

1. I am a member of a church which believes in the Bible.

2. If the elders suspect that I do not believe in the Bible, I might get myself excommunicated. This would not be good; it would take away my influence.

3. I teach in a humanist institution, so if I go around talking about the eternal standards of biblical ethics, I might get fired, and I would unquestionably be ridiculed. This would also not be good.

---

6. Greg L. Bahnsen, *By This Standard: The Authority of God's Law Today* (Tyler, Texas: Institute for Christian Economics, 1985).

4. If I adopt a lot of Dooyeweerdian verbiage, I can get out of my dilemma. After all, he got out of his.

We are now ready for a translation of the verbiage:

1. There are no eternal standards of right and wrong.

2. The Bible does not literally speak to concrete historical situations in terms of fixed ethical standards because there are no fixed ethical standards applicable to concrete historical circumstances.

3. There is a "creation order." It is an empty box. Into it I am entitled to pour anything that appeals to me, as a respectable, tax-financed intellectual.

4. The "cultural historical basic possibilities" tell me how much socialist drivel I can get unsuspecting Christian laymen to swallow in the name of Jesus.

It should be clear why Troost and the cosmonomic idea enthusiasts have had no influence anywhere outside of a very restricted circle of Dutch readers. Dutch-Christian intellectuals respect academic scholarship, especially pseudo-Germanic scholarship, almost to the point of idol worsip. They frequently model their writing style after German pagan scholars. Herman Ridderbos' orthodox book, *Paul* (1975), is a good example. Dooyeweerd and his followers have fallen into the Germanic verbal bog. Their style is best described as a form of verbal constipation. They are enmeshed in verbiage which cannot be translated into English, let alone translated into action. They have no consistent economic program. They just have verbiage.

Troost can wax incoherent—he thinks he is waxing eloquent—promoting jumbled economic programs that are borrowed from modern Keynesian socialism, but to what effect? He is unable to distance himself from the run-of-the-mill political liberalism of our era. He is worse than speechless; he is a motor-mouth. Noise keeps coming out, but nothing principled. His program will be swallowed up in the flux of historical change. He offers nothing uniquely Christian, uniquely socialistic, or uniquely anything positive.

Do I exaggerate? Am I unfair? Judge for yourself:

A detailed elaboration of this is not given in my essay. I did cite certain results: i.e., that we, under the guidance of what we learn in Holy Scripture, must see and experience our earthly property rights as *relative* both in regard to God as well as in regard to our fellow men. In other words, in our 'unraffling' we have to maintain a religious distance, or, as it is better phrased, as not possessing our possessions (I Corinthians 7:29-31). However, one cannot deduce from this religious *basic attitude* any concrete right of property, as many 'progressive theologians' think they can do. This can be done neither in civil property rights, nor in public government rights, nor yet in rights of private enterprise. These concrete and temporal relations of justice lie on the niveau [?] of our temporal earthly life in which that which is concretely just hic et nunc and that which is love for neighbor *in concreto* is co-determined by the normative social, economical and other principles. These principles are not — as the natural law tradition thinks — *given* as positively formulated prescriptions but must be searched out from the complex normative *structures* of the situation (p. 54).

Do you remember the story of the king who was led by his own vanity to buy a set of "invisible clothes" by a bunch of "con artists"? Then he went out in his new clothes to lead a parade. No adult in the awe-struck crowd would admit that the king was stark naked. Finally, a little boy asked his father why the king was wearing no clothes. His father saw the light, and yelled, "The king has no clothes!" The king's vanity was given a decisive blow by the howls of laughter that followed the innocent lad's remark. Dooyeweerd, for all his competence in exposing the myth of neutrality in humanists, philosopher by philosopher, was the self-deceived victim of his own academic pride. He adopted a non-biblical starting point — a reference point devoid of biblical content, which he called the "heart" — and he also adopted humanism's hostility to biblical law. So have his followers. Troost is a good example. I prefer to serve as the little boy for the petrified crowd of Dutch Calvinists who stand in awe of the Dooyeweerdian verbiage, and who seem incapable of saying out loud: "These academic con men are naked!"

Conclusion

Troost feels inhibited by Mosaic law. So do all sinners. But instead of repenting, and calling for the reconstruction of society in terms of God's law, Troost rejects biblical law. It is not normative in his system. "What is normative is the *ethical-religio basic attitude* of early Christianity, because this is required everywhere in the great love commandment of the Bible, including the Mosaic legislation" (p. 56). A man can get away with murder in the foggy mists of the "ethico-religio basic attitude" of *any* religion or philosophy. But Troost does not want to get away with murder. He wants to get away with guilt-manipulation: "But in this Bible history we have to do with a *fundamental religious attitude of christian mentality* which must be ready *every* day and under *all* circumstances to make a happy and voluntary renunciation of money and goods on behalf of those who are in need . . ." (p. 56). Under *all* circumstances? How are we to know *when?* These proponents of progressive taxation and opponents of the 10% tithe never tell us — the better to manipulate us.

Troost's original essay is irrelevant. It was irrelevant in 1966, and it is irrelevant today. It was simply symptomatic of a crisis in Western civilization. Those who should be preparing an intellectual and moral framework for comprehensive reform along biblical lines have joined the enemies of Christ, and have marched in the parade of statism. Why? Because they hate biblical law more than they hate humanism. This, above all, constitutes the crisis of twentieth century Christianity. Christians have dressed themselves in the rags of humanism and have imagined themselves in robes of splendor.

Update: 1985

I have included this appendix in order to call the reader's attention to a type of economic analysis which has become extremely popular since 1966. There is almost nothing in Troost's essay which was not implicit or explicit a decade later in Ronald Sider's *Rich Christians in an Age of Hunger.* The argumentation is almost identical: moralistic, vague, guilt-inducing, statist, and explicitly antinomian. Troost's essay is an example of a genre which has become the standard fare in neo-evangelical circles, whether in *The Other Side, Sojourners,* or some other pro-State, pro-enforced wealth redistribution magazine published in the name of Jesus.

What should also be apparent is that my response in 1966 is almost identical in approach to David Chilton's response to Sider in *Productive Christians in an Age of Guilt-Manipulators.* The emphasis is on the specific revelation of God in the Bible, especially in Old Testament law. Troost's rejection of biblical law and of the whole concept of Bible-based blueprints for economics is exactly the line pushed by

Sider, Evangelicals for Social Action, and the other neo-evangelical liberation theologians.

It is clear why Troost and his neo-evangelical clones are so hostile to the idea of biblical blueprints: the Bible unquestionably promotes free market institutional arrangements. This is why the three other authors in Clouse's book, *Wealth and Poverty: Four Christian Views of Economics* (InterVarsity Press, 1984) all agreed that the Bible must not be appealed to with respect to specific social and economic institutional arrangements, and why my essay kept returning to the theme of the ethical requirement of abiding by Old Testament principles. I was derided in the symposium for appealing to the Book of Deuteronomy (p. 66). Anyone who has read Deuteronomy should understand why I was derided: it promises economic and other external blessings to societies that conform to the external requirements of Old Testament law.

In short, the terms of the debate have not changed in two decades, nor are they likely to change in the next two hundred years. The issue is clear: God's word or man's word, God's law or man's law, God's blueprints or man's blueprints. Take your pick. Or as Elijah put it, choose this day whom you will serve. It is clear enough to see who serves God in this century, and who serves Baal. It shows even in the mundane academic discipline of economics.

SCRIPTURE INDEX

OLD TESTAMENT

NEW TESTAMENT

INDEX

345

jargon, 334-36
jealousy, 90, 195-96
Jefferson, Thomas, 48, 154
Jeremiad, 272, 274-75
Jericho, 17
Jerusalem, 88-89, 168, 324
Jesus
  activism, 227
  battle, 221
  covenant, 211
  dominion, 221
  Dominion Man, 16
  eating meal, 83
  lawyer &, 307-8
  name, 179
  new world order, 88
  oaths, 58
  O. T. Law, 306-7
  physician, 20-21
  power of death, 119
  redemption, 2
  resurrection, 81
  revolutionary, 221
  temptations, xxii-xxiii
  trial of, xxiii-xxiv
  yoke, 126
Jews, 90, 142 (*see also* Israel)
Johnson, Lyndon, 219
Jordan, James, 18n-19n, 59n, 266n
  language, 61
  third day, 86-87
Joseph, 66
journey, 279-80
jubilee, xxi
jubilee year, 129
Judaizers, 243
judging, 310-11, 312-13, 321
judgment, xvi-xvii, 50
judgment day, xvi-xvii
jury, 61
justice, 216

kidnapping, 134
kill, 116
kingdom of God, 37
kingdoms, 45-46
kings, 17

Kline, Meredith, 56n, 76n
knowledge, 151, 162, 185-86, 190, 194
Kohath, 42

Laban, 315
labor, 77, 126, 142, 143
Ladner, Gerhart, 35n
laissez-faire, 298
lamb, 45n
lambs, 239
land, 75, 85, 166, 293
Langley, Baxter, 297
language, 60
lashing, 60
Latouche, Robert, 224
law
  annulment, 4
  antinomianism, 318
  blessings, 112
  case-law, 18
  death, 317
  dominion &, xii
  evangelism, 315
  freedom, 24
  government &, 319
  grace, 152
  hatred of, 220
  history, 19
  internalization, 206-7
  life, 20
  love &, 308-12
  offensive strategy, 226
  outmoded, 14
  peace, 211
  permanent, 2
  predictable, 15, 285
  principles, 3, 306, 309
  prohibition, 26
  State &, 13
lawlessness, 197
law of averages, 47
law-order
  biblical, 97, 202
  decalogue &, 18
  Egypt's, 19
  polytheism, 21
  social co-operation, 206
  unity, 97

WHAT IS THE ICE?

by Gary North, President, ICE

The Institute for Christian Economics is a non-profit, tax-exempt educational organization which is devoted to research and publishing in the field of Christian ethics. The perspective of those associated with the ICE is straightforwardly conservative and pro-free market. The ICE is dedicated to the proposition that biblical ethics requires full personal responsibility, and this responsible human action flourishes most productively within a framework of limited government, political decentralization, and minimum interference with the economy by the civil government.

For well over half a century, the loudest voices favoring Christian social action have been outspokenly pro-government intervention. Anyone needing proof of this statement needs to read Dr. Gregg Singer's comprehensive study, *The Unholy Alliance* (Arlington House Books, 1975), the definitive history of the National Council of Churches. An important policy statement from the National Council's General Board in 1967 called for *comprehensive economic planning*. The ICE was established in order to *challenge* statements like the following:

> Accompanying this growing diversity in the structures of national life has been a growing recognition of the importance of competent planning within and among all resource sectors of the society: education, economic development, land use, social health services, the family system and congregational life. It is not generally recognized that an effective approach to problem solving requires a comprehensive planning process and coordination in the development of all these resource areas.

The *silence* from the conservative denominations in response to such policy proposals has been deafening. Not that conservative church members agree with such nonsense; they don't. But the con-

363

servative denominations and associations have remained silent because they have convinced themselves that *any* policy statement of any sort regarding social and economic life is *always* illegitimate. In short, there is no such thing as a correct, valid policy statement that a church or denomination can make. *The results of this opinion have been universally devastating.* The popular press assumes that the radicals who do speak out in the name of Christ are representative of the membership (or at least the press goes along with the illusion). The public is convinced that to speak out on social matters in the name of Christ is to be radical. *Christians are losing by default.*

The ICE is convinced that conservative Christians must devote resources to create alternative proposals. There is an old rule of political life which argues that "You can't beat something with nothing." We agree. It is not enough to adopt a whining negativism whenever someone or some group comes up with another nutty economic program. We need a comprehensive alternative.

Society or State

Society is broader than politics. The State is not a substitute for society. *Society encompasses all social institutions:* church, State, family, economy, kinship groups, voluntary clubs and associations, schools, and non-profit educational organizations (such as ICE). Can we say that there are no standards of righteousness—justice—for these social institutions? Are they lawless? The Bible says no. We do not live in a lawless universe. But this does not mean that the State is the source of all law. On the contrary, God, not the imitation god of the State, is the source.

Christianity is innately decentralist. *From the beginning, orthodox Christians have denied the divinity of the State.* This is why the Caesars of Rome had them persecuted and executed. They denied the operating presupposition of the ancient world, namely, the legitimacy of a divine rule or a divine State.

It is true that modern liberalism has eroded Christian orthodoxy. There are literally thousands of supposedly evangelical pastors who have been compromised by the liberalism of the universities and seminaries they attended. The popularity, for example, of Prof. Ronald Sider's *Rich Christians in an Age of Hunger,* co-published by Inter-Varsity Press (evangelical Protestant) and the Paulist Press (liberal Roman Catholic), is indicative of the crisis today. It has sold like hotcakes, and it calls for mandatory wealth redistribution by the

State on a massive scale. Yet he is a professor at a Baptist seminary.

The ICE rejects the theology of the total State. This is why we countered the book by Sider when we published David Chilton's *Productive Christians in an Age of Guilt-Manipulators* (3rd edition, 1985). Chilton's book shows that the Bible is the foundation of our economic freedom, and that the call for compulsory wealth transfers and higher taxes on the rich is simply *baptized socialism.* Socialism is anti-Christian to the core.

What we find is that laymen in evangelical churches tend to be more conservative theologically and politically than their pastors. But this conservatism is a kind of *instinctive conservatism.* It is *not* self-consciously grounded in the Bible. So the laymen are unprepared to counter the sermons and Sunday School materials that bombard them week after week.

It is ICE's contention that *the only way to turn the tide in this nation is to capture the minds of the evangelical community,* which numbers in the tens of millions. We have to convince the liberal-leaning evangelicals of the biblical nature of the free market system. And we have to convince the conservative evangelicals of the same thing, in order to get them into the social and intellectual battles of our day.

In other words, *retreat is not biblical,* any more than socialism is.

By What Standard?

We have to ask ourselves this question: *"By what standard?"* By what standard do we evaluate the claims of the socialists and interventionists? By what standard do we evaluate the claims of the secular free market economists who reject socialism? By what standard are we to construct intellectual alternatives to the humanism of our day? And by what standard do we criticize the social institutions of our era?

If we say that the standard is "reason," we have a problem: Whose reason? If the economists cannot agree with each other, how do we decide who is correct? Why hasn't reason produced agreement after centuries of debate? We need an alternative.

It is the Bible. The ICE is dedicated to the defense of the Bible's reliability. But don't we face the same problem? Why don't Christians agree about what the Bible says concerning economics?

One of the main reasons why they do not agree is that the question of biblical economics has not been taken seriously. Christian scholars have ignored economic theory for generations. This is why the ICE devotes so much time, money, and effort to studying what the Bible teaches about economic affairs.

There will always be some disagreements, since men are not perfect, and their minds are imperfect. But when men agree about the basic issue of the starting point of the debate, they have a far better opportunity to discuss and learn than if they offer only "reason, rightly understood" as their standard.

Services

The ICE exists in order to serve Christians and other people who are vitally interested in finding moral solutions to the economic crisis of our day. The organization is a *support ministry* to other Christian ministries. It is non-sectarian, non-denominational, and dedicated to the proposition that a moral economy is a truly practical, productive economy.

The ICE produces several newsletters. These are aimed at intelligent laymen, church officers, and pastors. The reports are non-technical in nature. Included in our publication schedule are these monthly and bi-monthly publications:

> **Biblical Economics Today** (6 times a year)
> **Christian Reconstruction** (6 times a year)
> **Dominion Strategies** (12 times a year)

Biblical Economics Today is a four-page report that covers economic theory from a specifically Christian point of view. It also deals with questions of economic policy. **Christian Reconstruction** is more action-oriented, but it also covers various aspects of Christian social theory. **Dominion Strategies** is a two-page question-and-answer format newsletter. Readers submit questions, and half a dozen or more are selected each month.

The purpose of the ICE is to relate biblical ethics to Christian activities in the field of economics. To cite the title of Francis Schaeffer's book, "How should we then live?" How should we apply biblical wisdom in the field of economics to our lives, our culture, our civil government, and our businesses and callings?

If God calls men to responsible decision-making, then He must have *standards of righteousness* that guide men in their decision-making. It is the work of the ICE to discover, illuminate, explain, and suggest applications of these guidelines in the field of economics.

We publish the results of our findings in the newsletters. *The ICE sends out the newsletters free of charge.* Anyone can sign up for six months to receive them. This gives the reader the opportunity of seeing "what we're up to." At the end of six months, he or she can renew for another six months.

Donors receive a one-year subscription. This reduces the extra trouble associated with sending out renewal notices, and it also means less trouble for the subscriber.

There are also donors who pledge to pay $10 a month. They are members of the ICE's *"Reconstruction Committee."* They help to provide a predictable stream of income which finances the day-to-day operations of the ICE. Then the donations from others can finance special projects, such as the publication of a new book.

The basic service that ICE offers is education. We are presenting ideas and approaches to Christian ethical behavior that few other organizations even suspect are major problem areas. *The Christian world has for too long acted as though we were not responsible citizens on earth,* as well as citizens of heaven. ("For our conversation [citizenship] is in heaven" [Philippians 3:20a].) *We must be godly stewards of all our assets,* which includes our lives, minds, and skills.

Because economics affects every sphere of life, the ICE's reports and surveys are relevant to all areas of life. Because *scarcity affects every area,* the whole world needs to be governed by biblical requirements for *honest stewardship* of the earth's resources. The various publications are wide-ranging, since the effects of the curse of the ground (Genesis 3:17-19) are wide-ranging.

What the ICE offers the readers and supporters is an introduction to a world of responsibility that few Christians have recognized. This limits our audience, since most people think they have too many responsibilities already. But if more people understood the Bible's solutions to economic problems, they would have more capital available to take greater responsibility — and prosper from it.

Finances

There ain't no such thing as a free lunch (TANSTAAFL). *Someone has to pay for those six-month renewable free subscriptions.* Existing donors are, in effect, supporting a kind of intellectual missionary organization. Except for the newsletters sent to ministers and teachers, we "clean" the mailing lists each year: less waste.

We cannot expect to raise money by emotional appeals. We have no photographs of starving children, no orphanages in Asia. We generate ideas. *There is always a very limited market for ideas, which is why some of them have to be subsidized by people who understand the power of ideas — a limited group, to be sure.* John Maynard Keynes, the most influential economist of this century (which speaks poorly of this century), spoke the truth in the final paragraph of his *General Theory of Employment, Interest, and Money* (1936):

> . . . the ideas of economists and political philosophers, both when they are right and when they are wrong, are more powerful than is commonly understood. Indeed, the world is ruled by little else. Practical men, who believe themselves to be quite exempt from any intellectual influences, are usually the slaves of some defunct economist. Madmen in authority, who hear voices in the air, are distilling their frenzy from some academic scribbler of a few years back. I am sure that the power of vested interests is vastly exaggerated compared with the gradual encroachment of ideas. Not, indeed, immediately, but after a certain interval; for in the field of economic and political philosophy there are not many who are influenced by new theories after they are twenty-five or thirty years of age, so that the ideas which civil servants and politicians and even agitators apply to current events are not likely to be the newest. But, soon or late, it is ideas, not vested interests, which are dangerous for good or evil.

Do you believe this? If so, then the program of long-term education which the ICE has created should be of considerable interest to you. What we need are people with a *vested interest in ideas*, a *commitment to principle* rather than class position.

There will be few short-term, visible successes for the ICE's program. There will be new and interesting books. There will be a constant stream of newsletters. There will be educational audio and video tapes. But the world is not likely to beat a path to ICE's door, as long as today's policies of high taxes and statism have not yet produced a catastrophe. We are investing in the future, for the far side of humanism's economic failure. *This is a long-term investment in intellectual capital.* Contact us at: **ICE, Box 8000, Tyler, TX 75711.**

Dr. Gary North
Institute for Christian Economics
P.O. Box 8000
Tyler, TX 75711

Dear Dr. North:

I read about your organization in your book, *The Sinai Strategy.* I understand that you publish several newsletters that are sent out for six months free of charge. I would be interested in receiving them:

☐ *Biblical Economics Today*
Dominion Strategies
Christian Reconstruction
and *Preface*

Please send any other information you have concerning your program.

_____
name

_____
address

_____
city, state, zip

☐ Enclosed is a tax-deductible donation to help meet expenses.